Tonal Harmony

with an Introduction to Twentieth-Century Music

FOURTH EDITION

Tonal Harmony

with an Introduction to Twentieth-Century Music

Stefan Kostka

The University of Texas at Austin

Dorothy Payne

The University of South Carolina

Boston   Burr Ridge, IL   Dubuque, IA   Madison, WI   New York   San Francisco   St. Louis
Bankok   Bogotá   Caracas   Lisbon   London   Madrid
Mexico City   Milan   New Delhi   Seoul   Singapore   Sydney   Taipei   Toronto

McGraw-Hill

A Division of The McGraw-Hill Companies

Tonal Harmony
with an Introduction to Twentieth Century-Music

This book is printed on acid-free paper.

1 2 3 4 5 6 7 8 9 0 FGR/FGR 9 0 9 8 7 6 5 4 3 2 1 0 9

ISBN 0-07-289782-1 (book)
ISBN 0-07-289785-6 (CD)
ISBN 0-07-235846-7 (book with CD)

Editorial director: *Phillip A. Butcher*
Sponsoring editor: *Christopher Freitag*
Developmental editor: *JoElaine Retzler*
Marketing manager: *David Patterson*
Senior project manager: *Gladys True*
Production supervisor: *Heather D. Burbridge*
Interior and cover designer: *Kristyn Kalnes*
Senior supplement coordinator: *Cathy L. Tepper*
Compositor: *A-R Editions, Inc.*
Typeface: *10/12 Times Roman*
Printer: *Quebecor Printing Book Group/Fairfield*

Library of Congress Cataloging-in-Publication Data

Kostka, Stefan M.
    Tonal harmony, with an introduction to twentieth-century music /
Stefan Kostka, Dorothy Payne. — 4th ed.
        p.   cm.
    Includes indexes
    ISBN 0-07-289782-1
    1. Harmony.   I. Payne, Dorothy.   II. Title.
MT50.K85   1999
781.2'5—dc21   99-17042

http://www.mhhe.com

About the Authors

STEFAN KOSTKA

Holds degrees in music from the University of Colorado and the University of Texas and received his Ph.D. in music theory from the University of Wisconsin. He was a member of the faculty of the Eastman School of Music from 1969 to 1973. Since that time he has been on the faculty of the University of Texas at Austin. Dr. Kostka initiated courses in computer applications in music at both the Eastman School and the University of Texas. More recently he has specialized in courses in atonal theory and contemporary styles and techniques, interests that led to a second book, *Materials and Techniques of Twentieth-Century Music*. He continues to be active in computer applications in music theory and frequently teaches a course in multimedia authoring. Dr. Kostka is active in various professional organizations and is a past president of the Texas Society for Music Theory.

DOROTHY PAYNE

Holds both bachelor's and master's degrees in piano performance and a Ph.D. in music theory, all from the Eastman School of Music. She has been on the faculty of the University of South Carolina since 1994. Former administrative positions include those of Dean at South Carolina, Director of the School of Music at the University of Arizona, and Music Department Head at the University of Connecticut. Prior faculty appointments were held at the University of Texas at Austin, the Eastman School of Music, and Pacific Lutheran University. In addition to remaining active as a performer, Payne has presented lectures and workshops on theory pedagogy at meetings of professional societies and has served the National Association of Schools of Music as visiting evaluator, member of the Accreditation Commission, and Secretary of the Executive Committee.

Preface

Tonal Harmony with an Introduction to Twentieth-Century Music is intended for a two-year course in music theory/harmony. It offers a clear and thorough introduction to the resources and practice of Western music from the seventeenth century to the present day. Its concise, one-volume format and flexible approach make the book usable in a broad range of theory curricula.

APPROACH

The text provides students with a comprehensive but accessible and highly practical set of tools for the understanding of music. Actual musical practice is emphasized more than rules or prohibitions. Principles are explained and illustrated, and exceptions are noted.

In its presentation of harmonic procedures, the text introduces students to the most common vocal and instrumental textures encountered in tonal music. Traditional four-part chorale settings are used to introduce many concepts, but three-part instrumental and vocal textures are also presented in illustrations and drill work, along with a variety of keyboard styles. To encourage the correlation of writing and performing skills, we have included musical examples in score and reduced-score formats as well as charts on instrumental ranges and transpositions. Some of the assignments ask the student to write for small ensembles suitable for performance in class. Instructors may modify these assignments to make them most appropriate for their particular situations.

PEDAGOGICAL FEATURES

The text employs a variety of techniques to clarify underlying voice leading, harmonic structure, and formal procedures. These include textural reductions, accompanying many of the examples, which highlight chordal motion. Our goal has been to elucidate tonal logic at the phrase and section level as well as from one chord to the next. Abundant musical illustrations, many with commentaries, serve as a springboard for class discussion and individual understanding.

The book provides an extensive series of review material. A large portion of the text is devoted to Self-Tests, consisting of student-graded drills in chord spelling, part writing, and analysis, with suggested answers given in Appendix B. The Self-Tests can be used for in-class drill and discussion, in preparation for the Workbook exercises, or for independent study. Periodic Checkpoints enable students to gauge their understanding of the preceding material. Chapter summaries highlight the key points of each chapter.

ORGANIZATION

Part One (Chapters 1–4) begins the text with a thorough but concise overview of the fundamentals of music, divided into one chapter each on pitch and rhythm. Chapters 3 and 4 introduce the student to triads and seventh chords in various inversions and textures, but without placing them yet in their tonal contexts.

Part Two (Chapters 5–12) opens with two chapters on the principles of voice leading, with practice limited to root position triads. Chapter 7 follows with a systematic discussion of normative harmonic progressions. Subsequent chapters deal with triads in inversion (Chapter 8 and 9), basic elements of musical form (Chapter 10), and non-chord tones (Chapters 11 and 12).

Part Three (Chapters 13–15) is devoted entirely to diatonic seventh chords, moving from the dominant seventh in root position and inversion (Chapter13) through the supertonic and leading-tone sevenths (Chapter 14) to the remaining diatonic seventh chords (Chapter 15).

Part Four begins the study of chromaticism with secondary functions (Chapters 16–17) and modulation (Chapters 18–19), concluding in Chapter 20 with a discussion of binary and ternary forms. Chromaticism continues to be the main topic in Part Five (Chapters 21–26), which covers mode mixture, the Neapolitan, augmented sixth chords, and enharmonicism. Some further elements, ninth chords and altered dominants among them, are the subject of the final chapter of this section.

Part Six begins in Chapter 27 with a discussion of the developments and extensions in tonal practice that occurred in later nineteenth-century music. The concluding chapter provides an extensive introduction to major twentieth-century practices.

SUPPLEMENTARY MATERIALS

The following ancillary items can be used with the fourth edition of *Tonal Harmony*. Please consult your local McGraw-Hill representative for policies, prices, packaging options, and availability.

Workbook

Each set of exercises in the Workbook (ISBN: 0-07-303512-2) is closely correlated with the corresponding chapter of the text and with a particular Self-Test within the chapter. Each set of Workbook exercises begins with problems similar to those found in the corresponding Self-Test, but the Workbook exercises also include problems that are too open-ended for the Self-Test format as well as more creative types of compositional problems for those instructors who like to include this type of work.

Recordings

The fifth edition is accompanied by recordings of virtually all the examples from music literature found in the text and the Workbook. A set of compact discs is available for the text (ISBN: 0-07-289785-6), and one compact disc comes with the Workbook, offering over 400 selections in all. All examples were recorded using the same instrumentations seen in text and Workbook examples.

 A listening icon, as shown at left, indicates that a piece is contained on the CDs.

Instructor's Manual

The Instructor's Manual (ISBN: 0-07-289784-8) follows the organization of the text and provides teaching notes, a key to "objective" exercises from the Workbook, sources from the literature for part-writing exercises and composition assignments, and chapter quizzes.

NEW TO THIS EDITION

A major addition to the textbook consists of examples from jazz and popular music. This begins in Chapter 3 with an introduction to lead sheet symbols, and musical examples that illustrate the use of common-practice harmonies appear throughout the text. Related to this is a new section of the text, "The 12-Bar Blues," which appears in Chapter 20. A discussion of the American popular ballad form appears in the same chapter.

A new section in Chapter 8, "Soprano-Bass Counterpoint," provides an introduction to this important topic with several examples from the literature. Other new headings include "Consonant and Dissonant Intervals" in Chapter 1, "Harmonizing a Simple Melody" in Chapter 7, and "Resolutions to Tonic" in Chapter 24. Finally, the "Set Theory" section in Chapter 28 has been completely revised.

Students have always found the Checkpoint sections to be useful in testing their reading comprehension, and every chapter now contains at least one of these.

Finally, a number of excerpts from two of the better-known women composers of the nineteenth century, Clara Wieck Schumann and Fanny Mendelssohn Hensel, have been added to the textbook and to the Workbook.

ACKNOWLEDGMENTS

Many colleagues and friends provided assistance and encouragement during the development of the first edition of this text, notably Professors Douglass Green, Jerry Grigadean, and Janet McGaughey. Reviewers of the manuscript contributed many helpful suggestions; our sincere thanks are extended to Judith Allen, University of Virginia; Michael Arenson, University of Delaware; B. Glenn Chandler, Central Connecticut State College; Herbert Colvin, Baylor University; Charles Fligel, Southern Illinois University; Roger Foltz, University of Nebraska, Omaha; Albert G. Huetteman, University of Massachusetts;

William Hussey, University of Texas at Austin; Hanley Jackson, Kansas State University; Marvin Johnson, University of Alabama; Frank Lorince, West Virginia University; William L. Maxson, Eastern Washington University; Leonard Ott, University of Missouri; John Pozdro, University of Kansas; Jeffrey L. Prater, Iowa State University; Russell Riepe, Southwest Texas State University; Wayne Scott, University of Colorado; Richard Soule, University of Nevada; James Stewart, Ohio University; William Toutant, California State University at Northridge; and John D. White, University of Florida.

We are also grateful to those who contributed to the development of the second edition: Richard Bass, University of Connecticut; James Bermighof, Baylor University; Richard Devore, Kent State University; Lora Gingerich, Ohio State University; Kent Kerman, University of Texas at Austin; James W. Krehbiel, Eastern Illinois University; Frank Lorince, West Virginia University (retired); Donald Para, Western Michigan University; Marian Petersen, University of Missouri at Kansas City; Donald Peterson, University of Tennessee; and John Pozdro, University of Kansas.

Contributors to the third edition included Shirley Bean, University of Missouri, Kansas City; Brian Berlin, University of Texas at Austin; Horace Boyer, University of Massachusetts; Polly Brecht, Middle Tennessee State University; John Buccheri, Northwestern University; Arthur Campbell, St. Olaf College; Lisa Derry, Western Michigan University; David Foley, Ball State University; Douglass Green, University of Texas at Austin; Andrew Grobengieser, University of Texas at Austin; Thom Hutcheson, Middle Tennessee State University; Robert Judd, California State University, Fresno; William Pelto, Ithaca College; H. Lee Riggins, Bowling Green State University; Lynne Rogers, University of Texas at Austin; and Judith Solomon, Texas Christian University.

Contributors to the fourth edition include Ron Albrecht, Simpson College; John Benoit, Simpson College; Claire Boge, Miami University; Lisa Derry, Albertson College of Idaho; Allen Feinstein, Northeastern University; Karl Korte, University of Texas at Austin; Jennifer Ottervick, University of South Carolina; Paul Paccione, Western Illinois University; William Pelto, Ithaca College; Timothy Smith, Northern Arizona University; William Schirmer, Jacksonville University; and Judith A. Solomon, Texas Christian University.

Finally, we would express gratitude to Mary Robertson for her love and inspiration and to our colleagues and students for their continued encouragement.

Stefan Kostka
Dorothy Payne

To the Student

HARMONY IN WESTERN MUSIC

One thing that distinguishes Western art music from many other kinds of music is its emphasis on harmony. In other words, just about any piece that you perform will involve more than one person playing or singing different notes at the same time or, in the case of a keyboard player, more than one finger pushing down keys. There are exceptions, of course, such as works for unaccompanied flute, violin, and so on, but an implied harmonic background is often still apparent to the ear in such pieces.

In general, the music from cultures other than our own European-American one is concerned less with harmony than with other aspects of music. Complexities of rhythm or subtleties of melodic variation, for example, might serve as the focal point in a particular musical culture. Even in our own music, some compositions, such as those for nonpitched percussion instruments, may be said to have little or no harmonic content, but they are the exception.

If harmony is so important in our music, it might be a good idea if we agreed on a definition of it. What does the expression *sing in harmony* mean to you? It probably evokes impressions of something like a barbershop quartet, or a chorus, or maybe just two people singing a song—one singing the melody, the other one singing an accompanying line. Because harmony began historically with vocal music, this is a reasonable way to begin formulating a definition of harmony. In all these examples, our conception of harmony involves more than one person singing at once, and the *harmony* is the sound that the combined voices produce.

Harmony is the sound that results when two or more pitches are performed simultaneously. It is the vertical aspect of music, produced by the combination of the components of the horizontal aspect.

Although this book deals with harmony and with chords, which are little samples taken out of the harmony, you should remember that musical lines (vocal or instrumental) produce the harmony, not the reverse.

Sing through the four parts in Example 1. The soprano and tenor lines are the most melodic. The actual melody being harmonized is in the soprano, whereas the tenor follows its contour for a while and then ends with an eighth-note figure of its own. The bass line is strong and independent but less melodic, whereas the alto part is probably the least distinctive of all. These four relatively independent lines combine to create harmony, with chords occurring at the rate of approximately one per beat.

EXAMPLE 1 *Bach "Herzlich lieb hab' ich dich, o Herr"*

The relationship between the vertical and horizontal aspects of music is a subtle one, however, and it has fluctuated ever since the beginnings of harmony (about the ninth century). At times the emphasis has been almost entirely on independent horizontal lines, with little attention paid to the resulting chords—a tendency easily seen in the twentieth century. At other times the independence of the lines has been weakened or is absent entirely. In Example 2 the only independent lines are the sustained bass note and the melody (highest notes). The other lines merely double the melody at various intervals, creating a very nontraditional succession of chords.

EXAMPLE 2 *Debussy, "La Cathédrale engloutie," from Preludes, Book I*

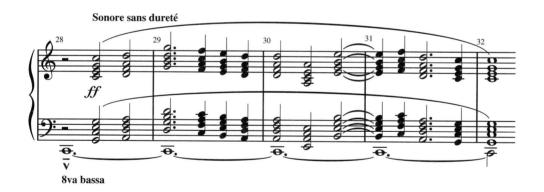

TONAL HARMONY DEFINED

The kind of harmony that this book deals with primarily is usually called *tonal harmony*. The term refers to the harmonic style of music composed during the period from about 1650 to about 1900. This would include such composers as Purcell, Bach, Handel, Haydn, Mozart, Beethoven, Schubert, Schumann, Wagner, Brahms, Tchaikovsky, and all their contemporaries.

Much of today's popular music is based on tonal harmony, just as Bach's music was, which means that both types have a good deal in common. First, both make use of a *tonal* *center*, a pitch class* that provides a center of gravity. Second, both types of music make use almost exclusively of major and minor scales. Third, both use chords that are tertian in structure. *Tertian* means "built of thirds," so a tertian chord might be C-E-G, a nontertian one C-F-B. Fourth, and very important, is that the chords built on the various scale degrees relate to one another and to the tonal center in fairly complex ways. Because each chord tends to have more or less standard roles, or functions, within a key, this characteristic is sometimes referred to as *functional* harmony. The details of these relationships between chords will be discussed more fully in the text; but to get an idea of what harmonic function is all about, play the chord of Example 3 on the piano.†

EXAMPLE 3

Play it several times. Arpeggiate it up and down. The "function" of this chord is clear, isn't it? Somehow, you know a lot about this chord without having to read a book about it. Play it again, and listen to where the chord "wants" to go. Then play Example 4, which will seem to follow Example 3 perfectly. This is an example of what is meant by the relationships between chords in tonal harmony and why we sometimes use the term *functional harmony*.

EXAMPLE 4

Tonal harmony is not limited to the period 1650–1900. It began evolving long before 1650, and it is still around today. Turn on your radio, go to a nightclub, listen to the canned music in the supermarket—it's almost all tonal harmony. Then why do we put the demise of tonal harmony at 1900? Because from about that time, most composers of "serious," or "legitimate," or "concert" music have been more interested in nontonal harmony than in tonal harmony. This does not mean that tonal harmony ceased to exist in the real world or in music of artistic merit. Also, it is important to realize that not all music with a

---

* Pitch class: Notes an octave apart or enharmonically equivalent belong to the same pitch class (all C's, B♯'s and D♭♭'s, for example). There are twelve pitch classes in all.
† If you cannot arrange to be at a piano while reading this book, try to play through the examples just before or right after reading a particular section or chapter. Reading about music without hearing it is not only dull, it's uninformative.

tonal center makes use of functional harmony—especially a good deal of the music of the twentieth century—music by composers such as Bartók and Hindemith, for example.

From our discussion we can formulate this definition of tonal harmony:

Tonal harmony refers to music with a tonal center, based on major and/or minor scales, and using tertian chords that are related to one another and to the tonal center in various ways.

USING THIS TEXT

The information in this text is organized in the traditional chapter format, but there are several additional features of which you should be aware.

Self-Tests

All chapters contain one or more such sections. These Self-Tests contain questions and drill material for use in independent study or classroom discussion. Suggested answers to all Self-Test problems appear in Appendix B. In many cases more than one correct answer is possible, but only one answer will be given in Appendix B. If you are in doubt about the correctness of your answer, ask your instructor.

Exercises

After each Self-Test section, we refer to a group of Exercises to be found in the Workbook. Most of the Workbook Exercises will be similar to those in the preceding Self-Test, so refer to the Self-Test if you have questions concerning completion of the Exercises. However, the Workbook will also often contain more creative compositional problems than appeared in the Self-Test, as it would be impossible to suggest "answers" to such problems if they were used as Self-Tests.

Checkpoints

You will frequently encounter Checkpoint sections. These are intended to jog your memory and to help you review what you have just read. No answers are given to Checkpoint questions.

Contents

PART I

Chapter 1

Elements of Pitch

THE KEYBOARD AND OCTAVE REGISTERS

Pitch in music refers to the highness or lowness of a sound. Pitches are named by using the first seven letters of the alphabet: A, B, C, D, E, F, and G. We will approach the notation of pitch by relating this pitch alphabet to the keyboard, using C's as an example. The C nearest the middle of the keyboard is called middle C, or C4. Higher C's (moving toward the right on the keyboard) are named C5, C6, and so on. Lower C's (moving left) are named C3, C2, and C1. Notes below C1 are followed by a 0, as in B0. All the C's on the piano are labeled in Example 1-1.

EXAMPLE 1-1

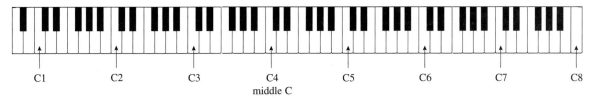

| C1 | C2 | C3 | C4 middle C | C5 | C6 | C7 | C8 |

From any C up to or down to the next C is called an *octave*. All the pitches from one C up to, but not including, the next C are said to be in the same *octave register*. As Example 1-2 illustrates, the white key above C4 would be named D4 because it is in the same octave register, but the white key below C4 would be named B3.

EXAMPLE 1-2

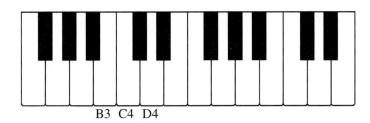

B3 C4 D4

NOTATION ON THE STAFF

Our system of musical notation is similar to a graph in which time is indicated on the X axis and pitch is shown on the Y axis. In Example 1–3, R occurs before S in time and is higher than S in pitch.

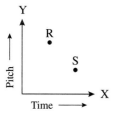

A *staff* is used in music to indicate the precise pitch desired. A staff consists of five lines and four spaces, but it may be extended indefinitely through the use of *ledger lines* (Ex. 1-4).

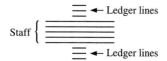

A *clef* must appear at the beginning of the staff in order to indicate which pitches are to be associated with which lines and spaces. The three clefs commonly used today are shown in Example 1-5, and the position of C4 in each is illustrated. Notice that the C clef appears in either of two positions.

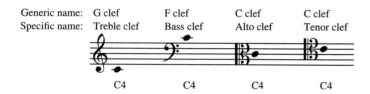

The clefs in Example 1-5 are shown in the positions that are in common use today, but you may occasionally find them placed differently on the staff in some editions. Wherever they appear, the design of the G clef circles G4, the dots of the F clef surround F3, and the C clef is centered on C4.

The grand staff is a combination of two staves joined by a brace, with the top and bottom staves using treble and bass clefs, respectively. Various pitches are notated and labeled on the grand staff in Example 1-6. Pay special attention to the way in which the ledger lines are used on the grand staff. For instance, the notes C4 and A3 appear twice in Example 1-6, once in relation to the top staff and once in relation to the bottom staff.

EXAMPLE 1-6

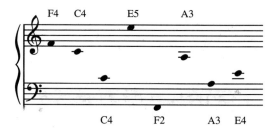

Self-Test 1-1
(Answers begin on page 571.)

A. Name the pitches in the blanks provided, using the correct octave register designations.

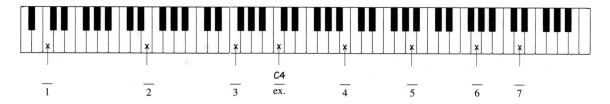

B. Notate the indicated pitches on the staff in the correct octave.

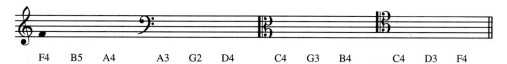

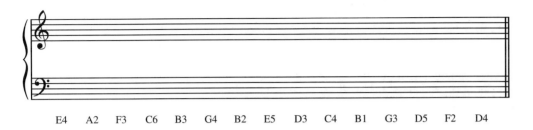

E4   A2   F3   C6   B3   G4   B2   E5   D3   C4   B1   G3   D5   F2   D4

Exercise 1-1 See Workbook.

THE MAJOR SCALE

In this chapter you will learn about major and minor scales, the scales that form the basis of tonal music. However, there are many other kinds of scales, some of which are covered in Chapter 28.

The *major scale* is a specific pattern of small steps (called half steps) and larger ones (called whole steps) encompassing an octave. A *half step* is the distance from a key on the piano to the very next key, white or black. Using only the white keys on the piano keyboard, there are two half steps in each octave (Ex. 1-7).

EXAMPLE 1-7

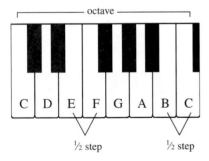

A *whole step* skips the very next key and goes instead to the following one. Using only the white keys on the piano keyboard, there are five whole steps in each octave (Ex. 1-8).

EXAMPLE 1-8

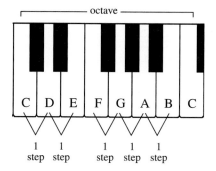

The major scale pattern of whole and half steps is the same as that found on the white keys from any C up to the next C. In the diagram below, the numbers with carets above them ($\hat{1}$, $\hat{2}$, etc.) are scale degree numbers for the C major scale.*

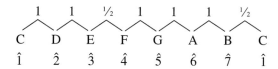

You can see from this diagram that half steps in the major scale occur only between scale degrees $\hat{3}$ and $\hat{4}$ and $\hat{7}$ and $\hat{1}$. Notice also that the major scale can be thought of as two identical, four-note patterns separated by a whole step.

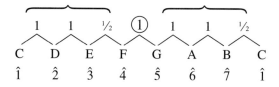

If we examine the steps on the white keys of a G-to-G octave, as in Example 1-9, we do not find the same pattern of whole and half steps that occurred in the C-to-C octave. In order to play a G major scale, we would need to skip the F key and play the black key that is between F and G. We will label that key with an *accidental*, a symbol that raises or lowers a pitch by a half or whole step. All the possible accidentals are listed in this table.

---

*Throughout this book we will refer to major scales with uppercase letters—for example, A major or A—and minor scales with lowercase letters—for example a minor or a.

Symbol	Name	Effect
×	Double sharp	Raise a whole step
♯	Sharp	Raise a half step
♮	Natural	Cancel a previous accidental
♭	Flat	Lower a half step
♭♭	Double flat	Lower a whole step

EXAMPLE 1-9

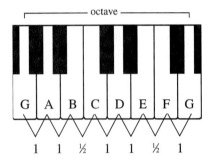

We can make our G scale conform to the major scale pattern by adding one accidental, in this case a sharp.

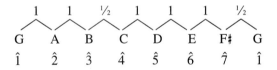

It is important to understand that major and minor scales always use all the letter names of the musical alphabet. It would not be correct to substitute a G♭ for the F♯ in a G major scale.

The scale is written on the staff in Example 1-10.

EXAMPLE 1-10

Notice that when we write or say the names of notes and accidentals, we put the accidental last (as in F♯ or F-sharp), but in staff notation the accidental always *precedes* the note that it modifies (as in Ex. 1-10).

THE MAJOR KEY SIGNATURES

One way to learn the major scales is by means of the pattern of whole and half steps discussed in the previous section. Another is by memorizing the key signatures associated with the various scales. The term *key* is used in music to identify the first degree of a scale. For instance, the *key of G major* refers to the major scale that begins on G. A *key signature* is a pattern of sharps or flats that appears at the beginning of a staff and indicates that certain notes are to be consistently raised or lowered. There are seven key signatures using sharps. In each case, the name of the major key can be found by going up a half step from the last sharp (Ex. 1-11).

EXAMPLE 1-11

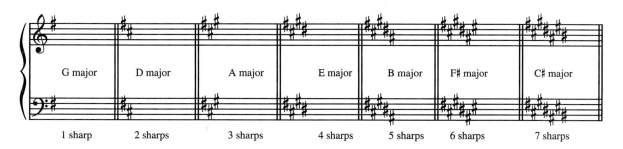

| G major | D major | A major | E major | B major | F♯ major | C♯ major |
| 1 sharp | 2 sharps | 3 sharps | 4 sharps | 5 sharps | 6 sharps | 7 sharps |

There are also seven key signatures using flats. Except for the key of F major, the name of the major key is the same as the name of next-to-last flat (Ex. 1-12).

EXAMPLE 1-12

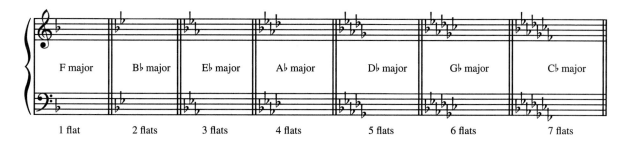

| F major | B♭ major | E♭ major | A♭ major | D♭ major | G♭ major | C♭ major |
| 1 flat | 2 flats | 3 flats | 4 flats | 5 flats | 6 flats | 7 flats |

You may have noticed that there are three pairs of major keys that would sound exactly the same—that is, they would be played on the very same keys of the piano keyboard.

B major	=	C♭ major
F♯ major	=	G♭ major
C♯ major	=	D♭ major

Notes that are spelled differently but sound the same are said to be *enharmonic*; so B major and C♭ major, for example, are *enharmonic keys*. If two major keys are not enharmonic, then they are *transpositions* of each other. To *transpose* means to write or play music in some key other than the original.

The key signatures in Examples 1-11 and 1-12 must be memorized—not only the number of accidentals involved but also their order and placement on the staff. Notice that the pattern of placing the sharps on the staff changes at the fifth sharp for both the treble and the bass clefs. Try repeating the order of accidentals for sharps (FCGDAEB) and for flats (BEADGCF) until you feel confident with them.

Key signatures are written in much the same way using the alto and tenor clefs as they are for treble and bass. The only exception is the placement of sharps in the tenor clef, as you can see in Example 1-13.

EXAMPLE 1-13

Some people find it easier to memorize key signatures if they visualize a *circle of fifths*, which is a diagram somewhat like the face of a clock. Reading clockwise around the circle of fifths below, you will see that each new key begins on $\hat{5}$ (the fifth scale degree) of the previous key.

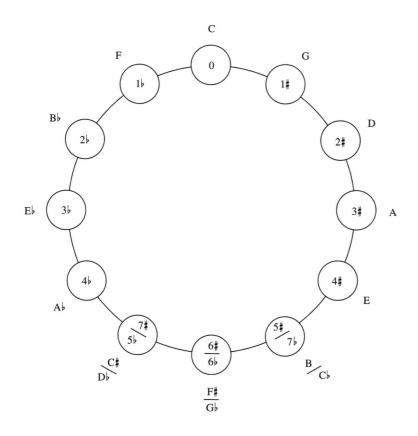

Checkpoint

1. Does G3 lie below or above middle C?
2. How is a double sharp notated?
3. Half steps in the major scale occur between scale degrees _____ and _____ as well as between scale degrees _____ and _____ .

Self-Test 1-2
(Answers begin on page 572.)

A. Notate the specified scales using accidentals, *not* key signatures. Show the placement of whole and half steps, as in the example.

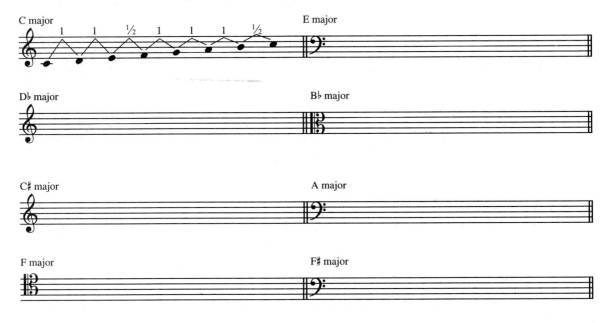

B. Identify these major key signatures

| _C_ major | ____ major | ____ major | ____ major | ____ major | ____ major | ____ major | ____ major |
| **ex.** | **1** | **2** | **3** | **4** | **5** | **6** | **7** |

C. Notate the specified key signatures.

| A major | Db major | F# major | Bb major | B major | Cb major | D major | C major |

D. Fill in the blanks.

Key signature	Name of key	Key signature	Name of key
1. Three flats	____ major	8. _____	B♭ major
2. Seven sharps	____ major	9. One sharp	____ major
3. _____	D major	10. Five flats	____ major
4. One flat	____ major	11. _____	F♯ major
5. _____	A♭ major	12. _____	C♭ major
6. _____	B major	13. Four sharps	____ major
7. Six flats	____ major	14. _____	A major

Exercise 1-2 See Workbook.

MINOR SCALES

Musicians traditionally memorize and practice three minor scale formations, although they are not used with equal frequency, as we shall see in a later chapter. One of these is the *natural minor scale*. You can see from the illustration below that the natural minor scale is like a major scale with lowered $\hat{3}$, $\hat{6}$, and $\hat{7}$.

C major	C	D	E	F	G	A	B	C
Scale degree	$\hat{1}$	$\hat{2}$	$\hat{3}$	$\hat{4}$	$\hat{5}$	$\hat{6}$	$\hat{7}$	$\hat{1}$
c natural minor	C	D	E♭	F	G	A♭	B♭	C

Another minor scale type is the *harmonic minor scale*, which can be thought of as major with lowered $\hat{3}$ and $\hat{6}$.

C major	C	D	E	F	G	A	B	C
Scale degree	$\hat{1}$	$\hat{2}$	$\hat{3}$	$\hat{4}$	$\hat{5}$	$\hat{6}$	$\hat{7}$	$\hat{1}$
c harmonic minor	C	D	E♭	F	G	A♭	B♭	C

The third type of minor scale is the *melodic minor scale*, which has an ascending form and a descending form. The ascending form, shown below, is like major with a lowered $\hat{3}$.

C major			C	D	E	F	G	A	B	C
Scale degree				$\hat{1}$	$\hat{2}$	$\hat{3}$	$\hat{4}$	$\hat{5}$	$\hat{6}$	$\hat{7}$	$\hat{1}$
c ascending melodic minor			C	D	E♭	F	G	A♭	B♭	C

The descending form of the melodic minor scale is the same as the natural minor scale.

The three minor scale types are summarized in Example 1-14. The scale degrees that differ from the major are circled. Notice the arrows used in connection with the melodic minor scale in order to distinguish the ascending $\hat{6}$ and $\hat{7}$ from the descending $\hat{6}$ and $\hat{7}$.

EXAMPLE 1-14

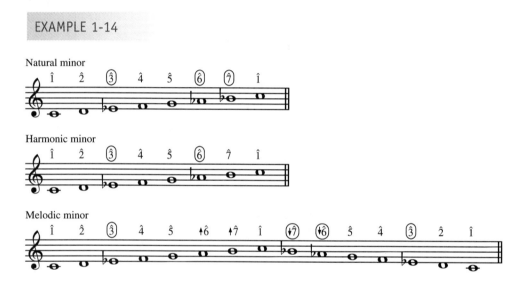

Natural minor

Harmonic minor

Melodic minor

MINOR KEY SIGNATURES

Minor key signatures conform to the natural minor scale, no matter which minor scale type is actually in use. Looking back at Example 1-14, you can see that the natural minor scale on C requires three accidentals: B♭, E♭, and A♭. The key signature of c minor, then, is the same as the key signature of E♭ major; c minor and E♭ minor are said to be *relatives* because they share the same key signature. The $\hat{3}$ of any minor key is $\hat{1}$ of its relative major, and the $\hat{6}$ of any major key is $\hat{1}$ of its relative minor. If a major scale and a minor scale share the same $\hat{1}$, as do C major and c minor, for example, they are said to be *parallels*. We would say that C major is the parallel major of c minor.

The circle of fifths is a convenient way to display the names of the minor keys and their *relative* majors as well as their key signatures.

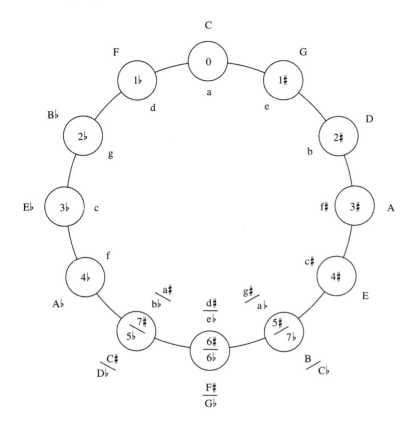

You may find it easier to learn the minor scales in terms of their relative majors, as in the circle-of-fifths diagram above, than in terms of their parallel majors, which is how minor scales were introduced on pages 13–14. This will be most helpful regarding the keys of g♯, d♯, and a♯, which have no parallel major forms. If you do use the relative major approach, remember that the key signature for any minor scale conforms to the *natural* minor scale and that accidentals must be used in order to spell the other forms. Example 1-15 illustrates the spellings for the related keys of F major and d minor.

EXAMPLE 1-15

F major scale

Relative minor, natural form

Harmonic minor raises $\hat{7}$

Melodic minor raises $\hat{6}$ and $\hat{7}$, ascending only

It is very important to practice faithfully all the major and minor scales on an instrument until they become memorized patterns. An intellectual understanding of scales cannot substitute for the secure tactile and aural familiarity that will result from those hours of practice.

Self-Test 1-3
(Answers begin on page 573.)

A. Notate the specified scales using accidentals, *not* key signatures. Circle the notes that differ from the *parallel* major scale. The melodic minor should be written both ascending and descending.

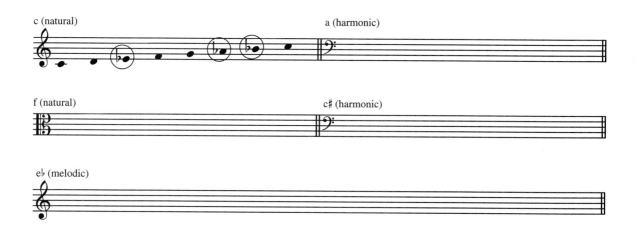

c (natural)   a (harmonic)

f (natural)   c♯ (harmonic)

e♭ (melodic)

b♭ (natural)   g♯ (harmonic)

f♯ (melodic)

B. Identify these minor key signatures.

_a_ minor ____ minor ____ minor ____ minor ____ minor ____ minor ____ minor ____ minor
ex.   **1**   **2**   **3**   **4**   **5**   **6**   **7**

C. Notate the specified minor key signatures.

b   d   g♯   c   f♯   a   b♭   a♯

D. Fill in the blanks.

Key signature	Name of key	Key signature	Name of key
1. _____	d minor	8. Two flats	____ minor
2. Six flats	____ minor	9. _____	f minor
3. Four sharps	____ minor	10. _____	b minor
4. _____	f♯ minor	11. Three flats	____ minor
5. Six sharps	____ minor	12. _____	a♭ minor
6. _____	b♭ minor	13. One sharp	____ minor
7. _____	a♯ minor	14. Five sharps	____ minor

Exercise 1-3 See Workbook.

SCALE DEGREE NAMES

Musicians in conversation or in writing often refer to scale degrees by a set of traditional names rather than by numbers. The names are shown in Example 1-16. Notice that there are two names for $\hat{7}$ in minor, depending on whether it is raised.

EXAMPLE 1-16

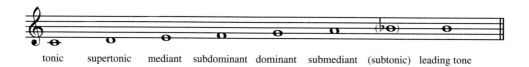

tonic   supertonic   mediant   subdominant   dominant   submediant   (subtonic)   leading tone

The origin of some of these names is not what you would probably expect from studying Example 1-16. For example, *subdominant* does not mean "below the dominant," as the chart below illustrates.

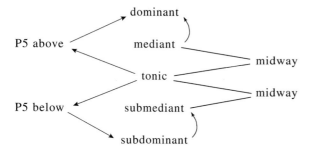

Checkpoint

Now is the time to start learning the scale degree names, if you do not know them already. Here are a couple of exercises that will help.

1.   Translate these numbers aloud to scale degree names as fast as possible. Repeat as often as necessary until speed is attained.

    $\hat{1}$ $\hat{2}$ $\hat{3}$ $\hat{4}$ $\hat{5}$ $\hat{6}$ $\hat{7}$ $\hat{1}$ $\hat{7}$ $\hat{6}$ $\hat{5}$ $\hat{4}$ $\hat{3}$ $\hat{2}$ $\hat{1}$

    $\hat{3}$ $\hat{5}$ $\hat{7}$ $\hat{6}$ $\hat{4}$ $\hat{2}$ $\hat{1}$ $\hat{6}$ $\hat{3}$ $\hat{7}$ $\hat{2}$ $\hat{5}$ $\hat{4}$ $\hat{3}$ $\hat{1}$

    $\hat{5}$ $\hat{2}$ $\hat{7}$ $\hat{4}$ $\hat{6}$ $\hat{3}$ $\hat{1}$ $\hat{2}$ $\hat{7}$ $\hat{5}$ $\hat{6}$ $\hat{4}$ $\hat{1}$ $\hat{3}$ $\hat{2}$

2. Call out or sing the scale degree names contained in each example below.

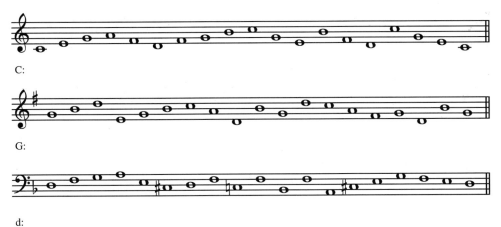

C:

G:

d:

INTERVALS

An *interval* is the measurement of the distance in pitch between two notes. A *harmonic interval* results if the notes are performed at the same time, whereas a *melodic interval* occurs when the notes are played successively (Ex. 1-17). The method of measuring intervals is the same for both harmonic and melodic intervals.

EXAMPLE 1-17

Harmonic intervals   Melodic intervals

There are two parts to any interval name: the numerical name and the modifier that precedes the numerical name. As Example 1-18 illustrates, the numerical name is a measurement of how far apart the notes are vertically on the staff, regardless of what accidentals are involved.

EXAMPLE 1-18

1   2   3   3   3   3   4   (etc.)

In speaking about intervals, we use the terms *unison* instead of 1 and *octave* (8ve) instead of 8. We also say 2nd instead of "two," 3rd instead of "three," and so on. Intervals smaller than an 8ve are called *simple intervals*, whereas larger intervals (including the 8ve) are called *compound intervals*.

It is important to notice in Example 1-18 that the harmonic interval of a 2nd is notated with the top note offset a little to the right of the bottom note. Accidentals are handled the same way for harmonic intervals of a 2nd, 3rd, or 4th, if both notes require an accidental.

Self-Test 1-4
(Answers begin on page 574.)

Provide the numerical names of the intervals by using the numbers 1 through 8.

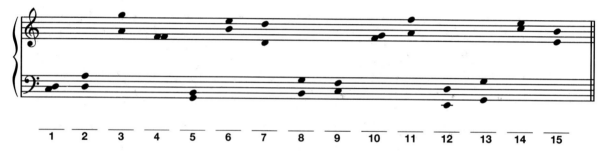

| 1 | 2 | 3 | 4 | 5 | 6 | 7 | 8 | 9 | 10 | 11 | 12 | 13 | 14 | 15 |

Exercise 1-4 See Workbook.

PERFECT, MAJOR, AND MINOR INTERVALS

One way to begin learning intervals is by relating them to the intervals contained in the major scale, specifically the intervals from $\hat{1}$ up to the other scale degrees. This method can then be applied in any context, whether or not the major scale is actually being used.

The term *perfect* (abbreviated P) is a modifier used only in connection with unisons, 4ths, 5ths, 8ves, and their compounds (11ths, and so on). As Example 1-19 illustrates, a P1, P4, P5, and P8 can all be constructed by using $\hat{1}$ in the major scale as the *bottom* note.

EXAMPLE 1-19

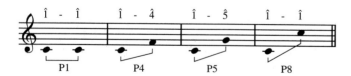

If we want to spell one of these intervals above E♭, for example, we need only to think of scale steps $\hat{1}$, $\hat{4}$, and $\hat{5}$ of the E♭ major scale. If the bottom note does not commonly serve as $\hat{1}$ of a major scale (such as D♯), remove the accidental temporarily, spell the interval, and then apply the accidental to both notes (Ex. 1-20).

EXAMPLE 1-20

P5 above   P5 above   P5 above
D♯ = ?   D♮ = A♮   D♯ = A♯

Usually, 2nds, 3rds, 6ths, and 7ths are modified by the terms *major* (M) or *minor* (m). The intervals formed by $\hat{1}$-$\hat{2}$, $\hat{1}$-$\hat{3}$, $\hat{1}$-$\hat{6}$, and $\hat{1}$-$\hat{7}$ in the major scale are all major intervals, as Example 1-21 illustrates.

EXAMPLE 1-21

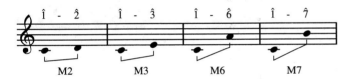

If a major interval is made a half step smaller without altering its numerical name, it becomes a minor interval (Ex. 1-22).

EXAMPLE 1-22

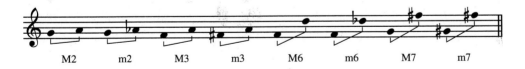

Self-Test 1-5
(Answers begin on page 574.)

A.   All the intervals below are unisons, 4ths, 5ths, or 8ves. Put "P" in the space provided
     only if the interval is a perfect interval.

B.   All the intervals below are 2nds, 3rds, 6ths, or 7ths. Write "M" or "m" in each space,
     as appropriate.

C.   Notate the specified intervals above the given notes.

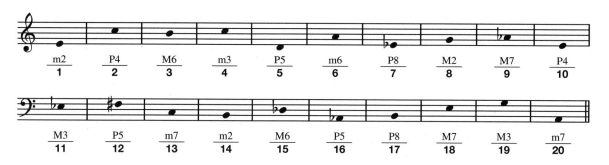

Exercise 1-5 See Workbook.

AUGMENTED AND DIMINISHED INTERVALS

If a perfect or a major interval is made a half step larger without changing the numerical name, the interval becomes *augmented* (abbreviated +). If a perfect or a minor interval is made a half step smaller without changing its numerical name, it becomes *diminished* (abbreviated °). These relationships are summarized below.

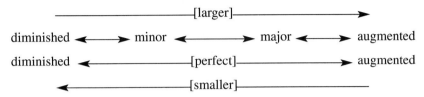

There is no such thing as a diminished unison. Doubly augmented and doubly diminished intervals are possible, but they seldom occur. *Tritone* is a term used for the +4 or its enharmonic equivalent, the °5.

INVERSION OF INTERVALS

Descending intervals, especially large ones, are often easier to spell and identify through the use of *interval inversion.* We invert an interval by putting the bottom pitch above the top one; for example, the interval D-A inverts to A-D. When we invert an interval, the new numerical name is always different from the old one. The new numerical name can be calculated by subtracting the old numerical name from 9.

Constant value of 9	9	9	9	9	9	9
Minus old numeric name	−2	−3	−4	−5	−6	−7
Equals new numeric name	7	6	5	4	3	2

You can see that an inverted 2nd becomes a 7th, a 3rd becomes a 6th, and so on (Ex. 1-23).

EXAMPLE 1-23

2   7   3   6   4   5   5   4   6   3   7   2

The modifier also changes when an interval is inverted, with the exception of perfect intervals.

Old modifier	m	M	P	+	o
New modifier	M	m	P	o	+

As an example of the usefulness of inversion, suppose you wanted to know what note lies a m6 below G3. Invert the m6 down to a M3 up, as in Example 1-24, transpose the B3 down an 8ve, and you find that the answer is B2.

EXAMPLE 1-24

m6↓ = ?   M3↑ = B3   m6↓ = B2

Fluency with intervals, as with scales, is necessary for any serious musician and will provide a solid foundation for your further study. As you did with scales, you will benefit from finding out how various intervals sound and feel on a musical instrument.

One exercise you can do (you can think of others) is to write out the notes of the chromatic scale in random order. Include each black key twice—once as a sharped note and once as a flatted note. Then play some interval above and below each note. Work for speed, using your ear to correct yourself.

CONSONANT AND DISSONANT INTERVALS

In tonal music, some harmonic intervals are considered to be consonant, whereas others are considered to be dissonant. The terms *consonant* and *dissonant* can be defined roughly as meaning pleasing to the ear and not pleasing to the ear, respectively, but these are very dependent on context. Some of the most exciting moments in tonal music involve dissonance, which is certainly not displeasing in that context, but the dissonances resolve eventually to the consonances that give them meaning. As you can imagine, this is a complex subject, and it is one with which much of this book is concerned.

For now it will suffice to say that major and minor 3rds and 6ths and perfect 5ths and 8ves are consonant. All other intervals are dissonant, except for the P4, which is dissonant only when it occurs above the lowest voice.

Checkpoint

1. What is the term for an interval in which the notes are played in succession instead of simultaneously?
2. Is there such a thing as a m5? A P6?
3. A perfect interval made a half step smaller without changing its numerical name becomes_____.
4. A °5 inverted becomes a _____.
5. Intervals that are relatively displeasing to the ear are classified as _____.

Summary

Pitch in music refers to the highness or lowness of a sound. Particular pitches are named by using the *musical alphabet*, consisting of the letters A through G, at which point the alphabet starts over. From one letter up or down to its next occurrence is called an *octave*, whereas the space from any C up to the next B is called an *octave register*. Octave registers are numbered, with the lowest C on the *piano keyboard* designated as C1. The C nearest the middle of the piano keyboard is called *middle C*, or C4.

Pitches are notated on the *staff*, an arrangement of five lines and four spaces that can be extended through the use of *ledger lines*. A staff always begins with one of several *clefs*, which determine exactly what pitch is represented by each line or space. A *grand staff* consists of two staves joined by a brace, with a treble clef on the top staff and a bass clef on the bottom.

The *major scale* consists of a particular arrangement of *whole steps* and *half steps*. Most major scales also have a *parallel minor* scale that begins on the same note but that lowers scale degrees $\hat{3}$, $\hat{6}$, and $\hat{7}$ by a half step. This form of the minor is called the *natural minor scale*. The *harmonic minor scale* lowers only scale degrees $\hat{3}$ and $\hat{6}$ of its parallel major, whereas the *melodic minor scale* lowers scale degree $\hat{3}$ when ascending and scale degrees $\hat{3}$, $\hat{6}$, and $\hat{7}$ when descending.

Every scale has an associated *key signature*, consisting of zero to seven sharps or flats arranged in a particular way on the staff. There are 15 key signatures in all, with one major and one minor scale associated with each. Major and minor keys that share the same key signature are said to be *relative keys*. The notes of a scale are all assigned *scale degree names*, which vary only slightly between major and minor. *Enharmonic* notes or keys sound the same but are spelled differently. To *transpose* music means to play it in another key.

The difference between any two pitches is called an *interval*. A *harmonic interval* separates pitches that are sounded simultaneously, whereas a *melodic interval* separates pitches that are sounded in succession. Intervals are defined by means of a numerical name and a modifier that precedes it. These modifiers include the terms *perfect, major, minor, augmented,* and *diminished.* To *invert* an interval, put the lower note above the upper one (or the reverse). The numerical name and modifier of an inverted interval can be predicted using the method explained in this chapter.

Consonant intervals include major and minor 3rds and 6ths, the P5, and the P8. The P4 is usually consonant, unless it occurs above the lowest voice.

Self-Test 1-6
(Answers begin on page 575.)

A. Most of the intervals below are either augmented or diminished. Label each interval.

B. Label what each interval becomes when it is inverted.

1. P4 becomes _____   **5.** °5 becomes _____

2. M7 becomes _____   **6.** m2 becomes _____

3. +2 becomes _____   **7.** m6 becomes _____

4. M3 becomes _____   **8.** +6 becomes _____

C. Notate the specified interval *below* the given note. (You may find it helpful to invert the interval first in some cases.)

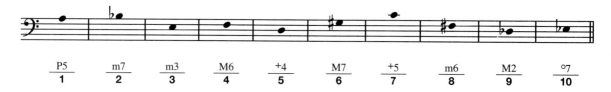

D.   Label each interval in this melody (from Wagner's *Götterdämmerung*).

Exercise 1-6 See Workbook.

Chapter 2

Elements of Rhythm

RHYTHM

This chapter is concerned with the time aspect of music—how sounds are notated so that they will occur at a predictable moment and in a predetermined pattern. *Rhythm* is a general term used to refer to the time aspect of music, as contrasted with the pitch aspect.

DURATIONAL SYMBOLS

Durations are notated by using symbols that are organized so that each symbol is twice the duration of the next shorter symbol and half the duration of the next longer symbol. The table below lists a number of these symbols.

Value	Note	Rest
Breve	𝅜 = o + o	= +
Whole	o = 𝅗𝅥 + 𝅗𝅥	= +
Half	𝅗𝅥 = ♩ + ♩	= 𝄽 + 𝄽
Quarter	♩ = ♪ + ♪	𝄽 = 𝄾 + 𝄾
Eighth	♪ = ♬ + ♬	𝄾 = 𝄿 + 𝄿
Sixteenth	♬ = 𝅘𝅥𝅲 + 𝅘𝅥𝅲	𝄿 = 𝅀 + 𝅀

The same series could be continued to thirty-seconds, sixty-fourths, and so on. Durations other than these must be indicated through the use of ties, dots, or other symbols. A *tie* is a curved line that connects two notes of the same pitch, creating a new duration that is equal to their sum. A *dot* always adds to the duration one-half the value of the note, rest, or dot that precedes it, for example ♩. = ♩ ♪ and ♩.. = ♩ ♪ 𝅘𝅥𝅲. When notated on the staff, a dot is never placed on a staff line. If the notehead itself is on a staff line, the dot is put to the right of the note but in the space *above* it.

BEAT AND TEMPO

The *beat* is the basic pulse of a musical passage. To determine the beat of a passage you are listening to, tap your foot to the music or try to imagine the way a conductor would conduct the passage—the conductor's arm movement. The resulting steady pulse is called the beat, and the rate at which the beats occur is called the *tempo*.

A composer commonly specifies the tempo of a passage by one of two methods—sometimes by both. The first method uses words, often in Italian, to describe the tempo.

Italian	English	German	French
Grave	Solemn	Schwer	Lourd
Largo	Broad	Breit	Large
Lento	Slow	Langsam	Lent
Adagio	Slow	Langsam	Lent
Andante	Moderately slow	Gehend	Allant
Moderato	Moderate	Mässig	Modéré
Allegretto	Moderately fast	Etwas bewegt	Un peu animé
Allegro	Fast	Schnell	Animé
Vivace	Lively	Lebhaft	Vif
Presto	Very fast	Eilig	Vite

The second method is more exact because it shows precisely how many beats are to occur in the space of one minute. For example, if the desired tempo would result in seventy-two quarter notes in one minute, the tempo indication would be ♩ = 72 or M.M. ♩ = 72. The M.M. stands for Maelzel's metronome, after Johann Maelzel, who widely promoted the device during the early nineteenth century.

METER

Beats tend to be grouped into patterns that are consistent throughout a passage; the pattern of beats is called the *meter*. Groups of two, three, and four beats are the most common, although other meters occur. Incidentally, a group of four beats could often also be interpreted as two groups of two beats each and vice versa. In any case, the groups of beats are called *measures* (abbreviated m. or mm.), and in notation the end of a measure is always indicated by a vertical line through the staff called a *bar line*. The words *duple, triple,* and *quadruple* are used to refer to the number of beats in each measure, so we have *duple meter, triple meter,* and *quadruple meter*. These terms are summarized below, along with the pattern of stresses usually found in each meter (referred to as *metric accent*).

Grouping	Meter type	Metric accent pattern
Two-beat measure	Duple	Strong-weak
Three-beat measure	Triple	Strong-weak-weak
Four-beat measure	Quadruple	Strong-weak-less strong-weak

As you might imagine, most marches are in duple meter because people have two feet, whereas contemporary popular music tends to be in duple or quadruple meter. Waltzes are always in triple meter, as are a number of traditional songs such as "Amazing Grace" and "Scarborough Fair."

The meter of many passages is clear and easily identified, but in other cases the meter might be ambiguous. For example, sing "Take Me Out to the Ball Game" quite slowly while you tap you foot or conduct, then decide on the meter type. Now sing it again, but very fast. The first time you probably felt the meter was triple, but at a faster tempo you should have identified the meter as duple (or quadruple). Between those extreme tempos are more moderate tempos, which two listeners might interpret in different ways—one hearing a faster triple meter, the other a slower duple meter. Both listeners would be correct because identifying meter is a matter of interpretation rather than of right and wrong.

Self-Test 2-1
(Answers begin on page 575.)

A. Show how many notes or rests of the shorter duration would be required to equal the longer duration.

ex. ♩ × __2__ = 𝅝

1. ♪ × ___ = ♩

2. ♩ × ___ = 𝅝

3. ♪ × ___ = ♩.

4. ♬ × ___ = 𝅗𝅥

5. 𝄾 × ___ = ▬

6. 𝄾 × ___ = 𝄾·

7. 𝄽 × ___ = ▬

8. ♬ × ___ = ♩..

9. ♪ × ___ = 𝅗𝅥 ♪

10. 𝅘𝅥𝅯 × ___ = ♪.

11. 𝄽· × ___ = ▬·

12. ▬ × ___ = 𝌀

13. 𝄾 × ___ = 𝄽

14. ♩ × ___ = 𝌀

15. ♪. × ___ = ♩.

16. ♪ × ___ = 𝅝·

B. Sing aloud each of the songs listed below. Then identify the meter type of each, using the terms *duple, triple,* and *quadruple.*

1. "Silent Night" (slow tempo)_____

2. "Jingle Bells"_____

3. "America the Beautiful"_____

4. "Seventy-Six Trombones"_____

5. "Home on the Range"_____

C. Scale review. Given the key and the scale degree, supply the note name. Assume the *melodic minor* form for each minor key.

ex. f♯:	$\hat{4}$	B		**8.** B♭:	$\hat{4}$	____
1. D♭:	$\hat{6}$	____		**9.** c:	$\downarrow\hat{6}$	____
2. f:	$\hat{3}$	____		**10.** e:	$\hat{4}$	____
3. A:	$\hat{5}$	____		**11.** A♭:	$\hat{7}$	____
4. B:	$\hat{3}$	____		**12.** F♯:	$\hat{2}$	____
5. g:	$\uparrow\hat{6}$	____		**13.** b♭:	$\hat{5}$	____
6. c♯:	$\downarrow\hat{7}$	____		**14.** E:	$\hat{6}$	____
7. E♭:	$\hat{5}$	____		**15.** d:	$\uparrow\hat{7}$	____

Exercise 2-1 See Workbook.

DIVISION OF THE BEAT

In most musical passages we hear durations that are shorter than the beat. We call these shorter durations *divisions of the beat.* Beats generally divide either into two equal parts, called *simple beat,* or into three equal parts, called *compound beat.* Be careful not to confuse beat type, which refers to how the *beat* divides (simple or compound), with meter type, which refers to how the *measure* divides (duple, triple, or quadruple). The common beat and meter types can be combined with each other in six possible ways.

Beat	Meter		
	Duple	**Triple**	**Quadruple**
Simple	Simple duple	Simple triple	Simple quadruple
Compound	Compound duple	Compound triple	Compound quadruple

For example, sing "Take Me Out to the Ball Game" quickly in duple meter, as you did in the discussion of meter on p. 30. You can hear that the beats divide into thirds, so this is an example of compound duple. Do the same with "I Don't Know How to Love Him" (from *Jesus Christ Superstar*) or "Around Her Neck She Wore a Yellow Ribbon," and you will find that both are simple duple (or simple quadruple).

Checkpoint

1. How many 16th notes are there in a half note?
2. Two dots following a quarter note add what durations to it?
3. What is the term that refers to the number of beats in a measure?
4. What term refers to the way that the beats divide?

Self-Test 2-2
(Answers begin on page 576.)

Sing aloud each of the songs listed below. Then identify the beat and meter types of each, using terms such as *simple duple* and so on.

   1. "Auld Lang Syne"_____   _____

   2. "Pop Goes the Weasel" _____   _____

   3. "Silent Night" _____   _____

   4. "Jingle Bells" _____   _____

   5. "Seventy-Six Trombones"_____   _____

SIMPLE TIME SIGNATURES

A time signature is a symbol that tells the performer how many beats will occur in each measure, what note value will represent the beat, and whether the beat is simple or compound. A time signature for a simple beat has 2, 3, or 4 as the top number. The top number indicates the number of beats in the measure; the bottom number indicates the beat note (2 = 𝅗𝅥, 4 = ♩, 8 = ♪, and so on). Some typical simple time signatures are listed in the following table.

Time signature	Beats per measure	Beat note	Division of the beat
$\frac{2}{4}$	2	♩	♫
$\frac{2}{2}$ or ¢	2	𝅗𝅥	♩ ♩
$\frac{3}{16}$	3	♬	♬♬
$\frac{3}{4}$	3	♩	♫
$\frac{4}{8}$	4	♪	♬
$\frac{4}{4}$ or C	4	♩	♫

Example 2-1 illustrates how some of the songs we have been considering might be notated. The beat values were chosen arbitrarily; "Jingle Bells," for example, could also be notated correctly in $\frac{2}{2}$ or $\frac{2}{8}$ or any other simple duple time signature.

EXAMPLE 2-1

"Jingle Bells"

"America the Beautiful"

"Home on the Range"

Self-Test 2-3
(Answers begin on page 576.)

A. Fill in the blanks.

	Beat and meter type	Beat note	Division of the beat	Time signature
1.	Simple duple	♩		
2.				$\frac{3}{8}$
3.			♩ ♩	2
4.	Simple quadruple		♫	
5.	Simple triple	♪		

B. Renotate the excerpts from Example 2-1 using the specified time signatures.

  1. $\frac{2}{8}$ "Jingle Bells"

  2. $\frac{4}{2}$ "America the Beautiful"

  3. $\frac{3}{4}$ "Home on the Range"

Exercise 2-3 See Workbook.

COMPOUND TIME SIGNATURES

If the beat divides into three equal parts, as in compound beat, the note value representing the beat will be a dotted value, as shown below.

Beat note	Division of the beat
𝅗𝅥.	♩ ♩ ♩
♩.	♫♪
♪.	♫♪
♪.	♫♪

Dotted values present a problem where time signatures are concerned. For example, if there are two beats per measure, and the beat note is ♩., what would the time signature be? $\frac{2}{4\frac{1}{2}}$? $\frac{2}{4+8}$? $\frac{2}{8+8+8}$? There is no easy solution, and the method that survives today is the source of much confusion concerning compound beat. Simply stated, a compound time signature informs the musician of the *number of divisions* of the beat contained in a measure and what the *division duration* is. This means that the top number of a compound time signature will be 6, 9, or 12 because two beats times three divisions equals six, three beats times three divisions equals nine, and four beats times three divisions equals twelve. Some examples are given in the table below.

Time signature	Beats per measure	Beat note	Division of the beat
$\frac{6}{8}$	2	♩.	♪♪♪
$\frac{6}{4}$	2	♩.	♩♩♩
$\frac{9}{16}$	3	♪.	♪♪♪
$\frac{9}{8}$	3	♩.	♪♪♪
$\frac{12}{8}$	4	♩.	♪♪♪
$\frac{12}{4}$	4	♩.	♩♩♩

Example 2-2 illustrates some familiar tunes that use compound beat. As before, the choice of the actual beat note is an arbitrary one.

EXAMPLE 2-2

"Take Me Out to the Ball Game"

"Down in the Valley"

"Pop Goes the Weasel"

You can see from this discussion that compound time signatures do *not* follow the rule, so often learned by the student musician, that "the top number tells how many beats are in a measure, and the bottom number tells what note gets the beat." Of course, there are some pieces in $\frac{6}{8}$, for example, that really do have six beats to the measure, but such a piece is not really in compound duple. A measure of $\frac{6}{8}$ performed in six does not sound like compound duple; instead, it sounds like two measures of simple triple, or $\frac{3}{8}$. In compound duple, the listener must hear two compound beats to the measure, not six simple beats. In the same way, a slow work notated in $\frac{2}{4}$ might be conducted in four, which would seem to the listener to be simple quadruple. In both cases, the usual division value has become the beat value.

The reverse also occurs—that is, the usual beat value sometimes becomes the actual division value. For example, a fast waltz or scherzo is almost always notated as simple triple, usually as $\frac{3}{4}$. But the aural effect is of one beat per measure, for which we might use the term *compound single*. If you didn't know the metric convention of such pieces, you would probably assume when hearing them that they were in compound duple because the measures tend to group in pairs.

Checkpoint

1. What three numbers are found on the top of simple time signatures?
2. What three numbers are found on the top of compound time signatures?
3. If the top number of a compound time signature is **9**, how many beats will there be in the measure?

Self-Test 2-4
(Answers begin on page 577.)

A. Fill in the blanks.

Beat and meter type	Beat note	Division of the beat	Time signature
1. Compound duple	♩.		
2.			9/4
3.	𝅗𝅥.		6
4. Compound quadruple		♫ (beamed sixteenths)	
5.		♫ (beamed eighths)	9

B. Renotate the excerpts from Example 2-2 using the specified time signatures.

1. ⁶₄ "Take Me Out to the Ball Game"

2. ⁹₈ "Down in the Valley"

3. ⁶₁₆ "Pop Goes the Weasel"

Exercise 2-4 See Workbook.

TIME SIGNATURES SUMMARIZED

There are two types of beat, simple and compound, and three common meters, duple, triple, and quadruple, which can be combined in a total of six ways. For each of these six combinations there is a number that will always appear as the top part of the time signature.

Beat type	Meter type		
	Duple	Triple	Quadruple
Simple	2	3	4
Compound	6	9	12

A listener can usually recognize the beat and meter types of a passage without seeing the music. Therefore, you can usually say what the top number of the time signature is (except that duple and quadruple are often indistinguishable). However, to know what the bottom number of the time signature is, you have to look at the music because any number representing a note value can be used for any meter.

Bottom number	Simple beat duration	Compound beat duration
1	𝅝	𝅝·
2	𝅗𝅥	𝅝·
4	𝅘𝅥	𝅗𝅥·
8	𝅘𝅥𝅮	𝅘𝅥·
16	𝅘𝅥𝅯	𝅘𝅥𝅮·

Remember that the bottom number of a time signature (the leftmost column in the table above) stands for the *beat* value in a *simple* time signature and the *division* value in a *compound* time signature.

MORE ON DURATIONAL SYMBOLS

When rhythms are notated, it is customary to use rests, beams, ties, and dots in such a way that the metric accent is emphasized rather than obscured. Several incorrect and correct examples are notated below.

Incorrect	Correct

Of course, it is correct to notate rhythms so as to obscure the metric accent when that is the desired result. *Syncopations* (rhythmic figures that stress normally weak beats or divisions) are frequently notated in that way, as below.

More involved figures, such as the following, are especially common in twentieth-century music.

$$\frac{2}{4} \; \text{♩. ♫ ♩ ♪ ♪ |} = \frac{3}{8} + \frac{2}{8} + \frac{3}{8}$$

A *grouplet* (or tuplet) refers to the division of an undotted value into some number of equal parts other than two, four, eight, and so on or the division of a dotted value into some number of equal parts other than three, six, twelve, and so on, as you can see below.

Original value	Grouplet
♩	(triplet eighths) also (triplet), etc.
𝅝 (half)	(triplet quarters)
♩.	(duplet)
𝅗𝅥.	(quadruplet)
♩	(quintuplet sixteenths)

Of all the possibilities, the superimposition of triplets on a simple beat is the most common. The note value of a grouplet is determined by the next longer available note value. For example, a third of a quarter note is longer than a sixteenth note but shorter than an eighth note, so the eighth note is chosen to represent it.

When a single-stem note is notated on the staff, the stem should go up if the note is below the middle line and down if the note is above the middle line. A note on the middle line theoretically can have its stem point in either direction, but most professional copyists consistently put a downward stem on notes that occur on the middle line (Ex. 2-3).

EXAMPLE 2-3

Beams are used to connect durations shorter than a quarter note when the durations occur within the same beat. Not all professional copyists follow the same rules for determining the stem direction of beamed notes. Our preference is to decide the direction of the stems on the basis of the note that is farthest the middle line. That is, if the note that is farthest from the middle line is below it, all the stems that are to be beamed together will point upward (Ex. 2-4).

EXAMPLE 2-4

Summary

Rhythm refers to the time aspect of music, as contrasted with the pitch aspect. The relative duration of a musical sound is specified by a *durational symbol*, such as a whole note, half note, and so on. One or more *dots* may follow a durational symbol, each one adding to the duration one-half the value of the note or dot that precedes it; a *tie* connects two notes, creating a value equal to their sum. Most durational symbols use *stems*, and there are conventions of notation regarding the direction of the stems. *Beams* are often used to group together (but not to tie) durations shorter than a quarter-note.

The basic pulse of a musical passage is called the *beat,* and the *tempo* is the rate at which the beats occur. The general tempo may be indicated by one of many terms in English or other languages, or it may be specified more exactly by a *metronome* marking.

Beats usually group into patterns of two, three, or four beats, referred to as *duple, triple,* and *quadruple meters,* respectively. Associated with each meter is its own pattern of *metric accents.* Beats in any meter usually divide into two equal parts (*simple beat*) or three equal parts (*compound beat*), giving rise to such terms as "triple simple" and "duple compound." A *grouplet* is used when a beat divides in a way that is contrary to the prevailing division of the beat.

A *time signature* is a symbol that tells the performer the beat and meter types and what note value will represent the beat. A listener can identify the beat and meter types, but not the note value that represents the beat, just by listening to the music. The beat values for simple time signatures are always undotted notes, whereas those for compound time signatures are always dotted notes.

Self-Test 2-5
(Answers begin on page 577.)

A.   Fill in the blanks.

	Beat and meter type	Beat value	Division of the beat	Time signature
1.				$\frac{4}{4}$
2.	Compound triple	𝅘𝅥𝅭.		
3.				$\frac{2}{8}$
4.	Compound duple		𝅘𝅥 𝅘𝅥 𝅘𝅥	
5.			𝅘𝅥 𝅘𝅥	**3**
6.			𝅘𝅥𝅮𝅘𝅥𝅮𝅘𝅥	**12**

B. Each measure below is incomplete. Add one or more rests to the end of each to complete the measure.

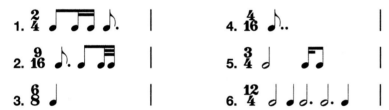

C. Provide the best time signature for each exercise. In some cases more than one correct answer might be possible.

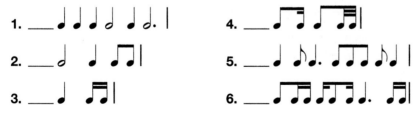

D. Each passage below is notated so that placement of the beats is obscured in some
    fashion. Rewrite each one to clarify the beat placement. This may involve breaking
    some of the long notes into tied shorter notes or rebeaming groups of notes.

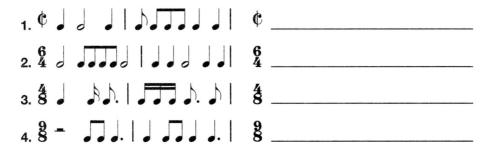

E. Add stems as required.

    1. Each duration is a quarter note.

    2. Each duration is an eighth note. Beam them in groups of three.

F. Listen to a recording of the beginning of each of the five movements of Beethoven's
    Symphony No. 6, Op. 68, and identify the beat and meter types of each. Then name
    three time signatures that *could* have been used to notate the movement.

Movement	Beat type	Meter type	Possible time signatures
I			
II			
III			
IV			
V			

G. Scale review. Given the scale degree, the note, and whether the key is major or minor, supply the name of the key. Assume melodic minor for all minor key examples.

ex. ↑6̂ is C♯ in __e__ minor

1. 4̂ is B♭ in ____ minor
2. 3̂ is B in ____ major
3. ↑7̂ is B♯ in ____ minor
9. ↑6̂ is G♯ in ____ minor
4. 6̂ is F♯ in ____ major
10. 5̂ is C in ____ major
5. 4̂ is E♭ in ____ major
11. 3̂ is B♭ in ____ minor
6. 5̂ is G in ____ minor
12. ↓7̂ is E in ____ minor
7. 6̂ is B in ____ major
13. 7̂ is D♯ in ____ major
8. 5̂ is B♭ in ____ major
14. 2̂ is B♭ in ____ major

H. Interval review. Notate the specified interval above the given note.

1 — m2 2 — P4 3 — P5 4 — M2 5 — M7 6 — +6 7 — M3 8 — M6 9 — °7

I. Interval review. Notate the specified interval below the given note.

1 — m3 2 — m6 3 — °5 4 — m7 5 — P5 6 — m2 7 — M7 8 — +2 9 — P4

Exercise 2-5 See Workbook.

Chapter 3

Introduction to Triads and Seventh Chords

INTRODUCTION

In this chapter we begin working with chords, the basic vocabulary of tonal harmony. We will not be concerned at this stage with how chords are used compositionally or even what kinds of chords occur in the major and minor modes, although we will encounter these topics soon enough. First we have to learn how to spell the more common chord types and how to recognize them in various contexts.

TRIADS

In "To the Student" (pp. xi–xiv), we explained that tonal harmony makes use of *tertian* (built of 3rds) chords. The fundamental tertian sonority is the triad, a three-note chord consisting of a 5th divided into two superimposed 3rds. There are four possible ways to combine major and minor 3rds to produce a tertian triad.

The names and abbreviations for these four triad types are given in Example 3-1.

EXAMPLE 3-1

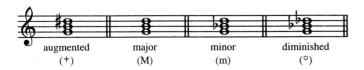

| augmented | major | minor | diminished |
| (+) | (M) | (m) | (°) |

Play these triads at the piano and compare the way they sound. You might be able to guess from listening to them that in tonal music the major and minor triads are found the most often, the augmented the least often. There are also names (in addition to note names) for the members of a triad (Ex. 3-2).

EXAMPLE 3-2

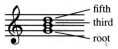

Study the preceding diagram and examples very carefully before going on.

Checkpoint

1. Which triad types contain a m3 as the bottom interval? As the top interval?
2. Which triad types contain a M3 as the top interval? As the bottom interval?
3. Which triad types contain a P5 between the root and the 5th? a°5? a +5?

Self-Test 3-1
(Answers begin on page 579.)

A. Spell the triad, given the root and type. (As with keys, uppercase letters indicate major, and lowercase letters indicate minor; augmented triads are represented by uppercase letters followed by + and diminished by lowercase letters followed by °.)

1. b♭ _____   **7.** A _____

2. E _____   **8.** d _____

3. g° _____   **9.** G♭ _____

4. f° _____   **10.** B _____

5. c _____   **11.** a♭ _____

6. D+ _____   **12.** c♯ _____

B. Notate the triad, given the root and type.

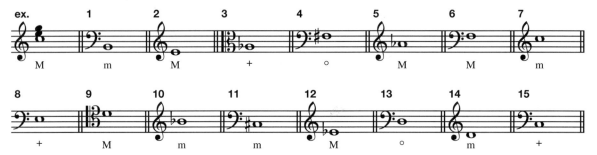

C. Fill in the blanks.

	ex.	1.	2.	3.	4.	5.	6.	7.	8.	9.	10.
Fifth	F	___	___	___	D♯	___	___	___	___	G♯	B
Third	D	A	G♭	___	___	___	F♯	C♯	___	___	___
Root	B♭	___	___	B	___	C♭	___	___	F	___	___
Type	M	+	m	m	+	M	°	M	°	m	M

D. Given the chord quality and one member of the triad, notate the remainder of the triad, with the root as the lowest tone.

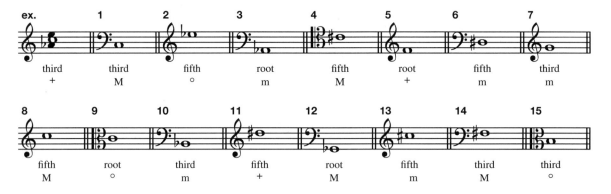

Exercise 3-1 See Workbook.

SEVENTH CHORDS

If we extend a tertian triad by adding another 3rd on top of the 5th of the triad, the result is a four-note chord. Because the interval between this added note and the root is some kind of 7th (major, minor, or diminished), chords of this sort are called *seventh chords.*

Because it would be possible to use more than one kind of 7th with each triad type, there are many more seventh-chord types than triad types. However, tonal harmony commonly makes use of only five seventh-chord types (Ex. 3-3). Below each chord in Example 3-3 you will find the commonly used name for each chord and the symbol used as an abbreviation. Be sure to play Example 3-3 to familiarize yourself with the sound of these chords.

EXAMPLE 3-3

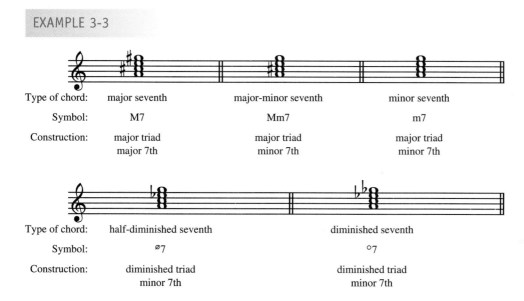

Type of chord:	major seventh	major-minor seventh	minor seventh
Symbol:	M7	Mm7	m7
Construction:	major triad major 7th	major triad minor 7th	major triad minor 7th

Type of chord:	half-diminished seventh	diminished seventh
Symbol:	ø7	°7
Construction:	diminished triad minor 7th	diminished triad minor 7th

Quite soon we will begin composition exercises using triads. Although seventh chords will not be used in composition exercises for some time, you will nevertheless be able to start becoming familiar with them from an analytical standpoint through examples and analysis assignments.

Checkpoint

1. Which seventh-chord types have a diminished triad on the bottom?
2. Which ones have a M3 between the 5th and the 7th of the chord?
3. Which ones have a m3 between the 3rd and the 5th of the chord?
4. Which ones contain at least one P5? Which contain two?

Self-Test 3-2
(Answers begin on page 580.)

A. Identify the type of each seventh chord, using the abbreviations given in Example
3-3 (M7, Mm7, m7, ᵒ⁷, ᵒ7).

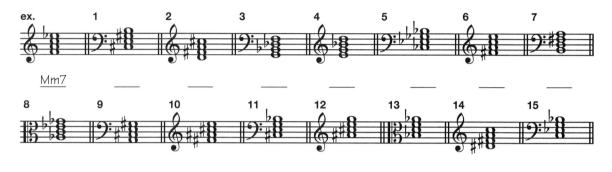

B. Notate the seventh chord, given the root and type.

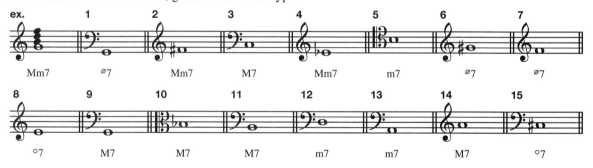

C. Given the seventh chord quality and one member of the chord, notate the rest of the
chord.

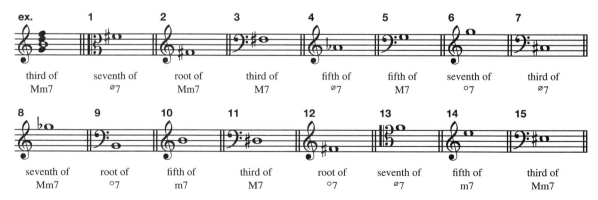

Exercise 3-2 See Workbook.

INVERSIONS OF CHORDS

Up to now, we have been notating all chords with the root as the lowest tone. However, in a musical context, any part of a chord might appear as the lowest tone. The three possible *bass positions* of the triad are illustrated in Example 3-4.

EXAMPLE 3-4

The bass position that we have been using, with the root as the lowest tone (or "in the bass"), is called *root position*. You might assume that "third position" would be the term for a chord with the 3rd as the lowest tone, but musical terminology is fraught with inconsistencies. Instead, this position is called *first inversion*. Reasonably enough, *second inversion* is used for chords with the 5th in the bass. The term *inversion* is used here to mean the transfer of the lowest note to some higher octave.

EXAMPLE 3-5

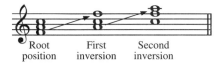

Root   First   Second
position   inversion   inversion

All the chords in Example 3-6 are first inversion F major triads. Notice that the upper notes of the chord can be spaced in any way without altering the bass position. Also, any of the notes can be duplicated (or *doubled*) in different octaves.

EXAMPLE 3-6

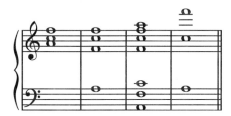

(All are in first inversion)

The inversion of seventh chords works just like the inversion of triads, except that three inversions (four bass positions) are possible (Ex. 3-7).

EXAMPLE 3-7

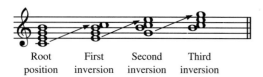

| Root | First | Second | Third |
| position | inversion | inversion | inversion |

INVERSION SYMBOLS AND FIGURED BASS

In analyzing music we often use numbers to indicate the bass positions of chords. Instead of using 1 for first inversion, 2 for second inversion, and so on, we use numbers derived from the Baroque system called *figured bass* or *thoroughbass*. During the Baroque period (approximately 1600–1750), the keyboard player in an ensemble read from a part consisting only of a bass line and some symbols indicating the chord to be played.

In the Baroque system, the symbols consisted basically of numbers representing *intervals above the bass* to be formed by the members of the chord, but the notes could actually be played in any octave above the bass. The system dealt only with intervals, not with roots of chords, because the theory of chord roots had not been devised when figured bass was first developed.

The table below illustrates the figured bass symbols for root position and inverted triads and seventh chords for a G major triad and a G Mm 7.

Sonority desired							
Complete figured bass symbol	$\begin{smallmatrix}5\\3\end{smallmatrix}$	$\begin{smallmatrix}6\\3\end{smallmatrix}$	$\begin{smallmatrix}6\\4\end{smallmatrix}$	$\begin{smallmatrix}7\\5\\3\end{smallmatrix}$	$\begin{smallmatrix}6\\5\\3\end{smallmatrix}$	$\begin{smallmatrix}6\\4\\3\end{smallmatrix}$	$\begin{smallmatrix}6\\4\\2\end{smallmatrix}$
Symbol most often used		6	$\begin{smallmatrix}6\\4\end{smallmatrix}$	7	$\begin{smallmatrix}6\\5\end{smallmatrix}$	$\begin{smallmatrix}4\\3\end{smallmatrix}$	$\begin{smallmatrix}4\\2\end{smallmatrix}$
How to find the root	Bass note	6th above bass	4th above bass	Bass note	6th above bass	4th above bass	2nd above bass

In the figured bass system, the number 6 designates a 6th above the bass. Whether it is a M6 or a m6 depends on the key signature. If the Baroque composer wished to direct the keyboard player to raise or lower a note, there were several methods that could be used, including the following three.

1. An accidental next to an arabic numeral in the figured bass could be used to raise or lower a note.

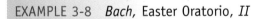

2. An accidental by itself always referred to the 3rd above the bass and could be used to alter that note.

3. A slash or plus sign in connection with an arabic numeral meant to raise that note.

Example 3-8 illustrates a portion of an actual figured bass part from the Baroque period, along with a possible *realization*. Some keyboard players may have added embellishments not shown in this realization. Bach included the numeral 5 at several places to remind the player to play a root position triad.

EXAMPLE 3-8 *Bach,* Easter Oratorio, *II*

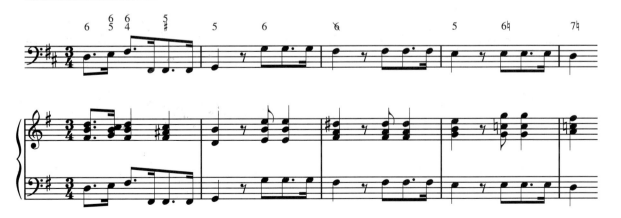

The realization of figured basses is still considered to be an effective way to learn certain aspects of tonal composition, and we will occasionally use exercises of this kind in the text.

The inversion symbols that we use today are summarized in the table below. These symbols are usually used with a roman numeral (as in I^6 or V^6_5) as part of a harmonic analysis. Notice that when a seventh chord is inverted, the 7 is replaced by the appropriate inversion symbol.

Bass position	Triad symbol	Seventh chord symbol
Root position	(none)	7
First inversion	6	$^6_5$
Second inversion	$^6_4$	$^4_3$
Third Inversion	(none)	$^4_2$ or 2

LEAD SHEET SYMBOLS

There are some intriguing parallels and contrasts between the figured bass system of the seventeenth and eighteenth centuries and the lead sheet symbols (sometimes called pop symbols) developed for use with jazz and other types of popular music in the twentieth century. Both facilitated the notation process and served to provide sufficient information to allow the performer to improvise within certain bounds. However, whereas the figured bass system provided the bass line with symbols indicating the chords that were to be constructed *above* it, lead sheet symbols appear along with a melody and indicate the chords that are to be constructed *below*.

There are various lead sheet symbol systems in use, just as there were frequently minor differences between the approaches taken by different composers to the use of figured bass symbols. Nevertheless, the system below is quite widely used today and would be understood by any competent jazz or pop musician. Example 3-9 illustrates the four triad types and the five common seventh chords with their associated pop symbols. Under each chord you will find the symbols introduced in Examples 3-1 and 3-3, and under each of these is the lead sheet symbol. With the exception of the half-diminished seventh, there is a clear correlation between the two systems.

EXAMPLE 3-9

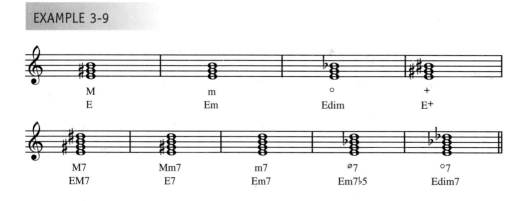

The list of symbols in Example 3-9 is incomplete because there are some chords that will be introduced in later chapters. A special case is the chord with an added sixth, as in C6, which calls for a triad with an added note a M6 above the root. Also, lead sheet symbols will occasionally specify a particular bass note, as in C/G, which calls for a C major triad over a G in the bass—a triad in second inversion. Finally, you may discover that lead sheet symbols frequently differ from one edition to the next because editors routinely make substitutions, simplifying or complicating the harmony as they see fit.

Example 3-10 is from the beginning of a typical American "standard" ballad, and it uses five of the chord types seen in Example 3-9. Notice that the ♭ in F♯m♭5 does not literally mean to flat the fifth but to lower it from C♯ to C♮.

EXAMPLE 3-10   *Kosma, "Autumn Leaves"*

English Lyric by Johnny Mercer; French Lyric by Jacques Prévert. Music by Joseph Kosma.
© 1947, 1950, 1987 Enoch et Cie. © Renewed 1975, 1978 Enoch et Cie. Sole selling Agent for North America Hal Leonard Corporation. International Copyright Secured. All rights reserved. Used by permission.

Self-Test 3-3
(Answers begin on page 581.)

A.   Identify the root and type of each chord, and show the correct inversion symbol.

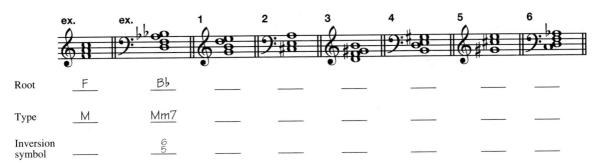

	ex.	ex.	1	2	3	4	5	6
Root	F	B♭	___	___	___	___	___	___
Type	M	Mm7	___	___	___	___	___	___
Inversion symbol	___	$\frac{6}{5}$	___	___	___	___	___	___

Root   ____   ____   ____   ____   ____   ____   ____

Type   ____   ____   ____   ____   ____   ____   ____

Inversion
symbol   ____   ____   ____   ____   ____   ____   ____

B. The bottom staff of this recitative is played on bassoon and keyboard, the keyboard
    player (the "continuo") realizing the figured bass. Fill in each blank below the bass
    line with the root and type of the chord to be played at that point. Remember that a
    numeral 5 by itself is simply a reminder to use a root position triad.

Bach, *Easter Oratorio,* II

C. Notate using whole notes on the bottom staff the chords indicated by the lead sheet symbols. Notate all chords in root position unless the symbol calls for an inversion. A 6 after a chord symbol means to add a note a M6 above the root.

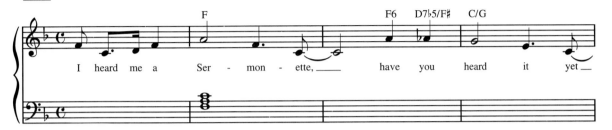

Hendricks and Adderley, "Sermonette"

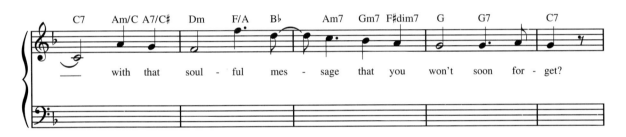

By John Hendricks and Julian Adderley. Copyright © 1955 by Silhouette Music Corp. Used by permission of Chappell & Co., Inc., Miami, FL 33014.

Exercise 3-3 See Workbook.

RECOGNIZING CHORDS IN VARIOUS TEXTURES

Some people, especially those without much keyboard experience, find it difficult at first to analyze a chord that is distributed over two or more staves, as in Example 3-11.

EXAMPLE 3-11

EXAMPLE 3-12

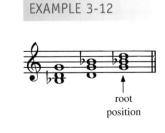

One procedure to follow with the chord is to make an inventory of all the *pitch classes** found in the chord (B♭, G, and D) and to notate the chord with each pitch class in turn as the lowest note. The other notes should be put as close to the bottom note as possible. The version that consists only of stacked 3rds is in root position. We can see from Example 3-12 that the chord in Example 3-11 is a g minor triad in first inversion.

The chord in Example 3-12 contains the pitch classes E, A, C♯, and G, allowing four bass positions.

EXAMPLE 3-13

Example 3-14 tells us that the chord in Example 3-11 is an A major-minor seventh chord in second inversion.

EXAMPLE 3-14

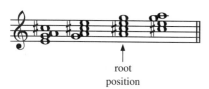

root
position

You might already be able to carry out this process in your head, which will speed things up considerably. If not, you will learn to do so with practice.

Checkpoint

1. What is the symbol for the first inversion of a triad? Of a seventh chord?
2. Explain $\frac{4}{2}$, $\frac{6}{4}$, and $\frac{4}{3}$.
3. Which bass position for which chord type requires no symbol?

*The term pitch class *is used to group together all pitches that have an identical sound or that are identical except for the octave or octaves that separate them. For example, all B♯'s, C's, and D♭♭'s belong to the same pitch class, no matter what octave they are found in.*

Summary

The fundamental sonority of tonal harmony is the *triad,* a three-note chord consisting of a 5th divided into two superimposed 3rds. The bottom note of the 5th is the *root,* and the top note is the *5th.* The note that divides the 5th is the *3rd.* There are four triad types: *major, minor, diminished,* and *augmented.*

A *seventh chord* may be thought of as a triad with another 3rd added above the 5th of the triad. The added note is a 7th above the root. Although many seventh chord types are possible, only five occur with any frequency in tonal harmony:

> *major seventh chord* (M7): major triad with a M7 above the root
>
> *major-minor seventh chord* (Mm7): major triad with a m7 above the root
>
> *minor seventh chord* (m7): minor triad with a m7 above the root
>
> *half-diminished seventh chord* (ø7): diminished triad with a m7 above the root
>
> *diminished seventh chord* (°7): diminished triad with a °7 above the root

Root position is the term for a chord with the root notated as the lowest tone. Any other arrangement is called an *inversion.* A chord with the 3rd as the lowest tone is in *first inversion,* whereas one with the 5th as the lowest tone is in *second inversion.* A seventh chord with the 7th as the lowest tone is in *third inversion.* There are symbols for most of the various bass positions:

Bass position	Triad symbol	Seventh-chord symbol	Root
Root position	none	7	Bass note
First inversion	6	$^6_5$	6th above bass
Second inversion	$^6_4$	$^4_3$	4th above bass
Third inversion	n/a	$^4_2$	2nd above bass

Inversion symbols are derived from *figured bass,* a method of abbreviated notation used in the Baroque era. *Lead sheet symbols* are used in jazz and most popular music to indicate chords to be played under a given melody. Both figured bass symbols and lead sheet (pop) symbols will be used occasionally throughout much of this text.

Self-Test 3-4
(Answers begin on page 582.)

A. Identify the root, type, and inversion symbol for each chord. All the notes in each
    exercise belong to the same chord. The lowest note is the bass note for the purpose
    of analysis.

Root   _____   _____   _____   _____   _____

Type   _____   _____   _____   _____   _____

Inversion
symbol   _____   _____   _____   _____   _____

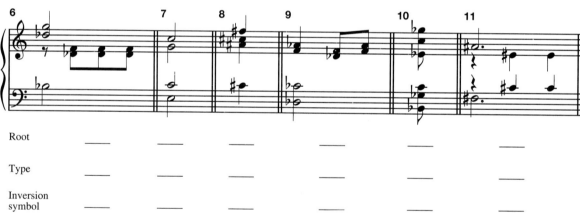

Root   _____   _____   _____   _____   _____   _____

Type   _____   _____   _____   _____   _____   _____

Inversion
symbol   _____   _____   _____   _____   _____   _____

B.   The excerpts below are to be analyzed in a similar fashion. Each chord is numbered.
     Put your analysis of each chord in the numbered blanks below the excerpt.

1. Schubert, Moment Musical, Op. 94, No. 6

Root   ___ ___ ___   ___   ___   ___ ___   ___ ___ ___   ___   ___

Type   ___ ___ ___   ___   ___   ___ ___   ___ ___ ___   ___   ___

Inversion
symbol ___ ___ ___   ___   ___   ___ ___   ___ ___ ___   ___   ___

2. Byrd, *Psalm LIV*

The *8* under the treble clef on the tenor staff (third staff from the top) means that the
notes are to be sung an 8ve lower than written.

Root   ___   ___   ___ ___ ___   ___   ___

Type   ___   ___   ___ ___ ___   ___   ___

Inversion
symbol ___   ___   ___ ___ ___   ___   ___

3. Fischer, "Blumen-Strauss"

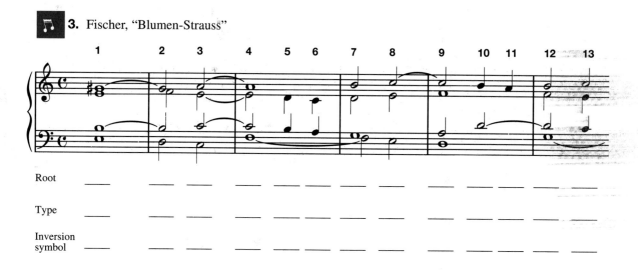

Root   ___   ___   ___   ___   ___   ___   ___   ___   ___   ___   ___   ___

Type   ___   ___   ___   ___   ___   ___   ___   ___   ___   ___   ___   ___

Inversion
symbol   ___   ___   ___   ___   ___   ___   ___   ___   ___   ___   ___   ___

Exercise 3-4 See Workbook.

Chapter 4

Diatonic Chords in Major and Minor Keys

INTRODUCTION

Now that we have presented the four triad types and the five common seventh-chord types, we can begin to look at how they are used in tonal music. Most chords in tonal music are made up only of notes from the scale on which the passage is based. That is, if a passage is in G major, most of the chords contain only notes found in the G major scale. Chords of this kind are called *diatonic* chords. All other chords—those using notes not in the scale—are called *altered* or *chromatic* chords. We will get to them later. At this point we are not going to worry about how you might *compose* music using diatonic chords, although that will come up soon. For now, we are going to concentrate on spelling and recognizing diatonic chords in various keys.

THE MINOR SCALE

Before we can begin talking about diatonic chords, we have to return to the problem of the minor scale. Because instrumentalists are taught to practice natural, harmonic, and melodic minor scales, we sometimes assume that the tonal composer had three independent minor scale forms from which to choose, but this is not how the minor mode works in tonal music.

We can make the following generalization about the three minor scales: there is, in a sense, one minor scale that has two scale steps, $\hat{6}$ and $\hat{7}$, that are variable. That is, there are two versions of $\hat{6}$ and $\hat{7}$, and both versions will usually appear in a piece in the minor mode. All the notes in Example 4-1 are diatonic to e minor. Notice the use of ↑$\hat{6}$ and ↑$\hat{7}$ to mean raised $\hat{6}$ and $\hat{7}$ and ↓$\hat{6}$ and ↓$\hat{7}$ to mean unaltered $\hat{6}$ and $\hat{7}$.

EXAMPLE 4-1

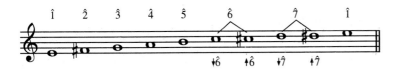

How do composers decide which version of $\hat{6}$ and $\hat{7}$ to use? Melodically, the most graceful thing for ↑$\hat{6}$ and ↑$\hat{7}$ to do is to ascend by step, whereas ↓$\hat{6}$ and ↓$\hat{7}$ tend naturally to descend by step; these tendencies conform to the melodic minor scale. Example 4-2 provides a good illustration of the use of the minor scale. If you look closely at Bach's treatment of $\hat{6}$ and $\hat{7}$ (circled notes), you will see that all the motion is stepwise, with two exceptions. The first leap involving $\hat{6}$ or $\hat{7}$ is from the G♭4 in m. 2. Here the eventual goal is F, not A, so the ↓$\hat{6}$ form is used. The other leap occurs in the bass in m. 4. Here the goal of the line is B♭, not G♭, so the ↑$\hat{7}$ form is used.

♫ EXAMPLE 4-2   *Bach,* Well-Tempered Clavier, *Book II, Prelude 22*

If a $\hat{6}$ or $\hat{7}$ is left by leap instead of by step, there will generally be an *eventual* stepwise goal for that scale degree, and the $\hat{6}$ and $\hat{7}$ will probably be raised or left unaltered according to the direction of that goal, as in Example 4-2. In the next excerpt, Example 4-3, the A♭4 in m. 1 (↓$\hat{6}$) is left by leap to the C5, but the eventual stepwise goal of the A♭4 is the G4 in the next measure, so the descending form of the melodic minor is used. Still, the use of the melodic minor is just a rule of thumb, not a law. It is not difficult to find passages in minor where ↑$\hat{6}$ and ↑$\hat{7}$ lead downward, as in m. 3.

♫ EXAMPLE 4-3   *Bach,* Well-Tempered Clavier, *Book I, Fugue 2*

And, in some cases, ↓$\hat{6}$ and ↓$\hat{7}$ lead upward (Ex. 4-4).

EXAMPLE 4-4   *Bach,* Well-Tempered Clavier, *Book I, Prelude 10*

In other instances, ↑7̂ and ↓6̂ appear next to each other, forming a harmonic minor scale (Ex. 4-5).

EXAMPLE 4-5   *Beethoven, Sonata Op. 2, No. 2, III, Trio*

The reasons for such exceptions to the melodic minor scale are usually harmonic. As we will see later in this chapter, the underlying harmonies generally conform to the harmonic minor scale.

Checkpoint

1. What is the term for chords that contain no notes outside of the scale? What about chords that do contain such notes?
2. Individual lines in tonal music tend to conform most closely to which of the three traditional minor scales?
3. Name the five common seventh-chord types.

DIATONIC TRIADS IN MAJOR

Triads may be constructed using any degree of the major scale as the root. Diatonic triads, as we have mentioned, will consist only of notes belonging to the scale. To distinguish the triads built on the various scale degrees from the scale degrees themselves, we use roman numerals instead of arabic numerals (for example, V instead of $\hat{5}$). The triad type is indicated by the form of the roman numeral itself.

Triad type	Roman numeral	Example
Major	Uppercase	V
Minor	Lowercase	vi
Diminished	Lowercase with a °	vii°
Augmented	Uppercase with a +	III+

Taking C major as an example, we can discover the types of diatonic triads that occur on each degree of the major scale.

EXAMPLE 4-6

You should memorize the following table.

Diatonic triad types in major	
Major	I, IV, and V
Minor	ii, iii, and vi
Diminished	vii°
Augmented	none

DIATONIC TRIADS IN MINOR

The construction of triads is somewhat more involved in the minor mode than in major. Because $\hat{6}$ and $\hat{7}$ are variable, and because nearly all triads contain $\hat{6}$ or $\hat{7}$, more diatonic triads are possible in minor. Nonetheless, there are seven triads in minor (one for each scale degree) that occur more frequently than the others, and these are the ones we will use in our exercises for now. The roman numerals of the more common diatonic triads are circled in Example 4-7.

EXAMPLE 4-7

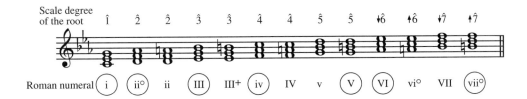

Scale degree of the root: $\hat{1}$ $\hat{2}$ $\hat{2}$ $\hat{3}$ $\hat{3}$ $\hat{4}$ $\hat{4}$ $\hat{5}$ $\hat{5}$ ↓$\hat{6}$ ↑$\hat{6}$ ↓$\hat{7}$ ↑$\hat{7}$

Roman numeral: (i) (ii°) ii (III) III+ (iv) IV v (V) (VI) vi° VII (vii°)

Notice that the *roots* of the triads circled above all belong to the *harmonic* minor scale. In fact, all the notes of the circled triads belong to the harmonic minor scale, with the exception of the 5th of the III chord. Here is the table of minor-key triads, which you should also memorize.

Common diatonic triads in minor	
Major	III, V, and VI
Minor	i and iv
Diminished	ii° and vii°
Augmented	none

Checkpoint

1. In a major key, which triads are minor?
2. In a minor key, which triads are major?
3. The triads on which two scale degrees are the same type in both major and minor?
4. Which of the four triad types occurs least often in tonal music?

Self-Test 4-1
(Answers begin on page 583.)

A. Given the key and the triad, supply the roman numeral. Be sure your roman numeral is of the correct type (uppercase and so on). Inversion symbols, where required, go to the upper right of the roman numeral (as in I⁶).

ex.   1   2   3   4   5   6   7

d: ___i___ B: _____ b: _____ A♭: _____ e: _____ F♯: _____ a: _____ D♭: _____

bb: ____   G: ____   d#: ____   C: ____   A: ____   c#: ____   Bb: ____   g: ____

B.   In the exercises below you are given the name of a key and a scale degree number. *Without using key signatures,* notate the triad on that scale degree and provide the roman numeral. In minor keys be sure to use the triad types circled in Example 4-7.

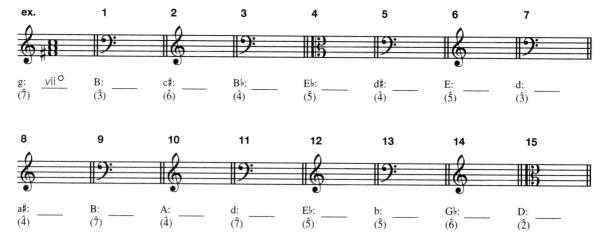

g: vii°   B: ____   c#: ____   Bb: ____   Eb: ____   d#: ____   E: ____   d: ____
(7̂)   (3̂)   (6̂)   (4̂)   (5̂)   (4̂)   (5̂)   (3̂)

a#: ____   B: ____   A: ____   d: ____   Eb: ____   b: ____   Gb: ____   D: ____
(4̂)   (7̂)   (4̂)   (7̂)   (5̂)   (5̂)   (6̂)   (2̂)

C.   Analysis. Write roman numerals in the spaces provided, making sure each roman numeral is of the correct type and includes an inversion symbol if needed. The tenor line sounds an octave lower than notated.

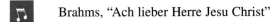

Brahms, "Ach lieber Herre Jesu Christ"

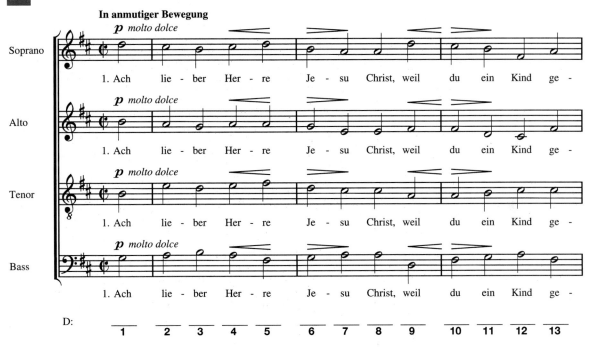

Exercise 4-1 See Workbook.

DIATONIC SEVENTH CHORDS IN MAJOR

In the next chapter we will begin simple composition exercises using triads, but seventh chords will not be used compositionally until Chapter 13. Nevertheless, we will continue to work with seventh chords in spelling exercises and in analysis to build a solid foundation for those later chapters.

The chords on each scale degree in major can include a 7th above the root. The roman numeral system for seventh chords is similar to that for triads, as you will see in the following table.

Seventh-chord type	Roman numeral	Example
Major seventh	Uppercase with M7	I^{M7}
Major-minor seventh	Uppercase with a 7	V^7
Minor seventh	Lowercase with a 7	vi^7
Half-diminished seventh	Lowercase with $^{\varnothing}7$	$ii^{\varnothing 7}$
Diminished seventh	Lowercase with $^{\circ}7$	$vii^{\circ 7}$

Four of the five seventh-chord types occur as diatonic seventh chords in major keys.

EXAMPLE 4-8

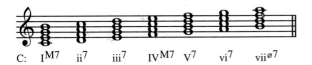

C:　I^{M7}　ii^7　iii^7　IV^{M7}　V^7　vi^7　vii^{ø7}

You should learn the following table, which summarizes major-key seventh chords.

Diatonic seventh chords in major	
M7	I^{M7} and IV^{M7}
Mm7	V^7
m7	ii^7, iii^7, and vi^7
ø7	vii^{ø7}
°7	none

DIATONIC SEVENTH CHORDS IN MINOR

Because of the variability of $\hat{6}$ and $\hat{7}$, there are sixteen possible diatonic seventh chords in minor. Example 4-9 shows the most commonly used seventh chords on each scale degree. The others will be discussed in later chapters. Notice that most of the notes in Example 4-9 belong to the harmonic minor scale.

EXAMPLE 4-9

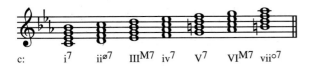

c:　　i^7　　ii^{ø7}　III^{M7}　iv^7　　V^7　　VI^{M7}　vii^{°7}

Here is the last chord table to learn.

Common diatonic seventh chords in minor	
M7	III^{M7} and VI^{M7}
Mm7	V^7
m7	i^7 and iv^7
ø7	ii^{ø7}
°7	vii^{°7}

Remember that the inversion symbols for seventh chords are $^6_5$, $^4_3$, and $^4_2$. This means that the V^7 in first inversion is symbolized as V^6_5, *not* as V^7_{65}.

Checkpoint

1. Most of the five common seventh-chord types appear diatonically in both major and minor. Which one type does not?
2. Does the m7 chord occur on more scale steps in minor than in major?
3. The seventh chords on most scale steps are different qualities in major and minor. Which chord is the exception to this?

Summary

Minor scale usage in tonal music is not really based on the natural, harmonic, and melodic minor scales, the three traditional minor scale forms presented in Chapter 1. In actual practice, scale steps $\hat{6}$ and $\hat{7}$ are variable. Although ascending and descending lines usually follow the conventions of the melodic minor scale, this is by no means always true. Both melodic and harmonic considerations must be taken into account.

We analyze the triads and seventh chords used in tonal music by means of *roman numerals* indicating the scale degree that is the root of the chord and the quality, or sound, of the chord. Although the issue of the minor scale is somewhat complicated, we can say that as a rule the following triad types are found on the various degrees of the major and minor scales:

Major	I	ii	iii	IV	V	vi	vii°
Minor	i	ii°	III	iv	V	VI	vii°

Similarly, we can generalize about the types of seventh chords:

Major	I^{M7}	ii^7	iii^7	IV^{M7}	V^7	vi^7	$vii^{ø7}$
Minor	i^7	$ii^{ø7}$	III^{M7}	iv^7	V^7	VI^{M7}	$vii^{°7}$

The roots of the triads and seventh chords in these tables all conform to the harmonic minor scale, but this is not necessarily true of the other notes in each chord.

In this chapter we have been concerned only with how diatonic triads and seventh-chords are spelled in tonal music. The more interesting and more complex topic of how they actually function in relation to each other will be the subject of later chapters.

Self-Test 4-2
(Answers begin on page 584.)

A. Given the key and the seventh chord, supply the roman numeral. Be sure your
    roman numeral is the correct type and includes inversion if applicable.

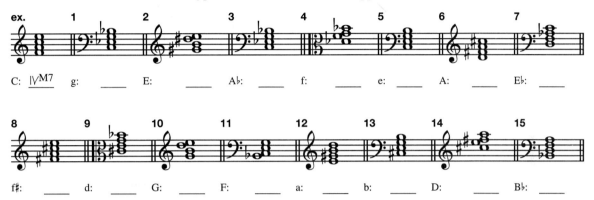

C: IVM7   g: ____   E: ____   Ab: ____   f: ____   e: ____   A: ____   Eb: ____

f#: ____   d: ____   G: ____   F: ____   a: ____   b: ____   D: ____   Bb: ____

B. In the exercises below you are given the name of a key and a scale degree number.
    Without using key signatures, notate the seventh chord on that scale degree and pro-
    vide the roman numeral. In minor keys be sure to use the chord types shown in
    Example 4-9.

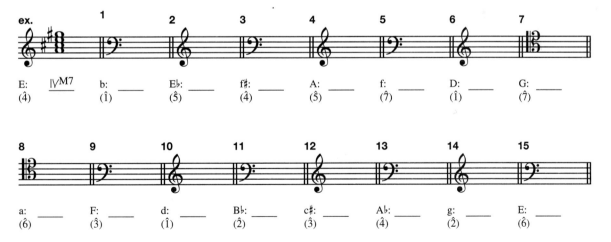

E: IVM7   b: ____   Eb: ____   f#: ____   A: ____   f: ____   D: ____   G: ____
(4̂)   (1̂)   (5̂)   (4̂)   (5̂)   (7̂)   (1̂)   (7̂)

a: ____   F: ____   d: ____   Bb: ____   c#: ____   Ab: ____   g: ____   E: ____
(6̂)   (3̂)   (1̂)   (2̂)   (3̂)   (4̂)   (2̂)   (6̂)

C.   Analysis. Put roman numerals in the spaces provided, making sure each roman
     numeral is of the correct type and includes an inversion symbol if needed.

1. Bach, "Nun lob', mein' Seel', den Herren"

2. Schumann, *Chorale,* Op. 68, No. 4

Exercise 4-2 See Workbook.

PART II
Diatonic Triads

Chapter 5

Principles of Voice Leading

INTRODUCTION

The compositional process, being a creative one, is not entirely understood. It is reasonable to assume that a composer thinks of several aspects more or less simultaneously—melody, harmony, rhythm, and so on. Naturally, a complete analysis of a composition must take all these factors into account. For the most part, however, this text concentrates on questions relating to the harmonic aspect of tonal music because it is this aspect that most clearly delineates tonal music from other types.

We could say that the basic vocabulary of tonal harmony consists of triads and seventh chords and that its grammar involves the ways in which these chords are selected (harmonic progression) and connected (voice leading). In this chapter and the next we will concentrate on some of the basics of the voice-leading aspect: How does a composer write out a given succession of chords for some combination of performers? How can he or she decide in which direction each vocal or instrumental line should go?

Voice leading (or *part writing*) may be defined as the ways in which chords are produced by the motions of individual musical lines. A closely related term is *counterpoint,* which refers to the combining of relatively independent musical lines. Naturally, the style of voice leading will depend on the composer, the musical effect desired, and the performing medium (for example, it is easier to play a large melodic interval on the piano than it is to sing it). However, there are certain voice-leading norms that most composers follow most of the time, and our study will concentrate on these norms.

For various reasons, many theory texts have based their approach to voice leading on the style of the four-voice choral harmonizations by J. S. Bach. Although the Bach chorales epitomize the late Baroque approach to choral writing, most musicians today feel the need to study other textures and styles as well. To answer this need, our study of voice leading will deal with a variety of textures in both vocal and instrumental styles.

THE MELODIC LINE

Our beginning exercises will make use of short and simple melodies in vocal style to avoid, for now, the complications involved with more ornate vocal and instrumental melodies. The following procedures should be followed for Chapters 5 through 9.

1. *Rhythm.* Keep the rhythm simple, with most durations being equal to or longer than the duration of the beat. The final note should occur on a strong beat.

2. *Harmony.* Every melody note should belong to the chord that is to harmonize it.

3. *Contour.* The melody should be primarily *conjunct* (stepwise). The shape of the melody should be interesting but clear and simple, with a single *focal point,* the highest note of the melody.

Example 5-1a is a good example of the points discussed so far. Example 5-1b is not as good because it has an uninteresting contour. Example 5-1c, although more interesting, lacks a single focal point and contains one incorrectly harmonized tone (E5).

EXAMPLE 5-1

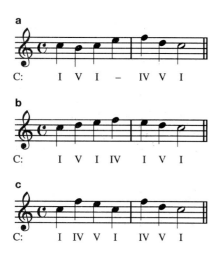

4. *Leaps.*

    a. Avoid augmented intervals, 7ths, and intervals larger than a P8. Diminished intervals may be used if the melody changes direction by step immediately after the interval.

    b. A melodic interval larger than a P4 is usually best approached and left in the direction *opposite* to the leap.

    c. When smaller leaps are used consecutively in the same direction, they should outline a triad.

5. *Tendency tones.* In tonal music $\hat{7}$ has a strong tendency to move up to $\hat{1}$. An exception to this is the scalewise line descending from $\hat{1}$: $\hat{1}$–$\hat{7}$–$\hat{6}$–$\hat{5}$. The only other tendency tone that needs to be considered is $\hat{4}$, which often moves down to $\hat{3}$, but not with the regularity with which $\hat{7}$ goes to $\hat{1}$.

Example 5-2a illustrates a good melody in the restricted style with which we are beginning. Example 5-2b, on the other hand, breaks all of rule 4 as well as rule 5.

EXAMPLE 5-2

a: i   V   i   V   –   i   V   i   V   i

a: i   –   V   i   V   i   V   i   iv   i

Self-Test 5-1
(Answers begin on page 585.)

A. Criticize each melody in terms of the rules for simple melodies discussed under "The Melodic Line" on pages 75–77.

G: I   V   I   IV   V   I   IV   V   I

Bb: I   –   V   I   IV   V   I   V   I

d: i   iv   V   i   iv   V   i   –   iv   V   i

B. Compose simple melodies that will conform to the given progressions. Slashes represent bar lines, and every chord except the last takes one beat.

  1. D: I   V   I   /   IV   I   I   /   vi   ii   V   /   I   //

  2. e: i   iv   i   i   /   V   V   i   i   /   iv   V   i   //

  3. F: I   V   vi   IV   /   I   IV   ii   V   /   I   //

Exercise 5-1 See Workbook.

NOTATING CHORDS

A *musical score* is a tool used by a composer, conductor, or analyst. A score shows all the parts of an ensemble arranged one above the other, enabling the experienced reader to "hear" what the composition will sound like. In a *full score* all or most of the parts are notated on their own individual staves. Any musician should be able both to read and to prepare a full score, and some of your theory exercises should be done in full score. However, a *reduced score,* notated at concert pitch on as few staves as possible, might be more practical for daily theory exercises. Your choice of full or reduced score will depend partly on the sort of musical texture that the exercise will use. That is, if you are composing for four parts in chorale style, two staves will probably suffice. On the other hand, four active and independent instrumental lines might require four staves.

When you are notating more than one part on a single staff, be sure that the stems of the top part always point up and those of the bottom point down, even if the parts have crossed. Example 5-3 illustrates some common notational errors. The score in this case is the familiar SATB (Soprano, Alto, Tenor, Bass) reduced score.

EXAMPLE 5-3

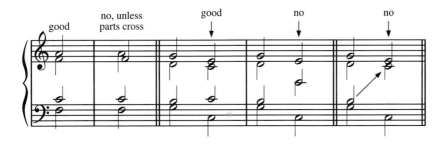

VOICING A SINGLE TRIAD

Once you have settled on the combination of instruments and voices for which you are writing and have selected the opening chord, the next consideration is *voicing:* how the chord is to be distributed or spaced. The way in which a chord is spaced has a great deal of influence on its aural effect. To convince yourself of this, play Example 5-4 at the piano. Each chord in the example contains five parts and covers the same range, but the aural effects are quite different. An even wider variety of effects could be obtained by playing Example 5-4 on various combinations of instruments. Although each of these spacings might be appropriate under certain circumstances, the spacing in Example 5-4e is the least commonly used because of its "muddy" effect.

EXAMPLE 5-4

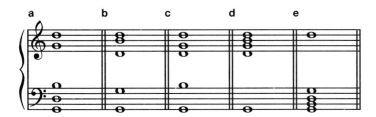

Because so much attention has been paid to four-part textures by authors of theory texts, a terminology concerning the voicing of chords in four-part textures has been developed.

Close structure: less than an octave between soprano and tenor

Open structure: an octave or more between soprano and tenor

Example 5-5 illustrates these spacings in traditional hymn style.

EXAMPLE 5-5   *"Old One Hundredth" (Protestant hymn)*

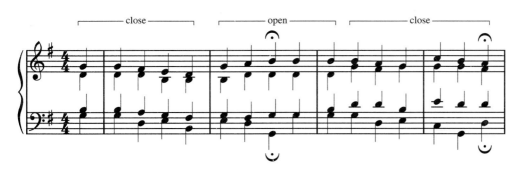

In your beginning part-writing exercises, it would be advisable for you to follow two simple conventions concerning spacing.

1. Do not allow any part to cross above the soprano or below the bass because the essential soprano/bass counterpoint might become unclear (see Example 5-6). The alto and tenor lines may cross briefly if there is a musical reason to do so (see Example 5-7).

EXAMPLE 5-6

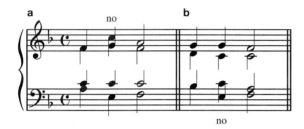

EXAMPLE 5-7   *Bach, "Gott, der du selber bist das Licht"*

2.   When writing for three or more parts, avoid overly spacious sonorities by keeping adjacent upper parts (excluding the bass) within an octave of each other. For example, in a four-part texture there should be no more than an octave between soprano and alto (Example 5-8a) or between alto and tenor (Example 5-8b), although there might be more than an octave between tenor and bass (Example 5-8c).

EXAMPLE 5-8

After you have gained some experience in composing, you may begin to experiment with exceptions to these conventions.

When you are composing for vocal ensembles, use the ranges given in Example 5-9.

EXAMPLE 5-9

Self-Test 5-2
(Answers begin on page 586.)

A. Analyze the excerpt from a Bach chorale below, using roman numerals. Then show beneath each roman numeral the structure of the chord by writing "O" or "C" for open or close structure. The note in parentheses in m. 3 is not part of the chord and should be ignored for the purpose of harmonic analysis.

Bach, "Wo soll ich fliehen hin"

g: ___ ___ ___ ___ ___ ___ ___ ___ ___ ___ ___

B. Review the two conventions concerning spacing on page 80. Then point out in the example below any places where those conventions are not followed.

C. Fill in the circled missing inner voice(s) to complete each root position triad, being sure that each note of the triad is represented. Follow the spacing conventions and stay within the range of each vocal part.

G: I   f: V   B♭: IV   f♯: III

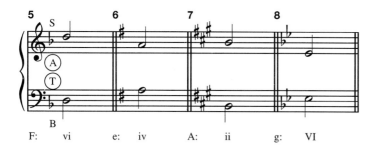

F: vi   e: iv   A: ii   g: VI

Exercise 5-2 See Workbook.

PARALLEL MOTION

As we will see, in tonal music it is important to consider the relationships between any voice in the texture and every other voice in the texture. So, for example, in a four-part texture we would look at the relationships between the soprano and alto, soprano and tenor, soprano and bass, alto and tenor, alto and bass, and tenor and bass. The relationships we are looking at have to do with how each pair of voices moves from chord to chord. There are five possibilities, each of which is illustrated in Example 5-10: static, oblique, similar, contrary, and parallel. Of these, parallel motion is most pertinent to the present discussion.

EXAMPLE 5-10

One of the basic goals of voice leading in tonal music is to maintain the relative independence of the individual parts. Because of this, voices moving together in parallel motion must be given special attention. Look at Example 5-11, and you will see that it consists of three versions of the i–V–i progression in the key of b. Each version uses the same chords, and each version contains parallel voice leading (indicated by the diagonal lines in the example). However, only one version, Example 5-11c, would be considered acceptable by a composer of tonal music.

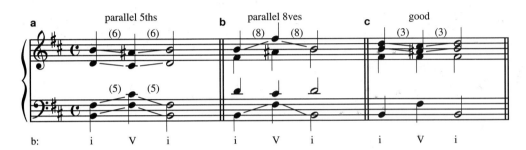

The reason that Examples 5-11a and 5-11b are unacceptable in the tonal style is that they contain parallel 5ths and 8ves. Although such parallels regained acceptance in the twentieth century, composers of tonal music generally followed the convention, dating from around 1450, of avoiding parallel 5ths and 8ves as well as their octave equivalents, such as 12ths and unisons. Note that this does *not* rule out the *duplication* of a line at the 8ve, which was common in orchestral writing (for example, see Ex. 7-8 on pages 109–110, in which the bass line is doubled at the 8ve because the double basses sound a P8 lower than written). The reason for avoiding parallel 5ths and 8ves has to do with the nature of counterpoint. The P8 and P5 are the most stable of intervals, and to link two voices through parallel motion at such intervals interferes with their independence much more than would parallel motion at 3rds or 6ths. We can deduce a rule of parallel motion: *Objectionable parallels* result when two parts that are separated by a P5 or a P8 or by their octave equivalents move to new pitch classes that are separated by the same interval.

If you apply this rule to the three parts of Example 5-12, you will find that all of them are acceptable. In Example 5-12a the soprano and tenor do not move to new pitch classes, whereas in Example 5-12b the 5ths do not occur between the same pair of parts. Finally, the parallel 4ths in Example 5-12c are allowed, even though a P4 is the inversion of a P5.

EXAMPLE 5-12

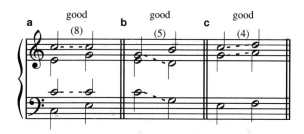

Consecutive perfect 5ths and 8ves by contrary motion were also generally avoided, at least in vocal music. This means that the composer usually did not "correct" parallels (Ex. 5-13a) by moving one of the parts up or down an octave (Ex. 5-13b).

EXAMPLE 5-13

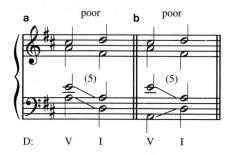

Octaves by contrary motion are occasionally found at cadences in instrumental music and especially in vocal writing, when both melody and bass outline $\hat{5}$–$\hat{1}$. You will see that this occurs in Example 5-14, below the arrow, but the listener probably understands that A4 and G4 are the basic notes of the melody in mm. 7–8, whereas the D4 is only a quick arpeggiation. Notice also in Example 5-14 that some of the notes are in parentheses. In many of the examples in this book, notes that do not belong to the chord are put in parentheses. Non-chord tones will be discussed in more detail in Chapters 11 and 12.

EXAMPLE 5-14   *Haydn, Quartet Op. 64, No. 4, II*

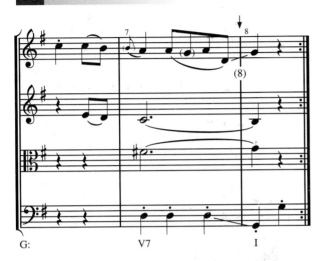

G: V7   I

The term *unequal 5ths* refers to a P5 followed by a °5 or the reverse. Apparently, some tonal composers avoided unequal 5ths involving the bass, and others used P5-°5 but not °5–P5, yet neither of these restrictions holds true for tonal music in general. For the purposes of our part-writing exercises, we will consider unequal 5ths acceptable *unless* they involve a °5–P5 between the bass and another voice. Several sets of unequal 5ths are illustrated in Example 5-15, with all but the last being acceptable.

EXAMPLE 5-15

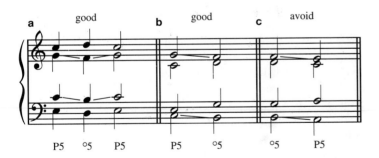

An objectionable *direct* (or *hidden*) *5th* or *8ve* occurs when the *outer* voices move in the same direction into a P5 or P8, with a leap in the soprano part. The aural result is similar to parallel 5ths and 8ves. In Examples 5-16a and 5-16b the interval of a P5 or P8 between the outer voices is approached from the same direction with a leap in the soprano. In Example 5-16c the 5th involves the bass and alto, not the bass and soprano, whereas in Example 5-16d the soprano moves by step, not by leap. Both Examples 5-16c and 5-16d are correct.

EXAMPLE 5-16

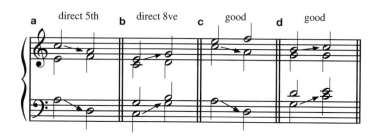

The avoidance of parallels of all types was somewhat less strictly maintained in instrumental than in vocal music. In piano writing, for instance, accompaniment figures frequently outlined 5ths or 8ves, as in Example 5-17.

EXAMPLE 5-17   *Mozart, Sonata K. 284, III*

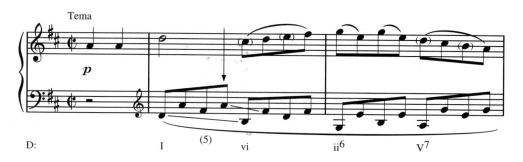

In most cases, such instances of parallels are confined to those textures and instrumental lines in which they are not obvious to the ear. When you attempt to compose music in the tonal style, you should use parallel 5ths and 8ves very sparingly, if at all, and in such a way that the listener's attention will not be drawn to them. Parallels involving both of the outer parts are especially rare and should be avoided. The few instances of such parallels, such as in Example 5-18, do not contradict the general validity of the rule. Possibly Beethoven was trying to evoke a rustic, unsophisticated atmosphere through the use of the parallels—the example is, after all, from the beginning of the *Pastoral* Symphony.

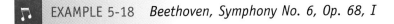

EXAMPLE 5-18   *Beethoven, Symphony No. 6, Op. 68, I*

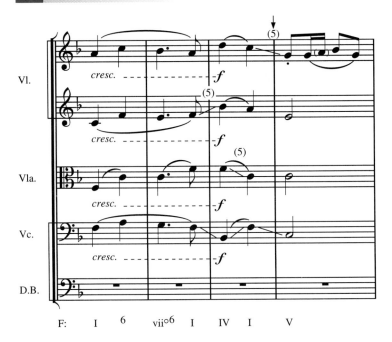

Checkpoint

1.   What do we mean by the focal point of a melody?
2.   What scale degree is the strongest tendency tone in tonal music?
3.   In a four-voice texture, adjacent upper parts should be kept within what interval?
4.   Under what circumstances are unequal 5ths unacceptable?
5.   What are direct octaves?

Summary

Chords in tonal music are produced by the motions of individual musical lines, and the manipulation of these lines is called *voice leading* or *part writing.* A closely related term is *counterpoint,* which refers to the combining of relatively independent musical lines.

In your first exercises you will use melodies that are relatively short and simple and that conform to the suggestions given on pp. 75–77, and you will usually notate your exercises in *reduced score* rather than in *full score.* When two parts are notated on a staff, the stems of the top part always point up, and those of the bottom point down.

   Spacing is an important consideration in voicing chords. In four-part textures, the space between the soprano and tenor parts categorizes a chord to be in *close structure* or *open structure*. Other suggestions regarding spacing are given on p. 79.

   Parallel 5ths and 8ves are avoided in most contexts in tonal music because they undermine the relative independence of the individual parts. Also generally avoided are *consecutive 5ths and 8ves by contrary motion* and, in certain circumstances, *unequal 5ths* and *direct 5ths and 8ves*. See pp. 84–87 for details.

Self-Test 5-3
(Answers begin on page 587.)

A. Label the chords in the excerpt below with roman numerals. Then label any examples of parallelism (objectionable or otherwise) that you can find.

♫   Bach, "Ermuntre dich, mein schwacher Geist"

B. Find and label the following errors in this example:

   1. Parallel 8ves
   2. Parallel 5ths
   3. Direct 5th
   4. 5ths by contrary motion
   5. Spacing error (review p. 79)

C. Find and label the following errors in this example:

   1. Parallel 8ves
   2. Parallel 5ths
   3. Direct 8ve
   4. 8ves by contrary motion
   5. Unacceptable unequal 5ths
   6. Spacing error

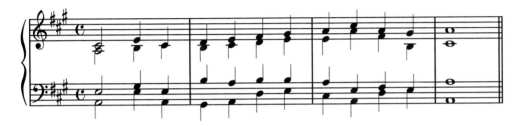

Exercise 5-3 See Workbook.

Chapter 6

Root Position
Part Writing

INTRODUCTION

We will begin our first efforts at tonal composition by exploring the relatively restricted environment of root position triads. Inverted triads, introduced in Chapters 8 and 9, will allow us to write more melodic bass lines, but for now we will have to accept the somewhat rigid contour of a root position bass. The inner voices, however, should be treated as melodies, even if they are seldom as interesting as the soprano line. It is especially important to observe even in the inner voices the rules concerning leaps that you learned in the previous chapter (see rule 4, p. 76).

Although you learned quite a bit about seventh chords in Chapters 3 and 4, we will not begin using them compositionally until Chapter 13. However, seventh chords will appear frequently in musical examples and Self-Test analysis problems as well as in exercises in the Workbook, so you will have the opportunity to become better acquainted with them before we launch into their special voice-leading requirements.

We can reduce to four the number of different intervals that can separate the roots of any two chords. This is because a 2nd and a 7th, for example, are the same in this context because the part writing of the upper voices is the same whether the bass moves by a 2nd or by a 7th. The four combinations, then, are:

2nd apart (same as a 7th apart)

3rd apart (same as a 6th apart)

4th apart (same as a 5th apart)

same roots—a repeated chord

As we deal with these four combinations (which will be taken up in reverse order from the way they are listed above), the conventions followed in writing for three and four parts are presented. In each section, the traditional four-part texture will be discussed first.

A major issue in part writing in the tonal style concerns which notes of a chord are doubled or even tripled. When we refer to a note being doubled or tripled, we mean that two or three of the parts are given that pitch class, although not necessarily in the same octave. For example, look at the Bach excerpt in Part A of Self-Test 5-3 (p. 88). The root of the first chord, G, is tripled in the alto, tenor, and bass. The root of the second chord, C, is doubled in the soprano and bass.

ROOT POSITION PART WRITING WITH REPEATED ROOTS

Four-Part Textures

1. All members of the triad are usually present. The final I chord is sometimes incomplete, consisting of a 3rd and a tripled root.

2. The root is usually doubled. The leading tone ($\hat{7}$) is almost never doubled because it is such a strong tendency tone (review p. 76).

Three-Part Textures

1. The 5th of the triad is often omitted. The final I chord may consist only of a tripled root.

2. An incomplete triad will usually have the root doubled. The leading tone ($\hat{7}$) is almost never doubled.

When a root position triad is repeated, the upper voices may be arpeggiated freely, as long as the spacing conventions are followed (review discussion of voicing a single triad, pp. 78–80). The bass may arpeggiate an octave. Example 6-1 illustrates appropriate part writing for repeated roots.

EXAMPLE 6-1

Self-Test 6-1   Using repeated roots.
(Answers begin on page 588.)

Test your understanding of the preceding section by filling in the inner voice or voices in the second chord of each pair. The key is C major throughout.

Exercise 6-1 See Workbook.

ROOT POSITION PART WRITING WITH ROOTS A 4TH (5TH) APART

As you will learn in the next chapter, one of the most fundamental root movements in tonal music is that of the descending P5 (or ascending P4). The part-writing principles involved in this root movement are identical to those concerned with the ascending P5 (or descending P4). Other principles that must always be kept in mind are those concerning spacing, parallelism, and the resolution of $\hat{7}$ to $\hat{1}$ when $\hat{7}$ occurs in the melody.

Four-Part Textures

1. One method for writing this root relationship in four parts is to keep in the same voice the tone that is common to both chords, whereas the remaining two upper parts move by step in the same direction. The stepwise motion will be ascending for root movement of a P5 down (Ex. 6-2a) and descending for root movement of a P5 up (Ex. 6-2b). The purpose of the ties here and in subsequent examples is only to point out the common tones and not to imply that they must be tied.

5th/4th — 3 methods

EXAMPLE 6-2

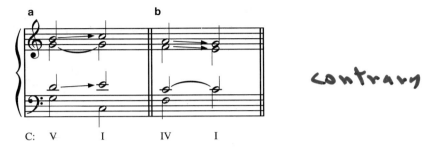

contrary

C: V   I   IV   I

2.   A second method moves all three upper parts in the same direction, with no leaps larger than a 3rd. The motion will be descending for a root movement of a P5 down (or P4 up) and ascending for a root movement of a P5 up (or P4 down). See Example 6-3.

EXAMPLE 6-3

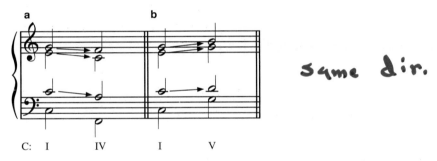

same dir.

C: I   IV   I   V

3.   A third method, although not as smooth as the first two, is useful for changing between close and open structures. Here we again keep in the same voice the tone that is common to both chords, whereas the voice that has the 3rd in the first chord leaps to provide the 3rd of the second chord. The remaining voice moves by step. See Example 6-4.

EXAMPLE 6-4

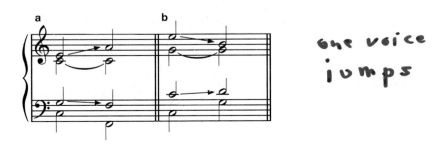

one voice jumps

Three-Part Textures

The more flexible nature of three-part writing makes it impossible to distill a few conventional methods, as was done for four-part textures. Remember that each chord must contain at least a root and 3rd, and observe conventions concerning spacing and parallelism (Ex. 6-5). Aim for smooth voice leading instead of complete chords.

EXAMPLE 6-5

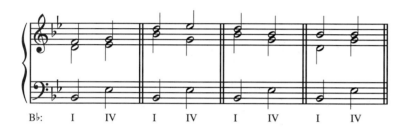

Bb: I   IV   I   IV   I   IV   I   IV

Self-Test 6-2   Using roots a 4th (5th) apart.
(Answers begin on page 589.)

A.   Add alto and tenor parts to each exercise below. Each progression involves roots a P5 (P4) apart. Use one of the three methods outlined on pages 92–93 in each case, and state which you have used.

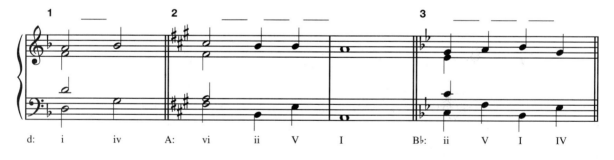

d: i   iv   A: vi   ii   V   I   Bb: ii   V   I   IV

e: V   i   iv   i   F: I   IV   I   V   Bb: I   V   I   IV   I

B.   Add an alto part to each example. Be careful to observe conventions concerning spacing, parallels, and doubling. Each triad should include at least a root and a 3rd.

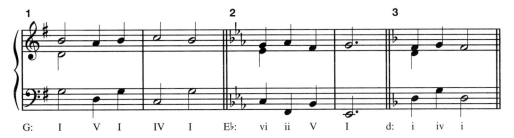

G: I   V   I   IV   I   Eb: vi   ii   V   I   d: i   iv   i

Exercise 6-2 See Workbook.

ROOT POSITION PART WRITING WITH ROOTS A 3RD (6TH) APART

The voice leading that involves root position triads a 3rd or 6th apart is often quite smooth because the two triads will always have two tones in common.

Four-Part Textures

Assuming that the first of the two root position triads has a double root, only one of the upper voices will need to move. The two upper voices that have tones in common with the second chord remain stationary, whereas the remaining voice moves by step. The stepwise motion will be upward for roots a descending 3rd apart (Ex. 6-6a) and downward for roots an ascending 3rd apart (Ex. 6-6b).

EXAMPLE 6-6

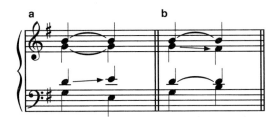

Three-Part Textures

Commonly encountered part-writing situations are more diverse in three-part textures. Some possibilities are illustrated in Example 6-7. Especially tricky is the ascending root movement. In that case, you should not omit the 5th of the second chord because the listener might assume that the music has progressed only from a root position triad to an inverted form of the same triad (compare Ex. 6-7c and d with Ex. 6-7e and f).

EXAMPLE 6-7

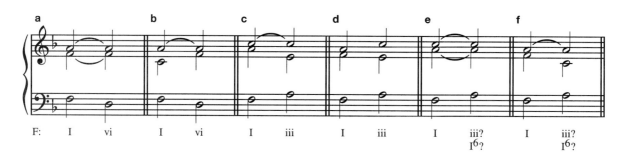

Self-Test 6-3   Using roots a P4th (P5th) and 3rd (6th) apart.

(Answers begin on page 590.)

A. Add alto and tenor parts to each exercise. Use the smoothest voice leading in each case.

B. Add an alto part to each exercise. Be careful to observe the conventions concerning parallels, spacing, and doubling.

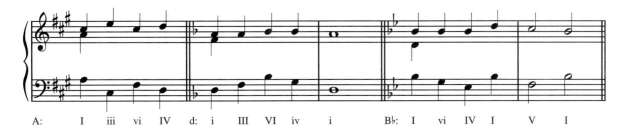

A: I   iii   vi   IV   d: i   III   VI   iv   i   Bb: I   vi   IV   I   V   I

Exercise 6-3 *See Workbook.*

ROOT POSITION PART WRITING WITH ROOTS A 2ND (7TH) APART

Two triads with roots a 2nd (or 7th) apart have *no* tones in common, so every part must move from the first chord to the second. In this discussion we will assume that the bass moves by 2nd rather than by 7th.

Four-Part Textures

If the root is doubled in the first chord, as is usually the case, the voice leading is usually quite simple: If the bass moves up by step, the upper voices move down to the next chord tone (Ex. 6-8a), whereas if the bass moves down by step, the upper voices move up to the next chord tone (Ex. 6-8b).

EXAMPLE 6-8

a   b

The progression V–vi (or V–VI) is known as the "deceptive progression," for reasons that will become clear in the next chapter. In terms of voice leading, deceptive progressions present some special problems. In most cases the leading tone ($\hat{7}$) moves parallel with the bass, resolving up to tonic ($\hat{1}$), whereas the other two voices move down, contrary to the bass, to the next available chord tones. This results in a doubled 3rd in the vi (or VI) chord, as in Example 6-9a and b. In the major mode, if the leading tone is in an inner voice, it may move down by step to $\hat{6}$, as in Example 6-9c, because the lack of resolution is not so apparent to the ear. This is not acceptable in the minor mode, however, because of the awkward interval of a +2 that results, as in Example 6-9d.

EXAMPLE 6-9

The voice leading away from a triad with a doubled 3rd must be handled carefully because the conventions discussed in this chapter all assume doubled roots.

Example 6-10 provides two examples of the deceptive progression, one in B♭ and one in g. In the first one, the V–vi progression in B♭, the leading tone is in an inner voice (the alto), and Bach avoids resolving it to tonic (as in Ex. 6-9c). Remember that this is only practicable when in major mode with the leading tone in an inner voice. In the V–VI progression, where the key has shifted briefly to g, Bach resolves the leading tone to tonic, resulting in a doubled 3rd in the VI chord (as in Ex. 6-9b).

♫ EXAMPLE 6-10   *Bach, "Herr Christ, der ein'ge Gott's-Sohn"*

Three-Part Textures

The smoothest voice leading will find a complete triad followed by a triad with two roots and a 3rd (Ex. 6-11a and b) or a triad consisting of two roots and a 3rd followed by a complete triad (Ex. 6-11c and d). In other words, with roots a 2nd apart, the sequence will usually be complete to incomplete or incomplete to complete. Remember to resolve $\hat{7}$ to $\hat{1}$ in the V–vi progression—with the possible exception of cases in which $\hat{7}$ is in the inner voice in a major key.

EXAMPLE 6-11

Checkpoint

1. How many tones are shared between triads with roots a 2nd apart? A 3rd apart? A 4th or 5th apart?
2. Describe the three methods of connecting triads with roots a 4th or 5th apart.
3. What is usually doubled in the second chord of a V–vi (or V–VI) progression? What is the possible exception to this?

Self-Test 6-4   Using all root relationships.
(Answers begin on page 590.)

A. Complete each progression. Make two versions of each: one for three parts and one for four parts.

G: I   vi   IV   d: i   iv   V   A: I   vi   ii   e: i   V   VI   B♭:   iii   vi   V

B. Fill in alto and tenor parts in these two exercises.

C. Name the keys and analyze the chords specified by these figured basses. Then compose a good melody line for each. Finally, fill in alto and tenor parts to make a four-part texture.

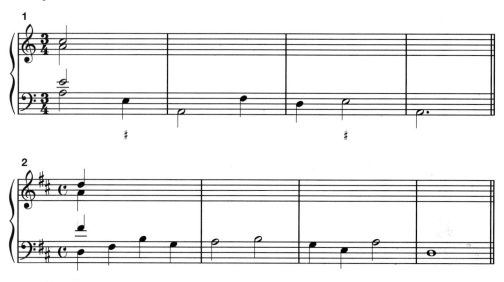

Exercise 6-4 See Workbook.

The given soprano here and elsewhere might make it impossible to follow the conventions. Watch out for parallels and spacing, and double the root in most cases.

INSTRUMENTAL RANGES AND TRANSPOSITIONS

Many of the exercises suggest that you compose examples for combinations of instruments in your class, and your instructor may make additional assignments that also call for instrumental combinations. To carry out these assignments successfully, you will need to understand the ranges and transpositions of the various instruments.

Appendix A provides suggested ranges for many of the instruments for which you may wish to write. A "written range" is given next to the "sounding range" for each instrument in Appendix A. This is necessary because, strange as it might seem at first, players of certain instruments of the band and orchestra do not read music at concert pitch. This means that the notes that they read in their parts produce pitches that are higher or lower than the notes that have the same names on the piano.

The reasons that we have transposing instruments are somewhat complicated, but we will try to explain two of them here as examples. The French horn was originally a valveless instrument that could play only the notes of the harmonic series. A harmonic series with C2 as a fundamental is illustrated in Example 6-12. The filled-in noteheads represent pitches that are quite out of tune in comparison to the modern equal-tempered system.

EXAMPLE 6-12

To play in different keys, the horn player had to insert the proper *crook,* a piece of tubing of a precisely calculated length. A longer crook lowered the instrument's *fundamental* and, correspondingly, its harmonic series, whereas a shorter crook did the reverse. No matter what crook was used, it was the custom to write for the horn as if it were in the key of C so that the C fundamental and its familiar harmonic series would remain unchanged. This practice was retained even after valves were introduced and the horn settled into its modern F fundamental.

Perhaps an easier example to understand is the saxophone family, which consists of eight different instruments, each of which has a different sounding range (only two of the saxophones are included in Appendix A). To make it easier for players to "double"—to switch from one saxophone to the other—saxophone music is written as if all saxophones had the same range, with the result that a G4, for example, is fingered the same way on every saxophone.

Naturally, a musician has to understand transpositions thoroughly to compose, arrange, or read instrumental music. To write music that you have composed or arranged from concert pitch for a transposing instrument, follow the instructions under "written range" in Appendix A. To write music from a transposing instrument into concert pitch, you have to reverse the process. Example 6-13 illustrates this. Notice that key signatures are transposed as well.

EXAMPLE 6-13

If you don't have Appendix A or a similar guide handy, remember that a transposing instrument "sees a C but sounds its key." This means that a horn player who sees a C will sound an F because the French horn is pitched in F. To go from concert pitch to the transposed part, remember that "to hear its key, you must write a C."

One procedure to use when writing for an ensemble is this:

1. Notate the sounding ranges of the performers at the top of your page of manuscript paper.
2. Compose the exercise in the form of a reduced score on as few staves as practicable. Keep an eye on the ranges.
3. Provide enough copies for the ensemble so that players will not have to huddle around a single stand. Instrumental parts should be copied onto separate sheets using correct transpositions.

Summary

The possible relationships between the roots of any two triads can be reduced to four. Part-writing conventions involving all four relationships are discussed in terms of both three- and four-part textures on the pages indicated below.

Repeated roots, pp. 92–94.

Roots a 4th (or 5th) apart, pp. 92–94.

Roots a 3rd (or 6th) apart, pp. 95–96.

Roots a 2nd (or 7th) apart, pp. 97–99.

Whereas the 5th of the triad is frequently omitted in three-part textures, this is seldom found in four-part textures, with the exception of the final I chord. In most cases, when a member of the chord is *doubled,* the doubled tone is the root. However, in the V–vi (or V–VI) progression, the 3rd of the vi chord is usually doubled.

You will need to understand instrumental transpositions if you want to write instrumental music or read instrumental scores. For various reasons, many musical instruments do not sound where written; instead, the music must be transposed, either *from* concert pitch so that you can notate the part or *to* concert pitch so that you can understand the score. Appendix A provides ranges and transpositions for a number of different instruments.

Self-Test 6-5
(Answers begin on page 592.)

A. Notate the chords below for the specified instruments. Each chord is written at concert pitch, so transpose as needed for the performers. Note that the instruments are listed in *score order,* the order used in Appendix A, which is not always the same as order by pitch. **Use the correct clef for each instrument.**

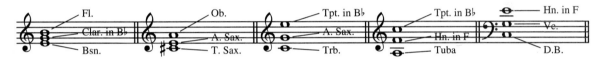

Fl.   Ob.   A. Sax.   Hn. in F   Hn. in F

Clar. in B♭   A. Sax.   Tpt. in B♭   Tpt. in B♭   Vc.

Bsn.   T. Sax.   Trb.   Tuba   D.B.

B. Here is a short chord progression to use in these exercises:
   F: I vi ii V I

   1. Make an arrangement for two alto saxophones and one tenor saxophone. Copy out the parts, using correct transpositions.
   2. Make a four-part arrangement for SATB chorus.

C.   Write a version of the excerpt below on a grand staff by transposing the parts to concert pitch. Play your version on the piano, and analyze the harmonies if you can
(there are some non-chord tones, so be sure to listen carefully).

E♭ Alto Sax

B♭ Tenor Sax

B♭ Trumpet

Trombone

Exercise 6-5 See Workbook.

Chapter 7

Harmonic Progression

INTRODUCTION

Before you can begin to compose convincing tonal music or to learn anything from harmonic analyses, you must learn which chord successions are typical of tonal harmony and which ones are not. Why is it that some chord successions seem to "progress," to move forward toward a goal, while others tend to wander, to leave our expectations unfulfilled? Compare the two progressions in Example 7-1. The first was composed following the principles that will be discussed in this chapter, but the chords for the second were selected through rolling a die. Although the random example has a certain freshness to it, there is no doubt that the first one sounds more typical of tonal harmony. This chapter will explore this phenomenon, but first we must turn to a topic that concerns melody as well as harmony.

EXAMPLE 7-1

SEQUENCES AND THE CIRCLE OF FIFTHS

One of the important means of achieving unity in tonal music is through the use of a *sequence,* a pattern that is repeated immediately in the same voice but begins on a different

pitch class. A *tonal sequence* will keep the pattern in a single key, which means that modifiers of the intervals (major, minor, and so on) will probably change, as in Example 7-2a.
A *real sequence,* as in Example 7-2b, transposes the pattern to a new key. Modulating
sequences will be discussed in more detail in a later chapter.

EXAMPLE 7-2

It is important to understand the difference between sequence and *imitation.* In
Example 7-3 the first violin (top staff) plays an exact transposition of the melody first
heard in the second violin (bottom staff), but this is an example of *real imitation,* not a real
sequence, because the repetition of the pattern occurs in a different voice.

EXAMPLE 7-3   *Bach, "Double" Concerto, II (solo violins only)*

However, in addition to imitation, there are also sequences in Example 7-3. There is a sequence in m. 1 (the ♩♪♪♪ pattern) that is imitated by the first violin in m. 3. Another sequence occurs in the second violin in m. 3 (the ♪♪♪♪♪ pattern), but notice that the interval of a 4th in the first occurrence of the pattern becomes a 3rd in the second and third occurrences. A sequence such as this, where the repetitions of the pattern are neither tonal nor real, is called a *modified sequence*. The sequence in the Handel excerpt involves not just the melody but the harmony as well. The harmonic sequence is:

```
I   -   IV   -   ii   -   V   -   iii   -   vi   -   IV   -   V
```

A sequence may be melodic or harmonic or both. One common sequential harmonic pattern is:

```
I   -   V   -   vi   -   iii   -   IV   -   I
```

This forms the basis of the famous Pachelbel "Canon" (Ex. 7-4).

♫ EXAMPLE 7-4 *Pachelbel, Canon in D*

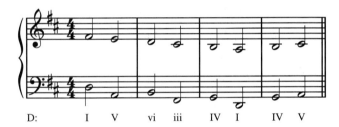

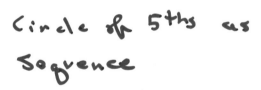
Circle of 5ths as Sequence

D: I   V   vi   iii   IV   I   IV   V

However, a sequential harmonic pattern that is far more significant to this chapter is the *circle-of-fifths progression*, which consists of roots related by descending 5ths (and ascending 4ths). Although most of the 5ths (and 4ths) will be perfect, if a diatonic circle-of-fifths progression goes on long enough, a °5 (or +4) will appear (Ex. 7-5).

EXAMPLE 7-5

Progressions of this sort often appear in connection with melodic sequences, as in Example 7-6.

EXAMPLE 7-6   *Vivaldi, Concerto Grosso Op. 3, No. 11, I (soloists only)*

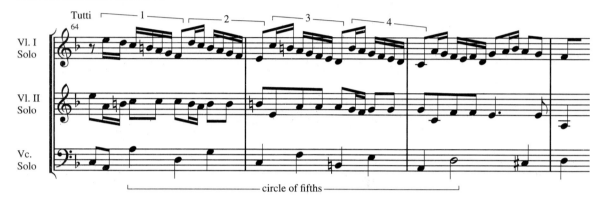

Although the chords in Example 7-6 are all in root position, if some or all of them were inverted, the progression would still contain a circle-of-fifths harmonic sequence.

Sequential progressions involving the circle of fifths are frequently found in twentieth-century popular music and jazz (see Ex. 7-7). Notice that both Example 7-6 and Example 7-7 include a °5 (or +4) in their root movements, which is not at all uncommon in circle-of-fifths progressions. In Example 7-6 the °5 occurs between the chords on F and B, and in Example 7-7 it occurs between the chords on B♭ and E.

EXAMPLE 7-7   *Richie, "Hello"*

By Lionel Richie. © 1983, 1984 Brockman Music (ASCAP). Used by permission of Chappell & Co., Inc., Miami, FL 33014.

Because the root progression of a 5th down (or 4th up) is so basic to tonal harmony, we will use the circle-of-fifths progression to show how diatonic chords are used in tonal music. We begin with the strongest of all such progressions, the V–I progression. (The following discussion applies equally to progressions in major and minor modes, except as noted.)

THE I AND V CHORDS

The ultimate harmonic goal of any tonal piece is the tonic triad, and this triad is often also the goal of many of the formal subdivisions of a composition. The tonic triad is most often preceded by a V (or V^7) chord, and it would be safe to say that $V^{(7)}$ and I together are the most essential elements of a tonal work. It is not difficult to find examples in which the harmony for several measures consists only of I and V chords, as in Example 7-8, which Mozart composed at the age of fifteen.

EXAMPLE 7-8   *Mozart, Symphony K. 114, III*

$$\text{i} \qquad \text{V}^4_3 \qquad \overset{6}{5} \qquad \text{i} \qquad 6 \qquad \text{V} \qquad \text{i}$$

It would be difficult to overstate the importance of the I–V–I progression at all levels of musical structure, from the phrase on up. In fact, a complex theory developed in the first third of the twentieth century by Heinrich Schenker takes the position that any tonal composition can be understood as an elaborated I–V–I progression. As the harmonic progression diagrams are developed in the course of this chapter, remember that chords other than I and V serve important but supporting roles.

THE II CHORD

If we extend our circle-of-fifths progression backward one step from the V chord, we have the following progression:

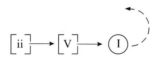

This diagram illustrates the normal function of ii to progress to V and of V to progress to I. The dotted line after the I indicates that if the piece continues, the I chord might be followed by anything.

Many phrases contain only a I–ii–V–I progression. Example 7-9 shows a typical soprano/bass framework for such a progression.

EXAMPLE 7-9

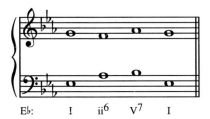

Eb: I   ii⁶   V⁷   I

Play Example 7-9 and then compare it with Beethoven's version of this progression in Example 7-10. Here Beethoven uses a ii$^6_5$ instead of a ii^6.

EXAMPLE 7-10   *Beethoven, Minuet*

Moderato

Eb: I   ii$^6_5$ V⁷   I

THE VI CHORD

One more step in the circle of fifths brings us to the vi chord.

$$\left[vi\right] \longrightarrow \left[ii\right] \longrightarrow \left[v\right] \longrightarrow \textcircled{I}$$

Put in root position, this progression illustrates an ostinato (repeated) bass pattern often found in popular tunes. Play example 7-11 and see whether it sounds familiar.

EXAMPLE 7-11

The same progression, but in minor, is seen in Example 7-12. As we will demonstrate in a later section, chord functions in minor are almost identical to those in major.

EXAMPLE 7-12   *Verdi,* La forza del destino, *Act II (piano-vocal score)*

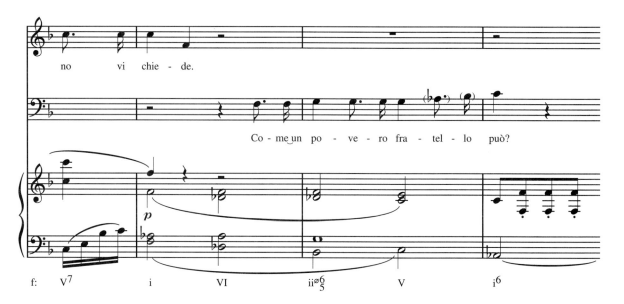

THE III CHORD

Another 5th backward brings us to the iii chord, far removed from the tonic triad.

Beginning theory students often assume that the iii chord is frequently encountered and that they should be sure to include at least one iii chord in each exercise they write. This is not at all the case, at least not in the major mode. When $\hat{3}$ is found in a bass line, the chord above it is almost always a I^6 rather than a iii. The iii chord does occur occasionally, of course. When it follows the natural descending 5ths progression, it will go to vi, as in Example 7-13. The use of the III chord in minor will be discussed on page 116.

EXAMPLE 7-13 *Bach, "O Ewigkeit, du Donnerwort"*

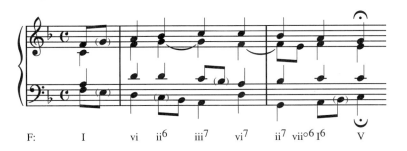

F: I   vi   ii^6 iii^7 vi^7 ii^7 vii°^{6}I^6 V

Also, the iii chord is useful for harmonizing a $\hat{1}$–$\hat{7}$–$\hat{6}$ soprano line, as in Example 7-14, although $\hat{7}$ is usually harmonized by V or vii° in other contexts.

EXAMPLE 7-14

D: I   iii   IV   I^6

THE VII CHORD

Continuing the circle of fifths backward from iii brings us to vii°. Although the vii°–iii progression does occur in sequential passages, the vii° usually acts instead as a substitute for V. Therefore, the customary goal of vii° outside of circle-of-fifths sequences is not iii but the I chord.

If vii° and V are used next to each other, V will usually follow the vii° because the V is the stronger sound.

The most common use of vii° is in first inversion between two positions of the tonic triad: I–vii°⁶–I⁶ or I⁶–vii°⁶–I (Ex. 7-15).

♫   EXAMPLE 7-15   *Handel,* Messiah

The vii°⁶ is also useful in harmonizing a $\hat{6}$–$\hat{7}$–$\hat{1}$ soprano line. Compare Examples 7-14 and 7-16.

EXAMPLE 7-16

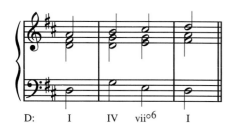

THE IV CHORD

Still missing from our diagram is the IV chord, which lies a P5 *below* the tonic. The IV is an interesting chord because it has three common functions. In some cases, IV proceeds to a I chord, sometimes called a *plagal* progression. More frequently, IV is linked with ii; IV can substitute for ii (going directly to V or vii°), or IV can be followed by ii (as in IV–ii–V). These three common uses of the IV are summarized in the chord diagram.

In Example 7-17 the IV appears in a plagal progression. (The I_4^6 in the last measure indicates that the notes of the tonic triad are present at that point. However, the bracket with the V under it means that everything within the bracket functions as V. The I_4^6 is actually a kind of embellishment called a *cadential six-four,* which will be explained further in Chapter 9.)

EXAMPLE 7-17   *Haydn, Sonata No. 35, II*

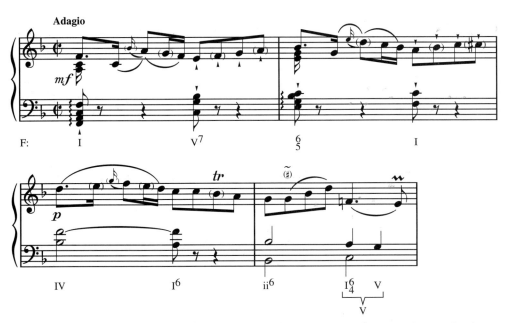

Later on in the same sonata in which Example 7-17 appears, IV is used in its pre-dominant function (Ex. 7-18).

EXAMPLE 7-18   *Haydn, Sonata No. 35, III*

COMMON EXCEPTIONS

The chord diagram on page 114 includes all the diatonic triads and gives a reasonably accurate picture of the chord progressions most often found in tonal music. However, to make our chart of chord functions more complete, we must include three commonly encountered exceptions to the norms discussed so far.

1.   V–vi (the deceptive progression)
2.   vi–V (skipping over IV or ii)
3.   iii–IV (see Ex. 7-14)

These additions are included in the diagram below, which may be considered complete for major keys. Remember that the dotted line after the I chord means that any chord may follow it.

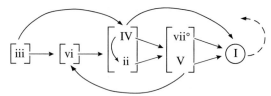

DIFFERENCES IN THE MINOR MODE

Most chords function the same way in minor as in major. However, the mediant triad, so seldom found in the major mode, is a common feature of the minor mode: It represents the relative major key, and minor-key music has a decided tendency to drift in that direction.

   In addition, the variability of $\hat{6}$ and $\hat{7}$ will occasionally produce chords of different quality and function. The most important of these are the following:

1.   The subtonic VII, sounding like the V in the key of the relative major—that is, a V of III.
2.   The minor v, usually v⁶, after which the ↓$\hat{7}$ will move to ↓$\hat{6}$, usually as part of a iv⁶ chord.

   The first of these possibilities is included in the chord diagram below.

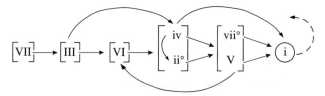

The second possibility, v⁶–iv⁶, is illustrated in Example 7-19.

♫ EXAMPLE 7-19 *Bach, "Als vierzig Tag' nach Ostern"*

e: i   v⁶   iv⁶   V

PROGRESSIONS INVOLVING SEVENTH CHORDS

We will not be using seventh chords in part-writing or composition exercises for a while, but they will occur in examples and in analysis exercises. You will see that in almost every case seventh chords function in the same way as triads; for example, both V and V7 tend to be followed by the I chord (or sometimes by the vi chord). The only exception is the tonic seventh chord (I^{M7} or i^7), which loses its stability as a harmonic goal. In most cases a tonic seventh is followed by a subdominant chord, although other possibilities will be discussed in Chapter 15.

Checkpoint

1. What is the difference between a tonal sequence and a real sequence?
2. Does a circle-of-fifths sequence use descending fifths or ascending fifths?
3. What are three conventional uses of the IV chord?

HARMONIZING A SIMPLE MELODY

Because we have so far discussed part writing only of root position chords, any melody harmonization exercises will have to be restricted to root position. For the best results, avoid using any root position diminished triads (this will be discussed in more detail in the next chapter). Your first step should be to select the chords for the very beginning and for the last two or three chords, as in Example 7-20.

EXAMPLE 7-20

D: I   ii   V   I

Next, write out the possibilities for each remaining chord, remembering that every melody note can serve as the root, third, or fifth of a triad, as in Example 7-21. Notice that we have not included the vii° chord as a possibility because we want to avoid root position diminished triads.

EXAMPLE 7-21

```
D:      I     ii    I     IV   ii   iii    V    iii   I     ii   V    I
              V     vi         ii   V      I    iii   I     vi
              IV               vi          I    vi    IV
```

The next step is to compose the rest of the bass line. The challenge here is to try to create a good harmonic progression while avoiding creating parallel or direct 5ths and 8ves with the melody. For example, parallel fifths would result if we began the third measure with a I–vi progression. Once you are satisfied with both the bass line and the progression, the final step is to add one or two inner voices, following as much as possible the conventions that you learned in Chapter 6. A possible harmonization is given in Example 7-22.

EXAMPLE 7-22

```
D:      I     V    vi   IV   V    I     I     I    IV   ii   V    I
```

CONCLUSION

The last two chord diagrams on page 116 are somewhat complex, but both are based on the circle-of-fifths progression. Keep this in mind while you are learning them. At the same time, be aware that Bach and Beethoven did *not* make use of diagrams such as these. They lived and breathed the tonal harmonic style and had no need for the information the diagrams contain. Instead, the diagrams represent norms of harmonic practice observed by theorists over the years in the works of a large number of tonal composers. They do not represent rules; they are just guidelines for your use in analyzing and composing tonal music.

Summary

A *sequence* is a pattern that is repeated immediately in the same voice but beginning on a different pitch class. A *diatonic sequence* keeps the pattern within a single key, whereas a *real* or *modulating sequence* transposes the pattern to a different key.

A sequential pattern may be melodic, harmonic, or both. A harmonic sequence that is very important in tonal music is the *circle-of-fifths sequence,* which consists of a series of root movements down a 5th (and/or up a 4th). The most important circle-of-fifths progression is the V–I (or V–i) progression, but the circle-of-fifths progression also forms the basis of the diagrams given on page 116 illustrating normative harmonic progressions in major and minor modes.

Self-Test 7-1
(Answers begin on page 593.)

A. Complete each progression to conform with the last two chord diagrams presented (p. 116). The chord in the blank should be different from those on either side of it. In most cases there is more than one correct answer.

1. I ___?___ vi (____ or ____)   **4.** I ___?___ IV (____ or ____)

2. IV ___?___ V (____ or ____)   **5.** vi ___?___ V (____ or ____)

3. V ___?___ IV (____ or ____)   **6.** vii° ___?___ V (____)

B. Bracket any portions of these progressions that do not conform to the complete major and minor chord diagrams (p. 116).

1. I   V   ii   vii° I
2. i   iv   i   VII   i   V   i
3. I   IV   iii   vi   ii   V   I
4. I   IV   ii   V   vi   ii   V   I

C. Analysis. Label all chords with roman numerals, and bracket any successions of chords that do not agree with the complete major and minor chord diagrams.

1. Bach, "O Herre Gott, dein göttlich Wort"

2. Vivaldi, Cello Sonata in G Minor, Sarabande*

In addition to labeling the chords, bracket any melodic sequences (including modified sequences) in the cello part. Non-chord tones in the solo part have not been put in parentheses, but the harmonic analysis can be done by concentrating on the accompaniment. The key is g minor despite what appears to be an incorrect key signature. Key signatures had not yet become standardized when this work was composed.

Unfigured bass realization by S. Kostka.

D. Analyze the chords specified by these figured basses and add inner voices to make a four-part texture. Bracket all circle-of-fifths progressions, even those that contain only two chords.

E. Analyze this figured bass, then add a good soprano line and inner voices. Bracket all circle-of-fifths progressions.

F. Harmonize the melodies below by using root position major or minor (not dimin-
    ished) triads in an acceptable progression. Try to give the bass a good contour while
    avoiding parallel and direct 5ths and 8ves with the melody. Be sure to include analy-
    sis. Finally, fill in one or two inner parts, as specified.

1. SAB

F:

2. SATB

e:

3. SATB

E♭:

4. SATB

d:

5. SAB

A:

G. Add an alto part (only) to mm. 1 to 2. Then compose a good soprano line for mm. 3 to 4 and fill in an alto part.

Bb:　　　I　　iii　　IV　V　　　vi　ii　V　　　I　　iii　vi　IV　　ii　V　I

H. Review. Label the chords with roman numerals and inversion symbols (where needed).

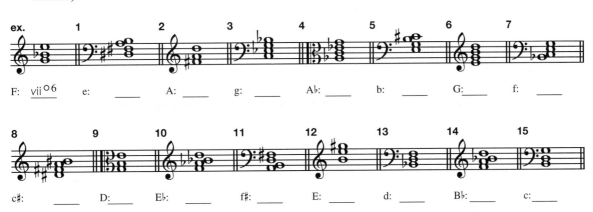

ex.　　　1　　　2　　　3　　　4　　　5　　　6　　　7

F: vii°6　　e: ____　　A: ____　　g: ____　　Ab: ____　　b: ____　　G: ____　　f: ____

8　　　9　　　10　　　11　　　12　　　13　　　14　　　15

c#: ____　　D: ____　　Eb: ____　　f#: ____　　E: ____　　d: ____　　Bb: ____　　c: ____

Exercise 7-1 See Workbook.

Triads in First Inversion

INTRODUCTION

Listen to the short phrase below, paying special attention to the bass line.

EXAMPLE 8-1

It's not bad, but it could be improved. The melody line is fine, having both shape and direction, but the bass seems too repetitive and too rigid. Compare Example 8-1 with Example 8-2.

EXAMPLE 8-2 *Haydn, Sonata No. 33, III*

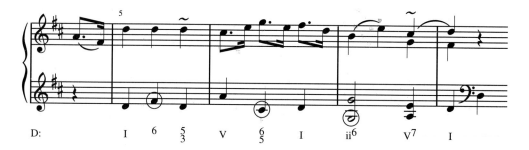

Now the bass line is improved through the use of inverted chords (indicated by circled bass notes in the example). Although the harmony is the same, the inverted chords have created a bass line with a more interesting contour and with more variety.

Most phrases of tonal music contain at least one inverted chord, and the inversions usually serve the purposes that we have just demonstrated. We are not saying that a phrase without inverted chords is poorly composed—it just depends on what effect the composer is after. For example, minuets from the Classical period often contain phrases with chords that are all in root position.

BASS ARPEGGIATION

One way in which first inversion triads often originate is simply through bass arpeggiation. If you look back at the first measure of Example 8-2, you will see that D4 is the primary bass note in the measure. The F♯4 serves the dual purpose of providing the 3rd of the chord and of giving the bass some variety. A similar situation is found in the first two beats of the second measure. When you analyze a bass arpeggiation such as these, you should identify the arpeggiations only with arabic numerals (as in Ex. 8-2) or omit symbols altogether (as in Ex. 8-3).

Accompaniment figures in keyboard music often involve faster arpeggiations. Two examples by Haydn are shown below (Exs. 8-3 and 8-4). In both, the fundamental bass line is the one shown in the textural reduction. The other pitches played by the left hand should be considered as inner voices that are simply filling in the chords. They are not part of the bass line, so we would not consider these notes to be creating inversions at all.

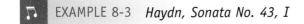

EXAMPLE 8-3   *Haydn, Sonata No. 43, I*

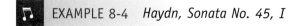

EXAMPLE 8-4   *Haydn, Sonata No. 45, I*

Textural reductions such as those of Examples 8-3 and 8-4 appear throughout this text. Their purpose is to simplify the texture and make the voice leading easier to understand. Notice that in the reduction of Example 8-4 the E♭5 has been transposed up one octave from the original. The octave transposition helps clarify the essentially conjunct (stepwise) nature of the melodic line.

SUBSTITUTED FIRST INVERSION TRIADS

First inversion triads are often used as *substitutes* for root position triads instead of coming about through bass arpeggiation. One reason for using such inversions is to improve the contour of the bass line. Another is to provide a greater variety of pitches in the bass line. A third reason is to lessen the importance of V and I chords that do not serve as goals of harmonic motion. Instances of this third type can be seen in Examples 8-3 and 8-4, where dominant chords are inverted. Example 8-5 contains a substituted inverted triad in the V[6], which allows the ascending stepwise motion of the bass to continue. The I[6] is an example of an arpeggiation following a structurally more important root position chord. The use of the I[6] provides variety and allows the bass to imitate the soprano figure from the previous beat.

EXAMPLE 8-5 *Bach, "Schmücke dich, o liebe Seele"*

F: I   V   vi   (V⁶)   I   (6)   V⁷   I

The diminished triad was used almost exclusively in first inversion throughout much of the tonal era. Earlier composers had considered a sonority to be acceptable only if all the intervals above the *bass* were consonant, and, as the diagram illustrates, a dissonant °5 or +4 occurs above the bass of a diminished triad unless it is in first inversion.

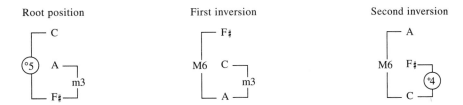

Tonal composers, although perhaps being unaware of the historical background, accepted for a time the tradition of using the diminished triad only in first inversion.

One first inversion triad that should *not* be freely substituted for the root position is vi⁶ (or VI⁶). A good rule to remember is that V in root position should not be followed by vi⁶. The reason for this can best be understood by playing Example 8-6 and comparing the effect of the V–vi and V–vi⁶ progressions. The V–vi sounds fine—a good example of a deceptive progression—but the vi⁶ sounds like a mistake.

EXAMPLE 8-6

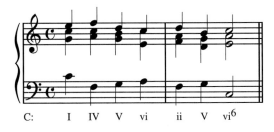

C: I   IV   V   vi   ii   V   vi⁶

One correct use of the vi⁶ chord is between a root position I and a root position ii, as in Example 8-7a. The vi⁶ will also occur occasionally as part of a sequential pattern, as in Example 8-7b.

EXAMPLE 8-7

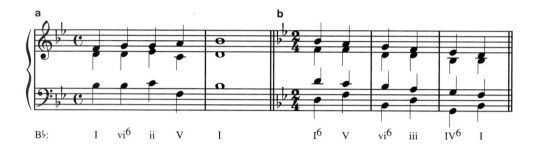

PARALLEL SIXTH CHORDS

Most passages use a reasonable balance of root position and first inversion triads, but there are many passages in which this is not true. Some styles call for a preponderance of root position chords. On the other hand, a whole series of parallel first inversion triads (or *sixth chords,* from figured bass symbols) is often found, especially in sequences. Chords used in parallel motion in this way generally do not function in the usual fashion. Instead, they serve as passing chords, connecting some chord at the beginning of the passage to some chord at the end of it. In Example 8-8 the parallel motion connects the root position I chord in m. 4 with another root position I chord in m. 7. The roman numerals in the sixth-chord passage are in parentheses to show that the chords are not functioning in their usual manner.

EXAMPLE 8-8   *Haydn, Symphony No. 104, I*

In the textural reduction of Example 8-8 the line in mm. 2–3 connecting D3 to C♯4 shows that a simplified version of the bass line would have stepwise motion here (m2 down) instead of the leap. Notice also the parallel 5ths in mm. 5–7. Haydn disguised the 5ths in the original through the use of non-chord tones. The usual technique used to avoid parallel 5ths in a sixth-chord passage is to put the root of each chord in the melody, thus producing acceptable parallel 4ths instead of objectionable parallel 5ths (Example 8-9a). In a four-voice texture, at least one voice will have to use leaps to avoid parallels, as in Example 8-9b.

EXAMPLE 8-9

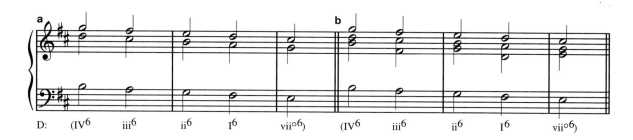

Checkpoint

1. What are the three uses of first inversion triads discussed in this chapter?
2. What type of triad (major, minor, or diminished) is usually used in first inversion?
3. How are inversions indicated in lead sheet symbols (review p. 53).

PART WRITING FIRST INVERSION TRIADS

Composition exercises using triads in first inversion as well as in root position are much more satisfying musically than are exercises restricted to root position only. Previous suggestions concerning spacing and voice leading still apply, of course, and should be considered together with those that follow.

Four-Part Textures

Inverted triads are nearly always complete in four-part textures. Because there are four voices and only three chord members, one of the members obviously will have to be doubled. The following suggestions should prove helpful.

1. In a contrapuntal texture—that is, in a texture consisting of relatively independent melodic lines—the doubling to use is the one that results from the best voice leading.

2. In a homophonic texture—that is, one that is primarily chordal or consists of a melody with chordal accompaniment—the doubling selected should be the one that provides the desired sonority.

3. In any texture, it is usually best not to double the leading tone.

The first of these suggestions probably needs no further explanation. Concerning the second suggestion, you should play Example 8-10, listening carefully to the different sonorities produced. If possible, you should also hear the example sung and performed by several combinations of instruments. The four parts of the example are presented in what is generally considered the order of preference on the part of composers of tonal music. However, this ordering is not to be interpreted as a rule. The quality of the sonority is affected as much by spacing as it is by doubling, as you will discover by comparing the last two chords in Example 8-10.

EXAMPLE 8-10

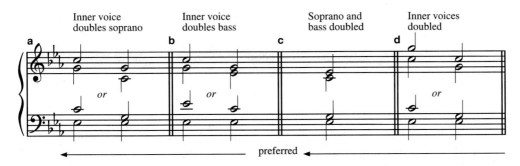

A doubled leading tone usually results in or implies parallel 8ves because of the strong tendency of $\hat{7}$ to resolve to $\hat{1}$. If you play Example 8-11a through c, you will probably agree that Example 8-11c produces the most pleasing effect. Example 8-11a is obviously incorrect because of the parallel 8ves. However, Example 8-11b, which avoids the parallels, still produces an unpleasant effect, probably because the parallels are still implied by the doubled leading tone.

EXAMPLE 8-11

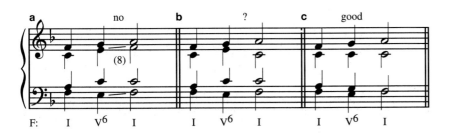

Three-Part Textures

Inverted triads are usually complete in three-part writing. Although incomplete inverted triads do occur, they are not used with the same frequency as incomplete root position triads. If a member of the triad is omitted, it will almost always be the 5th. The omitted member obviously cannot be the 3rd because that is the bass note. If the root is omitted, the resulting sonority might be heard *not* as an inverted triad but as a root position triad, as in Example 8-12.

EXAMPLE 8-12

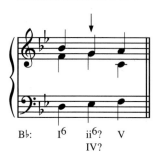

Example 8-13 is from a composition for TTB (Tenor, Tenor, Bass) chorus. The tenor parts sound an octave lower than written. There are two incomplete I⁶ chords in this excerpt. In the first of these the 5th is omitted, as we would expect. In the second incomplete I⁶, however, the root is omitted, but the listener recognizes the sonority as representing a I⁶ because it follows a V chord. Notice also that the IV at the beginning of m. 46 could also be analyzed as a ii⁶, as in Example 8-12. All the other inverted triads in the excerpt are complete.

EXAMPLE 8-13   *Schubert, "Bardengesang"*

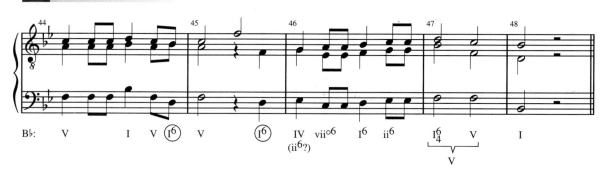

SOPRANO-BASS COUNTERPOINT

Now that we will be using triads in first inversion, the bass lines of your exercises can be much more interesting and musically satisfying than they were when you had only root position triads available. This bring us back to the subject of *counterpoint,* which was mentioned briefly on page 75, where it was defined as "the combining of relatively independent musical lines." We will now consider the idea of counterpoint a little more closely.

The words *relatively independent* are crucial to the understanding of counterpoint. The word *relatively* has to do with the style of the music in which the counterpoint is found. In tonal music, contrapuntal relationships are governed by certain voice-leading rules (restrictions against parallel fifths, and so on) and by conventions of harmonic progression. It would be unthinkable in tonal music, for example, for two lines to be in different keys. The word *independent,* in our definition of counterpoint, means that each line in a contrapuntal texture will ideally have its own unique contour and rhythm. Of these, the more important is contour. Let's begin with a counterexample. The opening of Haydn's Symphony No. 8, shown in Example 8-14, is pleasing and effective, but it is not contrapuntal because the lines have identical contours and rhythms and move in parallel motion throughout.

♫ **EXAMPLE 8-14**   *Haydn, Symphony No. 8, I (violins only)*

The instruments in Example 8-15 also have identical rhythms and contours, but they are offset by one measure, creating a contrapuntal form known as a *canon.* You no doubt have sung *rounds,* which are canons that are perpetual—there is no notated ending for the ensemble, as there is for Haydn's canon (not shown). Canons and rounds make use of a special type of counterpoint called *imitative counterpoint.* Most of the counterpoint discussed in this section is not imitative or is only incidentally imitative.

EXAMPLE 8-15   *Haydn, String Quartet Op. 76, No. 2, III*

In Example 8-16, Bach gives the soprano and bass different contours, although they have identical rhythms, so this is an example of counterpoint as well. Under the music, we show the relationships between the two lines as **p, s,** or **c,** for parallel, similar, or contrary (review p. 82). Notice that the prevailing relationships between the voices are contrary or similar.

EXAMPLE 8-16   *Bach, "Ermuntre dich, mein schwacher Geist"*
                (outer voices only)

Counterpoint, like that in the previous example, in which the two parts move with identical rhythms, is called 1:1 (one-to-one), or first species, counterpoint. In another harmonization of the same melody, shown in Example 8-17, Bach allows a little more rhythmic variety between the voices. Notice that he also uses a different time signature here.

EXAMPLE 8-17   *Bach, "Ermuntre dich, mein schwacher Geist"*
(outer voices only)

It is often instructive to simplify a texture by removing repetitions and embellishments to reveal the simpler underlying counterpoint. This is the approach frequently taken in the reductive examples in this text. For example, the reduction following Example 8-18 shows that the music begins with a step down and back up in the soprano and a step up and back down in the bass—figures that are known as *neighbor motions*. This is followed in the melody by a leap to $\hat{5}$ in the soprano and a stepwise descent to $\hat{7}$, against which the bass unfolds a somewhat more complicated counterpoint.

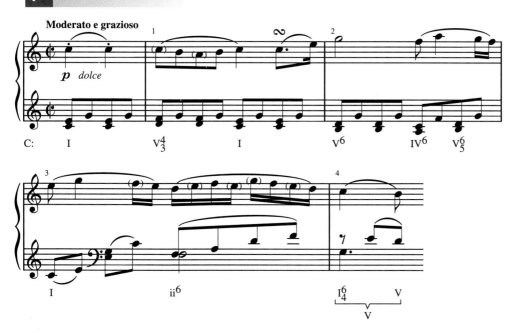

EXAMPLE 8-18   *Beethoven, Rondo, Op. 51, No. 1*

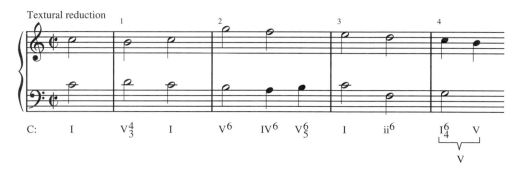

So, where in tonal music are we apt to encounter counterpoint? The music of the Baroque period (roughly 1600–1750) is known for contrapuntal textures. Although not all Baroque music is contrapuntal, much of it is, and it is not unusual in Baroque music for all the voices in a contrapuntal texture to have that relative independence that we have been talking about. This is also true in tonal music after the Baroque when the composer is working within one of the traditionally contrapuntal forms, such as the canon, discussed earlier. Another example is the *fugue,* a piece in which each voice states a short theme (the *subject*) in turn after which it is tossed about among the voices, fragmented, and developed. However, in most tonal music *after* 1750, the greatest contrapuntal interest is found between the soprano and bass lines. This is true not just of vocal music but of tonal music in general. The inner voice or voices in tonal music are frequently "filler" for the most part. In the previous Beethoven example, the inner voice comes to the fore only in m. 3, where it continues the eighth-note arpeggiations begun by the bass at the beginning of the measure.

When you are composing your harmony exercises, whether from scratch or with a given bass or soprano line, you should first try to create a good soprano/bass counterpoint, and only after that is accomplished should you fill in the inner parts. The melodies should be simple, like the ones you learned to write in Chapter 5. The bass line should also be effective, although bass lines tend to be more disjunct than soprano lines, especially at cadences, and the bass should move contrary to the soprano whenever practicable. Later, when you have learned more about adding embellishments, the results will be more musical if the basic contrapuntal framework between the soprano and bass is a good one.

As a final illustration, listen to Example 8-19 and the reduction that follows it. You can see that the counterpoint between the outer parts is basically quite simple. In fact, the reduction could easily be further simplified so that the top line would consists of $\hat{5}$ $\hat{1}$ $\hat{2}$ $\hat{3}$ in the first four measures and $\hat{5}$ $\hat{1}$ $\hat{2}$ $\hat{1}$ in the last four. Mozart took a very simple contrapuntal framework and embellished the top line to create a pleasing and interesting melody.

EXAMPLE 8-19 *Mozart, Quintet for Horn and Strings, K. 407*

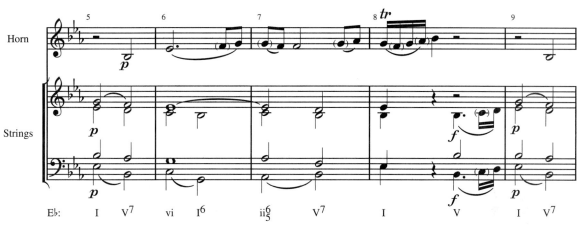

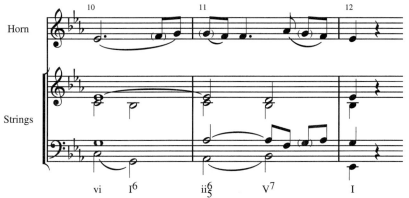

Textural reduction

Summary

Triads in inversion are not at all unusual in tonal music. In fact, most phrases include at least one. First inversions come about either as *arpeggiations* of triads by the bass or as *substitutions* for root position triads. First inversion triads are also called sixth chords, so *parallel sixth chords* is a term used for a passage that features first inversion triads in parallel motion.

Triads in first inversion are used for variety, to improve the bass line, and to lessen the weight of some I and V chords as well as for other reasons. First inversion also allows the use of diminished triads (and sometimes augmented ones) because these are not commonly used in root position.

Inverted triads in four-part textures are usually complete, with no tones omitted. In three-part textures, if a tone is omitted, it is usually the 5th of the chord. If a tone is to be doubled, any tone but the leading tone will do. In four parts, the preferred doublings are soprano or bass with alto or tenor.

Counterpoint is an important element of music throughout the tonal era. Some pieces, such as canons and fugues, feature counterpoint throughout and in all the voices, but in much tonal music the counterpoint is borne mostly by the soprano and bass lines.

Self-Test 8-1
(Answers begin on page 596.)

A. Analysis.

  1. Bracket the longest series of complete parallel sixth chords you can find in this excerpt. Do not attempt a roman numeral analysis. Does the voice leading in the sixth-chord passage resemble more closely Example 8-8 or Example 8-9?

Mozart, Sonata K. 279, III

2. Label all chords with roman numerals. Then classify the doubling in each inverted triad according to the methods shown in Example 8-10.

Bach, "Herzliebster Jesu, was hast du"

3. Label all chords with roman numerals. Write out the contour of the bass line in quarter-note heads (without rhythm). Can you find part or all of the bass line hidden in the melody?

Beethoven, Sonata Op. 2, No. 1, I

B. The following excerpt is from Mozart's *Eine kleine Nachtmusik.* Supply the missing tenor line (viola part in the original) and then compare your result with Mozart's (in Appendix B).

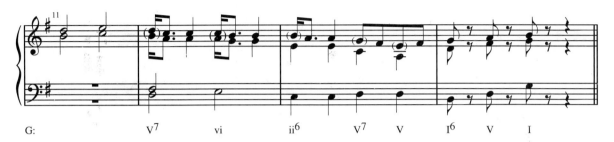

G: V⁷   vi   ii⁶   V⁷ V   I⁶ V   I

C. Supply alto and tenor lines for the following excerpts.

B♭: I ⁶ V   e: i   V⁶ ⁵₃ i   D: vi ii⁶ V   vi

E♭: IV V I⁶ IV⁶   f♯: i V⁶ i iv   d: i⁶ iv⁶ V i

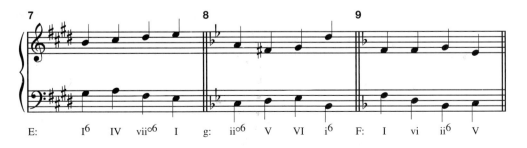

E: I⁶ IV vii°⁶ I   g: ii°⁶ V VI i⁶   F: I vi ii⁶ V

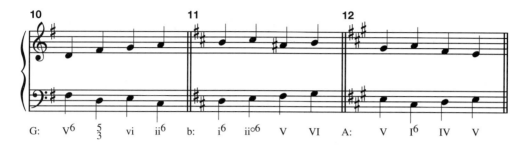

G: V⁶   ⁵₃   vi   ii⁶   b: i⁶   ii°⁶   V   VI   A: V   I⁶   IV   V

D. Using the first six problems from Part C, add an alto line to each to create a three-part texture.

E. Analyze the chords specified by these figured basses and then add alto and tenor parts.

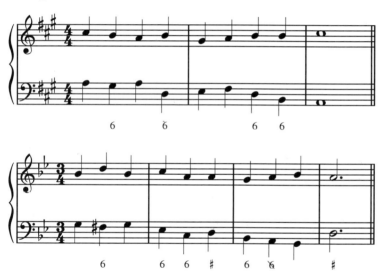

F. The excerpt below is from the Gavotte from Bach's French Suite No. 5. Supply the missing alto line (only) and then compare your result with Bach's original three-part version (Appendix B). Because this is written for a keyboard instrument, you do not need to worry about the range of the alto part.

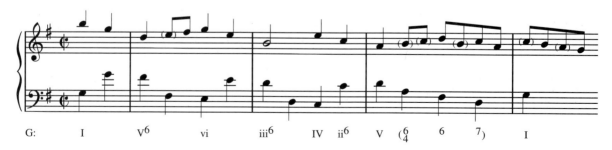

G: I   V⁶   vi   iii⁶   IV   ii⁶   V   (⁶₄   6   7)   I

G. Analyze the chords implied by the soprano and bass lines below, remembering to use only triads in root position and first inversion. Then add alto and tenor parts to make a four-part texture.

H. The following example is reduced from Beethoven's Sonata Op. 79, III. Analyze the implied harmonies (more than one good solution is possible) and add two inner parts, one on each staff.

I. Continue your solution to Part E with a second four-measure segment, similar to the first.

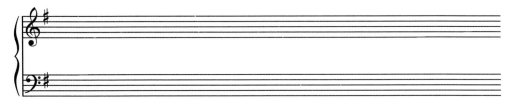

Exercise 8-1 See Workbook.

Chapter 9

Triads in Second Inversion

INTRODUCTION

It would be logical to assume that second inversion triads are used in tonal music in the same ways as first inversion triads: as bass arpeggiations and as substitutes for the root position. However, this is only partly true. Although both first and second inversion triads are created through bass arpeggiations, second inversion triads are *not* used as substitutes for the root position. The reason is that the second inversion of a triad is considered to be a much less stable sonority than either of the other two bass positions. For centuries before the development of tonal harmony, the interval of a P4 had been considered a dissonance if the *lowest voice* in the texture was sounding the bottom pitch of the P4. Although each of the sonorities in Example 9-1 contains a P4 (or a P4 plus a P8), the first two are considered to be consonant because the interval of a P4 does not involve the lowest voice (review the discussion of the diminished triad in first inversion on p. 127). The other two sonorities are dissonant in the tonal style, although our twentieth-century ears might not easily hear the dissonance.

EXAMPLE 9-1

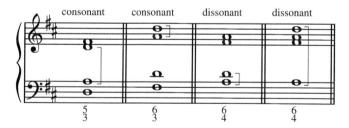

Notice that diminished and augmented $^6_4$ chords would also contain dissonant intervals above the bass—an +4 and a °4, respectively.

Because the composers of the tonal era recognized the instability of the $^6_4$ (six-four) chord (the only position in which there is a 4th above the bass), the chord is not used as a substitute for the more stable root position or first inversion sonorities. It is used in bass arpeggiations as well as in several other contexts to be described below.

BASS ARPEGGIATION AND THE MELODIC BASS

The six-four chord may come about through a bass arpeggiation involving a root position triad, a first inversion triad, or both (Ex. 9-2).

EXAMPLE 9-2   *Mendelssohn, Symphony No. 4, Op. 90, I*

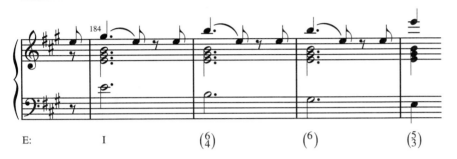

Your analysis of the "real" bass note will depend on the context, taking into account such factors as metric placement, duration, and register. The figures in parentheses in Example 9-2 are often omitted when analyzing a passage employing an arpeggiated bass.

Another somewhat incidental way in which six-four chords can be formed is through a melodic bass. If the bass part has an important melodic line instead of fulfilling its usual supporting role, any number of inverted chords may result. Because a melodic bass is no longer the harmonic foundation of the texture, inversions should not be indicated in such a passage. For example, the bass melody in Example 9-3 is accompanied only by repeated A's and C's, implying the tonic harmony in F major. It would not be correct to analyze the excerpt as beginning with a I$^6_4$.

EXAMPLE 9-3   *Beethoven, String Quartet Op. 59, No. 1, I*

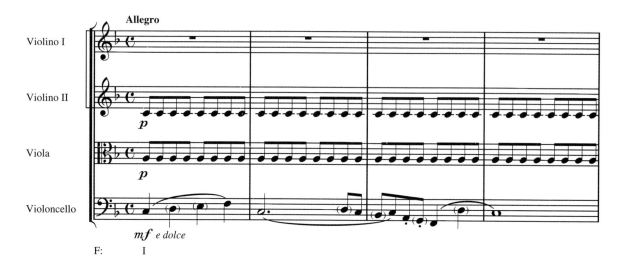

THE CADENTIAL SIX-FOUR

Besides its appearance in a bass arpeggiation or a melodic bass, the six-four chord tends to be used in three stereotyped contexts. If you compare the two halves of Example 9-4 below, you can see that they have much in common. Both begin with a tonic triad and end with a V–I progression. In Example 9-4b, however, the movement from ii^6 to V is momentarily delayed by a I$^6_4$ in a *metrically stronger position*. This is a very typical illustration of the cadential six-four, the most familiar of all six-four uses. Notice that the I$^6_4$ resolves to a *root position* V chord. Other resolutions of the cadential six-four will be introduced in Chapters 13 and 17.

EXAMPLE 9-4

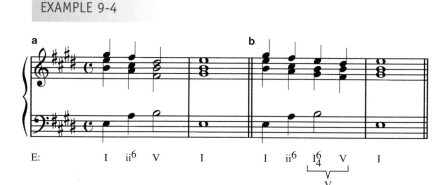

Theorists have long debated whether it is better to analyze the cadential six-four as I_4^6–V or simply as V, treating $\hat{1}$ and $\hat{3}$ as non-chord tones. On the one hand, all the notes of the tonic triad *are* present, but on the other hand, the *function* of the cadential I_4^6 is clearly decorative: It does not substitute for the root position tonic. The analytical symbols used in Example 9-4 and throughout this text are a compromise and reflect the validity of both schools of thought.

The voice leading in the upper parts into and away from the cadential I_4^6 is usually smooth, as in Example 9-4, and the resolution of the I_4^6 to V usually sees scale degrees $\hat{1}$ and $\hat{3}$ moving down by step to $\hat{7}$ and $\hat{2}$, respectively. The cadential I_4^6 occurs either on a stronger beat than the V, as in Example 9-4, or on a stronger *portion* of the beat, as in Example 9-5.

EXAMPLE 9-5 *Scarlatti, Sonata, L. 489*

However, in triple meter, if the V chord occurs on the third beat of a measure, the I_4^6 will frequently appear on the normally weak second beat, as in Example 9-6.

EXAMPLE 9-6 *Scarlatti, Sonata, L. 363*

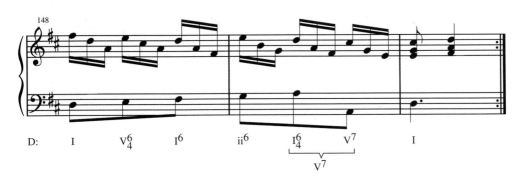

The most dramatic demonstration of the delaying character of the cadential I_4^6 is found at the cadenza of many solo concertos. In such cases, the orchestra usually stops on a I_4^6, after which the soloist performs the cadenza. No matter what the length of the cadenza, it eventually reaches V and, simultaneously with the return of the orchestra, resolves to I. In a cadenza played by a single-line instrument, the V chord will often be represented by a single tone or a trill, as in Example 9-7.

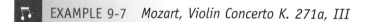

EXAMPLE 9-7 *Mozart, Violin Concerto K. 271a, III*

One special use of the III^{+6} in minor is so similar to the cadential six-four that it will be discussed here. If you play the progressions in Example 9-8 and compare them, it will be obvious to you that the same principle—the momentary delay of the dominant—is operating in each case. The cadential III^{+6}, which is not often used, is clearly a *linear event,* and not part of a III$^+$–V progression. A cadential iii^6 in the major mode is also a possibility, but it is not often found.

EXAMPLE 9-8

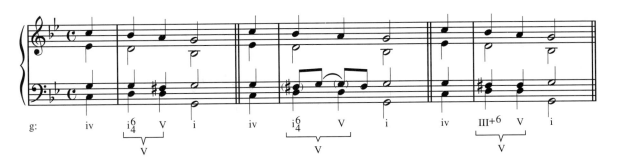

THE PASSING SIX-FOUR

Second inversion triads are frequently encountered harmonizing the middle note of a three-note scalar figure in the bass, a usage that is called a *passing* six-four chord. The figure may be ascending or descending. Although any triad may be used as a passing six-four chord, those in Example 9-9 are the most common and are found in both major and minor modes. The passing six-four usually falls on a *weak* beat and typically features smooth voice leading, as in Example 9-9. As with the cadential six-four, some theorists prefer not to assign a roman numeral to passing six-fours because of their weak harmonic function. In this text we will indicate this weak function by putting such roman numerals in parentheses.

EXAMPLE 9-9

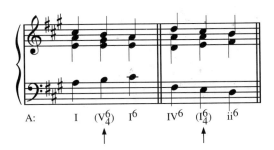

Example 9-10 contains both a passing I_4^6 (m. 25) and a cadential I_4^6 (m. 27) in a three-part texture. The first inversion chords in mm. 24–26 are all substituted first inversions. Notice that the melody in mm. 24–27 is an embellished stepwise descent from A5 to B4.

EXAMPLE 9-10   *Mozart, Sonata K. 309, III*

Textural reduction

Longer stepwise motions in the bass often use passing six-four chords, as in Example 9-11. The textural reduction shows that the melody is also essentially stepwise and moves for several measures in parallel 6ths with the bass.

EXAMPLE 9-11   *Mozart, Symphony No. 40, K. 550, IV (piano score)*

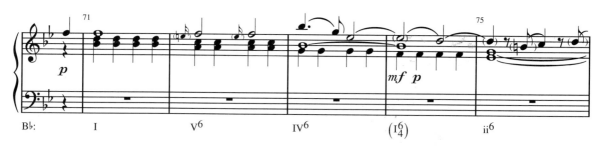

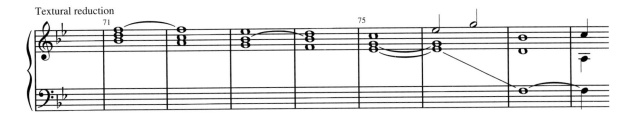

Textural reduction

THE PEDAL SIX-FOUR   *Neighboring*

One way of elaborating a static root position triad is to move the 3rd and 5th of the triad up by step then back down by step to their original positions. The sonority that results is a six-four chord (Ex. 9-12).

EXAMPLE 9-12

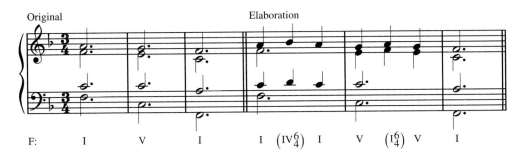

F: I   V   I   I   (IV$^6_4$)   I   V   (I$^6_4$)   V   I

Because this elaboration is similar to a pedal point (discussed in Chapter 12), it is called a *pedal six-four* (some theorists call it an embellishing or stationary six-four). The roman numeral beneath a pedal six-four is put in parentheses to indicate its weak harmonic function.

Pedal six-four chords usually work exactly like those in Example 9-12. That is, they involve either a I–(IV$^6_4$)–I progression or a V–(I$^6_4$)–V progression, with the six-four chord falling on a weak beat and with stepwise voice leading into and away from the six-four chord. Exceptionally, the bass may move after the six-four chord and before the return of the root position triad, as in Example 9-13.

♫ **EXAMPLE 9-13**   *Mozart, Quartet K. 465, I*

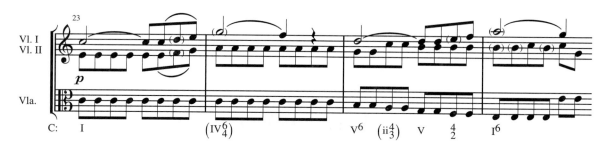

As with other types of six-four chords, pedal six-fours are occasionally seen in lead-sheet notation. Example 9-14 contains a clear instance of a pedal six-four employing a I–(IV$^6_4$)–I progression.

♫ **EXAMPLE 9-14**   *Webber, "Don't Cry for Me, Argentina"*

Words by Tim Rice, Music by Andrew Lloyd Webber. © Copyright 1976, 1977 by Evita Music Ltd. All Rights for the USA and Canada controlled and administered by MCA - On Backstreet Music, Inc. Used by permission.

Checkpoint

1. Two ways in which six-four chords are produced is through bass arpeggiation and by a melodic bass. Name the three other kinds of six-four chords discussed in this chapter.
2. The cadential six-four chord precedes what root position triad?
3. What two triads are most often used as passing six-four chords?
4. The pedal six-four usually involves one of two progressions. What are they?

PART WRITING FOR SECOND INVERSION TRIADS

In a four-part texture, the bass (5th of the chord) should be doubled. Exceptions to this are rarely encountered in tonal music. The other voices generally move as smoothly as possible—often by step—both into and out of the six-four chord. In a three-part texture, it is generally best to have all members of the triad present (Ex. 9-15a), but sometimes the root or 3rd is omitted, in which case the *5th* is doubled (Exs. 9-15b and 9-15c).

EXAMPLE 9-15

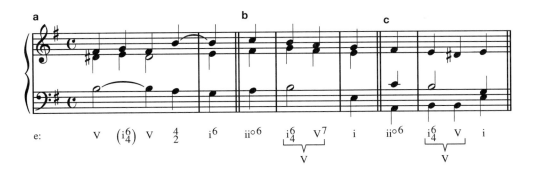

Summary

Six-four chords may come about incidentally through bass arpeggiation, or they may occur if the melody is in the bass. However, in other contexts, triads in second inversion are treated in special ways in tonal music because the six-four chord is considered dissonant in this style.

The *cadential six-four chord* is a tonic six-four that delays the arrival of the V chord that follows it. It depends totally on the V chord for its meaning, and it should not be thought of as a substitute for a tonic triad in root position or first inversion. The cadential six-four occurs in a metrically stronger position than the V chord that it delays.

A *passing six-four chord* harmonizes the middle note of a three-note scalar figure in the bass. The most common passing six-four chords are the V_4^6 and the I_4^6 chords, and they usually fall on a weak beat.

A *pedal six-four chord* elaborates the root position chord that precedes it and usually follows it as well. Most pedal six-four chords are I_4^6 or IV_4^6 chords.

The voice leading into and out of a six-four chord is usually as smooth as possible, with stepwise motion prevailing. In a four-voice texture, the bass (5th of the chord) is almost always doubled.

Self-Test 9-1
(Answers begin on page 601.)

A. Analysis. In addition to the specific instructions for each example, label each six-four chord by type.

   1. Label the chords with roman numerals. Be sure to include the F#5 at the beginning of m. 69 and m. 70 as a chord member.

   Mozart, Piano Sonata K. 333, III

   2. Label the chords with roman numerals.

   Schumann, "Little Morning Wanderer," Op. 68, No. 17

3. Label the chords with roman numerals.

Bach, "Wenn mein Stündlein vorhanden ist"

B. Fill in one or two inner parts, as specified. Identify any six-four chords by type.

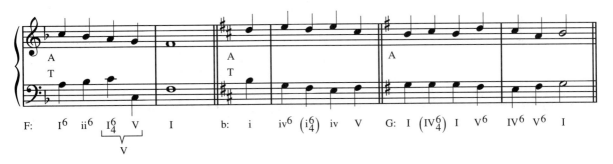

F: I⁶   ii⁶   I⁶₄   V   I   b: i   iv⁶ (i⁶₄)   iv   V   G: I (IV⁶₄)   I   V⁶   IV⁶ V⁶ I
                         V

C. Realize these figured basses for three or four voices, as specified. Notice the frequent use of ⁵₃ (or the equivalent, such as ⁵♯) to indicate a root position triad following an inverted chord. Analyze with roman numerals and label six-four types.

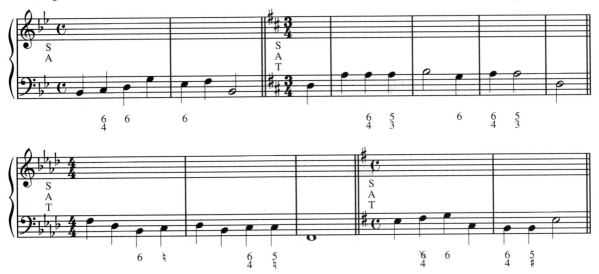

Exercise 9-1 See Workbook.

Chapter 10

Cadences, Phrases, and Periods

MUSICAL FORM

Understanding tonal harmony requires more than the knowledge of how each chord tends to function harmonically and how the voice leading might bring the chord into being. We must also give some consideration to musical *form*, the ways in which a composition is shaped to create a meaningful musical experience for the listener.

A study of the forms of lengthy compositions is beyond the scope of this text. However, it will be helpful for you to learn something of the harmonic basis of the smaller building blocks that combine to produce those larger forms.

CADENCES

Although the ultimate harmonic goal of a tonal composition is the final tonic triad, there will also be many interior harmonic goals found within the piece, some of them tonic tri-ads and some of them not. These interior goals might be reached at a fairly regular rate (often every four measures), or sometimes their appearances might not form a pattern at all. We use the term *cadence* to mean a harmonic goal, specifically the chords used at the goal. There are several types of cadences commonly found in tonal music. Some cadences sound more or less conclusive, or final, whereas others leave us off balance, feeling a need for the music to continue.

Locating the cadences in a composition is easier to do than it is to explain. Remember that what you are listening for is a goal, so there will often be a slowing down through the use of longer note values, but even a piece that never slows down (a "perpetuum mobile") will contain cadences. As you listen to the examples in this chapter, you will realize that you are already aurally familiar with tonal cadences and that finding them is not a com-plicated process.

There is a standard terminology used for classifying the various kinds of cadences, and the terms apply to both major and minor keys. One very important type of cadence consists of a tonic triad preceded by some form of V or vii°. This kind of cadence is called an *authentic cadence* (which is an unfortunate term because it implies that all the others are less than authentic). The *perfect authentic cadence* (abbreviated PAC) consists of a V–I (or V^7–I) progression, with both the V and I in root position and $\hat{1}$ in the melody over the

I chord (Ex. 10-1). The PAC is the most final sounding of all cadences. Most tonal compositions end with a PAC, but such cadences might also be found elsewhere in a piece.

🎵 EXAMPLE 10-1   *Bach,* Well-Tempered Clavier, *Book II, Prelude 10*

An *imperfect authentic cadence* (IAC) is usually defined simply as any authentic cadence that is not a PAC. However, it is useful to identify several subcategories, as follows:

1.   *Root position IAC:* Like a PAC, but $\hat{3}$ or $\hat{5}$ is in the melody over the I chord (Ex. 10-2).

🎵 EXAMPLE 10-2   *Bach,* Well-Tempered Clavier, *Book II, Prelude 12*

2.   *Inverted IAC:* V$^{(7)}$–I, but with either or both of the chords inverted (Ex. 10-3).

EXAMPLE 10-3   *Schumann, "Nachtlied," Op. 96, No. 1*

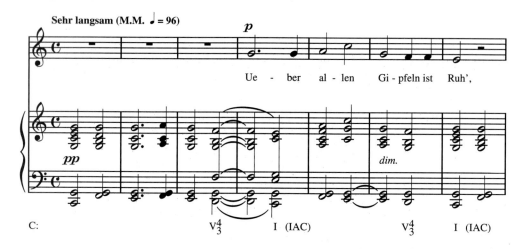

3.   *Leading-tone IAC:* Some form of vii°–I, the vii° substituting for a V chord
     (Ex. 10-4).

EXAMPLE 10-4   *Bach, "Befiehl du deine Wege"*

The root position IAC is certainly the most final sounding of the three IAC types, and you
might find some compositions that end with such a cadence. The other types are limited
almost exclusively to less important interior cadences.

Remember that not every V–I progression constitutes an authentic cadence. Only
when the I chord seems to serve as the goal of a longer passage—usually at least a few
measures—would we term a V–I progression a cadence. This same distinction also applies
to the other cadence types.

A *deceptive cadence* (DC) results when the ear expects a V–I authentic cadence but hears V–? instead. The ? is usually a submediant triad, as in Example 10-5, but others are possible. A DC produces a very unstable feeling and would never be used to end a tonal work. Remember that V–vi involves special part-writing problems. Review Example 6-9.

EXAMPLE 10-5   *Haydn, Sonata No. 4, II*

A deceptive progression is often used not to really *end* a phrase but to *extend* it a few measures until it reaches the true cadence.

The *half cadence* (HC) is a very common type of unstable or "progressive" cadence. The HC ends with a V chord, which can be preceded by any other chord (Ex. 10-6).

EXAMPLE 10-6   *Haydn, Sonata No. 44, II*

The *Phrygian half cadence* (Ex. 10-7) is a special name given to the iv⁶–V HC in minor. The name refers to a cadence found in the period of modal polyphony (before 1600), but it does not imply that the music is actually in the Phrygian mode.* Notice, incidentally, that Example 10-7 contains a deceptive progression (V⁷–VI) but not a deceptive *cadence* because the goal of the passage is the V in m. 4, not the VI in m. 3.

Phrygian half cadence

---

*Modal polyphony used a number of scalar patterns seldom employed by tonal composers. One of these was the Phrygian mode, which used a scale pattern the same as E to E with no accidentals.

EXAMPLE 10-7   *Schumann, "Folk Song," Op. 68, No. 9*

A *plagal cadence* (PC) typically involves a IV–I progression. Although plagal cadences are usually final sounding, they are not as important in tonal music as the authentic cadence. In fact, a plagal cadence is usually added on as a kind of tag following a PAC. A familiar example of this is the "Amen" sung at the end of hymns, as in Example 10-8.

EXAMPLE 10-8   *Dykes, "Holy, Holy, Holy!"*

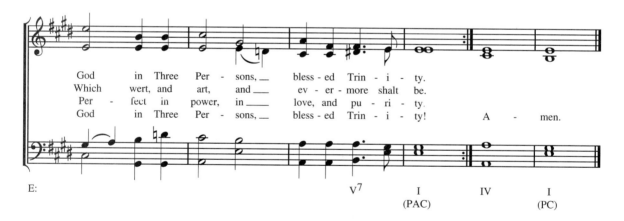

The definitions of cadence types given above are standard, for the most part, and they will apply to most cadences found in tonal music. Exceptions will be found, however, in which case the more general definition listed in the table below should be applied. For example, the Chapter 9 Self-Test included a phrase from a Bach chorale that concluded with a I⁶–IV cadence, but you can deduce from the table that this is a kind of half cadence.

Cadence type	First chord	Second chord
Authentic	Contains leading tone	Tonic
Plagal	Does not contain leading tone	Tonic
Deceptive	Contains leading tone	Not tonic
Half	Does not contain leading tone	Not tonic

A still more general but useful method of classifying cadences puts them into two groups: *conclusive* (authentic and plagal) and *progressive* (deceptive and half).

CADENCES AND HARMONIC RHYTHM

As a very general rule, the last chord of a cadence usually falls on a stronger beat than the chord that precedes it. This assumes that the rate at which the chords change—the harmonic rhythm—is faster than one chord per measure. The rhythmic examples below illustrate this using authentic cadences; possible cadential I_4^6 chords are shown in parentheses.

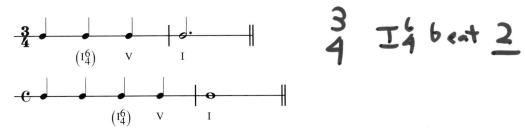

Checkpoint

Match the cadence-type abbreviations with the definitions and examples.

Conclusive cadences

1. PAC
   in
2. Root position IAC
3. Inverted IAC
4. Leading-tone IAC
5. PC

Definitions and examples

a. V–I, both in root position, with $\hat{3}$ or $\hat{5}$
        in the melody over the I chord
b. IV–I
c. ?–V
d. V–vi
e. vii°⁶–I

Progressive cadences

1. HC
2. Phrygian HC
   the
3. DC

a. V–I⁶
b. V–I, both in root position, with $\hat{1}$ in melody over the I chord
c. iv⁶–V in minor

a. $V-I^6$
b. $V-I$, both in root position, with $\hat{1}$ in melody over the I chord
c. iv^6-V in minor

MOTIVES AND PHRASES

A *motive* is the smallest identifiable musical idea. A motive can consist of a pitch pattern or a rhythmic pattern or both, as you can see below.

pitch motive   rhythm motive   pitch/rhythm motive

Of the two aspects of a pitch/rhythm motive, rhythm is probably the stronger and more easily identified when it reappears later in a composition. It is best to use *motive* to refer only to those musical ideas that are "developed" (worked out or used in different ways) in a composition.

A *phrase* is a relatively independent musical idea terminated by a cadence. A *phrase segment* is a distinct portion of a phrase, but it is not a phrase either because it is not terminated by a cadence or because it seems too short to be relatively independent. Essentially, a phrase segment is a melodic event, whereas a phrase is a harmonic event. Phrases are usually labeled with lowercase letters (a, b, c, and so on), as in Example 10-9.

🎵 EXAMPLE 10-9   *Beethoven, Symphony No. 6, Op. 68, I*

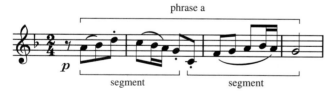

As you might guess from the definition of *phrase*, there is a good deal of subjectivity involved in identifying phrases. What sounds like a phrase to one listener might be a phrase segment to another listener. The issue cannot be decided by finding cadences because phrase segments frequently end with cadences. Also, phrases are often extended by means of a deceptive cadence followed by an authentic cadence, or they might be extended by repetition of the cadence, as in phrase a of Example 10-10 (mm. 1–6). The final phrase of this minuet, phrase a′, returns phrase a with an added repetition of the first

phrase segment, creating an eight-measure phrase. Phrases b and c also contain repetitions
of their opening phrase segments, but with some variation in each case.

EXAMPLE 10-10   *Haydn, Sonata No. 15, II*

The last note of one phrase sometimes serves as the first note of the next one, a process referred to as *elision*. An even more extreme overlap can be seen by looking back at Example 10-3, in which the fourth measure of the first phrase in the accompaniment serves also as the first measure of the first phrase of the song.

MOZART: "AN DIE FREUDE"

All the concepts we have presented so far in this chapter are well illustrated in Example 10-11. This deceptively simple song was composed by Mozart when he was eleven years old. The singer doubles the right hand of the piano part throughout, and a nice effect is obtained in performance if the left hand of the piano part is doubled by a cello or a bassoon.

EXAMPLE 10-11   *Mozart, "An die Freude," K. 53*

Cadences occur regularly every four measures in this song, each cadence marking the end of a phrase. Because the texture contains only two lines, the chords are necessarily incomplete, but the implied harmonies at the cadences are clear enough and have been labeled for you. The cadences illustrate all the types discussed in this chapter, with the exception of the PC. Notice that two cadences occur in the key of the dominant (C), and one occurs in the key of the supertonic (g). Because we do not lose track aurally of the key of F as we listen to the song, it would be appropriate to refer to mm. 13 to 24 as embellishments of V and ii rather than as a true change of tonal center. All the cadences are listed in the following table.

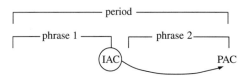

Notice that by definition the phrase endings in a period must be different. If both phrases are identical, the result is not a period but a *repeated phrase*. Repetition is important in tonal music, but it does not contribute to the growth of a musical form.

We use the term *parallel period* if both phrases *begin* with similar or identical material, even if that material is embellished. Example 10-12 illustrates a parallel period.

🎵 EXAMPLE 10-12   *Schubert, "Am Meer"*

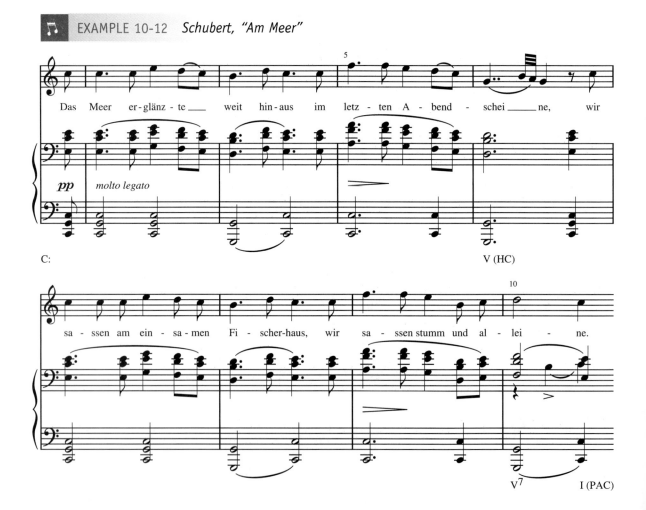

A formal diagram of Example 10-12 would show the parallel relationship between the phrases by labeling them a and a′ (pronounced "a prime").

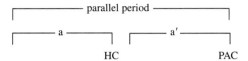

Sometimes the parallel relationship between the phrases is not so obvious. In Example 10-13, the melody of the second phrase begins like the first, but it is a third lower. Sequential relationships like this one are similar enough to be labeled a parallel period. The antecedent-consequent relationship here is established by the IAC in mm. 3 to 4 (V$_3^4$–I with $\hat{3}$ in the melody over the I chord) and the PAC in mm. 7–8.

♫ EXAMPLE 10-13   *Gershwin, "I Loves You Porgy"*

Copyright © 1935 by Gershwin Publishing Corporation. Copyright Renewed, Assigned to Chappell & Co., Inc. Used by permission of Chappell & Co., Inc., Miami, FL 33014.

A period in which the phrase beginnings are not similar is called a *contrasting period.* Example 10-14 illustrates a contrasting period.

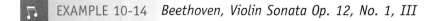

EXAMPLE 10-14   *Beethoven, Violin Sonata Op. 12, No. 1, III*

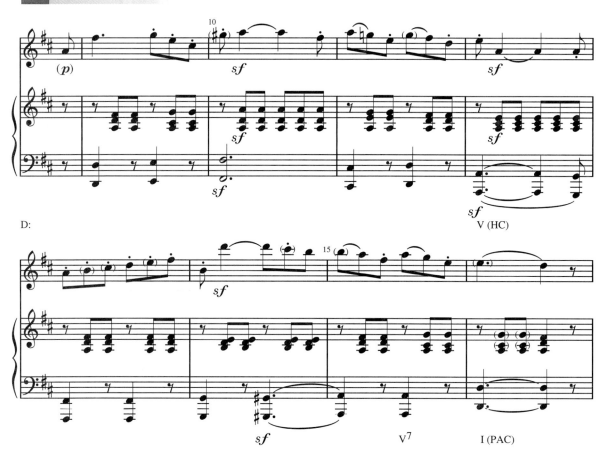

A common way of expanding a two-phrase period is by repeating the antecedent phrase (as in *aab*) or the consequent phrase (*abb*). It would also be possible to repeat both (*aabb*), which is not the same as a repeated period (*abab*).

A genuine *three-phrase period,** however, has three different phrases—two antecedents and a consequent or one antecedent and two consequents, as determined by the cadences. In Example 10–15 there are two antecedents because the first two phrases end with half cadences.

Some writers use the term phrase group *for what we call a three-phrase period.*

EXAMPLE 10-15 *Mozart, The Marriage of Figaro, K. 492, "Voi, che sapete."*

A *double period* consists typically of four phrases in two pairs, the cadence at the end of the second pair being stronger than the cadence at the end of the first pair.

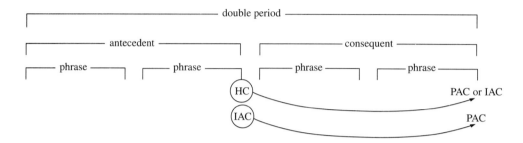

There are several things that should be pointed out about this diagram. First, notice that this structure is much like a period, with the only difference being that each half consists here of a pair of phrases instead of one phrase. Also notice that the first two phrases will probably not form a period according to our original definition. Finally, notice that a *repeated period* is not the same as a double period because a double period requires contrasting cadences.

Double periods are called *parallel* or *contrasting* according to whether the melodic material that begins the two halves of the double period is similar. Example 10-16 illustrates a parallel double period, and its structure is outlined in the following diagram.

♫ EXAMPLE 10-16   *Beethoven, Sonata Op. 26, I*

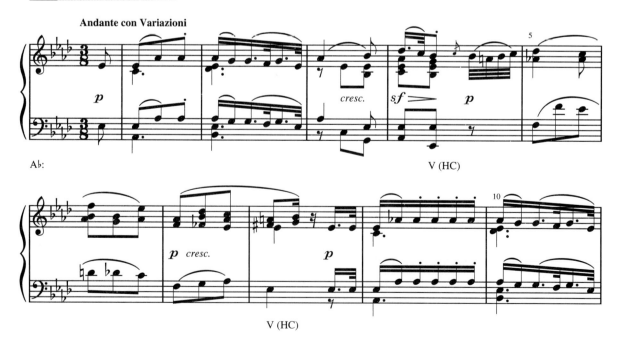

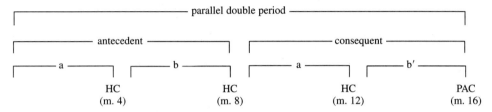

Because the first and third phrases have the same cadence, the third phrase in the diagram is labeled a, not a′, even though the original a is somewhat ornamented when it returns as the third phrase.

Often, several phrases will seem to constitute a formal unit other than a period or double period. The term *phrase group* is used for such situations. Before assigning this term, however, study the music (especially the cadences) closely to see whether a passage might be analyzed as a variant of some period form.

Summary

Musical form concerns the ways in which a composition is shaped to create a meaningful experience for the listener.

The term *cadence* can refer to a harmonic goal or the chords that are used at a harmonic goal. Cadence types in tonal music include:

authentic: some form of V or vii° followed by I or I⁶

perfect authentic (PAC): root position V or V⁷ followed by a root position I with
$\hat{1}$ in the soprano over the I chord

imperfect authentic (IAC): any authentic cadence that is not a PAC

deceptive (DC): V followed by some chord other than I, usually vi

half (HC): a cadence that ends on V

Phrygian half (HC): iv⁶–V in minor

plagal (PC): IV–I

A *motive* is the smallest identifiable musical idea. A *phrase* is a relatively independent musical idea terminated by a cadence. A phrase is usually constructed of two or more distinct portions called *phrase segments*.

Two phrases can be combined to form a *period* if they seem to go together as a musical unit and if the second phrase ends with a more conclusive cadence than the first. *Double periods* are just like periods, except that each half of the structure consists of two phrases rather than just one. Both periods and double periods may be either parallel or contrasting, according to whether the two halves begin with similar melodic material. A *repeated phrase* or *repeated period* does not produce a new kind of formal unit and should not be confused with a period or double period. A *phrase group* is a group of phrases that seem to belong together without forming a period or double period.

Self-Test 10-1
(Answers begin on page 602.)

A.   Analysis. The cadence chords have been analyzed for you in each example.

   1.   Make a diagram of this excerpt similar to the diagrams used in the text. Include phrase labels (a, b, and so on), cadence types and measure numbers, and the form of the excerpt. In addition, label the first seven chords in the first phrase.

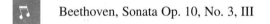   Beethoven, Sonata Op. 10, No. 3, III

2. Diagram the form of this excerpt as above. In addition, point out any *sequences* (review Chapter 7), either exact or modified, that occur in the melody.

Mozart, Sonata K. 284, II

3. There is certainly more than one way to interpret this famous theme. Most writers seem to prefer the three-phrase analysis shown here, the third phrase being
an unusually long one (mm. 9–17). What would the form of the theme have
been if it had ended in m. 8? Is there any way to hear the entire theme as an
expansion of that form? Diagram the theme to illustrate your interpretation.

Beethoven, Sonata Op. 13, III

4. Diagram this excerpt. See if you can find an example of 8ves by contrary motion (review pp. 84–85) between the melody and bass.

Chopin, Mazurka Op. 33, No. 2

B. Aural analysis. Sing through the following tunes and try to imagine aurally the
    cadence chords, or play the tunes on the piano and try to play the cadence chords.
    Then make a formal diagram of each song.

    1. "Daisy"
    2. "Take Me Out to the Ball Game" (four phrases)

C. Review. Notate the chords in the keys and bass positions indicated.

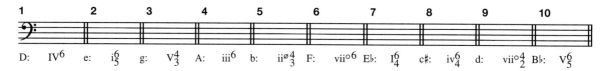

D: IV^6 e: i$^6_5$ g: V$^4_3$ A: iii^6 b: ii$^{\o4}_3$ F: vii$^{\circ6}$ E♭:   I$^6_4$ c♯:   iv$^6_4$ d: vii$^{\circ4}_2$ B♭:   V$^6_5$

Exercise 10-1 See Workbook.

Chapter 11

Non-Chord Tones 1

INTRODUCTION

Many of the examples in the preceding chapters contain notes that do not belong to the chord as analyzed. In many of those examples these notes have been put in parentheses to emphasize the embellishing quality of such non-chord tones, as opposed to chord tones, which are structurally more important. However, to understand tonal music we have to understand non-chord tones because most passages of tonal music contain at least a few of them.

A *non-chord tone* (abbreviated NCT) is a tone, either diatonic or chromatic, that is not a member of the chord. The tone might be an NCT throughout its duration, or, if the harmony changes before the tone does, the tone might be an NCT for only a portion of its duration.

Obviously, you have to analyze the chords before you can begin labeling NCTs, but the process is nearly simultaneous. In multipart music, recognizing the chords and the NCTs is often quite simple, as in Example 11-1.

♫ EXAMPLE 11-1 *Schubert, "Frühlingstraum," Op. 89, No. 11*

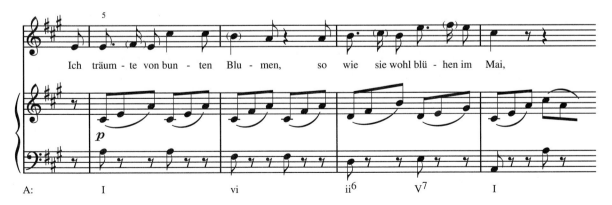

Other textures and compositional techniques may make the separation of chords from NCTs more problematic. This will be discussed in greater detail at the conclusion of Chapter 12.

CLASSIFICATION OF NON-CHORD TONES

One way of classifying NCTs is according to the ways in which they are approached and left.* The table below presents the basic definitions of the various types along with abbreviations. Those in the top half of the table will be discussed in detail in this chapter. The others are discussed in Chapter 12.

NCT name (and abbreviation)	Approached by	Left by
Passing tone (p)	Step	Step in same direction
Neighboring tone (n)	Step	Step in opposite direction
Suspension (s)	Same tone	Step down
Retardation (r)	Same tone	Step up
Appoggiatura (app)	Leap	Step
Escape tone (e)	Step	Leap in opposite direction
Neighbor group (n.gr)	(see p. 195)	
Anticipation (ant)	Step or leap	Same tone (or leap)
Pedal point (ped)	(see pp. 197–199)	

*doesn't
show

> ∨*

Example 11-2 provides illustrations of each of the NCT types in a three-part texture.

EXAMPLE 11-2

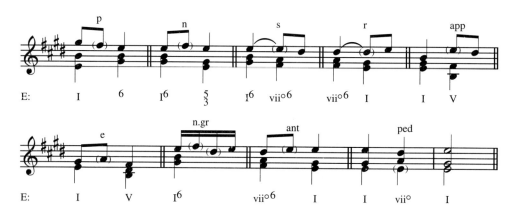

In addition to the basic definitions given above, NCTs can be further classified as to their *duration* and relative degree of *accent*.

---

*NCT terminology is not standardized. However, the definitions given here are widely used.

1. *Submetrical:* less than a beat in duration and occurring on either *accented* or *unaccented portions* of the beat (Ex. 11-3a).

2. *Metrical:* one beat in duration and occurring on either *accented* or *unaccented beats* (Ex. 11-3b).

3. *Supermetrical:* more than one beat in duration (Ex. 11-3c).

EXAMPLE 11-3

Admittedly, this terminology is cumbersome, but such considerations have much to do with the style and general effect of a passage. Remember that the beat in the definitions above is not always indicated by the bottom number of the meter signature.

Other terms used in the description of NCTs include *diatonic, chromatic, ascending, descending, upper,* and *lower.* These terms will be brought up in connection with the appropriate NCTs. The remainder of this chapter is devoted to a more detailed discussion of the NCT types that involve only stepwise motion: passing tones, neighboring tones, suspensions, and retardations.

PASSING TONES

The *passing tone* is used to fill in the space between two other tones. The two other tones may belong either to the same or to different chords, or they might be NCTs themselves. Usually the space between them is a 3rd, either up or down, and the passing tone is given whatever scale degree lies in between. In Example 11-1 the B4 in m. 6 is used to fill in the space between C♯5 and A4. The B4, then, is a passing tone or, more specifically, an *accented, submetrical, diatonic, descending passing tone.* You might think that this terminology is too detailed to be really useful, and you would be right. Most of the time we would refer to the B4 in Example 11-1 simply as a passing tone and let it go at that. However, a good musician, although perhaps not consciously using all the modifiers employed above, will still be aware of the possibilities and their influence on the musical effect.

Occasionally a passing tone fills the space between two notes that are only a M2 apart. Look at Example 11-4, from the *Jupiter* Symphony. The G♯5 in m. 56 is a passing tone, but the two tones that it connects, G5 and A5, are only a M2 apart. The G♯5, then, is a *chromatic passing tone,* as is the A♯3 in the bass line in m. 58.

Still referring to Example 11-4, look at the first violin part in m. 59. The tones G5 and D5, which are a P4 apart, are connected by two passing tones, F♯5 and E5. In m. 61 several passing tones appear in the first violin part. Technically, the A4, the D5, and the F♯5 are chord tones, and the others are passing tones. In a functional sense, however, *all* the tones after the A4 serve as passing tones filling in the m7 between A4 and G5, connecting the half cadence in m. 61 to the beginning of the next phrase.

Finally, notice that the A♯3 in the second violin part in m. 58 is a passing tone, as analyzed. Two lines are being played simultaneously by the second violins.

♫ **EXAMPLE 11-4**   *Mozart, Symphony No. 41 (Jupiter), K. 551, I*

Textural reduction

NEIGHBORING TONES

The *neighboring tone* is used to embellish a single tone. It may appear above the main tone (upper neighbor) or below it (lower neighbor), and it may be diatonic or chromatic. Example 11-1 contains neighboring tones in the voice line; all of them are *unaccented, upper neighboring tones.* The neighbors in Example 11-5 are all *accented.* The upper neighbors (the A's and the D) are *diatonic,* whereas the *lower neighbors* (the F♯'s and the B) are *chromatic.* (The vii°$^4_3$ in Example 11-5 is a fully diminished seventh chord instead of half-diminished because it is a "borrowed" chord, to be discussed more fully in Chapter 21.)

♫ **EXAMPLE 11-5** *Schumann, Scherzo Op. 32*

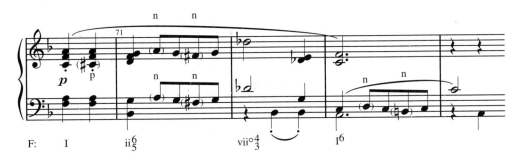

We can only guess about Schumann's reason for using the chromatic form of the lower neighboring tone here because diatonic neighbors would have been possible. A chromatic neighbor lends more tonal color to a passage, and it tends to draw more attention to the pitch that it is embellishing. A chromatic lower neighbor, like those above, acts as a leading tone to the tone it ornaments. As an experiment, try playing Example 11-5 four ways: (1) all diatonic neighbors, (2) chromatic upper neighbors, (3) chromatic lower neighbors, and (4) all chromatic neighbors. Compare the results.

SUSPENSIONS AND RETARDATIONS

The *suspension* holds on to, or suspends a chord tone after the other parts have moved on to the next chord. Although the suspension may not seem more important than any other type of NCT, considerably more study has been devoted to it. Part of the reason for this is that the suspension is the primary source of dissonance on the *accented* beat in much tonal and pretonal music. Suspensions may be submetrical, metrical, or supermetrical, but in any case they almost always fall on accented beats or accented portions of beats.

A special terminology has developed concerning the suspension. The *preparation* is the tone preceding the suspension, and it is the same pitch as the suspension. The *suspension* itself may or may not be tied to its preparation. The *resolution* is the tone following the suspension and lying a 2nd below it. The preparation and resolution are usually chord tones (Ex. 11-6).

EXAMPLE 11-6

Suspension terminology also provides a means of categorizing suspensions according to the vertical intervals created by the suspended tone and the resolution. For example, in Example 11-6, the vertical interval created by the suspension is a 7th and that created by the resolution is a 6th, so the entire figure is referred to as a 7-6 suspension.

Example 11-7 summarizes the common suspensions. Notice that the second number is larger than the first only in the 2-3 suspension, a type sometimes referred to as a *bass suspension.* In textures involving more than two parts, the vertical intervals are calculated between the *bass* and the suspended part. If the bass itself is suspended, the interval is calculated between the bass and the part with which it is most dissonant (generally a 2nd or 9th above in a 2-3 suspension). With the exception of the 9-8 suspension, the note of resolution should not be present anywhere in the texture when a suspension occurs.

EXAMPLE 11-7

The names of most suspensions remain constant, even if compound intervals are involved. For example, even if the 4-3 is actually an 11-10, as in Example 11-7, it is still referred to as a 4-3. The exception to this is the 9-8. It is always called a 9-8 suspension unless it does *not* involve a compound interval, in which case it is labeled a 2-1 suspension. The reason for this inconsistency is that the 2-1 suspension is found much less frequently than the 9-8, so it is appropriate that they have different labels.

When a suspension occurs in one of the upper voices, the bass will sometimes move on to another chord tone at the same time as the suspension resolves. This device is referred to as a *suspension with change of bass.* In such a case a 7-6 suspension, for example, might become a 7-3 suspension because of the movement of the bass. It is also possible to move the upper part of the dissonance as the bass resolves in a 2-3 suspension, creating a 2-6 suspension (Ex. 11-8).

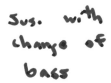

EXAMPLE 11-8

Although most suspensions are dissonant, consonant suspensions do occur. Example 11-9 contains a suspension in the second measure, even though no dissonance is present.

EXAMPLE 11-9

Suspensions are very often embellished. That is, other tones, some of them chord tones and some not, may appear after the suspended tone but before the true resolution. In Example 11-10 there is an embellished 7-6 suspension at the beginning of the second measure. In other words, the G5 is a suspension that resolves to F5, but ornamenting tones are heard before the F5 is reached. A similar figure appears at the beginning of the next measure, but here the 7th is a chord tone, part of the G^7 chord. In this case, the F5 is a chord tone that is treated as a suspension. Such *suspension figures,* in which the suspension is actually a chord tone, are quite common. Notice also in this example the use of the minor v^6 as a passing chord between i and iv^6.

EXAMPLE 11-10   *Bach, French Suite No. 2, Sarabande*

When the resolution of one suspension serves as the preparation for another, the resulting figure is called a *chain of suspensions.*

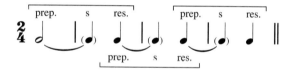

Example 11-10 above contains a chain suspension: The G5 is suspended, resolving to F5, which in turn is suspended (although not as an NCT), resolving to E♭5. A chain of 7-6 suspensions can be seen in Example 8-8 (p. 129).

Much of what has been said about the suspension applies also to the *retardation,* which is simply a suspension with an upward resolution. Retardations may occur anywhere in a passage, but they are especially common at cadences in Classical style, where they appear in combination with suspensions. As in Example 11-11, the retardation usually involves $\hat{7}$ resolving up to $\hat{1}$.

EXAMPLE 11-11

Ab: V⁷   I

Notice in this example that the I chord begins as soon as the tonic note is reached in the bass. It would be incorrect to analyze the first beat of the second measure as a vii° or V⁷ over a pedal point Ab. A pedal point starts out as a chord tone and only later becomes dissonant against the chords above it.

As if to help us summarize the suspension, Bach has provided us with a chorale phrase containing all the common suspensions as well as a less common one. To help you get the most out of Example 11-12, chord roots are provided along with the functional harmonic analysis. This is because the phrase *modulates* (changes key) from a to C and back again, and we have not yet presented the ways in which modulations are analyzed. After you understand the chords, follow each voice part through, looking at the NCTs and following the discussion below the example. Finally, play through Example 11-12 and listen to the effect of the suspensions.

EXAMPLE 11-12   *Bach, "Danket dem Herren, denn er ist sehr freundlich"*

| roots: | A | A | E | A | G | C | C | G | A | E |

Soprano
No NCTs

Alto

m. 1   The B4 is a submetrical 9-8 suspension. Its resolution, A4, becomes a submetrical 7-6 suspension on the next beat. Therefore, this is a chain of suspensions.

Tenor

m. 2   The D4 eighth note actually represents a metrical 9-8 suspension. The suspension
is ornamented by the two sixteenth notes that follow it, one of them being a chord
tone that anticipates the resolution, the other being a lower neighbor. Notice that
by the time the "real" resolution arrives (beat 2), the bass has moved to another
chord tone, so this is a 9-6 change of bass suspension.
     The B3 on beat 4 is an example of a relatively unusual suspension, the 2-1.

m. 3   The quarter note A3 represents a half note A3, which is a supermetrical 4-3 suspension. The suspension is ornamented with an augmentation of the figure used
to ornament the suspended D4 in m. 2.

Bass

m. 1   The empty parentheses on beat 2 remind us that the A3 is still sounding but is no
longer part of the chord. This is an example of a submetrical 2-3 suspension.

m. 3   The NCTs in this measure are unaccented, submetrical, ascending passing tones.

Checkpoint

1. A suspension is an NCT that is approached by _____ and left by
    _____ .

2. A neighboring tone is an NCT that is approached by _____   and left
    by _____ .

3. A retardation is an NCT that is approached by _____ and left by
    _____ .

4. A passing tone is an NCT that is approached by _____ and left by
    _____ .

5. What are some other terms that are sometimes used to describe NCTs? (Review pp.
    178–179.)

6. Provide the arabic numerals that are used to label the four common types of sus-
    pensions.

FIGURED BASS AND LEAD SHEET SYMBOLS

With the exception of suspensions, NCTs are generally not indicated in a figured bass or
in lead sheet symbols. Most suspensions in figured basses are shown by the use of sym-

bols identical or similar to the numbers we use to name suspension types. Some of the customary figured bass symbols are given in the table below.

Suspension	Symbols
9-8	9 8
7-6	7 6 or $\frac{7}{3}\frac{6}{\,}$
4-3	4 3 or 4 ♯
2-3	$\frac{5}{2}$ under first bass note, 6 under the next

Change of bass suspensions can be recognized by such combinations as "7 3" or "9 6" appearing over a moving bass.

In lead sheet symbols a sound that is related to the traditional 4-3 suspension is indicated by "sus" appended to the symbol, as in C7sus, which calls for a chord containing C, F, G, and B♭. The "suspension" may or may not have been prepared in the previous chord, and it will not necessarily resolve in the traditional sense. If the "suspension" does resolve, this could occur within the same chord, as in C7sus C7, or it may resolve in the next chord like a change of bass suspension, as in C7sus FM7. Often, as in Example 11-13, there is no resolution of the 4th at all, and instead it is carried into the next chord. Notice the G6 chord, which we have not encountered before. A lead sheet symbol with a 6 after it calls for a triad with an added note a M6 above the root. (The piano accompaniment in the example is provided for illustration only and does not necessarily reflect the way a jazz pianist would play this excerpt.)

 EXAMPLE 11-13 *Hampton and Kynard, "Red Top"*

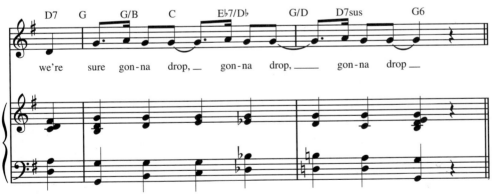

Words and Music by Lionel Hampton and Ken Kynard. © 1947 Cherio Corp. © Renewed 1957 Cherio Corp. Used by permission of Hal Leonard Corporation.

EMBELLISHING A SIMPLE TEXTURE

One way to compose in the tonal style is to begin with a simple texture that has an interesting soprano/bass counterpoint and then embellish it. Two common types of NCT embellishments are the neighbor and the passing tone. Another type of embellishment, although it is not an NCT, is arpeggiation. We have seen bass arpeggiations in connection with inverted triads, but arpeggiations can be used in any part to create motion or a more interesting line.

Adding neighbors, passing tones, and arpeggiations to the texture is not difficult, but you must be careful not to create objectionable parallels in the process. Example 11-14a illustrates a simple texture without parallels. Example 11-14b shows the same music embellished, but each embellishment has created objectionable parallels. Although parallels created by passing and neighboring tones may occasionally be found in tonal music, you should try to avoid them for now.

EXAMPLE 11-14

Adding suspensions to the texture does not usually create parallels, but it is still somewhat tricky at first. You may find the following suggestions helpful.

1. Find a step down in the bass. Is the harmonic interval between the bass and some upper voice over the second bass note a 3rd (or 10th)? If so, the 2-3 suspension will work.

2. Find in one of the upper voices a step down. Is the harmonic interval between the second note and the bass a 3rd, 6th, or 8ve? If so, the 4-3, 7-6, or 9-8 suspension, respectively, will work. Exception: Do not use the 4-3 or 7-6 if the resolution of the suspension would already be present in another voice. The aural result is very disappointing.

Below is a simple two-voice example (Ex. 11-15). Possible locations for suspensions are shown with an X. The second part of Example 11-15 is an embellished version containing all the embellishments discussed so far.

EXAMPLE 11-15

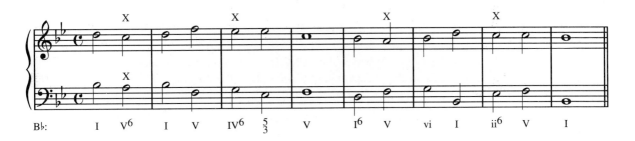

Summary

A *non-chord tone* (NCT) is a tone, either diatonic or chromatic, that is not a member of the chord. In addition to the usual nomenclature for NCTs, a number of adjectives may be used to describe the context of a particular NCT. These include the following:

Submetrical	Accented	Diatonic	Ascending	Upper
Metrical	Unaccented	Chromatic	Descending	Lower
Supermetrical				

A *passing tone* is an NCT that fills in the space between two other tones by moving stepwise between them. A *neighboring tone* is an NCT that embellishes a single tone by moving stepwise away from and then back to the tone.

A *suspension* is an NCT that delays a stepwise descent in a line. A suspension involves three phases: preparation, suspension, and resolution. Suspensions that occur in a voice other than the bass are classified by the intervals between the bass and the suspension and between the bass and the resolution. Most suspensions above the bass are 9-8, 7-6, or 4-3 suspensions. The only common bass suspension is the 2-3 suspension, in which the bass at the point of suspension forms the interval of a 2nd (or 9th) with some upper voice.

A *retardation* is similar to a suspension, but it delays a stepwise ascent and resolves upward.

Self-Test 11-1
(Answers begin on page 604.)

A.   Analysis.

   1.   Go back to Example 7-10 (p. 111) which shows NCTs in parentheses, and identify the type of each NCT in the blanks below. Always show the interval classification (7-6 and so on) when analyzing suspensions.

Measure	Treble	Bass
1	_____	
2	_____	_____
3	_____	
5	_____	
6	_____	_____
7	_____	

   2.   Do the same with Example 10-4 (p. 158).

   soprano: _____

   alto: _____   _____

   tenor: _____   _____   _____

   3.   Analyze chords and NCTs in this excerpt. Then make a reduction similar to
   those seen in this text by (1) removing all NCTs, (2) using longer note values or
   ties for repeated notes, and (3) transposing parts by a P8 when necessary to
   make the lines smoother. Study the simplified texture. Do any voice-leading
   problems appear to have been covered up by the embellishments?

   Bach, "Schmücke dich, o liebe Seele"

B. After reviewing the discussion of embellishment (pp. 187–189), decide what *one* suspension would be best in each excerpt below. Then renotate with the suspension and at least one other embellishment. Remember to put parentheses around NCTs and to label NCTs and arpeggiations.

C.   The example below is a simplified excerpt from a Bach chorale harmonization.
Analyze the chords with roman numerals and activate the texture with embellishments of various kinds. Although many correct solutions are possible, it will be
interesting to compare yours with Bach's, which may be found in Appendix B.

Exercise 11-1 See Workbook.

Chapter 12

Non-Chord Tones 2

APPOGGIATURAS

All the NCTs discussed so far are approached and left by step or by common tone. In most tonal music most NCTs will be of the types already discussed. NCTs involving leaps (appoggiaturas, escape tones, neighbor groups, and some anticipations) are not rare, however, and they tend to be more obvious to the listener.

As a very general rule, *appoggiaturas* (also called incomplete neighbors) are accented, approached by ascending leap, and left by descending step. The Tchaikovsky theme in Example 12-1 (notice the transposition) contains two appoggiaturas that fit this description. The first, A4, might also be heard as a suspension from the previous measure.

♫ EXAMPLE 12-1 *Tchaikovsky, Symphony No. 5, II*

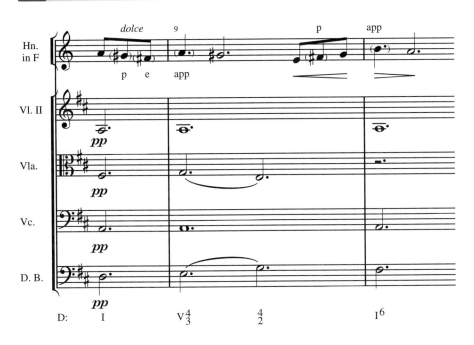

All appoggiaturas are approached by leap and left by step, but the sequence is not always ascending leap followed by descending step. In fact, Example 11-10 (p. 184) has already provided us with an example of an unaccented appoggiatura approached from above (the E5). Notice that it is also chromatic. Probably the only other generalization that could be made concerning the appoggiatura is that the appoggiatura, especially the supermetrical variety, is more typical of the nineteenth century than the eighteenth. As an illustration, consider Example 12-2. Four of the five NCTs in the phrase (not counting the A3s in m. 5, left hand, because they double the melody) are appoggiaturas, and two of the four are supermetrical. It is largely this aspect—though in combination with others (slow harmonic rhythm, disjunct melody, homophonic texture, wide range, and so on)—that gives this phrase its Romantic flavor.

♫   EXAMPLE 12-2   *Chopin, Nocturne Op. 27, No. 2*

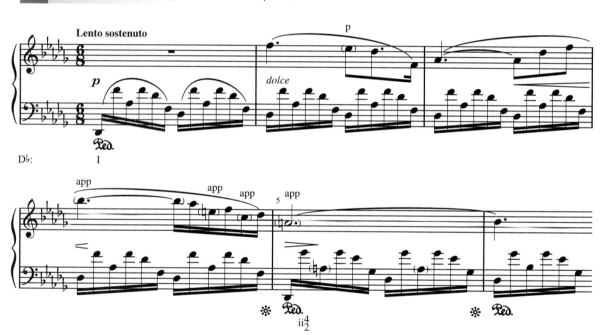

The reduction of Example 12-2 shows that when we move from the surface of the piece to a more background level, our interpretation of the supermetrical appoggiaturas changes considerably.

ESCAPE TONES

The contour of the escape tone (also called an incomplete neighbor) is the reverse of that of the appoggiatura because the escape tone is approached by step and left by leap in the opposite direction. Escape tones are usually submetrical, unaccented, and diatonic. They are often used in sequence to ornament a scalar line, as in mm. 59–60 of Example 11-4 (pp. 180–181). Notice in Example 11-4 that although *escape tone figures* ornament the line D5–C5–B4, actual escape tones occur only two times.

The escape tone is also frequently used at cadences to ornament the scale degree progression $\hat{2}$–$\hat{1}$. An instance of this can be seen in Example 12-3.

♪ EXAMPLE 12-3   *Haydn, Sonata No. 35, I*

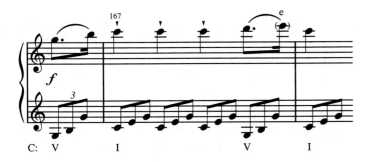

All the escape tones cited in this section have been *submetrical, unaccented,* and *diatonic;* these are all usually characteristic of the escape tone in tonal music.

THE NEIGHBOR GROUP   *Changing Tones*

A common method of embellishing a single tone involves a combination of two NCTs in succession, the first being an escape tone (also called a cambiata or "changing tone"), the second an appoggiatura. The figure is referred to as a *neighbor group*. As Example 12-4 illustrates, the neighbor group bears a resemblance to a neighboring tone figure.

EXAMPLE 12-4

ANTICIPATIONS

An *anticipation,* as the name implies, anticipates a chord that has not yet been reached. This NCT moves, by step or by leap, to some pitch that is contained in the anticipated chord but is not present in the chord that precedes it. For example, if the triad F/A/C were to proceed to the triad B♭/D/F, you could use either the note B♭ or the note D to anticipate the B♭/D/F chord while the F/A/C chord is still sounding. The note F could not be used as an NCT because it is common to both chords. Of the two notes B♭ and D, the B♭ is probably the better choice. In Example 12-5a the anticipated B♭4 forms a satisfying dissonance with the other pitches and is clearly an NCT, but in Example 12-5b the D5 forms no true dissonance with any other pitch.

EXAMPLE 12-5

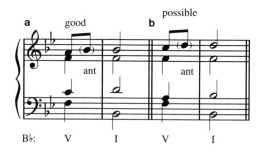

An anticipation very much like the one in Example 12-5a appears in Example 12-6.

EXAMPLE 12-6   *Bach,* Well-Tempered Clavier, *Book II, Fugue 22*

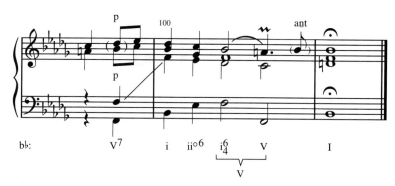

Most anticipations are approached by step, but the approach by leap is not rare. In Example 12-7 there are three *anticipation figures,* each approached by leap and left by common tone, but only one figure, that in the bass, is an NCT.

EXAMPLE 12-7 *Schumann, "Little Morning Wanderer," Op. 68, No. 17*

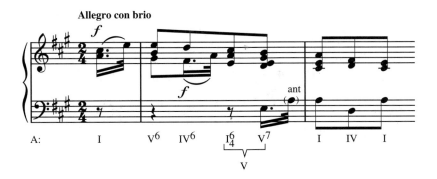

The least commonly encountered variety of NCT is the anticipation approached and *left* by leap. This is sometimes referred to as a *free anticipation*. Example 12.8 is an example from Mozart, in which the bass anticipates the tonic triad before the dominant chord has resolved, allowing the bass in mm. 7 to 9 to imitate the soprano in mm. 5 to 7.

EXAMPLE 12-8 *Mozart, Sonata K. 332, I*

THE PEDAL POINT

The pedal point has been saved for last in the discussion of NCTs because it is really in a class by itself. The *pedal point* is a compositional device that begins as a chord tone, then becomes a NCT as the harmonies around it change, and finally ends up as a chord tone when the harmony is once more in agreement with it. The other NCTs are clearly decorative and are always dependent on the harmony for their meaning. However, the pedal point often has such tonal strength that the harmonies seem to be embellishing the pedal point rather than the other way around. This sounds more complicated than it is. Look at Example 12-9, which shows the ending of a fugue by Bach.

EXAMPLE 12-9   *Bach, "Allein Gott in der Höh' sei Ehr"*

In one sense, the piece ends on beat 1 of mm. 88 with the IAC. What follows that cadence is a short codetta, with the tonic note sustained in the bass beneath a IV–vii°–I progression in the upper voices. The chords above the tonic pedal are analyzed, but in a very real sense the pedal overpowers the upper parts and represents the tonic harmony. Incidentally, the relatively weak inverted IAC is used to end this work because the bass line is presenting the melody on which the piece is based.

You might have noticed that inversions above the pedal point are not indicated in Example 12-9. This is generally a good practice to follow in the analysis of such passages. The aural effect of inversion is altered by the pedal, and there are no conventional symbols to represent this alteration.

The term *pedal point* comes from the frequent use of the device in organ compositions. At any point in the composition, but most frequently at the end of the work, the organist will be called on to sustain a single pitch with a pedal while continuing to play moving lines with the manuals (keyboards). Most frequently the sustained pitch is the tonic or the dominant, and the passage often includes the triad whose root is a P4 above the pedal point (hence the term *pedal six-four chord*). Therefore, if the tonic pitch is the pedal, the IV chord will often be used above it (as in Ex. 12-9), and if the dominant pitch is the pedal, the I chord will often be used above it.

Pedal points occasionally occur in parts other than the bass, in which case they are referred to as *inverted pedal points*. Anther possibility is for the pedal point to contain more than one pitch class (*double pedal point* and so on), as in Example 12-10. Although most pedal points are sustained, rearticulated pedal points, as in Example 12-10, are not uncommon.

EXAMPLE 12-10 *Schumann, "Reaper's Song," Op. 68, No. 18*

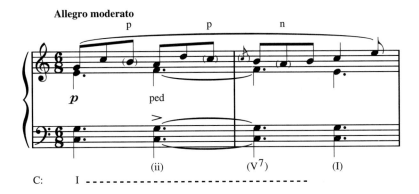

SPECIAL PROBLEMS IN THE ANALYSIS OF NON-CHORD TONES

In this section we will discuss three excerpts that demonstrate special problems that you might encounter from time to time in analyzing tonal music. First, the actual label that you assign to a tone may change as you reduce the passage. Such possibilities were mentioned in connection with Examples 12-1 and 12-2. For variety, we will do a reverse textural reduction of a similar passage. Example 12-11 shows two versions of a portion of a melody in E♭, the first melody being diatonic, the second incorporating chromatic and diatonic passing tones.

EXAMPLE 12-11

If we embellish each tone of Example 12-11b, we create the melody found in Example 12-12.

EXAMPLE 12-12   *Schubert, Impromptu Op. 90, No. 2*

E♭:   I⁶   V⁶₅   I

The labeling of the NCTs in Example 12-12 is problematic. For example, the first E♮4 in m. 3 is, on the surface, a neighboring tone (E♭4–E♮4–D♯4). However, Example 12-11b showed that the E♮4 is not a neighbor but a passing tone (E♭4–E4–F4), as are the F, F♯, and G that follow. The best solution is to label these notes as passing tones (as in Example 12-11) and the others as neighbors.

Example 12-13 is our second problematic excerpt. It is very unlikely that you would be able to determine the harmonic background of this excerpt just from looking at it, and actually it involves too many advanced harmonic concepts to allow detailed discussion of the harmonies at this time. However, if you play it slowly, you will discover that the right hand lags further and further behind the left. The cadence on f♯ in the right hand comes three eighth notes later than the cadence on f♯ in the left, and the cadences on A are four eighth notes apart. Both cadences are identified in the example.

EXAMPLE 12-13   *Brahms, Variations on a Theme by Schumann, Op. 9, Var. 2*

Once the two staves are "correctly" aligned, it becomes apparent that the texture contains no NCTs at all (except, perhaps, for the B♯4). Example 12-14 brings the right hand into alignment with the left. Play through both examples slowly and compare them.

 EXAMPLE 12-14

Conventional NCT terminology is inadequate to explain a passage such as this. Instead, it is better to use an approach such as the one we have demonstrated.

Finally, we consider the problem of implied harmonies and the analysis of unaccompanied melodies. As a general rule, NCT analyses based on melodies alone are arbitrary and uninformative. Nevertheless, the experienced musician can sometimes recognize the NCTs in an unaccompanied melodic line solely on the basis of implied harmonies. Example 12-15 shows one interpretation (others are possible) of the harmonies implied by a Bach fugue subject. The textural reduction shows that the melody is an elaboration of a simple stepwise line.

EXAMPLE 12-15   *Bach,* Well-Tempered Clavier, *Book II, Fugue 14*

Summary

An *appoggiatura* is an NCT that is approached by leap and resolved by step. In most cases, appoggiaturas are accented, approached by ascending leap, and resolved by descending step.

An *escape tone* is approached by step and resolved by leap in the opposite direction. Escape tones are usually submetrical, unaccented, and diatonic.

A *neighbor group* embellishes a single pitch by sounding its upper and lower neighbors in succession (in either order). The first neighbor is approached by step and left by leap, whereas the second one is approached by leap and resolved by step.

An *anticipation* anticipates a tone that belongs to the next chord. It may be approached by step or by leap. An anticipation almost always resolves to the tone it anticipated. An anticipation that resolves by leap is called a *free anticipation*.

A *pedal point* is a stationary pitch that begins as a chord tone, then becomes a NCT as the harmonies change, and finally ends up as a chord tone again. Pedal points usually occur in the bass, but they occasionally occur in other parts as well.

The analysis of chords and NCTs must always be carried out simultaneously. Although most NCTs are clearly recognizable as embellishments of the basic harmony, ambiguous cases will be encountered occasionally.

Self-Test 12-1
(Answers begin on page 605.)

A. Analysis.

   1. Go back to Self-Test 8-1, Part F (p. 142), which shows NCTs in parentheses, and identify the type of each NCT in the blanks below. Always show the interval classification (7-6 and so on) when you analyze suspensions.

   m. 1   _____

   m. 3   _____   _____   _____

   m. 4   _____   _____

   2. Analyze the NCTs in Example 9-10 (p. 150).

   m. 24   _____   _____

   m. 25   _____   _____

   m. 26   _____   _____   _____

   3. Analyze the NCTs in Example 9-11 (p. 150).

   m. 72   _____   _____   m. 76   _____

   m. 74   _____   m. 77   (melody)   _____

   m. 75   _____   _____   _____   (alto)   _____

   4. Label the chords and NCTs in this excerpt. Then make a simplified version without NCTs. Comment on the simplified version. Analyze two chords in m. 11, beat 3.

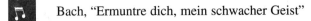

Bach, "Ermuntre dich, mein schwacher Geist"

5. The two excerpts below are from a theme and variations by Mozart. The first
excerpt is from the end of the theme, whereas the second excerpt is from the
end of the first variation. Analyze the harmonies (they are identical in the theme
and the variation) and label all NCTs.

Mozart, Piano Sonata, K. 284, III, Theme and Variation I

B. The example below is for three-part chorus. Analyze the chords with roman numer-
    als. Then add the specified NCTs at the points indicated. Show the interval classifi-
    cation of each suspension.

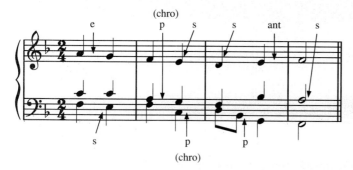

C. The excerpt below is a reduction of Mozart's Sonata K. 330, III, mm. 1–8. Use it as
    a framework for elaboration, employing arpeggiations and NCTs as you see fit. It is
    also possible to thicken the texture occasionally, if you wish.

Exercise 12-1 See Workbook.

PART III
Diatonic Seventh Chords

Chapter 13

The V⁷ Chord

INTRODUCTION

Diatonic seventh chords were introduced quite early in this text, in Chapter 4. Subsequent examples and exercises have included the analysis of many seventh chords, but we have not dealt with the details of how composers have used seventh chords in tonal music. The use of seventh chords is the subject of the next several chapters.

Before reading further, review the material on seventh chords on pages 68–70. In those sections you learned, among other things, that the five most common seventh-chord qualities are the major seventh, major-minor seventh, minor seventh, half-diminished seventh, and diminished seventh chords. Of these types, the major-minor seventh is by far the most frequently encountered. It is generally built on $\hat{5}$, with the result that the terms *dominant seventh* and major-minor seventh are used more or less interchangeably.

Dominant seventh chords are almost always major-minor sevenths—that is, when spelled in root position, they contain a major triad plus the pitch a m7 above the root. In major keys a seventh chord built on $\hat{5}$ will be automatically a major-minor seventh chord. But in minor keys *it is necessary to raise* $\hat{7}$ (the leading tone, not the seventh of the chord) to obtain the major-minor seventh quality. The seventh chord built on $\hat{5}$ without the raised $\hat{7}$ (v⁷ instead of V⁷) is not as common. It serves only as a passing chord, not as a true dominant, because it lacks the tonic-defining leading tone essential for a chord with a dominant function. When it does occur, it is the result of a descending line: $\hat{1}$–$\hat{7}\downarrow$–$\hat{6}\downarrow$.

EXAMPLE 13-1

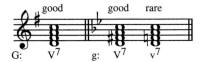

GENERAL VOICE-LEADING CONSIDERATIONS

The essential concept in the handling of *any* seventh chord involves the treatment of the 7th of the chord: *the 7th almost always resolves down by step.* We are naturally suspicious

of generalizations, as we should be, but the downward resolution of the 7th as a general
principle is extremely important. The 7th originated in music as a downward-resolving
suspension or descending passing tone, and the downward resolution came to be the only
one acceptable to the musical ear. To compare a 7th resolving down with one resolving up,
listen to Example 13-2. The difference may or may not seem startling to you, but tonal
music contains very few instances of the second resolution.

EXAMPLE 13-2

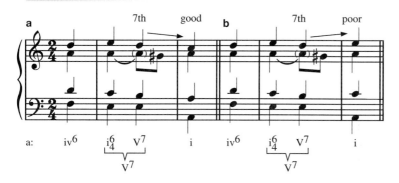

When you are working with the V⁷, you must also consider the leading tone: *When it
is an outer part, the leading tone almost always resolves up by step,* as in Example 13-3a.
To convince yourself of the reason for this, play Example 13-3b and notice the disappointing effect of the cadence.

EXAMPLE 13-3

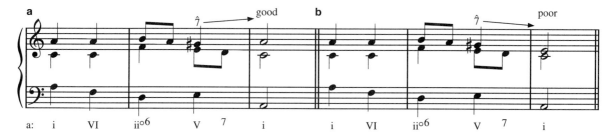

When you apply these two principles, remember not to confuse the 7th of the chord with
the seventh scale degree. We will summarize what we have presented so far in this chapter.

1.   The V⁷ chord is a major-minor seventh chord.

2.   The 7th of the chord ($\hat{4}$) resolves down to $\hat{3}$.

3.   The 3rd of the chord ($\hat{7}$) resolves up to $\hat{1}$, especially when it is in an outer part.

THE V⁷ IN ROOT POSITION

The resolution of the dominant seventh in root position to the tonic in root position is more difficult than that of any other combination. To master this technique, however, you need only to remember the principles we discussed earlier in this chapter.

1. The 7th ($\hat{4}$) must resolve *down* by step to $\hat{3}$.

2. The leading tone ($\hat{7}$), when in the *top* part, must resolve *up* by step to $\hat{1}$.

Another way of looking at these principles is in terms of the resolution of the tritone: the +4 tends to resolve outward to a 6th (Ex. 13-4a), the °5 inward to a 3rd (Ex. 13-4b). If we follow these principles, we find that the tonic triad is incomplete—it has no 5th.

EXAMPLE 13-4

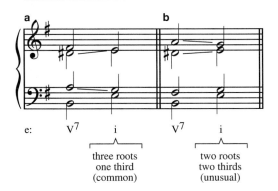

The resolution of V⁷ to an incomplete triad is not an "error" to be avoided and is, in fact, a very common occurrence, especially at final cadences. In Example 13-5 the leading tone, even though it is not in the top voice, resolves up by step, resulting in an incomplete tonic triad.

♫ EXAMPLE 13-5 *Schubert, Quartet (Death and the Maiden), Op. post., I*

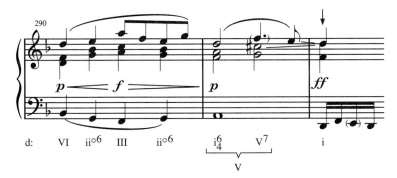

If you want to resolve the root position V[7] in four parts to a complete tonic triad, either of these methods will work.

1.   Use an incomplete V[7], omitting the 5th (or, less commonly, the 3rd) and doubling the root.

2.   Use a complete V[7], but put the leading tone (3rd of the V[7]) in an *inner* part and "frustrate" its natural resolution by taking it down a M3 to the 5th of the tonic triad.

The first solution works because the incomplete V[7] is a perfectly usable sonority. The second method, which is the more common, succeeds by tucking away the leading tone in an inner voice, where its lack of resolution is not so apparent to the listener. Both options are summarized in Example 13-6.

EXAMPLE 13-6

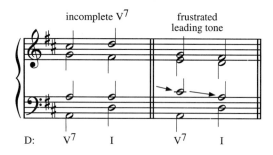

Illustrations of these two procedures from the literature are seen in the next two examples. In the first (Ex. 13-7) an incomplete V[7] (5th omitted) is used.

EXAMPLE 13-7   *Bach, "Nun ruhen alle Wälder"*

In the second (Ex. 13-8) Beethoven uses a complete V[7] but frustrates the leading tone.

EXAMPLE 13-8 *Beethoven, Quartet Op. 18, No. 1, IV*

You may have discovered by now that there *is* a way to resolve a complete V⁷ in four parts to a complete tonic triad while still resolving both the leading tone and the 7th of the chord: If the 5th of the V⁷ leaps to the 5th of the tonic triad, the complete tonic triad is obtained, but at the expense of parallel 5ths. This resolution is illustrated in Example 13-9.

EXAMPLE 13-9

In instrumental music this solution is occasionally found when the 5ths are taken by contrary motion, as in Example 13-10. Notice how the rests in the lower parts and the continued activity in the first violin distract the listener's attention from the 5ths.

EXAMPLE 13-10 *Haydn, Quartet Op. 76, No. 1, III (piano score)*

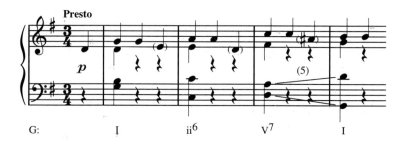

G: I   ii⁶   V⁷   I

However, the use of contrary 5ths or an upward resolution of the 7th (see the last sixteen measures of Beethoven's Quartet Op. 59, No. 2) to achieve a complete tonic triad is certainly the exception, and these devices should be avoided in beginning exercises.

THE V⁷ IN THREE PARTS

The V⁷ in a three-part texture will have to appear with one of the chord tones missing, unless one part articulates two pitches. Obviously, neither root nor 7th can be omitted without losing the flavor of the seventh chord. Of the two remaining members, the 5th is more commonly omitted, but examples with the 3rd omitted are not rare (Ex. 13-11).

EXAMPLE 13-11

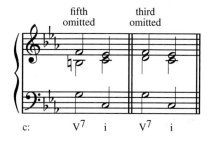

c: V⁷   i   V⁷   i

Example 13-12 illustrates the V⁷ with omitted 5th.

EXAMPLE 13-12   *Bach, Sinfonia No. 9*

A V⁷ with the 3rd omitted can be seen in Example 13-13.

EXAMPLE 13-13   *Mozart, Sonata K. 570, III*

OTHER RESOLUTIONS OF THE V⁷

The V⁷ in root position often moves deceptively to the submediant triad. The voice leading in this progression is just like that of the V–vi (or V–VI) progression discussed on pp. 97–98: The leading tone ($\hat{7}$) resolves up by step to tonic, and the other upper voices move down to the nearest chord tone, resulting in a doubled 3rd in the vi (or VI) chord. The only exception to this is when the leading tone is in an inner voice in the major mode, in which case it may move down by step to $\hat{6}$ instead.

    Some sample deceptive progressions are given in Example 13-14. Notice that in the four-voice versions the V⁷ chord is always complete; an incomplete V⁷ chord does not work well in a deceptive progression in four parts. Also notice that in every case it is only the bass that "deceives." That is, all the other voices move as they normally would in an authentic cadence.

EXAMPLE 13-14

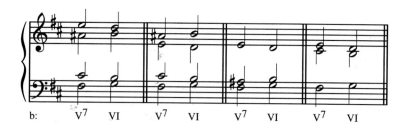

b: V⁷   VI   V⁷   VI   V⁷   VI   V⁷   VI

The only diatonic triads that commonly follow the V⁷ chord are the root position tonic and submediant triads. There are some altered chords that can embellish the deceptive progression, and we will see these in later chapters, but for now you should probably restrict your exercises to V⁷–I(i) and V⁷–vi(VI). The V⁷–I⁶(i⁶) resolution, seen in Example 13-15, is *not* a good choice because of the sound of the implied parallel 8ves.

EXAMPLE 13-15

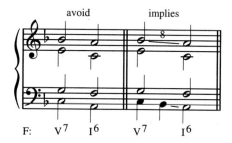

F: V⁷   I⁶   V⁷   I⁶

Checkpoint

1. In the resolution of any seventh chord, the 7th of the chord almost always moves (up/down) by (step/leap).

2. In the resolution of a V⁷ chord, the 3rd of the chord ($\hat{7}$) usually moves (up/down) by (step/leap). This principle is sometimes not followed when the 3rd of the chord is in an (inner/outer) part, in which case it may leap down to $\hat{5}$.

3. If a member of the V⁷ is to be omitted, it is usually the (3rd/5th).

4. If a member of the V⁷ is to be doubled, it is usually the _____ .

5. If the principles listed in questions 1 and 2 are followed in a four-part texture, the
    V^7–I progression will lead to (a complete/an incomplete) I chord.

6. Describe two good methods for attaining a complete I chord in a V^7–I progression
    in four parts.

7. Two good resolutions of the V^7 chord are V^7– _____ and V^7– _____ .

Self-Test 13-1
(Answers begin on page 607.)

A. The note given in each case is the root, 3rd, 5th, or 7th of a V^7 chord. Notate the chord
    in root position and name the major key in which it would be the V^7.

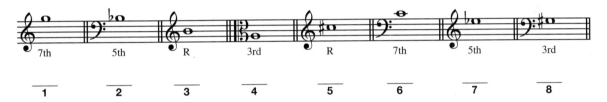

7th	5th	R	3rd	R	7th	5th	3rd
1	2	3	4	5	6	7	8

B. Go back to Self-Test 11-1, A.3, on pages 190–191. Study carefully the V^7 chords in
    mm. 1, 2, and 5 and comment on the voice leading. (Note: You may have analyzed the
    A♭3 in m. 1 as a passing tone, but it could also be considered a 7th.)

C. Resolve each chord below to a root position I. (Note: *c* means complete chord, *i* means
    incomplete chord.)

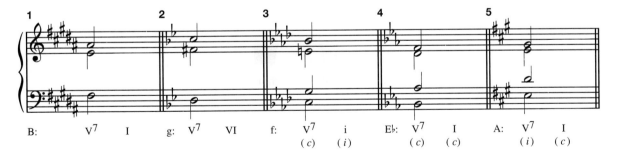

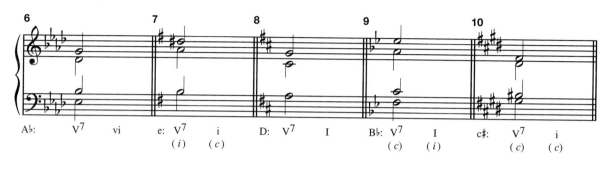

Ab: V⁷   vi   e: V⁷   i   D: V⁷   I   Bb: V⁷   I   c#:   V⁷   i
                            (i)   (c)   (c)   (i)   (c)   (c)

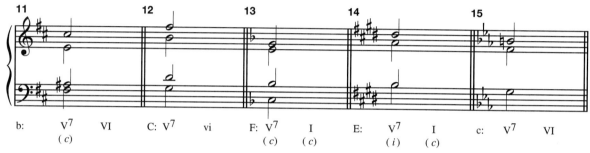

b: V⁷   VI   C: V⁷   vi   F: V⁷   I   E: V⁷   I   c: V⁷   VI
     (c)   (c)   (c)   (i)   (c)

D.   Notate the key signature and the V⁷ chord, then resolve it.

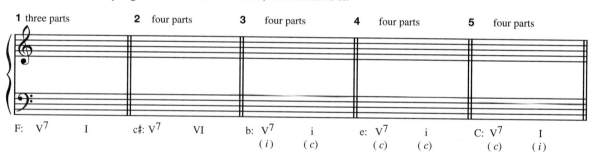

1 three parts   **2** four parts   **3** four parts   **4** four parts   **5** four parts

F: V⁷   I   c#: V⁷   VI   b: V⁷   i   e: V⁷   i   C: V⁷   I
                                                    (i)   (c)   (c)   (c)   (c)   (i)

E.   Analyze the harmonies implied by these soprano/bass frameworks. Then make four-
     part versions with embellishments and at least one root position V⁷.

F. Analyze the chords specified by this figured bass. Then make two harmonizations, one for SAB chorus and one for SATB chorus.

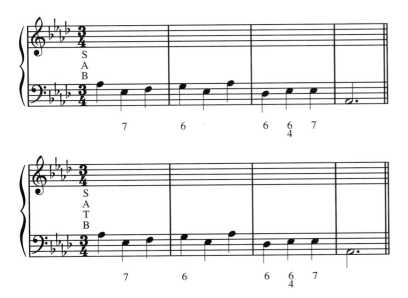

Exercise 13-1 See Workbook.

THE INVERTED V⁷ CHORD

The inversions of the V⁷ chord are actually easier to handle than the root position V⁷. However, no inversion of the V⁷ should be considered to be a possible substitution for the root position V⁷ at an important cadence. The voice-leading principles followed by composers in the resolution of inverted dominant sevenths are the following.

1. The 3rd ($\hat{7}$) resolves up by step to $\hat{1}$.

2. The 7th ($\hat{4}$) resolves down by step to $\hat{3}$.

The other members of the V⁷ have greater freedom, but they generally move by step ($\hat{2}-\hat{1}$) or are retained ($\hat{5}-\hat{5}$).

You will recall that the symbols used to indicate inverted seventh chords are these.

$\begin{smallmatrix}6\\5\end{smallmatrix}$ 3rd in the bass

$\begin{smallmatrix}4\\3\end{smallmatrix}$ 5th in the bass

$\begin{smallmatrix}4\\2\end{smallmatrix}$ (or 2) 7th in the bass

THE V$^6_5$ CHORD

Example 13-16 illustrates the basic voice leading in the resolution of the V$^6_5$.

EXAMPLE 13-16

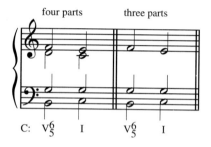

In practice, the V$^6_5$ is often used in a relatively weak position in the phrase. Example 13-17 is typical, with the V$^6_5$ harmonizing an F5 that is essentially a harmonized passing tone in the melody. The root position V that ends the passage has a much stronger effect than the V$^6_5$.

EXAMPLE 13-17 *Mozart, Sonata K. 309, III*

Textural reduction

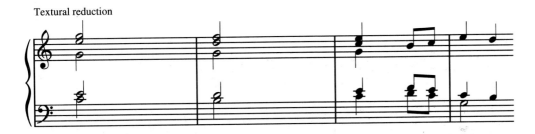

THE V⁴₃ CHORD

The V⁴₃ is often used in a fashion similar to that of the passing V⁶₄: to harmonize $\hat{2}$ in a $\hat{1}$–$\hat{2}$–$\hat{3}$ or $\hat{3}$–$\hat{2}$–$\hat{1}$ bass line. The V⁴₃ is seldom used in three-part textures, the V⁶₄ or vii°⁶ being used instead. Example 13-18 summarizes the treatment of the V⁴₃ in four parts.

EXAMPLE 13-18

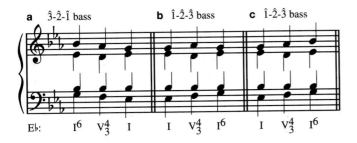

In the last progression above, the 7th of the V⁴₃ moves *up* to $\hat{5}$, one of the few situations in which composers frustrated the normal resolution of the 7th. The unequal 5ths seen between the soprano and alto in Example 13-18c are acceptable. Example 13-19 gives an example from Mozart of the I–V⁴₃–I⁶ progression with an unresolved 7th (in the horn and violin I).

EXAMPLE 13-19   *Mozart, Horn Concerto No. 3, K. 447, II*

THE V$^4_2$ CHORD

Because of the downward resolution of the 7th, the V$^4_2$ is almost always followed by a I^6. The V$^4_2$ is often preceded by a I^6 (Ex. 13-20a) or by some form of IV or ii chord (Ex. 13-20b), but it may also be preceded by a passing I$^6_4$ or a cadential I$^6_4$ chord (Ex. 13-20c).

EXAMPLE 13-20

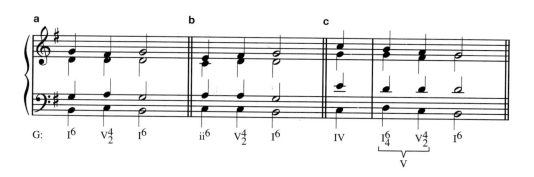

A less conventional but certainly effective treatment of the upper voices is seen in Example 13-21, in which the 5th of the V_2^4 leaps to the 5th of the I^6 chord.

EXAMPLE 13-21   *Beethoven, Sonata Op. 13, II*

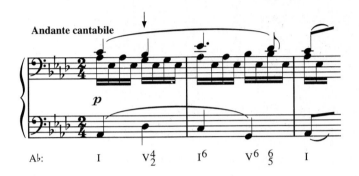

$A\flat$:   I V_2^4 I^6 V^6 $\begin{smallmatrix}6\\5\end{smallmatrix}$ I

THE APPROACH TO THE 7TH

We have seen that the resolution of the 7th of the V^7 (or of any seventh chord) is usually down by step. The way in which the 7th is approached should also be considered in any detailed analysis because different approaches have different musical effects. One way of doing this is to classify the contour of the voice that has the chord 7th. If the chord tone preceding the 7th is:

1.   the same pitch class as the 7th, we use the term *suspension figure* (Ex. 13-22a);

2.   a step above the 7th, we use the term *passing tone figure* (Ex. 13-22b);

3.   a step below the 7th, we use the term *neighbor tone figure* (Ex. 13-22c);

4.   none of the above, we use the term *appoggiatura figure* (Ex. 13-22d). This is historically the least common approach to the 7th. When used, the leap is almost always an ascending one.

EXAMPLE 13-22

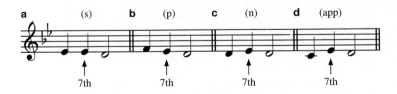

The contours defined above are put into context in Example 13-23.

EXAMPLE 13-23

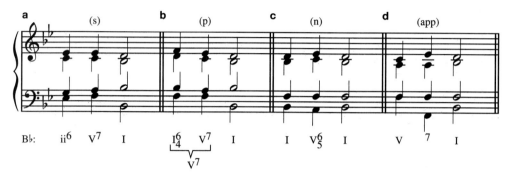

In the example, the 7th of the V⁷ is given to the soprano for purposes of illustration. In practice, of course, the 7th may occur in any voice.

To be sure that you understand this section, look at the approach to the 7th in the examples listed below.

Example 13-7 (p. 210)	Suspension figure (true of both the ii⁷ and the V⁷).
Example 13-8 (p. 211)	Neighbor tone figure.
Example 13-17 (p. 218)	Passing tone figure. The line is G5–F5–E5.
Example 13-19 (p. 220)	Ascending passage tone figure. The passing tone figure usually descends, the I–V$_3^4$–I⁶ progression being the only common exception.
Example 13-21 (p. 221)	Appoggiatura figure in the V$_2^4$, passing tone figure in the V$_5^6$.

Summary

The V⁷ is a major-minor 7th chord in both major and minor modes. This means that the leading tone must be raised in the V⁷ chord in the minor mode.

Two fundamental voice leadings should be followed when the V⁷ chord is used. First, the 7th of the chord ($\hat{4}$, not $\hat{7}$) should resolve down by step in the next chord (usually I or vi). The only common exception to this is the V$_3^4$–I⁶ progression, where the 7th may move up by step to the 5th of the I⁶ chord. Second, when it is in an outer part, the leading tone almost always resolves up by step.

The root position V⁷ usually moves to I or vi. When a V⁷ in a four-voice texture resolves to I, the I chord is frequently incomplete, with a tripled root and a 3rd. To arrive at a complete I chord, either the V⁷ must be incomplete itself (no 5th, with the root doubled) or the leading tone of the V⁷ must be in an inner voice so that it may leap down to the 5th of the I chord. When a V^7 in a four-voice texture resolves to vi, the leading tone must resolve to tonic if it is in the soprano voice or if the music is in the minor mode. In either case, the 3rd of the vi chord will be doubled.

The inverted V^7 is easy to use if you remember the basic principles outlined above concerning the leading tone and the 7th of the V^7. In general, the V6 resolves to I, the V$_3$ resolves to I or I^6, and the V$_2$ resolves to I^6.

The 7th of a V^7 chord in root position or inversion may be approached by means of a suspension figure, a passing tone figure, a neighbor tone figure, or an appoggiatura figure. Avoid approaching the 7th by a descending leap.

Self-Test 13-2
(Answers begin on page 610.)

A. Notate the specified chords. Use accidentals instead of key signatures.

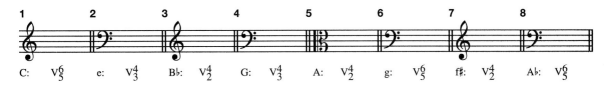

B. Comment on the resolution of the leading tone and both the approach to and the resolution of the 7th in the examples referred to below.

1. Self-Test 4-2, C.1, p. 72 (V_2^4).
2. Self-Test 4-2, C.2, p. 72 (V_3^4).
3. Example 7-18, p. 115 (V_2^4).

C.   Resolve each chord to a tonic triad (except as indicated). Analyze both chords.

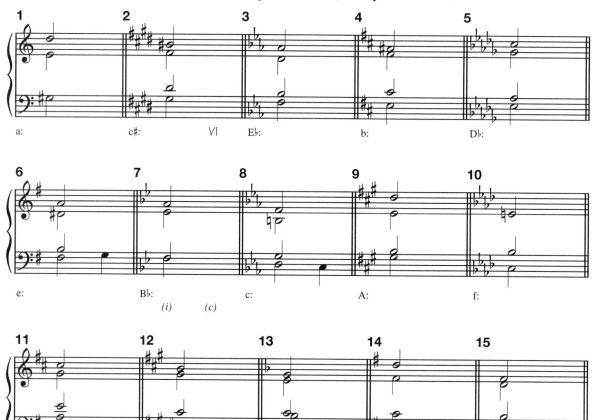

D.   Supply the key signature. Then notate and resolve the specified chord. Finally, begin
     the exercise with a chord that will allow good voice leading and provide the indicated
     approach to the 7th. Notate as quarter notes. Label all unlabeled chords.

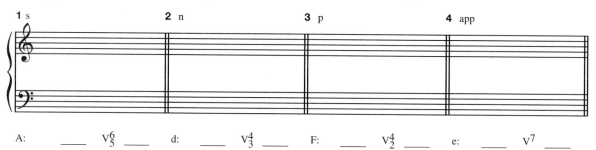

E.   Review. Identify the following keys. If the chord occurs diatonically in both major and
     minor, name both keys.

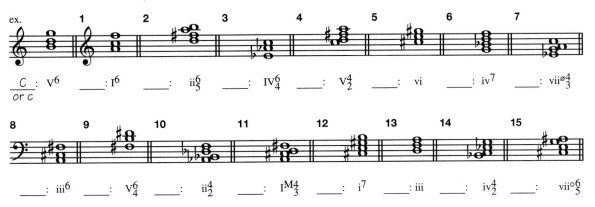

_C_ : V⁶   ___ : I⁶   ___ : ii⁶₅   ___ : IV⁶₄   ___ : V⁴₂   ___ : vi   ___ : iv⁷   ___ : vii°⁴₃
or c

___ : iii⁶   ___ : V⁶₄   ___ : ii⁴₂   ___ : I^M⁴₃   ___ : i⁷   ___ : iii   ___ : iv⁴₂   ___ : vii°⁶₅

Exercise 13-2 See Workbook.

Chapter 14

The II⁷ and VII⁷ Chords

INTRODUCTION

Any diatonic triad may appear with a 7th added, but the various diatonic seventh chords do not occur with equal frequency in tonal music. In fact, most seventh chords used are dominant sevenths, appearing either as the V⁷ or as a secondary V⁷ (to be discussed in Chapter 16). In the major mode, by far the most common diatonic seventh chord other than the V⁷ is the ii⁷. A ranking by frequency of the seventh chords in major would be approximately that shown below.

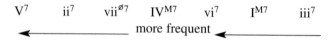

Because of the larger number of possible seventh chords in the minor (see pp. 69–70) a corresponding diagram for minor would be difficult to produce. The leading-tone seventh is more frequently found in minor than in major, but the supertonic seventh is still the more common of the two in minor. At any rate, a diagram showing the order of frequency of seventh chords in minor would not differ radically from that shown for major. In this chapter and the next each of the diatonic seventh chords is illustrated and discussed briefly. This chapter covers only the supertonic and leading-tone seventh chords, the remainder being discussed in Chapter 15.

You will not find the voice-leading principles to be difficult. Actually, Chapter 13 presented the most formidable part-writing problems to be found in tonal harmony. Because the principles are not difficult, there are not separate sections dealing with the handling of each chord in three and four voices. Instead, the following principles apply throughout.

1. The 7th of the chord almost always resolves down by step.
2. The 7th of the chord may be approached in various ways (review p. 221). Especially common is the suspension figure, although the passing tone figure also works well. Neighbor and appoggiatura figures are less common.
3. Incomplete chords must contain at least the root and the 7th.
4. Doubled tones should not be the chord 7th or the leading tone.

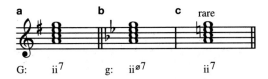

THE II⁷ CHORD

By far the most common of nondominant diatonic seventh chords, supertonic sevenths may be found in most compositions of the tonal era. In major the ii^7 is a minor seventh chord (Ex. 14-1a), whereas in minor keys the $ii^{\varnothing7}$ is almost always used (Ex. 14-1b). Another possibility in minor is the ii^7 chord created by a raised $\hat6$ (Ex. 14-1c); this chord is used rarely because the linear tendencies of both the $\uparrow\hat6$ and the chord 7th would usually resolve to a doubled leading tone in the V chord.

EXAMPLE 14-1

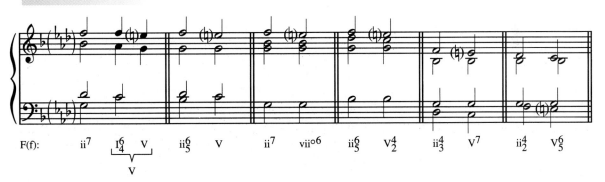

Like the supertonic triad, the supertonic seventh typically moves to V. The root position V may be delayed by the appearance of a cadential I_4^6 chord, or the V may be represented by a $vii^{\circ6}$ (see Ex. 14-2 for some typical resolutions).

EXAMPLE 14-2

Examples of all the cases above, as well as of others, are not difficult to find, but the first inversion of the ii^7 is the most common bass position. A ii_5^6–V^7 progression in a three-part texture is illustrated in Example 14-3. Notice the suspension figure that prepares the 7th of the ii_5^6.

EXAMPLE 14-3   *Mozart, Symphony No. 41, K. 551, IV*

A ii$^4_2$ chord appears in Example 14-4 with the 7th approached as a passing tone. The reduction clarifies the stepwise nature of the outer parts of the accompaniment. Notice that the voice attempts to escape the downward motion in mm. 16 to 17 for the climax of the song, but it soon rejoins the descent.

EXAMPLE 14-4   *Clara Wieck Schumann, "Beim Abschied"*

Used with permission of The Hildegard Publishing Company © 1993.

A much less typical use of the supertonic seventh chord is as a substitute for a IV chord in a plagal cadence. In such cases, the ii^7 is usually in first inversion, where its close resemblance to the IV is most obvious. In Example 14-5, which may be somewhat difficult to follow because of the clefs, Dvořák closes the phrase with a ii$^{\varnothing 6}_5$–i plagal cadence. The textural reduction makes the voice leading clearer and points out that most of the phrase is sequential.

♫ **EXAMPLE 14-5** *Dvořák, Symphony No. 9, Op. 95* (From the New World), *I*

Perhaps a better explanation of the ii$^{\varnothing 6}_5$ in the example above is that it is a iv chord with an added 6th (the F♯3). This is especially convincing in that it accounts for the E3, which is otherwise an unresolved 7th in the ii$^{\varnothing 7}$ chord.

THE VII^7 CHORD IN MAJOR

The leading-tone seventh in major is a half-diminished seventh chord,* possessing, as does the vii° triad, a dominant-like function. It normally resolves directly to the tonic, but it may first move to the V^7 simply by taking $\hat{6}$ (the 7th of the chord) down one step. Typical resolutions to tonic in four parts are demonstrated in Example 14-6. The third inversion, which is quite rare, is not shown, nor is vii$^{\varnothing 6}_5$–I, which would contain parallel 5ths.

---

*The fully diminished vii°^{7} in major is discussed in Chapter 21.

handwritten: // 5th with Vii⌀7

EXAMPLE 14-6

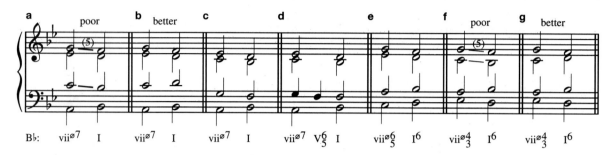

B♭:   vii⌀7   I   vii⌀7   I   vii⌀7   I   vii⌀7 V$^6_5$ I   vii⌀$^6_5$ I^6 vii⌀$^4_3$ I^6 vii⌀$^4_3$ I^6
         a   b   c   d   e   f   g

Notice that both the vii⌀7 and the vii⌀$^4_3$ resolutions must be handled carefully to avoid parallel 5ths (see Ex. 14-6a and f). This can be done by doubling the 3rd of the I chord or by revoicing the leading-tone chord so that parallel 4ths replace the parallel 5ths, as shown. The rare example from the literature of such parallels, as in Example 14-7, does not invalidate the principle.

EXAMPLE 14-7   *Haydn, Symphony No. 94, IV*

G: V$^6_5$ I   V   vii⌀$^4_3$ I^6 ii^6 I$^6_4$ V^7 I
                                                                      └──┬──┘
                                                                         V

A less common resolution of the vii⌀$^4_3$ is to a root position I chord, seen in Example 14-8 (from a composition for two four-part choruses). The vii⌀$^4_3$ is typically brought about, as it is here, by a IV chord that is left by parallel 3rds or 6ths outlining $\hat{1}$–$\hat{2}$–$\hat{3}$ in one voice and $\hat{6}$–$\hat{7}$–$\hat{1}$ in another (the two alto lines). The result is an interesting combination of both plagal and authentic cadences.

EXAMPLE 14-8 *Brahms, "Unsere Vater hofften auf dich," Op. 109, No. 1*

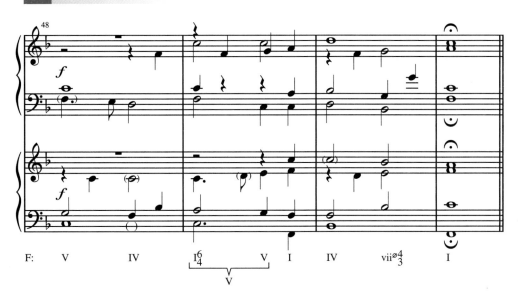

F: V   IV   I$^6_4$ V I IV vii$^{ø4}_3$ I

                       V

Otherwise, the vii^{ø7} poses no new problems. It should be remembered, however, that the vii^{ø7} is much less common than the other chords with dominant functions—V, V^7, and vii$^{o(6)}$.

THE VII⁷ CHORD IN MINOR

In the minor mode, the leading-tone seventh (Ex. 14-9a) appears as a fully diminished seventh chord (vii^{o7}). The subtonic seventh chord (Ex. 14-9b) generally is used in sequences, to be discussed in Chapter 15, or as a secondary dominant seventh (V^7 of III), a usage that is explained in Chapter 16. The vii^{o7} is found more frequently and is discussed in the following paragraphs.

EXAMPLE 14-9

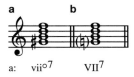

a: vii^{o7} VII^7

The vii^{o7}, whether in root position or inverted, tends to resolve to tonic. As with the vii^{ø7}, the vii^{o7} may move first to the V^7 simply by moving the 7th of the chord down to $\hat{5}$. The resolution of vii^{o7} to i, however, requires more discussion.

The vii°⁷ contains two tritones. The tendency of the tritone is to resolve inward by step when spelled as a °5, outward by step when spelled as a +4. If these tendencies are followed in four parts, as in Example 14-10, the tonic triad will have a doubled 3rd.

EXAMPLE 14-10

e:

Composers have not always cared to follow these tendencies, often taking $\hat{2}$ down to $\hat{1}$ instead of moving it up to $\hat{3}$ (compare Ex. 14-11a and b). In certain voicings, this can result in unequal 5ths (Ex. 14-11c).

EXAMPLE 14-11

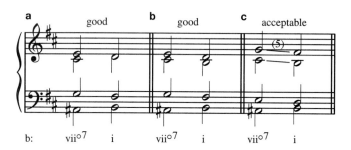

The 5ths, although acceptable, are often disguised through the use of NCTs, as in Example 14-12.

EXAMPLE 14-12 *Bach, Passacaglia in C Minor*

c: vii°⁶₅ i⁶ vii°⁷ i iv⁷ V⁷ i

Textural reduction

The members of the vii°⁷ usually move in the same ways when the chord is inverted as they do when it is in root position, and our discussion of the optionally doubled 3rd still applies (for example, see the first chord in Ex. 14-12). The vii°⁶₅ (Ex. 14-13a) usually is followed by i⁶ because resolution to the root position tonic creates unequal 5ths involving the bass (review p. 85). The vii°⁴₃ (Ex. 14-13b) moves smoothly to the i⁶; occasionally found is vii°⁴₃–i, which is similar to the vii°⁴₃–I cadence discussed in connection with Example 14-8. The vii°⁴₂ (Ex. 14-13c) is generally followed by V⁷ or by a cadential or passing i⁶₄.

EXAMPLE 14-13

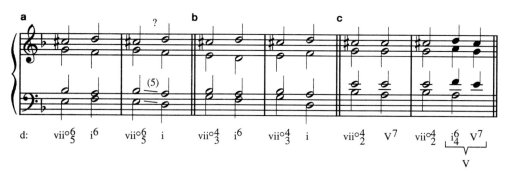

A vii°$^4_3$ in chorale texture is seen in Example 14-14, where it resolves to a i^6 with a doubled 3rd. An alternate analysis would eliminate two of the chords that occur in the same measure with the vii°$^4_3$—the ii$^{Ø6}_5$ and the ii^{Ø7}—by regarding the A4s as suspensions. It would not be equally good to analyze the G♯4s as lower neighbors, thereby eliminating the vii°$^4_3$ and the vii°^{6}, because that analysis turns up an unconvincing progression: ii$^{Ø6}_5$–i^6–ii^{Ø7}–i.

EXAMPLE 14-14   *Bach, "Als Jesus Christus in der Nacht"*

You may have noticed that Example 14-14 ends with a major tonic triad. In the Baroque period it was not at all uncommon to end a phrase or a composition in the minor mode in this way. This device, known as the *Picardy third,* is discussed further in Chapter 21.

Checkpoint

1. The most frequently used diatonic seventh chord is the V^7. Which one ranks second in frequency?
2. What tones of a seventh chord should not be omitted?
3. The 7th of a diatonic seventh chord resolves (up/down) by (step/leap).

4. Which types of seventh chords are found on $\hat{2}$ and $\hat{7}$ in major and minor? Which forms in minor are the most common?
5. The ii^7 tends to be followed by _____ , the vii$^{\emptyset 7}$ by _____ .
6. Which chord discussed in this chapter contains two tritones?
7. The natural tendency of the +4 is to resolve (inward/outward) by step, whereas the °5 resolves (inward/outward) by step.
8. Try to recall the implications of the preceding question in connection with the vii°^{7} chord.

Summary

The supertonic seventh chord is a minor seventh chord in the major mode (ii^7) and a half-diminished seventh chord in the minor mode (ii$^{\emptyset 7}$). Like the supertonic triad, it is usually followed by a V chord (or by a V delayed by a I$_4^6$). A less common usage finds the supertonic seventh, usually in first inversion, substituting for IV (or iv) in a plagal cadence.

The leading-tone seventh chord is a half-diminished seventh chord in the major mode (vii$^{\emptyset 7}$) and a fully diminished seventh chord in the minor mode (vii°^{7}). Like the leading-tone triad, it is usually followed by a I chord, but it may move first to a V^7 in root position or inversion simply by resolving the 7th down by step. The voice leading is usually stepwise in all voices as the leading-tone seventh chord resolves, although one occasionally encounters a vii°$_3^4$ (or vii$^{\emptyset 4}_3$) resolving to a root position tonic triad, which involves a leap of a 4th or 5th in the bass.

The most crucial aspect of part-writing supertonic and leading-tone seventh chords is the resolution of the 7th of the chord down by step in the following chord. In addition, incomplete seventh chords must contain at least the root and the 7th, and $\hat{7}$ should not be doubled in the leading-tone seventh chord.

Self-Test 14-1
(Answers begin on page 612.)

A. Notate the following chords. Use accidentals, not key signatures.

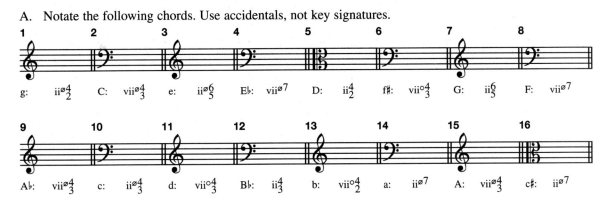

B.   Analyze the following chords. Be sure your symbols indicate chord quality and inversion.

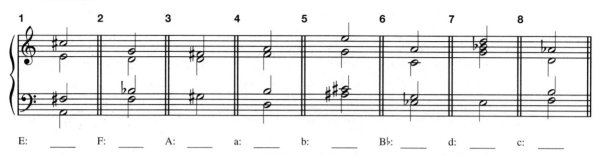

E: _____   F: _____   A: _____   a: _____   b: _____   B♭: _____   d: _____   c: _____

C.   Analyze the chords and NCTs in the following excerpts. Whenever you encounter a ii⁷ (ii⁰⁷) or vii⁰⁷ (vii⁰⁷) chord, discuss the voice leading into and out of the chord.

   1.   Each numbered blank indicates where a chord is to be analyzed. In many cases it would be equally valid to analyze the "chords" as NCTs.

Bach, "Gib dich zufrieden und sei stille"

   2.   Again, the chords are numbered. Also, the "real" bass notes of chords 1 to 3 are circled.

Mozart, Piano Sonata K. 284, III, Var. 5

3. Trace the predominant rhythmic idea in this excerpt.

Schubert, *Aufenthalt*

4. The melody notes on beat 2 of each odd-numbered measure are NCTs. Try to make a reduction that would show the simple model of which this excerpt is an elaboration. What is the meaning of the asterisks in mm. 9 and 15?

Chopin, Mazurka Op. 33, No. 3

D. Notate, introduce, and resolve the specified chords. Each chord 7th is to be approached as a suspension, as a neighbor, or as a passing tone, as specified. Include key signatures and roman numerals.

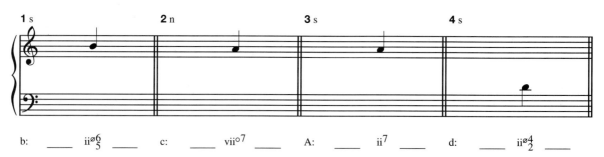

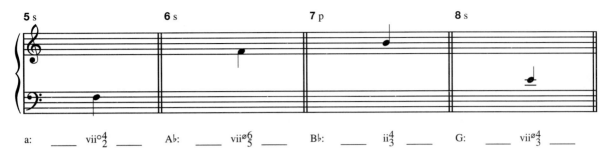

a: _____ vii°$\frac{4}{2}$ _____   A♭: _____ vii°$\frac{6}{5}$ _____   B♭: _____ ii$\frac{4}{3}$ _____   G: _____ vii°$\frac{4}{3}$ _____

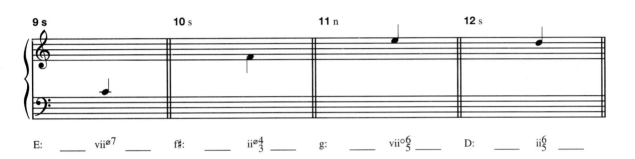

E: _____ vii°⁷ _____   f♯: _____ ii°$\frac{4}{3}$ _____   g: _____ vii°$\frac{6}{5}$ _____   D: _____ ii$\frac{6}{5}$ _____

E. Analyze the chords called for by this figured bass, analyzing in D major throughout. Then add two upper treble-clef parts conforming to those chords. Note: This trio would actually be performed by four musicians: two violinists, someone playing the bass line (probably a cellist), and a keyboard player realizing the figured bass. (The numerals 3 and 5 call for root position triads.)

Corelli, Trio Sonata Op. 3, No. 2, II

F.   Harmonize these chorale phrases for four-part chorus.

1.   Include a vii°⁷ and a ii⌀⁶₅.

2.   Include a ii⁷ (on the first half of beat 3 in m. 1).

Exercise 14-1 See Workbook.

Chapter 15

Other Diatonic Seventh Chords

THE IV^7 CHORD

The diatonic subdominant seventh chord is found in the forms shown in Example 15-1.

EXAMPLE 15-1

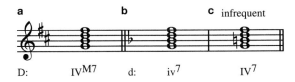

D: IV^{M7} d: iv^7 IV^7

Like the subdominant triad, the subdominant seventh moves to V (or vii°^{6}), often passing through some form of the ii chord on the way. The resolution to ii^7 (possibly inverted) is especially easy to handle because only the 7th needs to move. This is illustrated in Example 15-2.

EXAMPLE 15-2

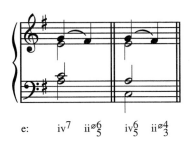

e: iv^7 ii°$^6_5$ iv$^6_5$ ii°$^4_3$

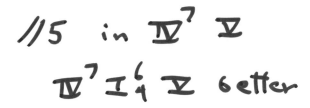

When iv^7 moves directly to V, parallel 5ths may result if the 7th of the chord is placed above the 3rd (Ex. 15-3a). This can be corrected through the use of a cadential six-four (Ex. 15-3b) or by doubling the 5th of the V chord (Ex. 15-3c). The solutions illustrated in

Example 15-3d and e, although less commonly used, are also acceptable. Bach's solution in Example 14-12 (p. 233) is especially elaborate. His voice leading combines elements of Example 15-3a and b and ornaments the result with a number of NCTs.

EXAMPLE 15-3

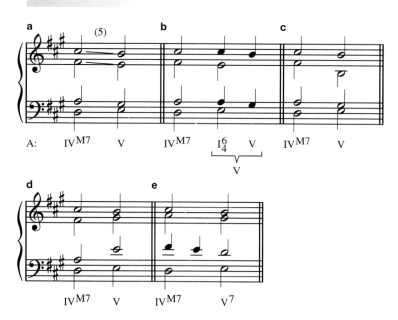

Otherwise, the voice leading to and from the root position or inverted subdominant seventh is smooth and offers no new problems. A iv^7 in a three-part texture is seen in Example 15-4, which features a circle-of-fifths sequence using seventh chords. Notice that mm. 200 to 201 sound as if they are in $\frac{2}{4}$ rather than in $\frac{3}{4}$. This metric device, which is known as *hemiola,* has been in use for many centuries and is still heard today. (The vii°^{7}/V shown beneath m. 202 is the subject of Chapter 17.)

EXAMPLE 15-4   *Mozart, Piano Sonata, K. 332, I*

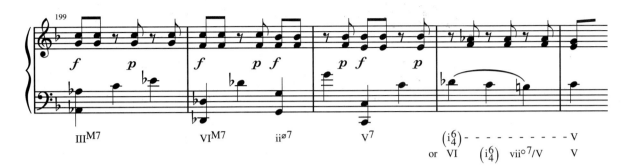

$$\text{III}^{\text{M7}} \qquad \text{VI}^{\text{M7}} \qquad \text{ii}^{\varnothing 7} \qquad \text{V}^{7} \qquad \left(\text{i}^{6}_{4}\right)\text{- - - - - - - - - V}$$
$$\qquad\qquad\qquad\qquad\qquad\qquad\qquad\qquad\qquad\qquad \text{or VI} \quad \left(\text{i}^{6}_{4}\right) \quad \text{vii}^{\circ 7}/\text{V} \qquad \text{V}$$

The subdominant seventh in minor with a raised $\hat{6}$ (see Ex. 15-1) has the same sound as that of a dominant seventh chord, but it does not have a dominant function. Instead, it results from ascending motion toward the leading tone ($\uparrow\hat{6}$–$\uparrow\hat{7}$–$\hat{1}$), as in the Bach example below (Ex. 15-5). This phrase is especially interesting in that it contains subdominant chords using both $\uparrow\hat{6}$ and $\downarrow\hat{6}$ and dominant chords using both $\uparrow\hat{7}$ and $\downarrow\hat{7}$.

♫ EXAMPLE 15-5   *Bach, "Als vierzig Tag' nach Ostern"*

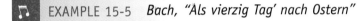

$$\text{e:} \qquad \text{i} \quad ^{6} \quad ^{5}_{3} \quad \text{V}^{6} \quad ^{5}_{3} \quad \text{i} \quad \text{IV}^{6}_{5} \quad \text{V}^{6} \quad \text{i} \quad \text{v}^{6} \quad \text{iv}^{6} \qquad\qquad \text{V}$$

THE VI⁷ CHORD

The submediant seventh is found in three forms (Ex. 15-6).

EXAMPLE 15-6

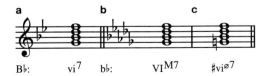

$$\text{B}\flat\text{:} \qquad \text{vi}^{7} \quad \text{b}\flat\text{:} \qquad \text{VI}^{\text{M7}} \qquad \#\text{vi}^{\varnothing 7}$$

Like their parent triads, the vi⁷ and the VI^M7 typically move toward V, usually passing through subdominant or supertonic chords, or both, on the way. The resolutions to IV and ii are not difficult, and some of the possibilities are illustrated in Example 15-7.

EXAMPLE 15-7

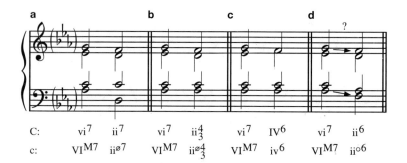

$$
\begin{array}{lllll}
\text{C:} & \text{vi}^7 \quad \text{ii}^7 & \text{vi}^7 \quad \text{ii}^4_3 & \text{vi}^7 \quad \text{IV}^6 & \text{vi}^7 \quad \text{ii}^6 \\[4pt]
\text{c:} & \text{VI}^{M7} \; \text{ii}^{ø7} & \text{VI}^{M7} \; \text{ii}^{ø4}_{3} & \text{VI}^{M7} \; \text{iv}^6 & \text{VI}^{M7} \; \text{ii}^{o6}
\end{array}
$$

If a root position vi⁷ or VI^M7 moves to a root position V, parallel 5ths are apt to result, as in Example 15-8a. In major this problem can be avoided by moving to V⁶ or V⁶₅, as in Example 15-8c.

EXAMPLE 15-8

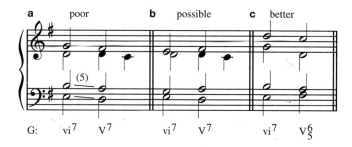

$$
\begin{array}{lll}
\text{a} \;\;\text{poor} & \text{b} \;\;\text{possible} & \text{c} \;\;\text{better}
\end{array}
$$

$$
\text{G:} \quad \text{vi}^7 \quad \text{V}^7 \qquad \text{vi}^7 \quad \text{V}^7 \qquad \text{vi}^7 \quad \text{V}^6_5
$$

Example 15-4 contains a typical VI^M7 in three voices in a circle-of-fifths progression. Notice the stepwise or common-tone voice leading in the upper voices. However, in freer textures, especially in piano music, composers sometimes paid less attention to voice-leading conventions. In Example 15-9 parallel 5ths are seen in the vi⁷–ii⁷ progression. Notice also the unresolved 7th in the cadence.

♫ EXAMPLE 15-9   *Chopin, Ballade Op. 38*

F: I   V⁷   I   IV   I⁶   iii⁶ vi⁷ ii⁷   V⁷   I

In minor, when the root of the submediant seventh moves up by step to $\hat{7}$, the $\hat{6}$ must be raised to avoid the interval of a ⁺2. The chord that results when $\hat{6}$ is raised is a half-diminished seventh: ♯vi⁰⁷. The origin of this chord is illustrated in Example 15-10.

EXAMPLE 15-10

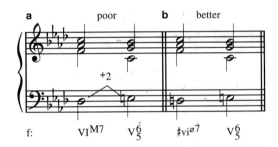

f: VI^M7   V⁶₅   ♯vi⁰⁷   V⁶₅

The ♯vi⁰⁷ usually serves as a passing chord between two chords of dominant function (V or vii°). It moves most smoothly to the otherwise unusual root position vii°, as in Example 15-11, but it can move to V⁶₅ if $\hat{1}$ leaps to $\hat{5}$ (as in Ex. 15-10b).

♫ EXAMPLE 15-11   *Bach, "Warum betrübst du dich, mein Herz"*

a: i   V (⁴₂) i⁶   V ♯vi⁰⁷ vii° i   V

THE I⁷ CHORD

The tonic seventh chord in its diatonic form is a M⁷ chord in a major key (Ex. 15-12a) and a m⁷ chord in a minor key (Ex. 15-12b). The minor-major seventh chord in minor (Ex. 15-12c), although possible, is quite rare in the tonal tradition, although it is used freely in jazz.

EXAMPLE 15-12

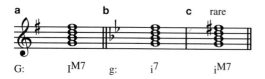

$$G: \qquad I^{M7} \qquad g: \qquad i^7 \qquad\qquad i^{M7}$$

Adding a 7th to the tonic triad obviously deprives it of tonal stability. Rather than being a harmonic goal or resting place, the tonic seventh is an active chord that demands resolution. It tends to move to a IV or sometimes to a ii or vi, any of which might also contain a 7th. The chord of resolution must be one that contains $\hat{6}$ so that the chord 7th ($\hat{7}$) can resolve down to it. Some possibilities are illustrated in Example 15-13.

EXAMPLE 15-13

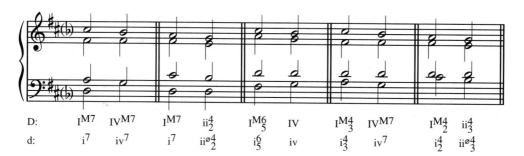

Although the tonic seventh is by no means a frequently encountered sonority, it can be very effective when handled well. Two examples from Schumann's *Album for the Young* appear below, with the 7th approached as a passing tone in each case. In both cases the chord 7th could be analyzed as a NCT, as is frequently the case with seventh chords. The decision to analyze a tone as a 7th will be influenced by such factors as its relative duration (Ex. 15-14) or its suspension into the next chord (Ex. 15-15). The textural reduction of Example 15-14 shows that the chord 7ths resolve down by step, even in this fairly free texture (see the bracketed notes). In the roman numeral analysis "V⁴₃/V" represents a secondary dominant, which will be discussed in Chapter 16.

EXAMPLE 15-14 *Schumann, "Mignon," Op. 68, No. 35*

EXAMPLE 15-15 *Schumann, "Spring Song," Op. 68, No. 15*

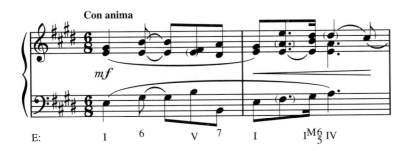

THE III⁷ CHORD

The diatonic mediant seventh chord takes the forms illustrated in Example 15-16. The first two chords in Example 15-16 (the other is rarely used) occur most often in sequences of seventh chords.

EXAMPLE 15-16

A typical instance of such a sequence is seen in Example 15-17. The music shown is played by the string orchestra, whereas the soloists have a somewhat embellished version. The iii[7] usually progresses to vi[(7)], as here, but it may also be followed by a IV chord.

EXAMPLE 15-17   *Corelli, Concerto Grosso Op. 6, No. 3, V*

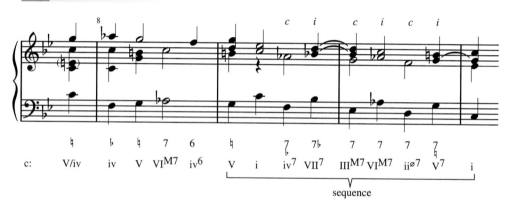

Checkpoint

1. The subdominant seventh chord often passes through some form of the _____ chord on its way to V.
2. What condition creates the IV[7] chord (not the iv[7] chord) and the #vi[ø7] chord in minor?
3. How does the addition of a seventh change the usual function of the tonic triad?
4. Which is more often encountered in the minor mode: III[M7] or III[+7]?

SEVENTH CHORDS AND THE CIRCLE-OF-FIFTHS SEQUENCE

As we explained in Chapter 7, the usual harmonic functions of most diatonic chords are closely related to the circle-of-fifths sequence. It is not surprising, then, that this is one of the most commonly used sequential patterns, and it can be found in various kinds of twentieth-century popular music as well (as in Example 3-10, on p. 53, which contains a iv^7–VII^7–III^{M7}–VI^{M7}–$ii^{ø7}$–V^7–i progression). If the chords used in a circle-of-fifths sequence are seventh chords, certain voice-leading conventions are almost always followed.

If the seventh chords are in root position in a four-part texture, complete chords will alternate with incomplete chords (5th omitted). If you look back at the iv^7 in Example 15-17, you will see that all notes of the chord are present, whereas the VII^7 that follows omits the 5th (F). This alternation between complete and incomplete chords continues through the V^7 chord. There is no other satisfactory way to handle the voice leading in this situation, as you can prove to yourself easily enough.

If the seventh chords are inverted in a four-part texture, either $^6_5$ chords will alternate with $^4_2$ chords, or $^4_3$ chords will alternate with 7 (root position) chords. All chords will be complete. These two situations are illustrated in Example 15-18.

EXAMPLE 15-18

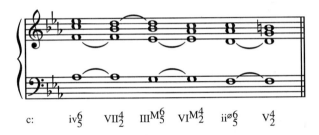

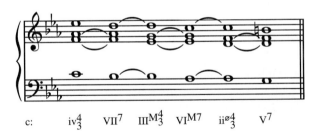

In three-part textures, a circle-of-fifths sequence will usually be in root position. A root position circle-of-fifths sequence in a three-part texture was illustrated in Example 15-4 (p. 242). The relevant part of that example is shown in reduction in Example 15-19, every chord omitting the 5th.

EXAMPLE 15-19

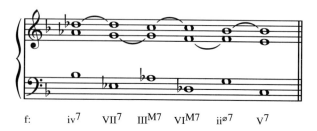

f: iv⁷   VII⁷   III^M7   VI^M7   ii°⁷   v⁷

The general principle followed in all of the circle-of-fifths examples that we have been discussing is that, with the exception of the bass in a root position sequence, *each voice either stays the same from one chord to the next or it moves down by step.* Look back over Examples 15-17 through 15-19 to verify this for yourself.

Summary

Some seventeen different seventh chords have been discussed in this chapter and the preceding one. Rather than trying to memorize the typical resolutions of these chords, we suggest that you simply remember and apply these principles:

1. The function of a triad is not changed by the addition of a 7th. Because, for example, iv tends to progress to ii° or V, you may assume that iv⁷ has these same tendencies. Exception: The tonic becomes an active chord instead of a stable harmonic goal.

2. Smooth approach to the 7th of the chord is a feature of many, but not all, passages employing diatonic seventh chords.

3. Chord 7ths almost always resolve down by step. It follows, therefore, that the chord of resolution must contain the note to which the 7th will resolve. The resolution is sometimes delayed, as in $\underset{V}{\underbrace{\text{iv}^7\text{-i}^6_4\text{-V}}}$, or, in rare cases, simply not employed.

4. In minor, the movement of the individual lines usually conforms to the melodic minor scale. Because of this, more seventh-chord types are possible in minor than in major.

5. In a circle-of-fifths progression of root position seventh chords in four parts, incomplete and complete chords must be used in alternation.

Self-Test 15-1
(Answers begin on page 617.)

A. Notate the following chords. Use accidentals, not key signatures.

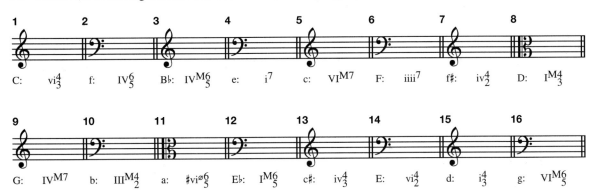

C: vi$^4_3$ f: IV$^6_5$ B♭: IV$^{M6}_5$ e: i^7 c: VI^{M7} F: iiii^7 f♯: iv$^4_2$ D: I$^{M4}_3$

G: IV^{M7} b: III$^{M4}_2$ a: ♯vi$^{ø6}_5$ E♭: I$^{M6}_5$ c♯: iv$^4_3$ E: vi$^4_2$ d: i$^4_3$ g: VI$^{M6}_5$

B. Analyze the following chords. Be sure your symbols indicate chord quality and inversion.

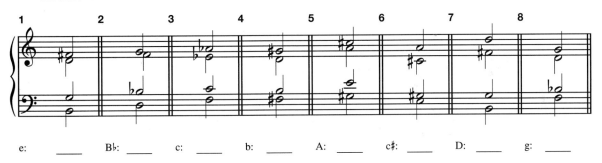

e: _____ B♭: _____ c: _____ b: _____ A: _____ c♯: _____ D: _____ g: _____

C. Analyze chords and NCTs in the excerpts below. Comment on the voice leading involving any of the chords discussed in this chapter.

1. What spacing "rules" are broken in this excerpt? Why do you suppose this was done?

Bach, "Nun ruhen alle Wälder"

2. Analyze two chords on beat 3 of the first measure.

Bach, "Warum sollt' ich mich denn grämen"

G:

3. A _____ progression occupies most of this excerpt. The seventh chords in this three-part texture each lack a _____. If you were to add a fourth voice beginning on F4, how would it proceed? (Do not label NCTs in this exercise.)

Mozart, Rondo, K. 494

D. Notate, introduce, and resolve the specified chords. Each chord 7th is to be approached as a suspension, as a neighbor, or as a passing tone, as indicated. Include key signatures and roman numerals.

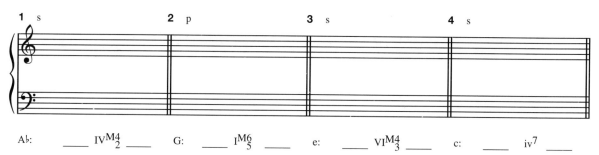

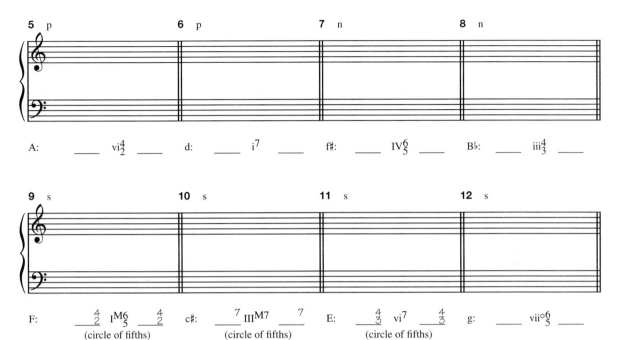

A: _____ vi$_2^4$ _____   d: _____ i^7 _____   f♯: _____ IV$_5^6$ _____   B♭: _____ iii$_3^4$ _____

F: _____ $_2^4$ IM$_5^6$ _____ $_2^4$ c♯: _____ ^{7} III^{M7} _____ ^{7} E: _____ $_3^4$ vi^7 _____ $_3^4$ g: _____ vii°$_5^6$ _____

(circle of fifths)   (circle of fifths)   (circle of fifths)

E. Add a top voice to create a three-part texture.

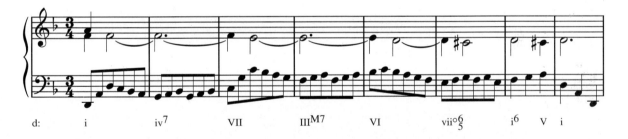

d: i   iv^7 VII   III^{M7} VI   vii°$_5^6$ i^6 V   i

F.   Analyze the chords specified by each figured bass and make a harmonization for four-part chorus.

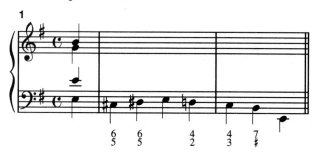

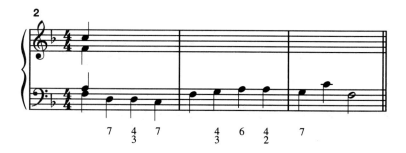

Exercise 15-1 See Workbook.

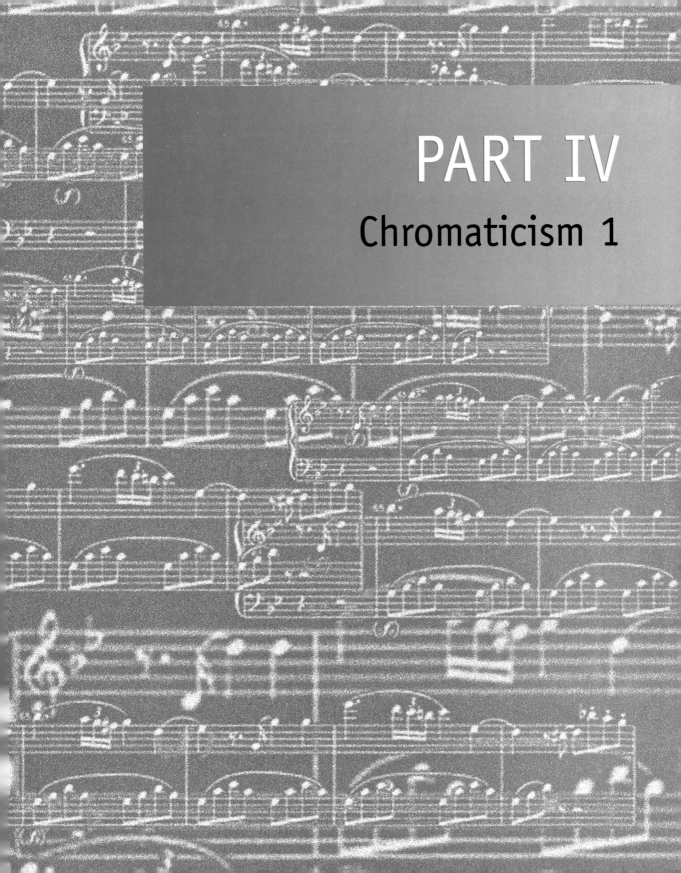

PART IV

Chromaticism 1

16

Secondary Functions 1

tonicizing chords

CHROMATICISM AND ALTERED CHORDS

The term *chromaticism* refers to the use of pitches foreign to the key of the passage. The only chromaticism we have discussed so far involves chromatic non-chord tones. For instance, Example 16-1 contains several notes not found in the B♭ major scale, but all of them are non-chord tones.

EXAMPLE 16-1   *Haydn, Quartet Op. 64, No. 3, I*

Some people use the term *nonessential chromaticism* to describe the use of chromatically altered tones as NCTs. *Essential chromaticism* refers to the use of tones from outside the scale as members of chords. Such chords are called *altered chords.*

SECONDARY FUNCTIONS

By far the most common sort of altered chord in tonal music is the *secondary function*. A chord whose function belongs more closely to a key other than the main key of the passage is called a secondary function. Listen to Example 16-2, paying special attention to the ending. Although the two-part texture means that incomplete chords will have to be used, it is clear that the F♯4 in m. 7 is not an NCT. In fact, the last two chords are D and G, and they sound like V-I in the key of G.

♫ **EXAMPLE 16-2**   *Haydn, Symphony No. 94, II*

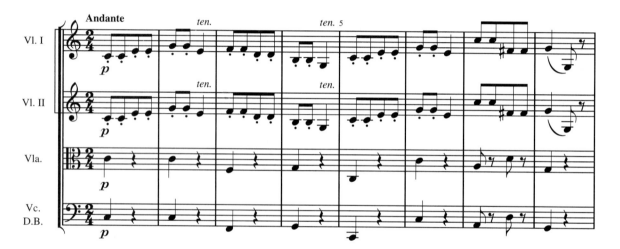

If our ears were to lose track of the original tonic at this point, or if the music were to continue in the key of G, employing F♯s and centering on G, we would analyze this as a change of key (a modulation). However, because we still hear the G chord as a V, and because the next phrase is a repeat of the first one, we label the G chord as V and call the D chord a *V of V* (the symbol is V/V). We say that the D chord has *tonicized* the G chord, giving it special emphasis, but that a change of tonic has not taken place.

Most secondary functions are either secondary dominants (*V of* and *V⁷ of*) or secondary leading-tone chords (*vii° of, vii°⁷ of,* and *vii⁰⁷ of*).

SECONDARY DOMINANT CHORDS

Because tonic triads are always major or minor, it makes sense that only major and minor triads can be tonicized by secondary dominants. This means that you would not expect to find V/ii° in minor or V/vii° in either major or minor. All other diatonic chords (other than I, of course) may be tonicized by secondary V or V7 chords. Example 16-3 illustrates the possibilities in F major. Notice that most of the accidentals create a leading tone to the root of the chord being tonicized.

EXAMPLE 16-3 *Secondary dominants in F major*

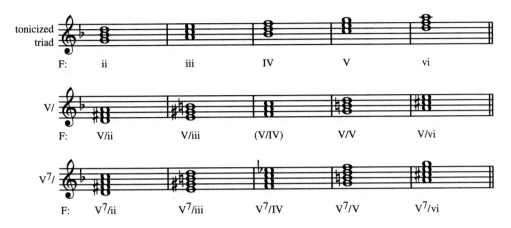

Only one of these chords, V/IV, is identical to a diatonic chord in F. Because V/IV sounds like I, composers most often use V⁷/IV instead of V/IV to make the secondary function clear.

The secondary dominants in d minor are illustrated in Example 16-4. Here three chords are identical to diatonic chords in d minor. The V/III (= VII) and the V⁷/III (= VII⁷) are both usable, even though they are not altered chords, because VII and VII⁷ usually function as dominants of III anyway. The V/VI, however, would usually be analyzed as III instead of as a secondary dominant.

EXAMPLE 16-4 *Secondary dominants in D minor*

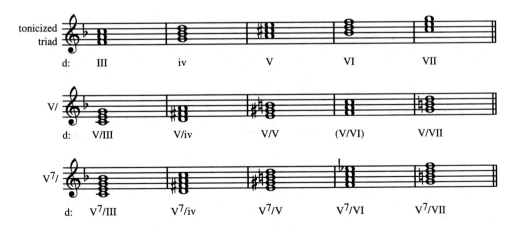

The major or minor triad that is tonicized by a secondary dominant may occur with its 7th, or the tonicized chord may itself be altered to become a secondary dominant. This means, for example, that any of the following progressions might be encountered.

V^7/ii–ii V^7/ii–V/V

V^7/ii–ii^7 V^7/ii–V^7/V

SPELLING SECONDARY DOMINANTS

There are three steps involved in spelling a secondary dominant.

1. Find the root of the chord that is to be tonicized.
2. Go up a P5.
3. Using that note as the root, spell a major triad (for V of) or a major-minor seventh chord (for V^7 of).

For example, to spell a V/vi in E♭, the steps are the following (Ex. 16-5).

1. The root of vi in E♭ is C.
2. A P5 above C is G.
3. A major triad on G is G–B♮–D.

EXAMPLE 16-5

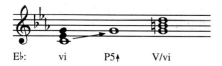

E♭:   vi   P5↑   V/vi

Or, to spell a V^7/V in b minor (Ex. 16-6),

1.   The root of V in b is F♯.
2.   A P5 above F♯ is C♯.
3.   A Mm^7 on C♯ is C♯–E♯–G♯–B.

EXAMPLE 16-6

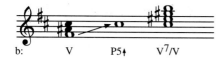

b: V   P5↑ V^7/V

RECOGNIZING SECONDARY DOMINANTS

If you encounter an altered chord in a passage, there is a good chance that it will be a secondary dominant. These steps will work in most cases.

1. Is it a major triad or major-minor seventh chord? If not, it is not a secondary dominant.

2. Find the note a P5 below the root of the altered chord.

3. Would a major or minor triad built on that note be a diatonic triad in this key? If so, the altered chord is a secondary dominant.

Self-Test 16-1
(Answers begin on page 620.)

A. Review how to spell secondary dominants (p. 260). Then notate these secondary dominants in the specified inversions. Include key signatures.

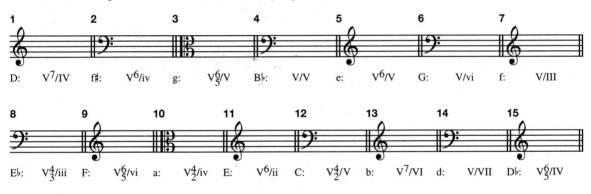

B. Label any chord that might be a secondary dominant according to the steps outlined above. Label all others with an X.

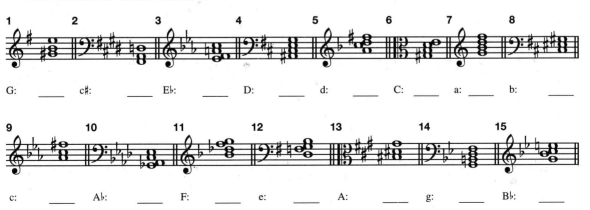

Exercise 16-1 See Workbook.

Checkpoint

1. What is the definition of a secondary function?
2. Most secondary functions are either secondary dominants (*V of* and *V⁷ of*) or
    _____ .
3. Why is a V/IV in major less convincing than a V^7/IV?
4. The root of a secondary dominant is how far above the root of the chord being
    tonicized?

SECONDARY DOMINANTS IN CONTEXT

Secondary dominants generally resolve just as primary dominants do. That is, a V^6_5/V in
C will resolve the same way as V^6_5 would in the key of G (Ex. 16-7a). The only exception
is that sometimes the chord of resolution contains a 7th. In that case, the leading tone slides
down a half step to become the 7th of the chord of resolution (Ex. 16-7b). Notice that complete seventh chords alternate with incomplete ones in Example 16-7c. This part-writing
principle should be familiar to you from the discussion of circle-of-fifths sequences in
Chapter 15 (pp. 248–250).

EXAMPLE 16-7

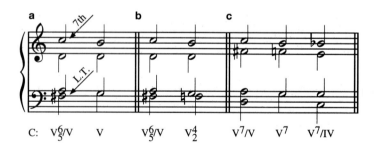

The V^7/V is the most frequently encountered secondary dominant. In Example 16-8 the V
is delayed by a cadential six-four. This is not an irregular resolution of the V^7/V because,
as we know, the I^6_4–V together stands for V.

🎵 EXAMPLE 16-8 *Schumann, Noveletten, Op. 21, No. 1*

Textural reduction

In our discussion of Example 16-7b above, we pointed out that the leading tone of the secondary dominant will move down by half step if the chord that follows contains a 7th. This is illustrated in Example 16-9.

🎵 EXAMPLE 16-9 *Chopin, Mazurka Op. 68, No. 1*

The common deceptive progression V⁽⁷⁾–vi is often given added impetus by inserting a dominant of vi between the V and the vi, as in Example 16-10.

♫ EXAMPLE 16-10   *Schumann, Eintritt, Op. 82, No. 1*

B♭:   I   V   I   IV   V⁷   V⁶/vi vi   IV   ii⁷ V⁷   I

The only deceptive progression that we have discussed up to this point is the progression from V or V⁷ to vi (or VI), but there are other kinds of deceptive progressions that we will encounter through the next several chapters. In general, a deceptive progression is the result any time that a dominant chord is followed by something other than a tonic triad, as in the V⁶₅–V⁴₂/IV progression in Example 16-11. Notice also the stepwise bass line.

♫ EXAMPLE 16-11   *Tchaikovsky, Trio Op. 50, II*

E: I⁶   V⁴₃   I   V⁶₅   V⁴₂/IV   IV⁶ (I⁶₄) ii⁶₅ I⁶   ii⁷

A much less smooth introduction to a V⁷/IV is seen in Example 16-12. Here we see the ending of a phrase that concludes with a deceptive cadence (m. 24). All parts then immediately leap to C♮, which is ♭7̂, to state the three-note motive that began the piece. This example also illustrates the V/ii.

EXAMPLE 16-12 *Haydn, Quartet Op. 20, No. 4, I*

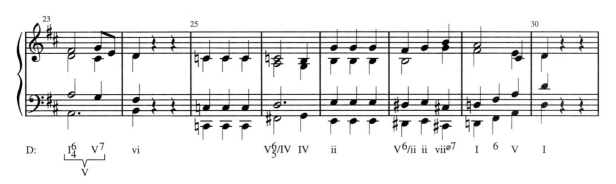

Examples of dominants of iii in major are not frequently encountered because the iii itself is the least often used diatonic triad. However, the III in minor, which represents the relative major key, is very often tonicized. Play through Example 16-13 and then compare it to the simple sequence below it. This circle-of-fifths sequence is the background of many passages of tonal music.

EXAMPLE 16-13 *Bach, French Suite No. 1, Minuet II*

Textural reduction

Secondary dominants abound in jazz and popular music, as do many other kinds of chromaticism. The harmonically simple but effective film theme in Example 16-14 reaches a half cadence in mm. 7 to 8 with a V^7/V–V progression. Notice the stepwise descent in the bass in mm. 1 to 5 (C–B–A–G–F), specified by the lead sheet symbols and including a passing I_4^6 chord.

 EXAMPLE 16-14   *Bacalov, "Il Postino"*

Music by Luis Enrique Bacalov. Copyright © 1994 C.A.M. S.R.I.-Rome (Italy), Via Cola di Rienzo, 152; and Ernesto Mediterraneo Film S.R.I.-Rome (Italy), Via Leprignano, 4. Used by permission.

Summary

Chromaticism refers to the use of pitches that are foreign to the key of the passage. Chords that employ chromaticism are called *altered chords,* and the most commonly encountered altered chord in tonal music is the *secondary function.* A secondary function is a chord whose function belongs more closely to a key other than the main key of the passage. Most secondary functions are either secondary dominants (*V of* and *V⁷ of*) or secondary leading-tone chords (*vii° of, viiø⁷ of,* and *vii°⁷ of*).

Secondary dominants can tonicize only major or minor triads or major or minor triads with a 7th. This means that the vii° chord, for example, cannot be tonicized by a secondary dominant.

To spell a secondary dominant, go up a P5 from the root of the chord to be tonicized and spell a major triad (for V of) or a major-minor seventh chord (for V⁷ of).

To determine whether an altered chord that you encounter in analysis might be a secondary dominant, see whether it is a major triad or a major-minor seventh chord with a root that is a P5 above a scale degree that usually carries a major or minor triad in that key. If so, the altered chord is a secondary dominant.

Secondary dominants resolve just as primary dominants do, except that the chord of resolution frequently contains a 7th. In that case, the leading tone of the secondary dominant moves down by half step to become the 7th of the chord of resolution.

The V^7/V is the most frequently encountered secondary dominant. Two variations on the deceptive progression that employs secondary dominants are $V^{(7)}$–V^7/vi–vi and $V^{(7)}$–V^7/IV. The $V^{(7)}/iii$ in major is seldom used, but the $V^{(7)}/III$ in the minor mode is quite common.

Self-Test 16-2
(Answers begin on page 621.)

A. Analysis

1. Analyze with roman numerals. Find the sequence and enclose it in brackets. Although the voice leading is conventional throughout most of this excerpt, parallel 5ths do occur. Find them. Be sure to play this example so that you can appreciate the effect of the last four measures.

Schumann, *Papillons,* Op. 2, No. 12

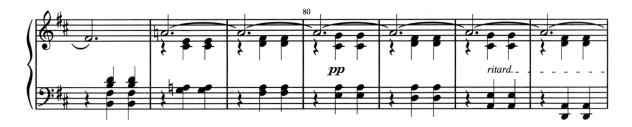

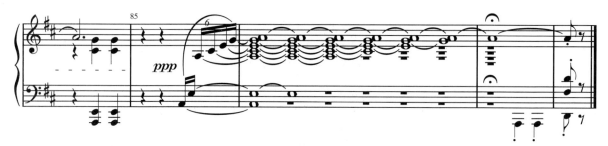

2. Label the chords and NCTs.

Schubert, Symphony in B♭, II

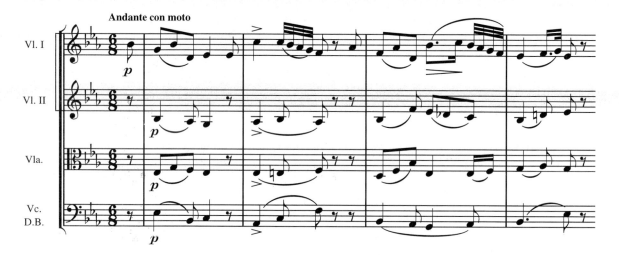

3. Analyze chords and NCTs. To what extent is this example sequential? If you play the first half of m. 1 as a chord, you will discover that there are seven different parts in the texture. To what extent are some of these voices doubling another voice at the octave? Except for this, are there any parallel 8ves to be found?

Schumann, *Romanze,* Op. 28, No. 1

4. Analyze chords and NCTs. To what extent is this example sequential?

♫ Mozart, Violin Sonata K. 481, II

5. This passage, from the beginning of Verdi's *Requiem,* is a beautiful example of *a cappella* writing. It features two circle-of-fifths progressions that employ secondary dominants. Label all chords and NCTs. (The ii°$^{\varnothing 4}_3$ in m. 53 is an example of mode mixture, the subject of Chapter 21.)

Verdi, *Messa da Requiem,* "Requiem aeternam"

ii°$\frac{4}{3}$

6. This excerpt is the introduction to a piece for chorus and piano. Label chords and NCTs.

Schumann, "Beim Abschied zu singen," Op. 84

7. Analyze chords and NCTs, but ignore the grace notes for the purpose of your analysis. Study the four voices that accompany the melody. Do they follow conventional voice-leading principles? What about the melody? Does it contribute an independent fifth voice, or is it sometimes doubling an accompanying line?

Schumann, *Arabesque,* Op. 18

B. For each of the following problems, first analyze the given chord. Next, find a smooth way to lead into the chord. Although there are many possibilities, it will often work to use a chord whose root is a P5 above the root of the secondary dominant. Experiment with other relationships also. Then resolve each chord properly, taking special care with the leading tone and the 7th resolutions. Analyze all chords.

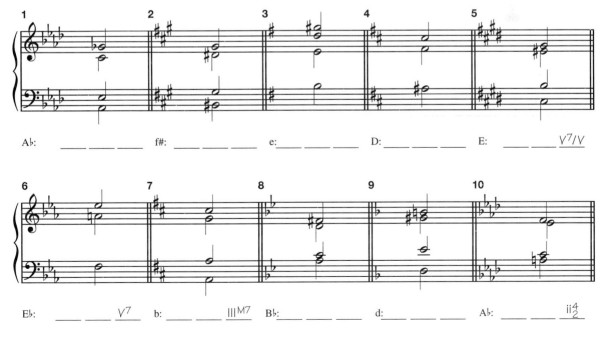

Ab: _____ _____ _____   f#: _____ _____ _____   e: _____ _____ _____   D: _____ _____ _____   E: _____ _____ V^7/V

Eb: _____ _____ V^7 b: _____ _____ III^{M7} Bb: _____ _____ _____   d: _____ _____ _____   Ab: _____ _____ ii^4_2

C. Below each note list the secondary V and V⁷ chords that could harmonize that note.
    You might find it helpful to refer to the charts on page 259.

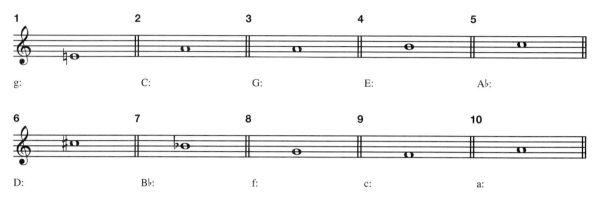

D. Provide roman numerals to show how the first note could be harmonized as a second-
    ary dominant. The second note should be harmonized by the tonicized chord.

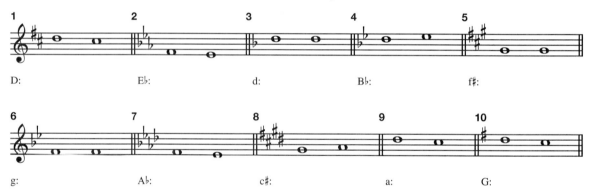

E. Harmonize each chorale phrase for SATB chorus. Include one or more secondary
    dominants in each phrase and activate the texture with some NCTs. Note that the key
    of the phrase does not always agree with the key signature.

F:

e:

F.   Analyze the harmonies specified by each figured bass and make a setting for SATB chorus.

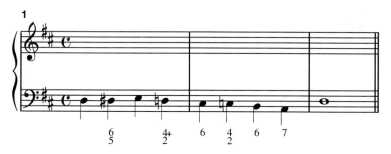

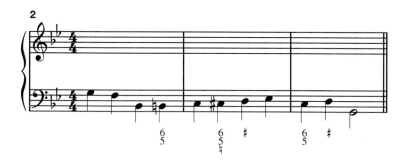

Exercise 16-2 See Workbook.

Chapter 17

Secondary Functions 2

SECONDARY LEADING-TONE CHORDS

The $V^{(7)}$ and vii°$^{(7)}$ chords have similar functions in tonal music (review p. 113), the main difference being that $V^{(7)}$, which contains a P5 above the root, sounds like a more substantial sonority. The same generalizations hold true for secondary functions, which means that any chord that can be tonicized by a $V^{(7)}$ can also be tonicized by a vii°$^{(7)}$.

One small complication arises when a leading-tone seventh chord (as opposed to a leading-tone *triad*) is used as a secondary function. Should the resulting chord be a vii°^{7}/ or a vii^{ø7}/? Almost all examples follow these principles:

1. If the triad to be tonicized is minor, use vii°^{7}/.

2. If the triad to be tonicized is major, use either vii^{ø7}/ or vii°^{7}/, although the fully diminished version appears to be used more often.

Examples 17-1 and 17-2 list all the secondary leading-tone chords in major and minor. While all these chords are theoretically possible, leading-tone chords of ii, IV, iv, V, and vi are more common than the others. One chord, the vii°/III in minor, is identical to a diatonic triad (ii°), and the vii^{ø7}/III is identical to a diatonic seventh chord (ii^{ø7}). The functions of these chords can be made clear only by the context. You might also notice that there is no vii^{ø7}/V in the minor mode, even though the V chord is major. This is an exception to rule 2 above, and the reason for it is that the dominant *key* is minor, even though the dominant triad is major.

EXAMPLE 17-1 *Secondary leading-tone chords in G major*

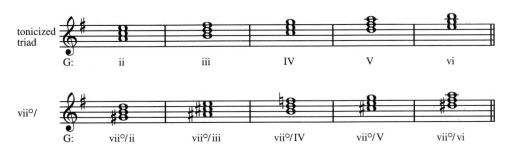

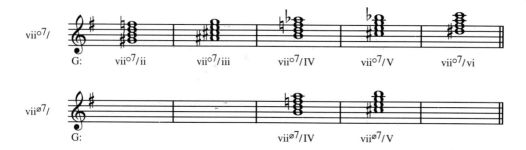

EXAMPLE 17-2   *Secondary leading-tone chords in E minor*

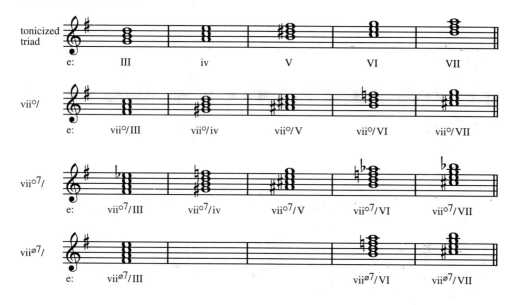

SPELLING SECONDARY LEADING-TONE CHORDS

The procedure for spelling secondary leading-tone chords is not difficult and can be summarized as follows.

1.   Find the root of the chord that is to be tonicized.

2.   Go down a m2.

3.   Using that note as the root, spell a diminished triad (for vii° of), a diminished seventh chord (for vii°7 of), or a half-diminished seventh chord (for viiø7 of).

For example, to spell a vii°⁷/vi in E♭,

1.   The root of vi in E♭ is C.

2.   A m2 below C is B.

3.   A °⁷ chord on B is B–D–F–A♭.

RECOGNIZING SECONDARY LEADING-TONE CHORDS

If you find an altered chord in a passage and it is not a V$^{(7)}$/, there is a good chance it will
be a secondary leading-tone chord. These steps will work in most cases.

1.   Is the chord a diminished triad, a diminished seventh, or a half-diminished seventh
     chord? If not, it is not a secondary leading-tone chord.

2.   Find the note a m2 above the root of the altered chord.

3.   Would a major or minor triad built on that note be a diatonic triad in this key? If so,
     the altered chord is probably a secondary leading-tone chord.

Self-Test 17-1
(Answers begin on page 627.)

A.   Review how to spell secondary leading-tone chords (pp. 276–277). Then notate these
     secondary leading-tone chords in the specified inversion. Include key signatures.

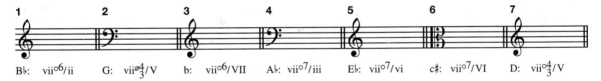

| 1 | 2 | 3 | 4 | 5 | 6 | 7 |

B♭: vii°⁶/ii   G: vii⌀⁴₃/V   b: vii°⁶/VII   A♭: vii°⁷/iii   E♭: vii°⁷/vi   c♯: vii°⁷/VI   D: vii°⁴₃/V

| 8 | 9 | 10 | 11 | 12 | 13 | 14 | 15 |

F: vii°⁶/V   a: vii⌀⁷/VII   E: vii°⁶/vi   G: vii°⁴₃/ii   f: vii°⁶/V   C: vii⌀⁷/IV   g: vii°⁶₅/iv   A: vii°⁶/IV

B. Label any chord that could be a secondary leading-tone chord according to the steps
    outlined on page 277. Label all others with an X.

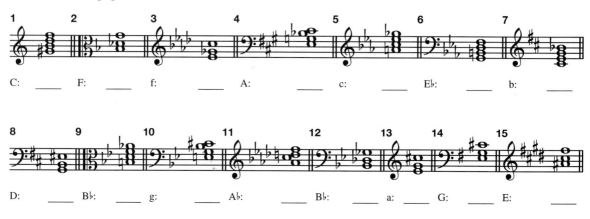

Exercise 17-1 See Workbook.

SECONDARY LEADING-TONE CHORDS IN CONTEXT

Secondary leading-tone chords resolve in the same way as do primary leading-tone
chords—leading tone up, 7th down—but be careful not to double $\hat{7}$ in resolving a vii°⁷/V
or a viiø⁷/V. Smooth voice leading is usually, but not always, a feature of the progressions.
A few examples will give you the idea.

In Example 17-3, Schubert intensifies the motion toward the first cadence by means
of a viiø⁷/V. As with the V/V, the motion to a I$_4^6$ is not considered an irregular resolution
because the I$_4^6$ only delays the V chord.

We noted on page 263 that the V⁽⁷⁾–vi deceptive progression is often embellished by
inserting a V⁽⁷⁾/vi between the V and the vi. Just as common in this context is the vii°⁷/vi,
as in the second phrase of Example 17-3.

EXAMPLE 17-3   *Schubert, "An die Musik," Op. 88, No. 4*

In Example 17-4 we encounter still another variant of the deceptive progression. Here the cadential I_4^6 in m. 2 is followed not by a V but by a vii°^{7}/vi.

EXAMPLE 17-4   *Schumann, "Herberge," Op. 82, No. 6*

A vii°$^4_3$/iv and a vii°$^4_2$ of V both appear in Example 17-5. There is a cadential six-four in m. 67, but there is not a real modulation to F♯ here. You can prove this for yourself by playing through the example. You will almost certainly hear the last chord as V, not I.

EXAMPLE 17-5   *Schumann, "Die feindlichen Brüder," Op. 49, No. 2*

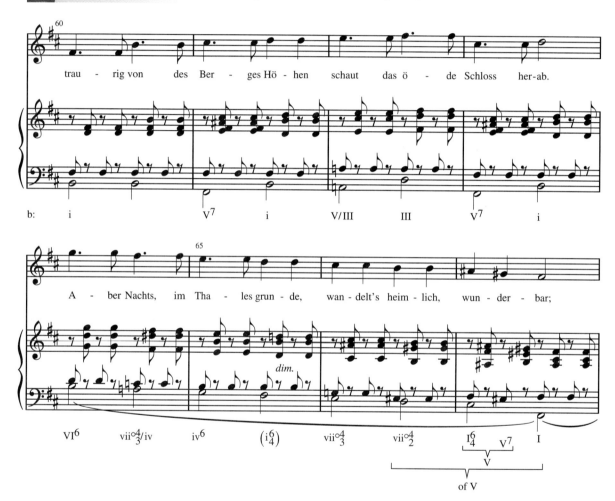

Example 17-6 is interesting in several respects. Notice that the V$^6_5$/V in m. 41 is followed not by a V, as expected, but by a V$^4_3$/IV (we have chosen the A in m. 43 as the bass of the V$^4_3$/IV). This and other unexpected resolutions of secondary functions will be discussed more fully later in this chapter. The V$^4_3$/IV itself resolves normally, as do the vii°$^4_3$/ii and the vii°$^6_5$/ii, except for some liberties taken with the viola part.

EXAMPLE 17-6   *Beethoven, Symphony No. 2, Op. 36, I*

SEQUENCES INVOLVING SECONDARY FUNCTIONS

Sequential patterns often use secondary functions. One that is especially common is the circle-of-fifths sequence, but with one or more secondary functions (V/ or vii°/) substituting for diatonic chords. Below is a short circle-of-fifths sequence, with possible substitutions shown for the first three chords.

Diatonic circle of fifths in C	e^7(iii^7)	$-a^7$(vi^7)	$-d^7$(ii^7)	$-G^7$(V^7)–C(I)
V^7/substitutes	E^7(V^7/vi)	$-A^7$(V^7/ii)	$-D^7$(V^7/V)	
vii°^{7}/substitutes	$g\sharp°^7$(vii°^{7}/vi)	$-c\sharp°^7$(vii°^{7}/ii)	$-f\sharp°^7$(vii°^{7}/V)	

By choosing one chord from each of the first three columns in the chart above, we can make up some variations on the circle-of-fifths progression.

Diatonic version	e^7	–	a^7	–	d^7	–	G^7	–	C
Variation	E^7	–	a^7	–	D^7	–	G^7	–	C
Variation	E^7	–	$c\sharp°^7$	–	d^7	–	G^7	–	C
Variation	$g\sharp°^7$	–	A^7	–	$f\sharp°^7$	–	G^7	–	C

An instance of substitutions of this sort is seen in Example 17-7. There is a circle-of-fifths progression in mm. 2 to 5 that is essentially a VI–ii°–V–i progression, with two °7 chord substitutions.

Diatonic circle of fifths in e	C (VI)	$-f\sharp°$ (ii°)	$-B$ (V)–e (i)
vii°^{7}/substitutes		$a\sharp°^7$	$d\sharp°^7$
		(vii°^{7}/V)	(vii°^{7})

🎵 **EXAMPLE 17-7**   *Beethoven, Piano Sonata Op. 14, No. 1, II*

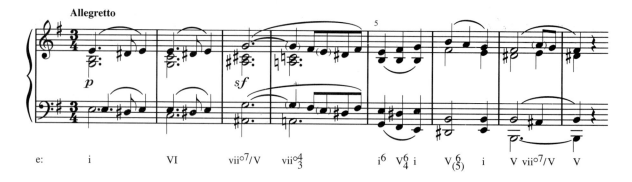

When a series of major-minor seventh chords is used in a circle-of-fifths sequence, certain voice-leading problems come up. For one thing, as you learned on page 262, each leading tone will resolve down by chromatic half step to become the 7th of the next major-minor seventh chord. Also, as you might recall from page 249, if the chords are in root position in a four-part texture, incomplete seventh chords must alternate with complete seventh chords. These points are illustrated in Example 17-8.

EXAMPLE 17-8

The voice leading in Example 17-8 is the precise voice leading Mozart uses in Example 17-9. However, he goes a step "too far," to an E♭⁷ in m. 58, implying a resolution to A♭. A change of key from B♭ to A♭ would be quite unexpected here. For five measures Mozart prolongs the suspense, until the E♭ in the bass is finally bent up to E♮, creating a vii°⁷/V in B♭. This leads back to a PAC in B♭. Notice also the A♭⁶₄ chords (pedal six-fours) that occur in mm. 58 to 61, adding to the listener's anticipation of A♭ as the goal. In studying this example, remember that the basses on the bottom staff sound an octave lower than written.

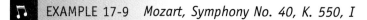 EXAMPLE 17-9   *Mozart, Symphony No. 40, K. 550, I*

Checkpoint

1. The root of a secondary leading-tone chord is how far below the root of the chord being tonicized?
2. Which of these is correct?
    vii°⁷/ii
    vii^ø⁷/ii
3. Name the only major triad that is never tonicized by a secondary vii^ø⁷.
4. Name two substitutes for a d⁷ chord in a circle-of-fifths progression.

DECEPTIVE RESOLUTIONS OF SECONDARY FUNCTIONS

Although you will find that most secondary $V^{(7)}$ and $vii^{\circ(7)}$ chords resolve as expected, you might encounter many interesting exceptions. One that is especially common is the resolution of a $V^7/$ up to the vi (or VI) of the chord that was being tonicized. For example, in the key of C:

Chords	D^7	e
Analysis	V^7/V	vi/V
		(iii)

A beautiful example of a deceptive resolution involving $V^7/vi–VI/vi$ occurs near the end of one of Schumann's songs (Ex. 17-10). The $vii^{\circ 7}/V$ that follows appears to be misspelled (B–D–F–G♯ instead of B–D–F–A♭), but $vii^{\circ 7}/V$ is frequently notated enharmonically when it is followed by a cadential I^6_4, as it is here, producing G♯–A instead of A♭–A♮. The use of enharmonic spellings will be discussed in more detail in Chapter 25. (Incidentally, does the beginning of Ex. 17-10 remind you of a familiar Christmas carol?)

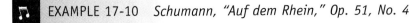 **EXAMPLE 17-10**   *Schumann, "Auf dem Rhein," Op. 51, No. 4*

Another kind of deceptive resolution was seen in Example 17-6, in which a V^6_5/V was followed by as V^4_3/IV. One of the reasons this progression "works" here is that it features smooth voice leading, summarized in Example 17-11a. Even smoother is the connection between any two Mm7 chords a m3 apart (Ex. 17-11b and c) or, surprisingly, a tritone apart (Ex. 17-11d) because all such pairs of Mm7 chords share two pitch classes. In the example, the common tones are tied. Notice that the remaining voices move by half step in contrary motion. Play through the example and notice how surprisingly convincing these progressions sound.

EXAMPLE 17-11

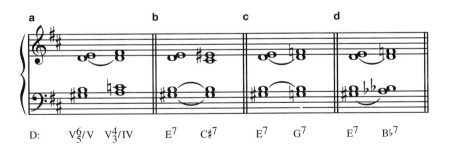

In Example 17-12 there is a root movement down a m3 from the V^4_2/IV (F^7) to the V^7/ii (D7). Notice that the composer (who was Felix Mendelssohn's sister) retains the common tones A and C in the same registers and moves the outer voices chromatically in contrary motion.

EXAMPLE 17-12   *Fanny Mendelssohn Hensel, "Von dir, mein Lieb, ich scheiden muss"*

OTHER SECONDARY FUNCTIONS

We have discussed secondary dominants, secondary leading-tone chords, and, in the preceding section, secondary submediants. Other secondary functions do occur, but less commonly. We tend to hear a change of key when we encounter several chords that are drawing our attention away from the original tonic. However, a short progression of chords will generally not be enough to accomplish a change of key, and it is in such passages that other secondary functions occasionally occur.

Listen to Example 17-13. Although one could argue in favor of a quick change of key to C in mm. 69 to 70, it is unlikely that we would really lose track of G as the tonal center so quickly. In this case, IV^6/IV would seem to be a better analysis than IV^6 in the key of C.

EXAMPLE 17-13 *Mozart, Sonata K. 545, II*

Example 17-14 is considerably more complicated, but it is worth the effort. You might want to begin by playing through the textural reduction that follows the example. The basic outline of the progression is I–V–I–iii–ii–V–I, but the iii and ii chords are elaborated by ii–V–i progressions of their own. Underlying all of this is an unusually long circle-of-fifths progression that involves the root of every chord in the excerpt except the first: A–D–G♯–C♯–F♯–B–E–A–D. Despite the harmonic complexity, the passage flows seamlessly, part of a famous theme that surely must be listened to, if you don't know it already.

Finally, notice that although the chords that are the point of this discussion—the ii^{ø7}/iii and the ii^{ø7}/ii—are spelled the same as a vii^{ø7}/V and a vii^{ø7}/IV, respectively, we can tell from the context that they are secondary ii^{ø7} chords, not secondary vii^{ø7} chords.

EXAMPLE 17-14   *Tchaikovsky, Symphony No. 5, Op. 64, II*
(Instruments sound where written)

Summary

Any chord that can be tonicized by a secondary dominant can also be tonicized by a secondary leading-tone chord. The vii°/ and vii°⁷/ chords may be used to tonicize major or minor triads, but the vii°⁷/ may tonicize only major triads. However, a major chord that is never tonicized by vii°⁷/ is the V chord in minor.

To spell a secondary leading-tone chord, go down a m2 from the root of the chord that is to be tonicized and spell a diminished triad (for vii° of), a diminished seventh chord (for vii°⁷ of), or a half-diminished seventh chord (for vii°⁷ of). To determine whether an altered chord that you encounter in analysis might be a secondary leading-tone chord, see whether it is a diminished triad, a diminished seventh chord, or a half-diminished seventh chord with a root that is a m2 below a scale degree that usually carries a major or minor triad in that key. If so, the altered chord is probably a secondary leading-tone chord.

Secondary dominant or leading-tone chords are frequently substituted for diatonic chords in circle-of-fifths sequences. A substituted secondary dominant will have the same root as the diatonic chord for which it substitutes, whereas a substituted secondary leading-tone chord will have a root a M3 higher.

The vii°⁷/vi is used in two more variants of the deceptive progression: V⁷–vii°⁷/vi–vi and I⁶₄–vii°⁷/vi–vi. In addition, secondary dominants may themselves resolve deceptively, usually to the vi (or VI) of the chord being tonicized. Secondary functions other than V, vii°, and vi also occur occasionally.

Self-Test 17-2
(Answers begin on page 627.)

A. Analysis

   1. Label chords and NCTs.

     Bach, "Warum betrübst du dich, mein Herz"

2. Label chords and NCTs. Review pages 284–285, then find two circle-of-fifths
   progressions that contain more than three chords. Remember that a leading-tone
   chord may substitute for a chord in the circle-of-fifths.

Haydn, Sonata No. 43, Minuetto I

3. Label chords and NCTs. Remember that the bass notes continue sounding until
   the pedal is lifted. The last eighth note in the melody is a rather unusual NCT.
   Discuss how it might be analyzed.

Mendelssohn, *Song without Words,* Op. 102, No. 1

4. Label chords and NCTs. Analyze the chords in m. 47 in two ways: once in the key of F, once in some key hinted at in m. 46.

Mozart, Sonata K. 333, I

5. Label chords and NCTs. Explain why this excerpt is not a period. Do not
include the grace notes in your analysis.

 Mozart, Violin Sonata K. 379, I

6. Label the chords with roman numerals. Label NCTs in the bassoon part only.
Analyze the chords from the middle of m. 88 to the middle of m. 90 in some
key other than B♭. Bracket the longest circle-of-fifths progression you can find.

Mozart, Bassoon Concerto K. 191, I

B. For each of these problems, first analyze and resolve the given chord, being espe-
    cially careful with the 7th chord and the leading tone. Then find a smooth way to
    lead into the given chord. Analyze all chords.

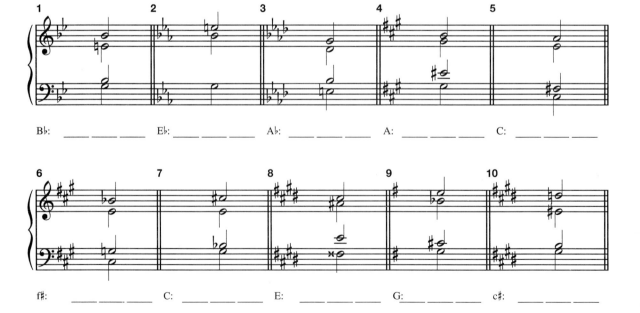

C. Harmonize each of these chorale phrases for SATB chorus. Include at least one secondary leading-tone chord or incorporate some other aspect discussed in this chapter
   in each harmonization.

e:

A:

b:

D. Analyze the harmonies specified by each figured bass, then make an arrangement of
   each for SATB chorus.

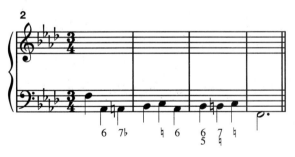

Exercise 17-2 See Workbook.

Chapter **18**

B^6 ii^6

$c: i^6$

Modulations Using
Diatonic Common Chords

MODULATION AND CHANGE OF KEY

Almost all compositions from the tonal era begin and end in the same key. Sometimes the *mode* will be changed, usually from minor to major, but the *keynote* (tonic note) remains the same. A piece that begins in c minor and ends in C major is still in C. Even multi-movement works begin and end in the same key if the movements are intended to be performed together as a unit. (An interesting exception to this is the song cycle.) The principle also holds for single movements from multimovement works (sonatas, symphonies, song cycles, and so on), although the interior movements will often be in different keys. We will use the term *change of key* for such situations, as in "There is a change of key from C major in the first movement to F major in the second movement."

 Modulation is another matter. A modulation is a shift of tonal center that takes place *within* an individual movement. Although a tonal work or movement begins and ends in the same key, other tonalities generally will be hinted at, referred to, or even strongly established. The longer the work, the more time is likely to be devoted to tonalities other than the tonic and the more keys are likely to be touched on.

 The tonal structure of a composition is closely related to its overall form. For example, a Classical piano sonata might have the following tonal structure. The crooked arrows represent modulations, and roman numerals represent other keys in relation to the tonic.

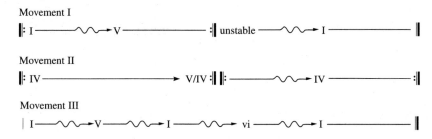

MODULATION AND TONICIZATION

The line between modulation and tonicization (using secondary functions—V/V and so on) is not clearly defined in tonal music, nor is it meant to be. One listener might find that a very short passage tonicizing a new tonality is enough to make a convincing modulation. For instance, you might have heard some of the excerpts in Chapters 16 and 17 as modulations, whereas other listeners might not have. The single most important factor in convincing the listener of a modulation is time, although other elements, such as a cadential I_4^6–V or V/V in the new key, contribute as well. Listen to Example 18-1. At the end of the excerpt, do you hear C or A as tonic? You could analyze this passage as *tonicizing* C or as *modulating* to C major. The difference in the analyses would not be an important one. There is no right or wrong here—there are just the interpretations of different listeners.

♪ **EXAMPLE 18-1** *Beethoven, Symphony No. 7, Op. 92, II*

It seems clear, however, that composers have always hoped the sophisticated listener (surely a minority of the audience) would manage to follow the modulations aurally. If not, many important effects would be lost. For example, if a composer has brought back a tune in another key when we had expected it to return in tonic, the composer expects us to be surprised. Otherwise, why bother? The fact that such effects might be lost on many listeners should not keep us from trying to appreciate what the composer is doing.

KEY RELATIONSHIPS

Two keys that sound the same but that are spelled differently are called *enharmonically equivalent keys.* C♯ major and D♭ major are enharmonically equivalent. If a composer for some reason respells C♯ as D♭, no modulation has occurred because the keynote is unchanged.

If a major key and a minor key have the same tonic tone, they are called *parallel keys.* The parallel minor of C major is c minor. Because parallel keys share the same tonic, we do not use the term *modulation* when talking about movement from one key to its parallel. The term *change of mode,* or *mode mixture,* is used instead. (Mode mixture is discussed in more detail in Chapter 21.)

If a major key and a minor key share the same key signature, they are called *relative keys.* The relative minor of C major is a minor. The term *modulation* is appropriate here because movement from one tonic to another is involved. Modulations between relative keys are common, especially from minor to relative major.

Most modulations in tonal music are between *closely related keys.* Two keys are said to be closely related if there is a difference of no more than one sharp or flat in their key signatures. Because this definition applies to both major and minor keys, it includes the relative major or minor key, where there is no difference at all in the key signatures. Here are the keys closely related to C major and c minor.

Starting Key: C major		
1♯	G	e
0♯, 0♭	Ⓒ	a
1♭	F	d

Starting Key: c minor		
2♭	g	B♭
3♭	ⓒ	E♭
4♭	f	A♭

Another way to find the keys closely related to some starting key is to take the keys represented by the tonic, subdominant, and dominant triads and their relatives. In minor use the natural minor scale in determining the closely related keys.

closely related key — 1♯ or ♭ difference

Starting Key: C major		
Dominant	G	e
Tonic	Ⓒ	a
Subdominant	F	d

Starting Key: c minor		
Dominant	g	B♭
Tonic	ⓒ	E♭
Subdominant	f	A♭

Still another method is to take the keys represented by the diatonic major and minor triads (only) of the home key. Again, use natural minor for the minor keys. The diatonic major and minor triads are also those that can be tonicized by secondary dominant or secondary leading-tone chords.

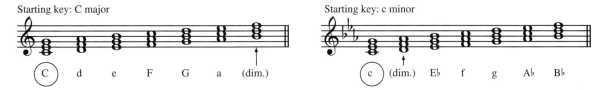

Starting key: C major
C   d   e   F   G   a   (dim.)

Starting key: c minor
c   (dim.)   E♭   f   g   A♭   B♭

If you compare the three methods above, you will see that each approach yields the same result. There are always five keys closely related to the starting key. Use whichever method seems easiest to you.

All key relationships that are not enharmonic, parallel, relative, or closely related are called *foreign relationships,* and such pairs of keys are said to be *distantly related.* Some relationships are more foreign than others. Often we describe foreign key relationships in terms of simpler relationships used in the composition. Thus, a modulation from C major to D major might be described as a modulation to the dominant of the dominant; one from C major to E♭ major might be called a modulation to the relative major of the parallel minor.

Checkpoint

1. Is movement from E major to e minor a modulation? Explain. If not, what is it called? What about a♯ minor to b♭ minor?
2. Compare and contrast *modulation* and *change of key.*
3. Name the five kinds of key relationships (discussed on pp. 302–303).
4. Describe three ways to find the five keys closely related to some starting key.

Self-Test 18-1
(Answers begin on page 633.)

A. Name the relative key in each case.

    1. D _____   **2.** b♭ _____   **3.** f♯ _____   **4.** C♭ _____   **5.** F _____

    6. d♯ _____   **7.** E _____   **8.** f _____   **9.** E♭ _____   **10.** g♯ _____

B. Name all the closely related keys to the given key. Be sure to use uppercase for major, lowercase for minor.

    1. B♭: _____   _____   _____   _____   _____

    2. D♭: _____   _____   _____   _____   _____

    3. c: _____   _____   _____   _____   _____

    4. a♯: _____   _____   _____   _____   _____

    5. c♯: _____   _____   _____   _____   _____

    6. A: _____   _____   _____   _____   _____

C. Name the relationship in each case (enharmonically equivalent, parallel, relative and closely related, closely related, or foreign).

    1. G/f _____   **6.** C♭/G♭ _____

    2. B/E _____   **7.** d/D _____

    3. a♯/b♭ _____   **8.** E♭/D♭ _____

    4. c/A♭ _____   **9.** B♭/g _____

    5. f♯/A _____   **10.** c♯/F♯ _____

Exercise 18-1 See Workbook.

COMMON-CHORD MODULATION

Most modulations are made smoother by using one or more chords that are common to both keys as an intersection between them. The *common chord* (or chords) serves as a hinge or pivot linking the two tonalities. In the diagram below, the shaded rectangle represents the common chord (also called a pivot chord) in a modulation from B♭ to F.

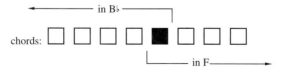

Whereas any pair of closely related keys will have at least one diatonic triad in common, this is not always the case with foreign key relationships. Modulation to a foreign key often requires the use of an altered chord as a common chord; techniques for such modulations are presented in Chapter 19.

To discover the potential common chords between two keys, simply consider the diatonic triads found in the first key to see whether they also occur in the second key. For example, there are four triads in common between B♭ and F.

First key, B♭	I	ii	iii	IV	V	vi	vii°
Triads in B♭	B♭	c	d	E♭	F	g	a°
Triads in F	B♭	C	d	e°	F	g	a
Second key, F	IV	V	vi	vii°	I	ii	iii

In minor keys, we usually consider the chord types commonly found on each scale degree: i, ii°, III, iv, V, VI, vii° (less frequently, other chords that occur in minor, such as IV and v, are used as common chords). This yields two common chords between B♭ major and c minor.

First key, B♭	I	ii	iii	IV	V	vi	vii°
Triads in B♭	B♭	c	d	E♭	F	g	a°
Triads in c	b°	c	d°	E♭	f	G	A♭
Second key, c	vii°	i	ii°	III	iv	V	VI

Example 18-2 illustrates a modulation from B♭ major to c minor, using the ii in B♭ as the common chord. Notice the symbol used to show the common-chord modulation.

EXAMPLE 18-2

When you are composing a modulation, you will find that the V or vii° in either key is often the least successful choice as common chord. As Example 18-3a illustrates, such a modulation can sound too abrupt. The modulation will be smoother if the V–I progression in the new key is delayed by several chords, especially through the use of a deceptive progression, a cadential six-four, or both, as in Example 18-3b.

EXAMPLE 18-3

The smooth voice leading in the outer voices of Example 18-3b also contributes to making this modulation to a foreign key convincing and successful.

ANALYZING COMMON-CHORD MODULATION

In analyzing modulations, the procedure to follow is this.

1. Listen to the passage carefully.

2. Find the first chord that seems to be functioning more naturally in the second key than in the first one. (This step is open to differing interpretations, but often this chord contains an accidental not found in the first key.)

In Example 18-4 the f♯° chord in the middle of m. 5 serves as a vii°⁶ in G but only as a secondary leading-tone chord in C. This is the chord that signals the modulation. Backing up one chord to the beginning of the measure brings us to the common chord, C (I = IV).

EXAMPLE 18-4 *Mozart, Viennese Sonatina No. 6, II*

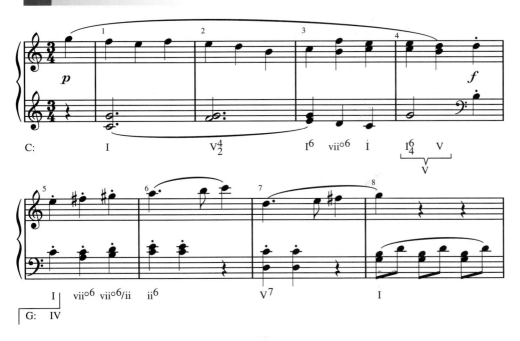

Example 18-4 is "recomposed" in Example 18-5 to illustrate the fact that the common chord itself does not signal the modulation but just smooths it out. In Example 18-5 the C chord is followed not by a modulation to G but by a cadence in C.

EXAMPLE 18-5

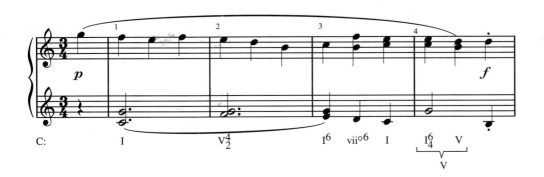

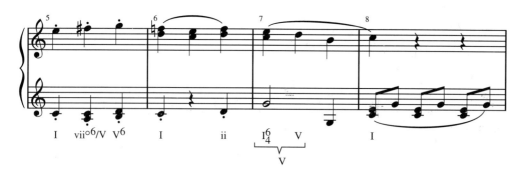

The most common modulation in major keys is I–V, as in Example 18-4. In minor keys, modulations to III or to v are the most frequently encountered. Example 18-6 illustrates a i–III modulation. The C7 chord (B♭ is the implied bass note) functions more naturally in F than in d and is preceded by the common chord.

EXAMPLE 18-6   *Tchaikovsky, Mazurka Op. 39, No. 10*

Incidentally, you might hear some of the examples and exercises in this chapter as tonicizations instead of true modulations. Analyze them as modulations anyway for practice in locating common chords.

Although I–V and i–III are the most frequently encountered modulations, all other closely related modulations do occur. In Example 18-7, the tonality moves briefly from I to iii. Notice that there is no change of key signature here. Indeed, the key signature of the main tonality is usually maintained throughout the work, no matter how many modulations occur.

EXAMPLE 18-7 *Dvořák, Quartet Op. 51, IV*

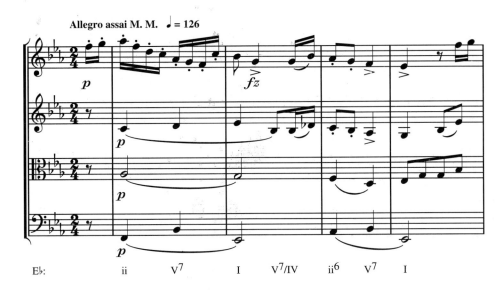

E♭:   ii   V⁷   I   V⁷/IV   ii⁶   V⁷   I

ii   V⁷   I   vi   i⁶₄   V⁷   i

g: iv

Summary

A modulation is a shift of tonal center that takes place within an individual movement. A tonicization is like a short modulation, and listeners frequently will disagree as to whether a particular passage really modulates.

Enharmonically equivalent keys sound the same but are spelled differently. If major and minor keys have the same tonic note, they are called *parallel keys*. A *change of mode* (or mutation), but not a modulation, occurs when music moves between two parallel keys. If two major and minor keys share the same key signature, they are called *relative keys*. Two keys are said to be *closely related* if their key signatures differ by no more than one accidental. All key relationships that are not enharmonic, parallel, relative, or closely related are called *foreign relationships,* and such pairs of keys are said to be *distantly related*.

Common-chord modulations use one or more chords that are diatonic to both keys as a kind of hinge or pivot linking the two tonalities. Whereas any two closely related keys will have at least one diatonic triad in common (and therefore available as a common chord), this will not necessarily be true of two distantly related keys.

To discover the potential common chords between two keys, list the diatonic triads found in the first key to see whether they also occur in the second key. To analyze a common-chord modulation, find the first chord that functions more convincingly in the second key than in the first, then back up one chord. If there is a diatonic common chord between the two keys, this should be where it is found.

Self-Test 18-2
(Answers begin on page 634.)

A. Analysis.

   1. This excerpt begins and ends in e, with a modulation to the relative major in between. Label chords and NCTs, showing the common chords as demonstrated in this chapter.

Bach, "Keinen hat Gott verlassen"

2. Label chords and NCTs. Why is it unlikely that Bach was thinking of the sonority on the last eighth of m. 7 as a seventh chord?

Bach, "Jesu, Jesu, du bist mein"

3. This song firmly establishes e minor at the beginning and then briefly modulates to a foreign key. Label chords and NCTs. (You will probably not be able
to analyze this modulation if you do not play it slowly on the piano.)

Schubert, "Auf dem Flusse," Op. 89, No. 7

4. Label chords and NCTs. Remember this is an excerpt; don't be fooled by the
key signature.

Schubert, "Am Feierabend," Op. 25, No. 5

5. Label chords and NCTs. Find the longest circle-of-fifths harmonic progression in the excerpt. To what extent does that progression generate a sequence in the melody and bass lines?

Schumann, "Freisinn," Op. 25, No. 2

euren Hüt-ten, eu-ren Zel - ten! Und ich rei - te froh in al - le

Fer - ne, ü - ber mei - ner Mü-tze nur die Ster - ne.

B. Fill in the name of the new key on the second line of each exercise.

1. B♭:   I   V   I   ii⁶   V   vi

                         ___: ii   V$_3^4$ I   V⁷   I

2. f♯:   i   V   VI   iv⁶

                         ___: ii⁶   V   vi   IV   V   I

3. d: i   V$_5^6$/iv   iv   V$_2^4$ i⁶

                         ___: iv⁶   (i$_4^6$)   ii°$_5^6$ V$_2^4$ i⁶   vii°⁶   i

4. A: I   V   vi   ii⁶   vii°⁶

                         ___: ii°⁶   i$_4^6$ V   i
                                             V

5. E♭   I   V$_3^4$ I⁶   IV

                         ___: I   vii°⁶   I⁶   V$_2^4$ I⁶   ii⁶   V   I

C. List the diatonic triads that could serve as common chords between each pair of keys. In minor keys, assume the usual chord qualities: i, ii°, III, iv, V, VI, vii°.

Example:	First key:	C:	I	iii	V	vi
	Triads:		C	e	G	a
	Second key:	G:	IV	vi	I	ii

1. First key, A♭:

Triads:

Second key, D♭:

2. First key, c:

Triads:

Second key, f:

3. First key, a:

Triads:

Second key, F:

4. First key, G:

Triads:

Second key, D:

5. First key, c♯:

Triads:

Second key, E:

6. First key, D:

Triads:

Second key, f♯:

D. Make choral settings of part B, progressions 1 (SATB) and 2 (SAB). Activate the texture with NCTs and/or arpeggiations. Arrange the metric structure so that the last chord comes on a strong beat.

E.   Harmonize the following chorale tune for SATB chorus. The first phrase should modulate to V; the second should return to I.

F.   Analyze the chords specified by this figured bass, then make an arrangement for SATB chorus.

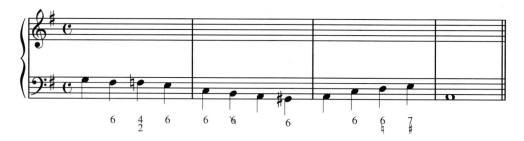

Exercise 18-2 See Workbook.

Chapter 19

Some Other Modulatory Techniques

ALTERED CHORDS AS COMMON CHORDS

In Chapter 18 we discussed modulations using chords that are diatonic in both keys as common chords. Although diatonic common-chord modulation is probably the most frequently used modulatory technique, there are many others. This chapter will present a few of them.

In Chapter 18 we listed a three-step procedure for the analysis of modulations. These steps bear repeating here.

1. Listen to the passage carefully.
2. Find the first chord that seems to be more directly related to the second key than to the first one.
3. Back up one chord. If there is a diatonic common chord, it should be in this position.

The phrase "if there is a diatonic common chord" might have suggested to you that altered chords may sometimes be used as common chords. For example, consider the modulation represented below:

Key of G: ————————▶

...D^7 G   a   A^7 D...

Key of D: ————————▶

Here the first chord that is more directly related to D than to G is the A^7 (V^7 in D). However, the a minor triad that precedes it cannot serve as a common chord because it makes no sense in the context of D major. Instead, the A^7 is itself the common chord, functioning as V^7/V in G. This modulation is illustrated in Example 19-1.

317

EXAMPLE 19-1   *Beethoven, Sonata Op. 14, No. 2, I*

G: V$^4_3$ I^6 ii^6 V$^6_5$/V   I

                                                                         D: V$^6_5$

Secondary V$^{(7)}$ and vii°$^{(7)}$ chords can be used as common chords. The chord might be a secondary function in the first key, in the second key, or in both keys. Sometimes the secondary function coincides with the *point of modulation* (the first chord in the new key), as in Example 19-1, while at other times the secondary function precedes it.

A number of other altered chords, to be discussed in Chapters 21 and 22, frequently serve as the common chord in a modulation, as examples in those chapters will illustrate. An additional common-chord technique involving enharmonic reinterpretation of the common chord is the principal topic of Chapter 25.

SEQUENTIAL MODULATION

It is not uncommon for a modulation to come about through the use of a sequence. This is a simple device: the composer merely states something at one pitch level and then states it again immediately at another pitch level. However, the modulating sequence, instead of being diatonic, tonicizes a different pitch. Often a common chord could be analyzed in such a modulation, but the sequence is equally important in establishing the new tonal center.

Example 19-2 is a clear instance of a sequential modulation. The first phrase, in C major, is transposed with little change up to d minor to create the second phrase. Sequences up by step are very frequently encountered. Notice that the d:i could also have functioned as C:ii, so this modulation is both sequential and by common chord.

EXAMPLE 19-2 *Schubert, Sonata in E Major, III*

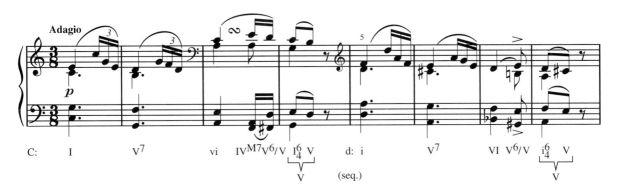

Whereas the sequential motion in Example 19-2 is up by step, that in Example 19-3 is down by step, from C major to B♭ major. (Some would analyze these measures as G: IV–V$_2^4$–I^6 followed by the same progression in F.)

EXAMPLE 19-3 *Beethoven, Sonata Op. 53, I*

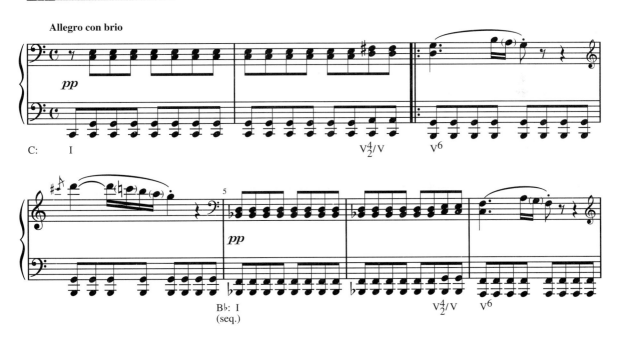

Keep in mind that many modulations are of short duration and might more properly be called tonicizations. Both Examples 19-2 and 19-3 return to the first key immediately after the sequence.

Another common pattern for sequential modulation is the circle of fifths. The circle-of-fifths sequences we have studied so far have been diatonic (such as vi–ii–V–I), with occasional secondary functions thrown in. However, the circle of fifths can be used to get from one key to another. In Example 19-4 Haydn moves from B major to the IV of G major through the progression B–E–A–D–G–C, each chord except the last becoming a V of the chord that follows. The sequence could have been stopped earlier, or it could have been carried past C to F, B♭, and so on, options that are basically open in any sequential modulation.

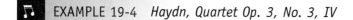 EXAMPLE 19-4   *Haydn, Quartet Op. 3, No. 3, IV*

MODULATION BY COMMON TONE

In some modulations the hinge between the two keys is not a common chord but a common tone. Unlike the common-chord modulation, where the progression usually makes the modulation smooth and undramatic, common-tone modulations often announce themselves clearly to the listener by isolating the common tone. This is the case in Example 19-5, where the note F♯ joins the keys of b minor and D major.

EXAMPLE 19-5 *Mozart, Fantasia K. 475*

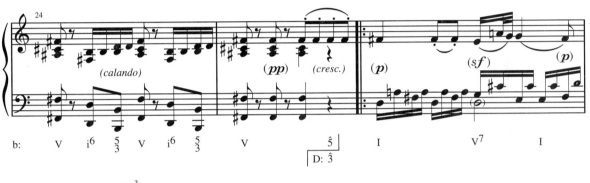

Even more dramatic is Example 19-6, which occurs at the end of the slow introduction to Beethoven's Symphony No. 4. Here an A links a pianissimo V in d minor with a fortissimo V⁷ in B♭ major.

EXAMPLE 19-6   *Beethoven, Symphony No. 4, Op. 60, I*

The two chords linked by the common tone in a common-tone modulation usually exhibit a *chromatic mediant relationship,* which has the following characteristics.

1.   The roots of the chords are a m3 or M3 apart. Sometimes the m3 or M3 is spelled enharmonically.

2.   They are either both major triads or both minor triads (or, in the case of seventh chords, the triad portions of the chords are both major or both minor).

Some examples of chromatic mediant relationships are illustrated in Example 19-7.

EXAMPLE 19-7

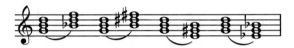

The chromatic mediant relationships that were used by Mozart and Beethoven in Examples 19-5 and 19-6 are shown in Example 19-8.

EXAMPLE 19-8

In both the Mozart and the Beethoven examples the two keys involved were closely related. However, the chromatic mediant relationship used in common-tone modulations makes it easy to modulate to foreign keys as well. In Example 19-9 Brahms begins a movement from a symphony with a melody that emphasizes E, C, and G—the notes of a C major triad. The listener might expect the music to continue in C major, but in the fourth measure the note E is isolated, after which it becomes the tonic of E major. C major and E major are in a chromatic mediant relationship to each other.

EXAMPLE 19-9   *Brahms, Symphony No. 4, Op. 98, II (piano arrangement)*

C: $\hat{3}$
E: $\hat{1}$

MONOPHONIC MODULATION

Sometimes a modulation is carried out by a single vocal or instrumental line. This is done by introducing and emphasizing the tones that are found in the second key but not in the first. Although harmonies are more or less clearly implied in a monophonic modulation, it is often best just to label the keys, as we have done in Example 19-10.

EXAMPLE 19-10   *Mozart, Sonata K. 576, II*

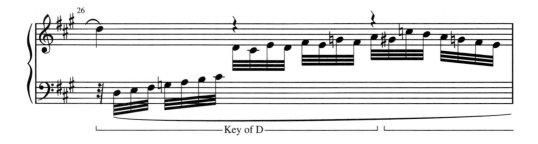

Key of D

This passage is also sequential, but it is not an example of a sequential modulation. The pattern in mm. 26 to 27 (D to e) is moved up a step (e to f♯), but the modulation is not caused by the sequence itself.

DIRECT MODULATION

Sometimes modulations occur without any attempt to smooth them over through the use of common chords or common tones. Such modulations most frequently occur between phrases, so this kind of direct modulation is often called a *phrase modulation*. A typical example from a chorale appears in Example 19-11.

EXAMPLE 19-11   *Bach, "Für Freuden, lasst uns springen"*

Most phrase modulations could also be analyzed as common-chord or common-tone modulations or both, as is the case here: the I in B♭ could be analyzed as a III in g minor,
whereas the D4 in the tenor provides a common tone between the V in g minor and the I
in B♭ major. Such analyses are not incorrect, but we prefer the term *phrase modulation*
because it more accurately reflects the way we hear this excerpt—as one phrase ending in
g minor and another beginning in B♭ major, with little effort being made to bridge the gap.

Some direct modulations occur *within* the phrase. However, this kind of modulation is
not frequently encountered, and you should try to eliminate all the other possibilities for
explaining the modulation before labeling it a direct modulation.

Example 19-12 shows a textural reduction of the kind of difficult modulatory passage
that you might occasionally encounter. Play through the example slowly (you will defi-
nitely need to hear it), observing the analysis below.

EXAMPLE 19-12   *Mozart, Fantasia K. 475, mm. 6–16 (simplified)*

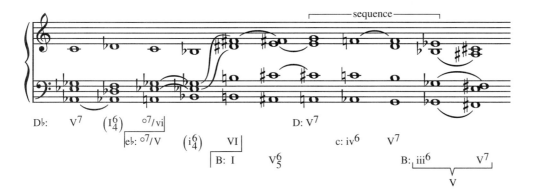

The first two tonicizations (these are too short to be called modulations), D♭ → e♭ and e♭ → B, are achieved by common chords. Next, a short sequence hints at D major (or minor) and c minor. The key of B then emerges as the goal of the passage. In a larger sense, the sequence connects the V_5^6 in B to the root position V^7 in B, which makes the sequence somewhat less important harmonically than the rest of the passage. The fleeting tonicizations of D and c would be considered direct because no other reasonable explanation is available.

Checkpoint

1. What do we call a modulation that is carried out by a single vocal or instrumental line?
2. What kind of modulation involves transposing a pattern up or down to a new key?
3. What is the term for a modulation in which a single tone joins the two keys?
4. Name the other two types of modulation discussed in this chapter.

Summary

Although diatonic common-chord modulations are the type most frequently encountered, other kinds of modulation do exist. For example, a chord that is an *altered chord* in one or both keys may serve as the common chord. The only altered chords we have studied so far are secondary functions, but we will study others in later chapters. Another possibility is the *sequential modulation,* in which the transposition of a pattern causes the change of tonal center. In a *modulation by common tone,* a single tone serves as the common element between the two keys. The chords joined by the common tone usually exhibit a *chromatic mediant* relationship. A single unharmonized line establishes the new tonal center in a *monophonic modulation.* A modulation that uses no common chords or common tones is a *direct modulation.* Because most direct modulations occur between phrases, this kind of modulation is often called a *phrase modulation.*

Self-Test 19-1
(Answers begin on page 640.)

A. Analysis

   1. Analyze chords and NCTs. In addition, label the approach to the 7th of each seventh chord (review pp. 221–222).

 Bach, "Die Nacht ist kommen"

2. This excerpt begins in D♭ major and ends in A major. Are these two keys in a chromatic mediant relationship? Listen to the excerpt carefully to determine the modulatory technique employed. Label all chords and NCTs.

Schubert, "Im Gegenwartigen Vergangenes," D. 710

3. In this excerpt mm. 10 to 12 and 17 to 19 are all in the same key. Label the chords in those measures with roman numerals. Label the chords in mm. 13 to 16 with roman numerals in another key. Listen to mm. 11 to 14. How is the second key achieved? The return to the first key comes with the last chord in m. 16. What would be the best way to describe this kind of modulation?

Schubert, "Der Wegweiser," Op. 89, No. 20

mir ver - steck-te __ Ste - ge durch ver - schnei-te __ Fel - sen - höhn, _ durch _ Fel - sen - höhn?

4. Name the two keys established in this excerpt. How is the modulation accomplished? What is the relationship between the two keys?

Mozart, Symphony No. 41, K. 551, I

B. Analyze the harmonies implied by the soprano-bass framework below. Then add alto and tenor parts. Identify the modulatory technique used.

C.   Follow the same instructions as for part B, but enliven the texture with NCTs and
     arpeggiations.

g:

Exercise 19-1 See Workbook.

Chapter 20

Binary and Ternary Forms

FORMAL TERMINOLOGY

In Chapter 10 you learned the terminology of period forms—such terms as *phrase, contrasting period,* and *parallel double period.* These terms are widely used and have generally accepted meanings. The terms we introduce in this chapter are also widely used, but writers on musical form disagree on some important aspects of their meanings. In addition, some writers recognize and name subcategories and modifications of the formal types discussed in this chapter. Although our approach attempts to find a common ground among the various systems, you should be aware that any book on musical form that you might read will disagree with our definitions to some extent.

BINARY FORMS

The word *binary* has to do with the concept of twoness. You are probably familiar with binary arithmetic, in which only two digits are used. In music a *binary form* is one that consists of two approximately equivalent sections, although they may be of unequal length. "Approximately equivalent" means that we would not use the term *binary* for a piece just because it has an introduction; the introduction is obviously not equivalent to the main body of the work.

Periods and double periods are binary forms, but we do not usually use the term *binary* for them, either, because a term like *parallel period* is more informative. However, in Example 20-1 we see a familiar tune whose four phrases do not add up to a double period.

EXAMPLE 20-1   *"Greensleeves"*

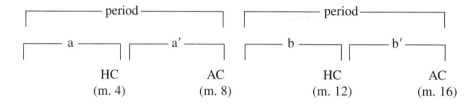

A diagram of the phrase structure reveals two parallel periods.

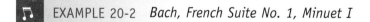

Although the structure is not a double period (because of the two authentic cadences), it is a binary form. Furthermore, "Greensleeves" is in *sectional* binary form because the first part ends with tonic harmony. If the first part of a binary form ends with something other than a tonic triad in the *main key* of the form, it is called a *continuous* binary form. The distinction between sectional and continuous forms is an important one, involving tonal independence in the first case and large-scale tonal drive in the second.

The two parts of the binary form in Example 20-2 are quite unequal in length, the second being twice as long as the first. The first half ends with a PAC in a minor, but because the main key of the piece is not a minor but d minor, this is an example of a continuous binary form.

♫ EXAMPLE 20-2   *Bach, French Suite No. 1, Minuet I*

Notice in this example that the second section is constructed largely from the two main motives of the first section. However, there is no area of contrast followed by a clearly stated return of the opening material, so the example is not in ABA form. Instead, like most binary examples, it lies somewhere between AA′ and AB, the second section containing elements of both contrast and continuation. This is also true of "Greensleeves" (Ex. 20-1), where the endings of phrases 3 and 4 were identical to the endings of phrases 1 and 2.

The Bach example (Ex. 20-2) repeats each of the two sections exactly. Repetition does not usually change our formal analysis. The minuet is a continuous binary form whether both, one, or no repeats are taken. However, movements or themes that consist of two repeated sections are so commonly encountered that a special term, *two-reprise,* is often used for them. To be thorough, then, we would say that Example 20-2 is a two-reprise continuous binary form. Incidentally, composers sometimes write out the repeats instead of using repeat signs, but we would still use the term *two-reprise.* Schumann and Chopin were especially fond of writing out repeats.

Notice in "Greensleeves" that the two parts of the binary form are of equal length (8+8), whereas in the Bach the second part is much longer (8+16). Some writers used the terms *balanced binary* and *unbalanced binary* for these situations.

TERNARY FORMS

The idea of statement-contrast-return, symbolized as ABA, is an important one in musical form. The ABA, or *ternary form,* is capable of providing the structure for anything from a short theme to a lengthy movement of a sonata or symphony. The B section of a ternary form can provide contrast with the A sections by using different melodic material, texture, tonality, or some combination of these.

The minuet from an early Haydn keyboard sonata is seen in Example 20-3. Notice that this example is a two-reprise structure, that part one ends on the dominant (m. 8), and that all of part 1 returns (mm. 17–24), with an adjustment of the cadence to allow an ending on the tonic triad. Therefore, this minuet is an example of two-reprise continuous ternary form.

EXAMPLE 20-3   *Haydn, Sonata No. 11, III, Minuet*

In short ternary forms the B section often is clearly based on the A material. This was true of the Haydn minuet throughout the B part, but especially in the first few measures. Example 20-4 is the trio that completes the movement begun in Example 20-3. Again there is a two-reprise structure, but here the A section ends in tonic (m. 10). The B part (mm. 11–19) is based on the A material, but some of the figures are inverted (compare mm. 1–2 with mm. 11–12), and it is in the key of the relative major. The return of A at m. 20 is quite obvious to the listener, although this A section is slightly longer than the original and considerably varied and even includes some of the inverted figures from B. The form is two-reprise sectional ternary.

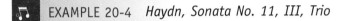 EXAMPLE 20-4   *Haydn, Sonata No. 11, III, Trio*

As with most minuets and trios, Haydn's minuet (Ex. 20-3) is played both before and after the trio (Ex. 20-4), so that the entire movement is itself a sectional ternary form.

At first glance, Example 20-5 might appear to be a five-part form.

$$\|: \quad A \quad :\| \quad B \quad A' \quad B \quad A'$$

However, on closer inspection we see that Schumann has written out only the second repeat of a two-reprise continuous ternary form.

$$\|: \quad A \quad :\|: \quad B \quad A' \quad :\|$$
$$\qquad V$$

♫ EXAMPLE 20-5   *Schumann, "Melody," Op. 68, No. 1*

A great number of twentieth-century popular songs, especially those composed before the advent of rock music, adhered to a sectional ternary pattern that we will call the American popular ballad form. It consists of an eight-bar period that is repeated with a different text, followed by an eight-measure "bridge" that is often in another key and a return to the opening period. The diagram below summarizes this form.

Music:	A	A	B	A
Text:	1	2	3	4
Measures:	1–8	9–16	17–24	25–32

Hundreds of songs ("The Lady Is a Tramp," "Moonlight in Vermont," and so on) follow this same general format.

ROUNDED BINARY FORMS

Frequently, the last part of what appears to be a ternary form returns only half of the first A section.

A　　　B　　　½A

The term that some writers use for this form is *rounded binary*. Often the phrase structure of a sectional rounded binary example will be:

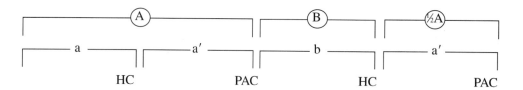

This is the form of many traditional tunes, such as "Oh, Susannah" (Ex. 20-6).

EXAMPLE 20-6 *"Oh, Susannah"*

   Example 20-7 is the theme from a set of variations. This is an example of a two-reprise sectional rounded binary form. Its form differs from "O Susannah" only in that the return of the a′ phrase is extended by two measures.

EXAMPLE 20-7 *Mozart, Sonata, K. 331, I*

THE 12-BAR BLUES

The 12-bar blues is an important form in jazz, rock, and related styles. It consists of three four-bar phrases, sometimes in an aab pattern ("You Ain't Nothin' but a Hound Dog") and sometimes in an abc pattern ("Rock around the Clock"). If the blues has a text (there are many purely instrumental blues compositions), the text may also be either aab or abc.

The most basic harmonic pattern for the 12-bar blues is:

Phrase 1   Phrase 2   Phrase 3
| I | I | I | I | IV | IV | I | I | V | IV | I | I |

However, although this pattern is always perceivable in a blues, there are a great many variants, and few blues heard today will follow this simple pattern exactly. In Example 20-8 notice first that all the chords are Mm7 chords, which, in the case of F7 and B♭7, introduces into the harmony tones that do not belong to the F major scale. Notice also the substitution of a IV^7 for I in m. 3 and the addition of a C^7 in m. 12 to lead back to the beginning. Finally, observe how many of the notes of this melody, especially the longer notes, create a sharp dissonance against the underlying harmony.

EXAMPLE 20-8   *Carpenter, "Walkin'"*

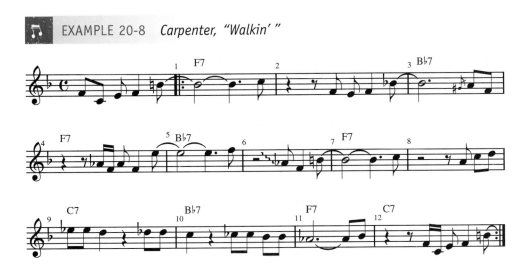

By Richard Carpenter. © Richcar Music 1955. Copyright Renewed. Used by permission.

Checkpoint

1. What is the difference between sectional binary and continuous binary?
2. What is the difference between rounded binary and ternary?
3. What does the term *two-reprise* mean?
4. What is the basic harmonic outline of the 12-bar blues?

OTHER FORMAL DESIGNS

Binary and ternary forms, especially the latter, provide the structure for many pieces and movements from multimovement works. The typical minuet and trio, for example, is sectional ternary because the minuet is played both before and after the trio.

A	B	A
Minuet	Trio	Minuet

The minuet itself is generally a two-reprise ternary or a two-reprise rounded binary, as is the trio.

Slow movements are also often in ternary form. For example, the second movement from Brahms's Symphony No. 1 is in ternary form. It makes use of *transitions,* which are passages that connect different themes or tonal centers, and a *coda,* which is a special concluding section.

Section:	A	trans.	B	trans.	A	coda
Tonality:	E	mod.	c♯	mod.	E	E
	(I)		(vi)		(I)	(I)
Mcasures:	1–27	28–38	39–57	57–66	67–100	101–128

Many other musical forms are beyond the scope of this text, but two of the more important forms will be discussed briefly here. We will refer those who want to learn more about these forms to complete movements found in two widely used anthologies:

Charles Burkhart, *Anthology for Musical Analysis,* 5th ed. Fort Worth: Harcourt Brace, 1994.

Ralph Turek, *Analytical Anthology of Music,* 2nd ed. New York: McGraw-Hill, 1992.

Sonata form (or sonata-allegro form) is usually found as the first movement of a sonata, string quartet, symphony, or similar work, although other movements may also be in sonata form. Early examples of sonata form resemble two-reprise continuous ternary form.

```
     ┌──────Exposition──────┐ ┌────Development────┐ ┌──Recapitulation──┐
     ╟:   A    trans.   B   :╟:   Working out of old      A    trans.   B   :╢
                                 material. Introduction
                                 of new material.

Major key:   I    mod.    V         unstable . . . . . . . . . . .I    unstable    I

Minor key:   i    mod.   III        unstable . . . . . . . . . . .i    unstable    i
```

The A and B in the diagram stand for themes or groups of themes that appear in different keys in the exposition but in tonic in the recapitulation. The repeats are seen less often in nineteenth-century music than in eighteenth-century music, although lengthy introductions and codas are more commonly found. The number of themes presented in the two key areas also tends to be larger in the later music.

Below are formal diagrams of the broad outlines of two movements in sonata form, one in major and one in minor. A more detailed formal analysis would include phrases and cadences.

Mozart, *Eine kleine Nachtmusik,* K. 525, I (Turek p. 222)

Exposition

mm. 1–18	A theme	G major
mm. 18–27	transition	G major → D major
mm. 28–35	1B theme	D major
mm. 36–55	2B theme	D major

Development

mm. 56–76		D major, C major, a minor, g minor, G major

Recapitulation

mm. 76–93	A theme	G major
mm. 93–100	transition	G major
mm. 101–108	1B theme	G major
mm. 109–132	2B theme	G major
mm. 133–137	Coda	G major

Beethoven, Piano Sonata, Op. 2, No. 1, I (Burkhart p. 238)

Exposition

mm. 1–8	A theme	f minor
mm. 9–20	transition	f minor → A♭ major
mm. 21–41	1B theme	A♭ major
mm. 42–48	2B theme	A♭ major

Development

mm. 49–101		A♭ major, b♭ minor, c minor, b♭ minor, A♭ major, f minor

Recapitulation

mm. 101–108	A theme	f minor
mm. 109–119	transition	f minor

mm. 120–140	1B theme	f minor
mm. 141–152	2B theme	f minor

Rondo form is found most frequently as the final movement of a sonata, string quartet, or symphony, although slow movements are also sometimes in rondo form. There are three common types.

Five-part rondo	A	B	A	C	A		
	I	V	I	x	I		
Five-part rondo	A	B	A	B	A		
(variant)	I	V	I	?	I		
Seven-part rondo	A	B	A	C	A	B	A
	I	V	I	x	I	I	I

The x in the diagrams above symbolizes some key other than I or V; ? means that a number of common possibilities exist.

As we did with sonata form, we provide below outlines of two movements in rondo form. The Haydn example is somewhat unusual in its tonal structure and in its symmetrical proportions.

Haydn, Piano Sonata No. 37, III (Turek p. 192)

mm. 1–20	A theme	D major
mm. 21–40	B theme	d minor
mm. 41–60	A theme	D major
mm. 61–80	C theme	G major
mm. 81–93	transition	G major → D major
mm. 94–134	A theme	D major

Beethoven, Piano Sonata, Op. 13, III (Burkhart p. 263)

mm. 1–17	A theme	c minor
mm. 18–25	transition	c minor → E♭ major
mm. 26–51	B theme	E♭ major
mm. 51–61	transition	E♭ major → c minor
mm. 62–78	A theme	c minor
mm. 79–94	C theme	A♭ major
mm. 95–120	transition	A♭ major → c minor
mm. 121–128	A theme	c minor
mm. 129–134	transition	c minor
mm. 135–170	B theme	C major
mm. 171–182	A theme	c minor
mm. 183–210	coda	c minor

Summary

The term *binary form* is applied to a movement or portion of a movement that consists of two main sections (except that periods and double periods are not usually referred to as binary forms). If the first section of a binary form ends on the tonic triad in the main key of the form, it is *sectional binary;* if the first section ends with any other chord, it is *continuous binary.* Most binary forms could be symbolized as AA', with the A' section containing elements of both continuation and contrast.

Music that is in *ternary form* is in three parts, with the middle section providing contrast through the use of different melodic material, texture, tonality, or some combination of these and the third part returning all or most of the first. Ternary form is symbolized as ABA and may be sectional or continuous, depending on whether the first A section ends with the tonic triad in the main key of the form.

Rounded binary form refers to music in which the opening A section returns after contrasting material but in a considerably abbreviated form, as in AB½A. In many instances the choice between rounded binary and ternary is difficult to make. Like binary and ternary forms, rounded binary forms may be sectional or continuous.

Many binary, ternary, and rounded binary forms are also *two-reprise* forms, meaning that they consist of two repeated sections. The first repeated section is always the first A section, whereas the second repeated section is the rest of the form. The repeats are sometimes written out, perhaps with ornamentation or changes in register. Also, the main sections of a binary, ternary, or rounded binary form may be connected by *transitions,* and the form may end with a special concluding section called a *coda.*

The American popular ballad form is a 32-bar AABA ternary design. The 12-bar blues form consists of three phrases with a basic harmonic structure that is in most cases elaborated on in any particular blues composition.

Other musical forms are beyond the scope of this text, although they are discussed briefly in the chapter. Among these are *sonata form,* a very important form in tonal music, and *rondo form.*

Self-Test 20-1
(Answers begin on page 642.)

A. Sing "America" ("My Country, 'Tis of Thee"), then diagram its phrase structure. Include measure numbers and cadence types in your diagram. What is the form?

B. Diagram the piece below down to the phrase level and name the form. Assume there is a HC in m. 12, although there are other ways to hear this. Also, complete the following exercises.

1. Explain the G♮4's in mm. 1 and 2.
2. If there were a modulation at the end of the first section (most people hear it as a tonicization), where would the common chord be?
3. Can you relate mm. 9 to 12 to anything in mm. 1 to 4?
4. Find a 9-8 suspension with change of bass.
5. Find consecutive octaves by contrary motion.

Beethoven, Bagatelle, Op. 119, No. 4

C. Diagram this trio down to the phrase level and name the form. Assume that the phrases are four measures long. Also, complete these exercises.

1. The violas double what part (until m. 39)?
2. Explain the C♯5 in m. 36.
3. Find parallel 5ths between the outer voices.

Mozart, Symphony K. 97, III

D. Diagram this piece down to the phrase level and name the form. Assume that all
    phrases are four measures in length, except for an eight-measure phrase in mm. 9 to
    16. Also, complete these exercises.

   1. Discuss the choice of keys (tonicizations) in this piece.
   2. Label the chords in mm. 17 to 24. Assume that the modulation back to f♯ is a
       phrase modulation.
   3. Find a disguised set of parallel 5ths in the same measures.
   4. What about this piece is reminiscent of two-reprise form?

 Schumann, *Album Leaf,* Op. 99, No. 1

Exercise 20-1 See Workbook.

PART V

Chromaticism 2

Chapter 21

Mode Mixture

INTRODUCTION

The term *mode mixture* refers to the use of tones from one mode (*mode* here refers to the major and minor modes) in a passage that is predominantly in the other mode. Usually the mixture involves coloring a passage in the major mode with notes from its parallel minor. Mode mixture often serves an expressive purpose, and it is a frequently encountered source of altered chords. Other terms used for mode mixture are *borrowed chords* and *mutation*.

BORROWED CHORDS IN MINOR

Some writers feel that the use of raised $\hat{6}$ and $\hat{7}$ in minor is an example of mode mixture. According to that view, every V, for example, is borrowed from major, which makes mode mixture in minor a very common occurrence. Our approach is that scale degrees $\hat{6}$ and $\hat{7}$ each have two versions (review pp. 61–63), which means that the raised $\hat{3}$ is the only scale degree that can be borrowed in a minor key.

As it happens, there is a chord frequently borrowed from major that contains the raised $\hat{3}$, and that chord is the major tonic triad itself. The raised $\hat{3}$ in the tonic triad is called the *Picardy third,* and it was used to end most compositions in minor from the early 1500s until around 1750. A typical use of the Picardy third is seen in Example 21-1. Notice that the uppercase roman numeral I is enough to indicate the mode mixture. It is not necessary to add any explanatory note in the analysis. The voice leading in this example is worth examining, especially the descending tenor line and the alto part, which actually contains two lines. The textural reduction shows a simplification of the texture.

EXAMPLE 21-1   *Bach, "Helft mir Gottes Güte preisen"*

b: i   V   VI   i⁶   ii∅⁶₅   V⁷   V⁷/iv   iv⁶₄   I

Textural reduction

The idea of the Picardy third is sometimes used on a very large scale. For example, Beethoven's Symphony No. 5 begins in c minor, but the main key of the last movement is C major.

THE USE OF ♭6̂ IN MAJOR

The most frequently encountered examples of mode mixture in the major mode involve chords that employ ♭6. The "♭6" here refers to the lowered sixth scale degree. The accidental to be used in the music might be a ♮, a ♭, or a ♭♭, depending on the key signature, but we will refer to the lowered sixth scale degree as ♭6̂ in any case. Borrowing ♭6̂ from the parallel minor creates four borrowed chords that are frequently used in major: vii°⁷, ii°, ii∅⁷, and iv. Example 21-2 illustrates these in the key of A major. Notice that the roman numerals are identical to those used in minor.

EXAMPLE 21-2

A: vii°⁷   ii°   ii∅⁷   iv

The vii°⁷ is actually a more useful chord than the viiø⁷ because parallel 5ths are never a problem in its resolution. The vii°⁷ chord is one of the primary motivic elements in Example 21-3, where it is accented each time it occurs. Although the $\flat\hat{6}$, F♭, is in an inner voice, it forms the beginning of an important line begun in the first phrase and completed in the second: F♭–E♭–D♭ | F♭–E♭–D♭–C. Notice also the nice effect created by the unusual V–ii–V in m. 15.

EXAMPLE 21-3 *Chopin, Mazurka, Op. 17, No. 3*

Incidentally, you will recall that either viiø⁷/ or vii°⁷/ may be used to tonicize a major triad (review p. 275). We can now understand that the use of vii°⁷ of a major triad is an example of mode mixture. The vii°⁷/V in Example 21-3 illustrates this, the C♭ being the $\flat\hat{6}$ "borrowed" from E♭ minor.

Frequently, the vii°⁷ does not resolve directly to I but is followed instead by V⁷. Only one voice needs to move to accomplish this, as Example 21-4 illustrates.

EXAMPLE 21-4

The borrowed iv is frequently used in first inversion as part of a stepwise descending bass line, as in Example 21-5. The imitation between soprano and tenor in mm. 4 to 5 and the soaring tenor line in mm. 5 to 6 are among the many points to appreciate in this beautiful phrase.

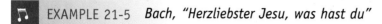

EXAMPLE 21-5 *Bach, "Herzliebster Jesu, was hast du"*

The borrowed ii°⁷ is probably used more often than the borrowed ii° because of the added direction provided by the 7th. Example 21-6 is typical.

EXAMPLE 21-6 *Bach, "Christus, der ist mein Leben"*

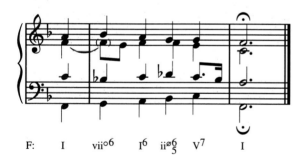

In general, ♭6̂ in vii°⁷, iv, or ii°⁽ø⁷⁾ moves down by half step to 5̂. It is often also approached by step, either from ♮6̂ or from 5̂.

OTHER BORROWED CHORDS IN MAJOR

The most frequently encountered examples of mode mixture in major are the vii°⁷, iv⁽⁷⁾, and ii°⁽ø⁷⁾ chords. Other possible borrowed chords are shown in Example 21-7. Of these, the ♭III and the ♭VII are relatively rare. Notice that the symbols for the borrowed submediant and mediant triads are preceded by a flat to show that the root is lowered. Use the flat in your analysis regardless of the actual accidental found in the notation, which might be a natural, flat, or double flat, depending on the key.

EXAMPLE 21-7

A: i   ♭VI   ♭III   ♭VII

Whereas vii°⁷, iv, and ii°(∅⁷) are often found alone in major-mode passages, the minor tonic triad frequently occurs in longer passages in the parallel minor. In Example 21-8 the minor mode takes over in m. 31, and major is not reestablished until the arrival of the D♮ in m. 36. Notice that this is *not* a modulation because B♭ is the tonal center throughout. This example also illustrates the ♭VI, preceded here by its secondary dominant. The ♭VI is sometimes used with dramatic effect in deceptive cadences: V–♭VI. The V$^{+6}_5$/IV in Example 21-8 is an augmented dominant, which is discussed in a later chapter.

EXAMPLE 21-8   *Haydn, Quartet Op. 9, No. 2, I*

B♭:   I   6   V$^{+6}_5$/IV   IV   vii°⁷/V

The ♭VII and ♭III chords are by no means commonly encountered. The ♭VII, when it occurs, frequently functions as a V/III, just as the same chord does in the minor mode. In Example 21-9 the ♭III is preceded by its secondary dominant and followed by a borrowed vii °7. The sonorities in mm. 26 to 27 with C and C♯ in the bass are passing chords that connect the V7 to the V$_5^6$ (see the textural reduction). These chords do not require roman numerals.

EXAMPLE 21-9 *Schumann, "Ein Jüngling liebt ein Mädchen," Op. 48, No. 11*

Textural reduction

Checkpoint

1. What is the name for the raised $\hat{3}$ in the tonic triad in the minor mode?
2. Show the chord symbols for the borrowed chords in major discussed in this chapter.
3. To what does *secondary mode mixture* refer?
4. How does ♭$\hat{6}$ most often proceed: up by step, down by step, or down by leap?

MODULATIONS INVOLVING MODE MIXTURE

Mode mixture in the new key is often employed as a signal to the listener that a modulation is taking place. In Example 21-10 a modulation from f to E♭ occurs. In m. 5 Beethoven uses an f minor chord, which is the common chord linking the two keys. The f^{ø7} chord that follows announces the modulation to the listener because this chord is a very unlikely one in the key of f. (The Ger^{+6} chord in m. 3 is discussed in Chapter 23.)

♪ EXAMPLE 21-10   *Beethoven, Horn Sonata, Op. 17, II*

Mode mixture also simplifies modulation to certain foreign keys. If a passage in major slips into the parallel minor, all the keys that are closely related to the parallel minor come within easy reach. For example, mixture in the key of F gives us access to all the keys in the chart below:

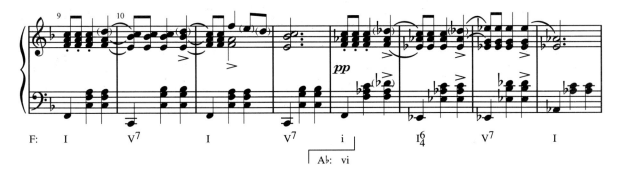

Schubert uses mode mixture in Example 21-11 to move to the relative major of the parallel minor: F →(f) → A♭.

♫ **EXAMPLE 21-11** *Schubert, Originaltanze, Op. 9, No. 33*

F: I   V⁷   I   V⁷   i   I⁶₄   V⁷   I

A♭: vi

Summary

The term *mode mixture* refers to the use of tones from one mode in a passage that is predominantly in the other mode. The only case in which a chord is "borrowed" from the major mode for use in minor is the *Picardy third,* a major tonic triad that was used to end most minor mode compositions in the early tonal era.

Borrowing from minor into the parallel major, on the other hand, is more common and involves a large number of chords. Several of these come about through the use of ♭6̂. These include vii°⁷, ii°, ii°⁷, and iv. Other borrowed chords require the use of ♭3̂ and even ♭7̂. These chords include the i, ♭VI, ♭III, and ♭VII chords, and of these the i and the ♭VI are the most commonly encountered.

Mode mixture is often a factor in modulations. Sometimes it is used only in the new key after a common chord as a signal to the listener that a modulation is taking place. At other times the common chord itself is a borrowed chord, a technique that simplifies modulations to some foreign keys.

Self-Test 21-1
(Answers begin on page 644.)

A. Notate the following chords in the specified inversions. Include key signatures.

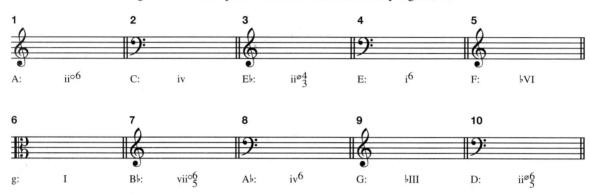

A: ii°6   C: iv   E♭:   ii⌀4/3   E: i6   F: ♭VI

g: I   B♭:   vii°6/5   A♭:   iv6   G: ♭III   D: ii⌀6/5

B. Label the following chords. Include inversion symbols.

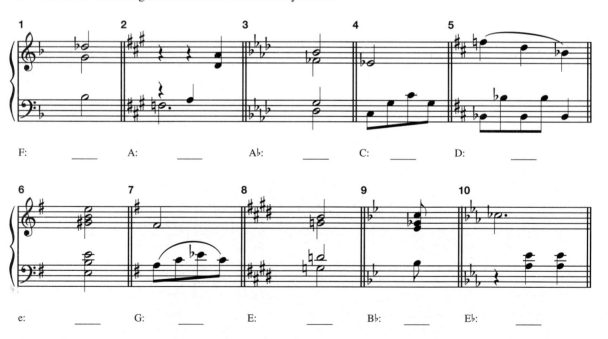

F: _____   A: _____   A♭: _____   C: _____   D: _____

e: _____   G: _____   E: _____   B♭: _____   E♭: _____

C. Analysis.

   1. Label chords and NCTs. Circle the roman numerals of any borrowed chords.

Bach, "Warum sollt' ich mich denn grämen"

G:

2. Label the chords and NCTs, and circle the roman numerals of any borrowed chords.

Verdi, *Il Trovatore,* Act II, No. 11

3. Label the chords, circling the roman numerals of any borrowed chords. Which part is doubling the violas in mm. 47 to 51? The horn in D sounds a m7 lower than written.

Haydn, Symphony No. 73, I

4. Label the chords, circling the roman numerals of any borrowed chords. Discuss any diminished seventh chords that occur in terms of the resolution of their tri-tones.

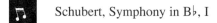

Schubert, Symphony in B♭, I

5. In this remarkable excerpt, Beethoven manages to modulate from a♭ minor to D major, a tritone away. Explain how he accomplishes this (it is not necessary to label every chord in the excerpt).

Beethoven, Sonata Op. 26, III

D. Part writing. Analyze the chords implied by the soprano-bass framework. Then fill in alto and tenor parts. Be sure to use the specified mode mixture.

1. Include a vii°⁷.

2. Include a ii⁰⁶₅.

E. Analyze the chords specified by this figured bass, then make an arrangement for
    SATB chorus.

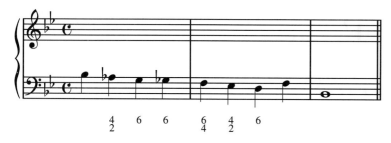

Exercise 21-1 See Workbook.

Chapter 22

The Neapolitan Chord

INTRODUCTION

Although the I–V–I progression is the basic organizing force in tonal harmony, much of the foreground harmonic interest in a tonal passage may be provided by the ways in which the dominant is approached. One of the more colorful chords that can be used to precede the dominant is the Neapolitan.

The *Neapolitan chord* derives its name from an important group of eighteenth-century opera composers who were associated with the city of Naples. Although the composers of the "Neapolitan school" frequently used this chord in their music, they did not originate it but inherited it from earlier composers. Nevertheless, the term *Neapolitan* has survived, and we will make use of it and its abbreviation, N. Simply stated, the Neapolitan triad is a *major triad* constructed on the *lowered second scale degree*. One accidental is required to spell the Neapolitan in a minor key and two in a major key, as is illustrated in Example 22-1.

EXAMPLE 22-1

CONVENTIONAL USE OF THE NEAPOLITAN

The Neapolitan is usually found in the minor mode and in first inversion. In fact, the first inversion is so typical that the Neapolitan triad is often referred to as the *Neapolitan sixth chord*. It functions much like a diatonic ii^6 (or ii^{o6}) chord, going eventually to V, but its aural effect is strikingly different. Example 22-2 illustrates several contexts in which the N^6 is commonly found. At the piano, establish the key of e minor and play through the example so you will become familiar with the distinctive sound of the N^6.

EXAMPLE 22-2

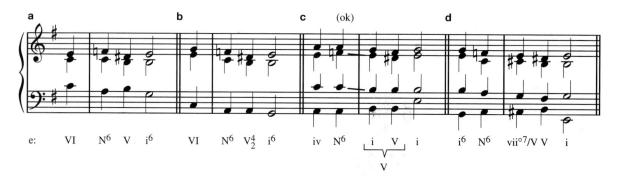

Example 22-2 illustrates several characteristics of the N⁶.

1. When a tone is doubled, it is usually the 3rd of the N^6.

2. The N^6 moves to V (or i_4^6–V), but vii°⁷/V may appear between the N^6 and the V. The N^6 would usually not be followed by iv or ii°.

3. The $\flat\hat{2}$ (the root of the N^6) moves down, especially when it appears in the melody. Its goal is the leading tone, which lies at the unusual interval of a °3 below $\flat\hat{2}$ (see the soprano line in Ex. 22-2a and b). However, the °3 is filled in by the tonic pitch when the N^6 moves first to i_4^6 or vii°⁷/V (Ex. 22-2c and d).

4. When the N^6 moves to i_4^6, as in Example 22-2c, parallel 4ths should be used to avoid parallel 5ths. Parallel 5ths would be created in Example 22-2c by transposing the alto line an octave lower.

5. The N^6, like the unaltered ii°⁶, is usually preceded by VI, iv, or i.

Example 22-3 illustrates the N^6 in a three-part texture. Notice the leap in the tenor voice from A3 to E4 to provide the 3rd for the i_4^6 chord. The textural reduction brings out the stepwise ascent in the bass from $\hat{1}$ up to $\hat{5}$.

EXAMPLE 22-3   *Haydn, Sonata No. 36, I*

Textural reduction

In Example 22-4 the N⁶ appears in a more complicated keyboard texture. Both Neapolitans in the example proceed directly to V. In the resolution of the first N⁶, the interval of a °3 in the melody is filled in by a supermetrical passing tone (the A5). Notice that the freer treatment of the inner parts allows the ♭$\hat{2}$ (B♭3) in the left hand to move upward to ♮$\hat{2}$. This does not disturb the listener, whose attention is drawn to the resolution of the more significant B♭5 in the melody.

EXAMPLE 22-4 *Beethoven, Bagatelle Op. 119, No. 9*

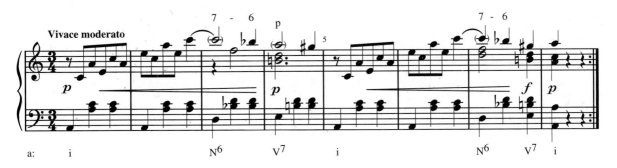

The N^6 chord occurs occasionally in popular music as well. Example 22-5, a theme from a film score, ends with a VI–N^6–V^7–i progression.

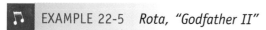

EXAMPLE 22-5   *Rota, "Godfather II"*

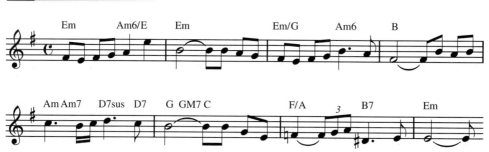

By Nino Rota. Copyright © 1974 by Famous Music Corporation. Used by permission of Hal Leonard Corporation.

OTHER USES OF THE NEAPOLITAN

The Neapolitan is usually employed in first inversion in the minor mode, and it usually moves toward V. However, several other contexts for the Neapolitan might be encountered.

1. The Neapolitan may appear in root position (N) or, rarely, in second inversion (N$^6_4$). In both cases, the bass will probably be doubled in a four-part texture.

2. The Neapolitan may occur in the major mode.

3. The Neapolitan may be tonicized. This can take the form of a single chord (such as V^7/N), or it might be a genuine modulation to the key of the Neapolitan. In some cases VI (or ♭VI) may function as V/N.

4. In a modulation the common chord may be a Neapolitan in either key. Foreign key relationships might be involved in such a modulation.

5. The Neapolitan may, on occasion, serve a function other than that of a pre-dominant chord.

6. In rare instances the Neapolitan may have a structure other than that of a major triad, including n (minor triad), N^{M7} (M7 chord), and N^7 (Mm7 chord).

The examples below illustrate most of these uses of the Neapolitan.

Both a V^7/N and a root position Neapolitan occur in Example 22-6. Notice the tritone root relationship between the N and V chords.

EXAMPLE 22-6   *Chopin, Mazurka Op. 7, No. 2*

a: V⁷   VI   V⁷/N   N   V⁷   i

In Example 22-7 Verdi uses the N in a major key (and in root position). However, he does prepare for the N by using mode mixture in the previous two measures. (Only the main chords are analyzed in the first five measures.)

EXAMPLE 22-7   *Verdi,* Il Trovatore, *Act I, No. 5*

An earlier excerpt from popular music, Example 7-7 (p. 108), also used a root position N, this time in a long circle-of-fifths progression: iv–VII–III–VI–N–V–i.

Example 22-8 begins in A major and ends in a♭ minor (although neither key signature agrees with that analysis). The I⁶ chord before the double bar is enharmonically the same as a B♭♭ major triad, which is the Neapolitan in a♭. It then moves normally to i⁴₆–V in a♭.

EXAMPLE 22-8   *Schubert,* Moment Musical, *Op. 94, No. 6*

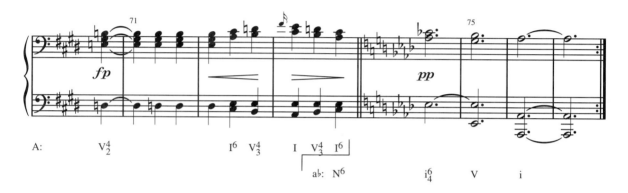

The chord in m. 108 of Example 22-9 contains all the notes of a Neapolitan chord, but it does not move to V. Instead, as the textural reduction shows, the N⁶ serves as a neighbor chord to the i⁶ that appears on either side of it.

EXAMPLE 22-9   *Mozart, Sonata K. 310, I*

Textural reduction

An occurrence of n^6, a minor Neapolitan, occurs in Example 22-10, and Schubert emphasizes it with the last *forte* to be heard in the movement.* The n^6 is followed by a Ger^{+6}, a chord that is discussed in the next chapter. Interestingly, it is enharmonically the same as a V^7/n^6.

EXAMPLE 22-10 *Schubert, String Quartet in D Minor ("Death and the Maiden"), D. 810, I*

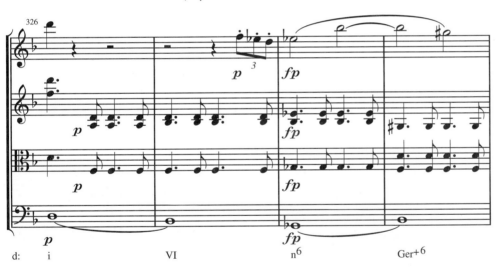

*We are indebted to Professor Graham Phipps of the University of North Texas for this example.

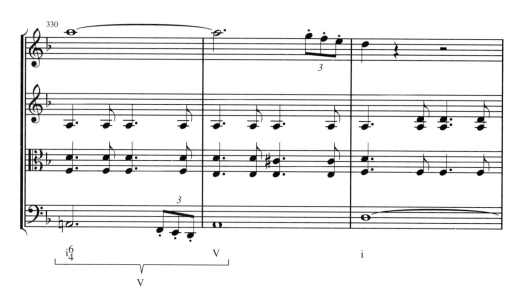

In Example 22-11, a V^7 chord is preceded by a N^7 (a Mm7 chord), resulting in two Mm7 chords a tritone apart. This is one of three combinations of Mm7 chords that share two pitches (review p. 289), in this case D and A♭/G♯. Notice the dynamic emphasis on the unusual Neapolitan chord, as in the previous example.

EXAMPLE 22-11 *Clara Wieck Schumann, "Impromptu—Le Sabbat," Op. 5, No. 1*

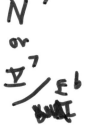

Checkpoint

1. Name four chords that commonly follow a N⁶ chord.
2. What is usually doubled in a N⁶ chord?
3. Does the ♭2̂ in a N⁶ tend to move up or down?
4. Name several less common uses of the Neapolitan chord.

Summary

The Neapolitan chord (symbolized as N) is a major triad constructed on the lowered second scale degree. The Neapolitan chord occurs most often in the minor mode and typically appears in first inversion, so it is often called the Neapolitan sixth chord.

Like the diatonic supertonic triad, the N⁶ progresses to V, sometimes passing through i⁶₄ or vii°⁷/V, or both, on the way. In four parts, the 3rd of the N⁶ is doubled and—in the resolution of the N⁶—the ♭2̂ moves down to the nearest chord tone.

Although the Neapolitan chord is characteristically found in the minor mode and in first inversion, it also occurs in the major mode and in other bass positions. In addition, the Neapolitan may serve as a common chord in a modulation and may itself be tonicized. Less commonly, the Neapolitan chord may progress toward some chord other than V and may, in rare instances, have a structure other than that of a major triad, including n (minor triad), N^{M7} (M7 chord), and N⁷ (Mm7 chord).

Self-Test 22-1
(Answers begin on page 647.)

A. Label each chord. Include inversion symbols, if any.

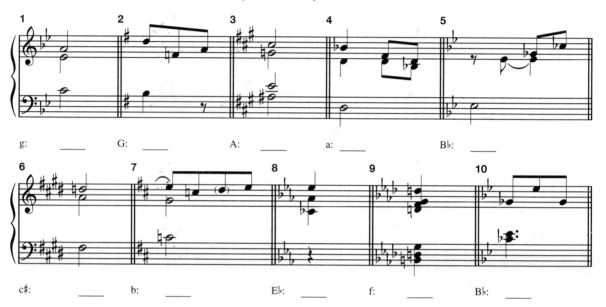

g: _____   G: _____   A: _____   a: _____   B♭: _____

c♯:   _____   b: _____   E♭: _____   f: _____   B♭: _____

B. Notate each chord. Include key signatures.

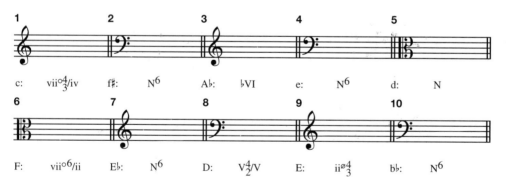

c: vii°$^4_3$/iv   f♯:   N^6 A♭:   ♭VI   e: N^6 d: N

F: vii°^{6}/ii   E♭:   N^6 D: V$^4_2$/V   E: ii$^{ø4}_3$ bb: N^6

C. Analysis.

1. Label chords with appropriate symbols. Try to think of two interpretations of
the first chord in m. 16.

Haydn, Sonata No. 37, II

2. a. Label the chords.
   b. Identify any six-four chords by type.
   c. Name the form of the excerpt.

Mozart, Piano Trio, K. 542, III

3. Label chords and NCTs. Assume that the F4 in m. 11 is a chord tone. Omit inversion symbols because the bass has the melody in this example.

Chopin, Prelude Op. 28, No. 6

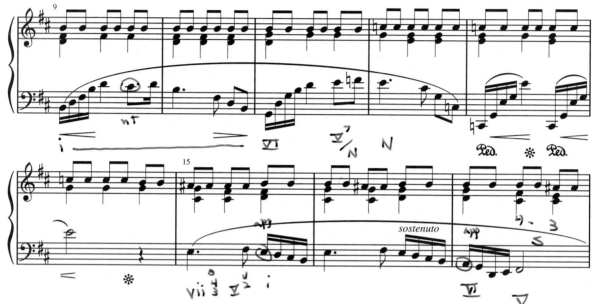

4. This excerpt from a well-known Mozart sonata begins in a minor and ends in F, with the first chord in m. 41 serving as the common chord. Label all the chords.

Mozart, Sonata K. 545, I

D. For each exercise provide the correct key signature and notate the specified chords preceding and following the N⁶. Use the given three- or four-part texture in each case.

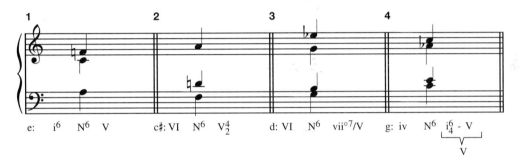

e: i⁶ N⁶ V   c♯: VI N⁶ V₂⁴   d: VI N⁶ vii°⁷/V   g: iv N⁶ i₄⁶ - V
                                                                          V

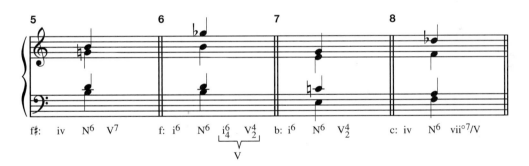

f♯: iv N⁶ V⁷   f: i⁶ N⁶ i₄⁶ V₂⁴   b: i⁶ N⁶ V₂⁴   c: iv N⁶ vii°⁷/V
                        V

E. Analyze the harmonies implied by the soprano-bass framework. Then fill in inner voices to make a four-part texture. Each excerpt should include a Neapolitan chord.

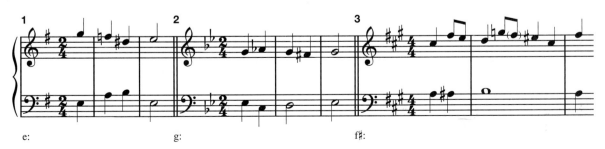

e: g: f♯:

F.   Analyze the harmonies specified by this figured bass, then make a setting for four-part chorus. It does contain a modulation.

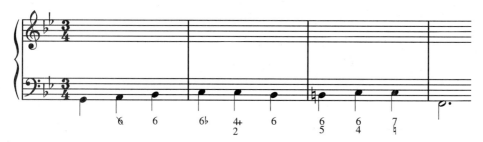

G.   Make a setting of the following progression in d minor for three-part chorus. Then make another setting in b minor for four-part chorus. Arrange the rhythm and meter so that the final chord comes on a strong beat.

i V^6 V^4_2/iv iv^6 V V^4_2/N N^6 V^4_2 i^6 vii^{o6} i   V

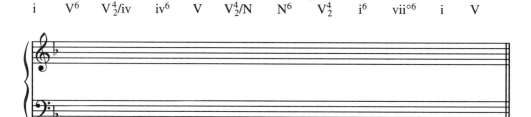

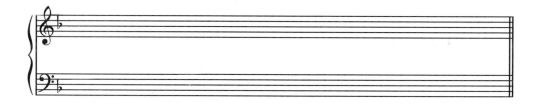

Exercise 22-1 See Workbook.

Chapter 23

Augmented Sixth Chords 1

THE INTERVAL OF THE AUGMENTED SIXTH

One way to emphasize a tone is to approach it by a half step, either from above or from below. In Examples 23-1a and b the dominant in g minor is approached by half steps. Approaching the dominant by half steps from above *and* below at the same time makes for an even stronger approach to the dominant, which is illustrated in Example 23-1c. You will notice that the two approaching tones form a vertical interval of an *augmented 6th.* This method of approaching the dominant distinguishes a whole category of chords called *augmented sixth chords.*

EXAMPLE 23-1

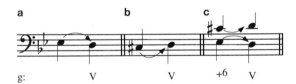

g: V   V   +6   V

The characteristic elements of most augmented sixth chords are those illustrated in Example 23-1c.

1. The chord being approached is the V chord.

2. The minor-mode $\hat{6}$ (chromatically lowered if in a major key) appears in the bass.

3. The $\sharp\hat{4}$ is in an upper part.

The interval of an $^+6$ formed by these pitches is enharmonically equivalent to a m7, but the difference between the effect of the $^+6$ and that of the m7 is easily detected by the ear. The m7 tends to resolve as in Example 23-2a, the $^+6$ as in Example 23-2b. Play both parts of Example 23-2 and notice the contrast in the effect of these two intervals.

EXAMPLE 23-2

In a two-part texture the augmented sixth chord appears as in Examples 23-1c and 23-2b. The analytical symbol to be used is simply $^+6$. Notice that the numeral is an arabic $^+6$ and not a roman +VI.

The interval of the $^+6$ usually resolves outward by half step, following the tendencies of the tones to lead to the dominant. Less commonly, the top pitch of the $^+6$ may descend chromatically to produce the 7th of a V^7. This generally occurs only in $^+6$ chords that have three or more pitch classes (see below), with the top pitch of the $^+6$ interval in an inner part.

For the reasons mentioned above, the $^+6$ chord is among the strongest of all approaches to the dominant, and it generally moves directly to V (or i_4^6–V). It is frequently used just after a modulation to make it clear to the listener that a modulation has, in fact, occurred. Like the N^6, the $^+6$ originated in the minor mode, but it was soon found to be equally useful in major keys. When used in major keys, it is often preceded by mode mixture.

THE ITALIAN AUGMENTED SIXTH CHORD

In most cases $^+6$ chords contain more than two pitch classes. When a third pitch class is included, it is usually the tonic pitch, which lies a M3 above the bass note. This combination of tones is referred to as an *Italian augmented sixth chord* (It^{+6}), which is illustrated in Example 23-3. This geographical term, like the others we will be using, has no historical authenticity—it is simply a convenient and traditional label.

EXAMPLE 23-3

The It^{+6}, like any other $^+6$ chord, resolves to V or I_4^6–V. In a four-part texture the tonic pitch is doubled. Typical resolutions are shown in Example 23-4.

EXAMPLE 23-4

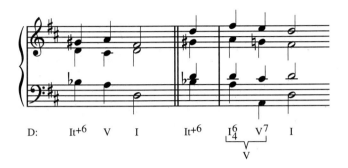

D: It^{+6} V   I   It^{+6} I$^6_4$ V^7 I

                      V

Example 23-5 includes an illustration of the It^{+6} in a three-part texture. Most of the excerpt consists of parallel 6ths (soprano and bass) surrounding a tonic pedal (alto). Notice that the bass reaches $\hat{5}$ four times, with different harmony in each case.

EXAMPLE 23-5   *Mozart, The Magic Flute, K. 620, Overture (piano reduction)*

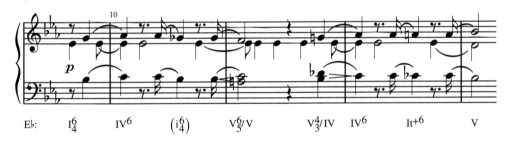

E♭:   I$^6_4$ IV^6 (i$^6_4$)   V$^6_5$/V   V$^4_3$/IV IV^6 It^{+6} V

THE FRENCH AUGMENTED SIXTH CHORD

There are two common $^{+6}$ chords that contain four pitch classes, and both of them may be thought of as It^{+6} chords with one pitch added. If the added tone is $\hat{2}$, the sonority is referred to as a *French augmented sixth chord* (Fr^{+6}), which is shown in Example 23-6.

EXAMPLE 23-6

c: $^{+6}$ It^{+6} Fr^{+6}

The Fr^{+6} works best in four-part or free textures. Typical resolutions are illustrated in Example 23-7.

EXAMPLE 23-7

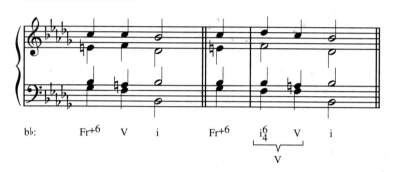

In Example 23-8, a Fr^{+6} provides the harmonic color for the climax of an entire movement. At this point, in m. 38, Beethoven shifts to a seven-part texture, which explains why $\hat{\sharp4}$ is doubled. In the following measure there is a sudden return to *piano* and a thinner texture, with the note of resolution ($\hat{5}$) appearing only in the bass. Notice that the bass and "tenor" move in parallel 3rds throughout.

EXAMPLE 23-8   *Beethoven, Sonata Op. 10, No. 3, III*

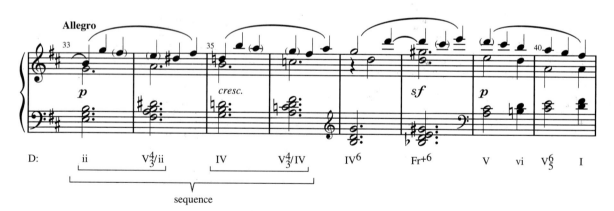

The Fr^{+6} chord occurs occasionally in popular music and jazz as well. The symbol used calls for a Mm7 chord with a lowered 5th, as in C: A♭7♭5, which is enharmonically the same as the Fr^{+6} chord in Example 23-6. In Example 23-9 the Fr^{+6} chord is the B♭7♭5.

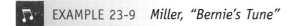

EXAMPLE 23-9 *Miller, "Bernie's Tune"*

Music by Kenneth Bernard Miller. © Copyright 1953-1954-1955 Atlantic Music Corp.
© Renewed 1981–1982 Assigned to Atlantic Music Corp. Used by permission.

THE GERMAN AUGMENTED SIXTH CHORD

The other common $^+6$ chord that contains four pitch classes is the *German augmented sixth chord* (Ger^{+6}, not G6). It may be thought of as an It^{+6} with the addition of a minor-mode $\hat{3}$ (chromatically lowered if in a major key). The Ger^{+6} is shown in Example 23-10.

EXAMPLE 23-10

As with any $^+6$ chord, the usual resolutions of the Ger^{+6} are to V and to i_4^6–V. When the Ger^{+6} moves directly to V, parallel 5ths are apt to result, as in Example 23-11. Because the ear is distracted by the resolution of the interval of the $^+6$, the parallels are not so objectionable here, and they might occasionally be encountered.

EXAMPLE 23-11

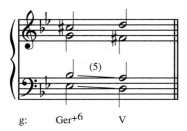

However, composers usually manage either to hide the parallels through anticipations or suspensions or to avoid them through the use of leaps or arpeggiations. In Example 23-12 Mozart first avoids the 5ths by leaping the E♭4 to B3 (a °4) and then, in the second Ger^{+6}, by arpeggiating the B♭3 to G3 before the resolution, turning the Ger^{+6} into an It^{+6}.

♫ EXAMPLE 23-12 *Mozart, Quartet K. 173, I*

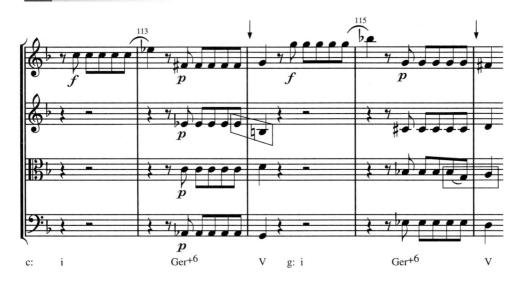

A simpler resolution to the problem of the parallels is to delay the V through the use of a cadential six-four, as in Example 23-13.

EXAMPLE 23-13

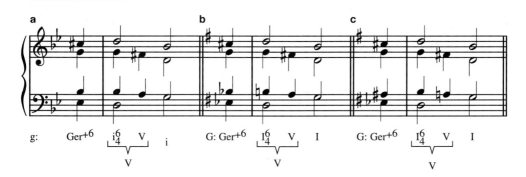

You might have noticed that the last Ger^{+6} in Example 23-13 is spelled differently from the others, although it sounds the same (A♯ = B♭). This is a fairly common enharmonic spelling of the Ger^{+6}, used in the major mode only, when the Ger^{+6} is going to I$^6_4$. The reason for its use is more for the eye than for the ear: A♯ to B♮ looks more reasonable than B♭ to B♮ because we expect raised notes to ascend and lowered ones to descend.

Enharmonic spellings are also involved when we compare the Ger^{+6} with the V^7/N. The listener can tell the Ger^{+6} from a dominant seventh chord only by its resolution, a feature that can lead to some interesting modulations (to be discussed in Chapter 25). For example, the Ger^{+6} in m. 33 of Example 23-14 sounds like a V^7/N (a D♭^{7}), especially because it is preceded by a N^6. The resolution to V^7 is needed before its function is clear to us. Notice also that the ♯$\hat{4}$ (B♮3) moves down chromatically to ♮$\hat{4}$ (B♭3) to provide the 7th of the V^7 chord.

EXAMPLE 23-14   *Beethoven, Quartet Op. 18, No. 1, II*

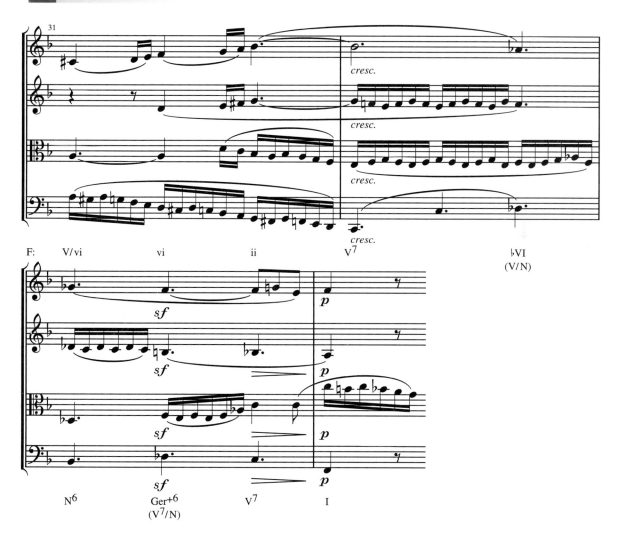

Ger^{+6} chords are encountered frequently in lead sheet symbols, where they are indicated as a Mm7 chord on the minor sixth scale degree, as in C: A♭7–G7, which represents C: Ger^{+6}–V^7.

Checkpoint

1. The $^+$6 in an augmented sixth chord results from a combination of what two scale degrees?
2. To create an It^{+6} chord, what scale degree do you add to the $^+$6?
3. What scale degree do you add to an It^{+6} chord to form a Fr^{+6} chord?
4. What scale degree do you add to an It^{+6} chord to form a Ger^{+6} chord?

OTHER USES OF CONVENTIONAL AUGMENTED SIXTH CHORDS

The conventional $^+$6 chord, as described in this chapter, usually functions as the final element of a series of chords leading to a dominant or cadential six-four chord. However, a number of other contexts might be encountered, even with what would be considered conventional $^+$6 chords. A few examples will give you an idea.

The $^+$6 may be used as a neighbor chord, as in V–$^+$6–V, which is in some ways a weaker function than its use as a pre-dominant chord. An instance of this was seen in Example 21-10 on p. 362.

Less commonly, another chord, usually some form of V/V or vii°/V, comes between the +6 and V chords, as in Example 23-15, where vii°^{7} substitutes for V.

EXAMPLE 23-15   *Mozart, Piano Sonata, K. 533 and K. 494, III*

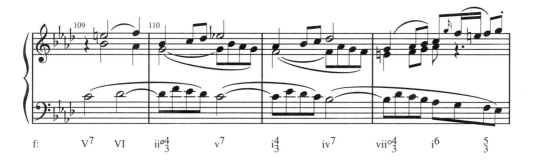

f: V^7 VI   ii$^{ø4}_3$ v^7 i$^4_3$ iv^7 vii$^{°4}_3$ i^6 $^5_3$

Measures 110 to 112 of Example 23-15 contain an interesting variant on the circle-of-fifths patterns that were discussed in Chapter 15 (review Exx. 15-17 and 15-18). Example 23-16a shows a much simpler model, whereas Example 23-16b elaborates that model slightly. Finally, compare Example 23-16b with mm. 110 to 112 in Example 23-15.

EXAMPLE 23-16

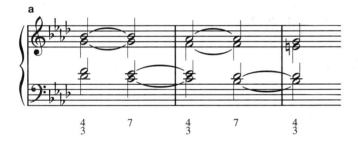

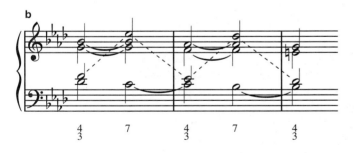

In Example 23-17 the Ger^{+6} resolves normally to a i$^6_4$ chord, but it turns out to be a passing six-four instead of the expected cadential six-four. Notice also the contrary motion in mm. 11 to 12 between the melody and the bass.

EXAMPLE 23-17   *Fanny Mendelssohn Hensel, "Auf der Wanderung"*

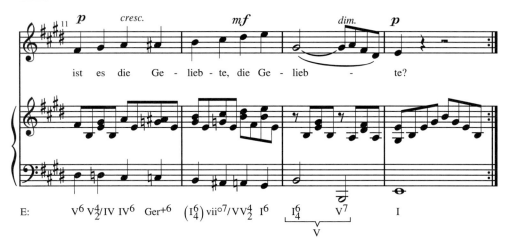

Summary

The class of chords known as augmented sixth chords get their name from the interval of an augmented 6th. The $^{+}6$ is typically formed between the minor sixth scale degree ($\flat\hat{6}$ if in major) in the bass voice and $\sharp\hat{4}$ in some upper voice. The interval of a $^{+}6$ expands to an octave on $\hat{5}$, harmonized by V or I_4^6–V.

In textures of three or more voices, the tonic scale degree usually appears along with $\flat\hat{6}$ and $\sharp\hat{4}$, and this combination of intervals is called an *Italian augmented sixth chord*. The other two conventional augmented sixth chords add a fourth tone to the Italian augmented sixth chord: the *French augmented sixth chord* adds a second scale degree, whereas the *German augmented sixth chord* adds $\hat{3}$ from the minor mode (in major either $\flat\hat{3}$ or $\sharp\hat{2}$).

Augmented sixth chords typically progress to V, although the V chord may, of course, be delayed by a tonic $^6_4$ chord. The tonic $^6_4$ chord is especially useful in avoiding parallel 5ths in the resolution of the Ger^{+6} chord, although the 5ths might also be avoided or hidden by other means.

Exceptional uses of conventional augmented sixth chords are occasionally encountered. A few of these are discussed on pp. 392–393.

Self-Test 23-1
(Answers begin on page 650.)   old p 394

A. Label each chord, using inversion symbols where appropriate.

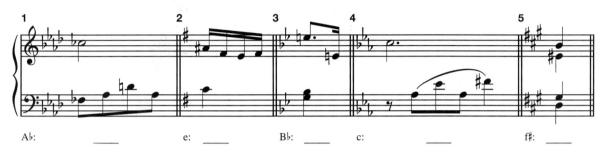

Ab: _____   e: _____   Bb: _____   c: _____   f#: _____

d: _____   B: _____   A: _____   bb: _____   G: _____

B. Notate each chord in close position. Augmented sixth chords should be in their customary bass position (b6 in the bass). Include key signatures.

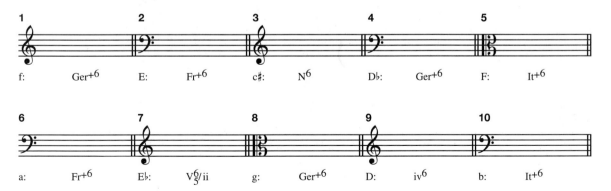

f: Ger+6   E: Fr+6   c#: N6   Db: Ger+6   F: It+6

a: Fr+6   Eb: V$^6_5$/ii   g: Ger+6   D: iv6   b: It+6

C. Label the chords in each excerpt below. Also, discuss the details of the resolution of each $^{+}6$ chord. Do $\#\hat{4}$ and $\flat\hat{6}$ follow their expected resolutions to $\hat{5}$? How are parallel 5ths avoided in the Ger^{+6} resolution(s)?

new

1. Clara Wieck Schumann, Polonaise, Op. 6, No. 6

2. This excerpt modulates.

Haydn, Quartet Op. 64, No. 2, III   ♩ ♩ p 395

3. Find in this excerpt two chords that are enharmonically equivalent but very different in function.

Reinecke, Flute Concerto, Op. 283, I

(3) **4.** Label all chords and find an example of a chromatic passing tone.

Haydn, Quartet Op. 20, No. 5, I

(4) 5. The two excerpts below are from the same song.

Beethoven, "Die Ehre Gottes aus der Natur," Op. 48, No. 4

D. Supply the missing voices for each fragment below. All but Exercise 5 are four-part textures.

E. Analyze the harmonies implied by this soprano-bass framework and try to include a Fr^{+6} and an example of mode mixture in your harmonization. Then complete the piano texture by filling in two inner parts in the treble-clef staff, following good voice-leading procedures.

F.   Analyze the chords specified by this figured bass, then make an arrangement for
     SATB chorus.

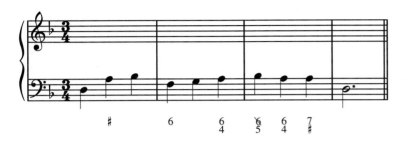

Exercise 23-1 See Workbook.

Chapter 24

Augmented
Sixth Chords 2

INTRODUCTION

Chapter 23 presented augmented sixth chords as they usually occur in tonal music: with $(\flat)\hat{6}$ in the bass, $\sharp\hat{4}$ in some upper part, and resolving outward to form a P8 on $\hat{5}$, which serves as the root of a V chord. Augmented sixth chords are sometimes used in other ways, however, including these:

1. A chord member other than $(\flat)\hat{6}$ may be used as the bass note.
2. The augmented sixth chord may serve a cadential function, resolving directly to a root position tonic triad.
3. The interval of the $^+6$ may be created by scale degrees other than $(\flat)\hat{6}$ and $\sharp\hat{4}$ to lead to some scale degree other than $\hat{5}$.
4. The interval of the $^+6$ may expand to the 3rd or the 5th of a chord instead of to its root.
5. The augmented sixth chord may not be one of the three commonly encountered types.

These five possibilities are discussed in more detail in the following sections. The list is organized according to frequency of occurrence, which means that you would rarely encounter the uses listed toward the bottom.

OTHER BASS POSITIONS

We have not yet discussed what pitch serves as the root of an augmented sixth chord. The reason for this is that the augmented sixth chord is a linear sonority that *has no root*. One can arrange the notes of a Fr^{+6} to resemble an altered V^7/V, and the It^{+6} and Ger^{+6} sonorities can be likened to altered iv^7 chords. Indeed, many theorists prefer to use modified roman numerals as a convenient way to represent augmented sixth chords. Still, these chords are rootless; they have only a most common bass position, that position having the $(\flat)\hat{6}$ in the bass.

Although the minor mode $\hat{6}$ usually constitutes the bass of an $^+6$ chord, other bass positions do occur, especially in music of the Romantic period. Generally, the voice leading will be identical or similar to that found in the standard resolutions discussed in

Chapter 23, but the interval of the $^{+}6$ will often be inverted to become a $^{\circ}3$. The most common of the various possibilities is that with $\sharp\hat{4}$ in the bass, as in Example 24-1. Notice also the enharmonic spelling of the Ger^{+6}

♫ EXAMPLE 24-1   *Brahms, "Ruf zur Maria," Op. 22, No. 5*

A progression very similar to the one in Example 24-1 is seen in an excerpt from a jazz tune in Example 11-13. If you will turn back to that example, you will see that it ends with a IV–Ger^{+6}–I$^6_4$–V^7–I progression with $\sharp\hat{4}$ in the bass of the Ger^{+6} chord. The lead sheet symbol in this case is E♭7/D♭, the D♭ functioning enharmonically as a C♯.

The only other bass position that occurs with any frequency is that with the tonic pitch in the bass, as in Example 24-2.

♫ EXAMPLE 24-2   *Brahms, Symphony No. 1, Op. 68, II (piano reduction)*

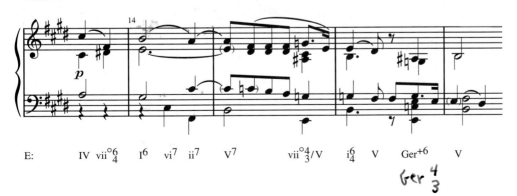

Because $^+6$ chords have no root and therefore technically cannot be inverted, it is not necessary to show the bass position of the chord in the analytical symbol. Just use It^{+6}, or whatever is appropriate, regardless of the bass position.

RESOLUTIONS TO TONIC

Occasionally an augmented sixth chord will progress directly to a root position triad without passing through a dominant chord on the way.* In Example 24-3, a Ger^{+6} chord appears in its usual position, with $\flat\hat{6}$ in the bass, but it is followed by a I chord instead of the usual V chord. Notice the enharmonic spelling of E♮ and F♭ in m. 253, a practice that is discussed in more detail in the next chapter.

♫ EXAMPLE 24-3   *Tchaikovsky,* Romeo and Juliet, *Op. 45 (strings and winds)*

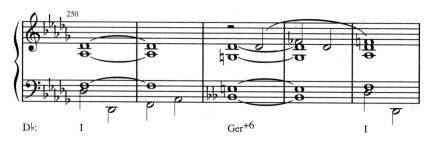

Db: I   Ger^{+6} I

Augmented sixth chords that resolve to tonic may occur in any bass position. In the previous example, the usual $\flat\hat{6}$ is in the bass, whereas in Example 24-4 the bass note is $\hat{3}$. Once again we see an enharmonic spelling, this time substituting G♮ for F𝄪. Notice that no special symbol is needed for the sorts of augmented sixth chords discussed in this section.

♫ EXAMPLE 24-4   *Dvořák,* Symphony No. 9 ("From the New World"), II
                  (simplified texture)

c#:   ii$^{\varnothing6}_{5}$ V   i   Ger^{+6} i   Ger^{+6} i   I

We are indebted to Charles J. Smith for Examples 24-3 and 24-4.

RESOLUTIONS TO OTHER SCALE DEGREES

As we have shown, the interval of the ⁺6 is usually created by the half steps above and below $\hat{5}$. Especially in the Romantic period, this same principle is occasionally applied to other scale degrees as well. In such cases we will employ analytical symbols similar to those used with secondary functions to indicate that the ⁺6 is embellishing some scale degree other than the dominant. The ⁺6 chords we have presented so far have all embellished the dominant, and we could have used symbols like Fr⁺⁶/V for these chords. However, we have followed the custom of symbolizing Fr⁺⁶/V as Fr⁺⁶. But when the ⁺6 embellishes some scale degree other than $\hat{5}$, we will make this clear by using the method shown in Example 24-5.

EXAMPLE 24-5

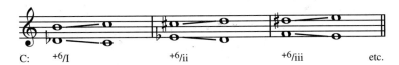

C: ⁺⁶/I   ⁺⁶/ii   ⁺⁶/iii   etc.

To spell or recognize the various ⁺6 types in these contents, you will have to be familiar with the intervallic structure of the three kinds of augmented sixth chord. In Example 24-6, ⁺6 chords embellishing $\hat{1}$ are formed by transposing the intervals from the more familiar ⁺6/V spellings.

EXAMPLE 24-6

C: It⁺⁶   It⁺⁶/I   Fr⁺⁶   Fr⁺⁶/I   Ger⁺⁶   Ger⁺⁶/I

The Ger⁺⁶/I–I cadence in Example 24-7 comes at the very end of a song, following a more conventional V$_3^4$–I cadence a few measures earlier.

EXAMPLE 24-7   *Chausson,* Sérénade italienne, *Op. 2, No. 5*

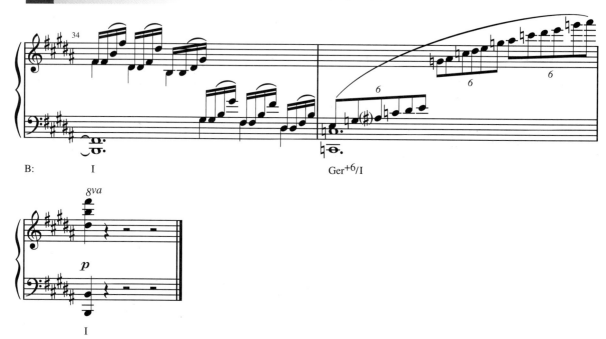

Often when an augmented sixth chord resolves to something other than V, the chord that it resolves to is a secondary dominant. In that case, it is probably better to show the analysis in relationship to the chord being tonicized. For example, the chord in m. 44 of Example 24-8 could be analyzed as an It^{+6}/vi, but it is better understood as part of a tonicization of F minor (ii).

EXAMPLE 24-8   *Mozart,* Sonata K. 457, I

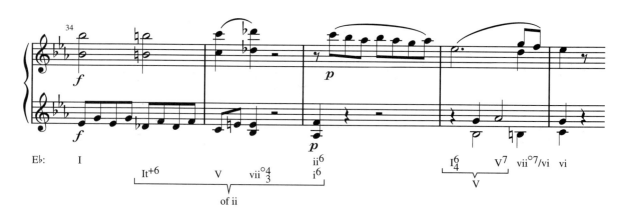

RESOLUTIONS TO OTHER CHORD MEMBERS

In all the resolutions discussed so far, the interval of the $^{+}6$ (or $^{\circ}3$) has resolved to the root of the next chord (which was sometimes ornamented with a cadential six-four chord). Much less common is the resolution of the $^{+}6$ or $^{\circ}3$ to the 3rd of a chord (as in Ex. 24-9a) or to the 5th of a chord (Ex. 24-9b). Such a use of the augmented sixth sonority is very different from those discussed so far. To signify this, the chord symbol is placed in brackets. It is important to realize that Examples 24-9b and c have little in common, even though they both show identically spelled Ger^{+6} chords followed by tonic triads. The tonic triad in Example 24-9b is in the relatively stable six-three position, whereas the tonic triad in Example 24-9c is a cadential six-four standing for the root position dominant that follows.

EXAMPLE 24-9

An example of a Ger^{+6} resolving to the 5th of a I chord is seen in Example 24-10. The textural reduction shows that the voice leading is very smooth. Be sure to listen to both versions.

EXAMPLE 24-10 *Chopin, Nocturne Op. 55, No. 2*

[Ger⁺⁶]

Textural reduction

OTHER TYPES OF AUGMENTED SIXTH CHORDS

Only rarely will you encounter an augmented sixth chord that is not one of the three standard types: Italian, French, or German. When you do encounter such a sonority, the symbol $^{+}6$ will suffice to show the characteristic interval found in the chord. One such chord is seen in Example 24-11. Here the $^{+}6$ sonority resembles a Fr^{+6}, but the D♭ would have to be a D♮ for it to be a Fr^{+6}. We enclose the $^{+}6$ symbol in brackets because the interval of the $^{+}6$ expands to the third of the I^{6} chord, as in Example 24-9a.

♫ EXAMPLE 24-11   *Strauss,* Till Eulenspiegel's Merry Pranks, *Op. 24 (piano reduction)*

[+6]   I⁶

The $^{+}6$ symbol may also be used for what is actually a very common occurrence—the use of two or three augmented sixth sonorities within the span of a single $^{+}6$ interval. In

Example 24-12 the pitches of all three types of augmented sixth chord appear in m. 15. In such cases the symbol ⁺6 would seem to be a good solution, although you could label the sonority that has the longest duration (Ger.⁺⁶) or the sonority that appears last (It⁺⁶) in Example 24-12.

EXAMPLE 24-12   *Mozart, Symphony No. 40, K. 550, I (piano reduction)*

g: ♯vi°⁷   ⁺6   V

Checkpoint

1. This chapter discusses five nonstandard ways in which augmented sixth chords may be used. List these five ways.
2. We enclose the augmented sixth chord symbol in brackets, as in [Fr⁺⁶], for which of those five uses?
3. What symbol do we use for the rare occurrence of an augmented sixth chord that is not one of the three standard types?

Summary

Most augmented sixth chords conform to the types discussed in the previous chapter, but variations do occur. For one thing, augmented sixth chords may appear with scale degrees other than (♭)6̂ in the bass—most commonly ♯4̂, but other chord members may appear in the bass as well. Another possibility is for the augmented sixth chord to resolve to a root position tonic triad. Also, the interval of the augmented 6th may embellish scale degrees other than 5̂, the chord of resolution often being a secondary dominant. Yet another possibility is to resolve the interval of an augmented 6th not to the root of a chord but to the 3rd or 5th. (This does not include the resolution to I⁶₄–V, where the I⁶₄ really represents the V chord.) Finally, you might on occasion encounter an augmented sixth chord that is not one of the three standard types (Italian, French, or German).

Self-Test 24-1
(Answers begin in page 653.)

A. Label the following chords.

B. Analysis.

1. Label the chords in this short excerpt.

Brahms, Quartet No. 2, Op. 51, No. 2, III

2. Label the chords in this excerpt.

Tchaikovsky, "The Witch," Op. 39, No. 20

3. This is the ending of one of Schumann's better-known songs. What national anthem is hinted at in the vocal part? Notice also the contrast between the diatonic setting of the text and the more chromatic codetta that ends the song. Label chords and NCTs.

Schumann, "Die beiden Grenadiere," Op. 49, No. 1

Schwer-ter ___ klir - ren und bli - tzen; dann steig' ich ge-waff - net her - vor ans dem Grab, den

Kai - ser, den Kai - ser zu schü - tzen!"

4. Label the chords, but not NCTs, in this excerpt. (Hint: Analyze the E♭ in m. 4 as a D♯.) Notice that in the first measure, for example, the A2 is the bass note through the entire measure.

Chopin, Mazurka, Op. 67, No. 4

Exercise 24-1 See Workbook.

Chapter 25

Enharmonic Spellings and Enharmonic Modulations

ENHARMONIC SPELLINGS

Enharmonic spellings are used by composers for a variety of reasons. One reason is to indicate clearly the direction in which a pitch will move. For example, consider the vii°⁷/V in Example 25-1a. When the vii°⁷/V moves to the cadential I$^6_4$, there is nowhere for the A♭ to go but up to A♮. This motion looks a little more sensible when the A♭ is spelled as G♯, as it is in Example 25-1b, but the aural result with any fixed-pitch instrument is the same. This new spelling changes the chord visually from a b°⁷ to a g♯°⁷, but it does not change its function or the analysis. Of course, when the vii°⁷/V moves directly to V, as in Example 25-1c, the A♭ spelling poses no problem because the seventh resolves immediately downward to the G.

EXAMPLE 25-1

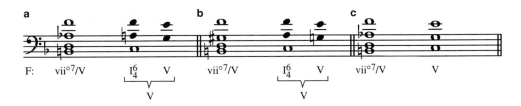

If you turn back to an earlier excerpt (Ex. 17-10 on p. 289), you will see an illustration of the enharmonically spelled vii°⁷/V, voiced exactly as in Example 25-1b. Very similar to the enharmonically spelled vii°⁷/V is the enharmonically spelled Ger^{+6} chord (review Ex. 23-13 on p. 390). Notice that both involve the respelled ♭$\hat{3}$/♯$\hat{2}$ preceding a I$^6_4$ in the major mode.

Another reason for enharmonic spellings is the desire on the part of the composer to make things easier for the performer. This is presumably the case in Example 25-2, which tonicizes F♭, the ♭VI of A♭. In the ♭VI portion (mm. 89–92) Mendelssohn notates the second violin and viola enharmonically in the key of E, presumably to make their tremolos easier to read.

EXAMPLE 25-2   *Mendelssohn, Quartet Op. 80, IV*

Instead of enharmonically spelling only some of the parts, as Mendelssohn did in the example above, composers usually respell the key entirely. In Schubert's String Trio there is a modulation from B♭ to G♭ (♭VI), which then changes by mode mixture into g♭ minor. To avoid this awkward key (the key signature would contain nine flats!), Schubert quite reasonably notates it in f♯ minor. The harmonic skeleton of this passage is shown in Example 25-3.

EXAMPLE 25-3   *Schubert, String Trio D. 581, I (textural reduction)*

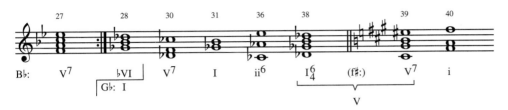

Examples of enharmonically spelled keys abound in nineteenth-century music. One of Schubert's impromptus contains a passage with the following tonal structure: E♭–e♭–c♭, the last being spelled as b minor. The e♭–c♭ portion of that passage is given in Example 25-4.

♫   EXAMPLE 25-4   *Schubert, Impromptu Op. 90, No. 2*

Composers will often—but not always—change the key signature in situations such as this. Otherwise, they will use whatever accidentals are required. This is the case with the Self-Test 21-1, part C5 (pp. 368–369), where Beethoven used accidentals to notate passages in b minor and D major, even though the key signature contains seven flats. However it is notated, the enharmonically spelled key is an example of enharmonic spelling for convenience; the listener is entirely unaware of the enharmonic spelling, and no special analytical symbols are required. Enharmonic spelling for convenience is *not* the same as enharmonic modulation, which is a much more interesting topic and which is the subject of the rest of this chapter.

ENHARMONIC REINTERPRETATION

The enharmonic spelling discussed so far in this chapter is intended primarily for the eye, not the ear. However, there are four sonorities used in tonal music that can be reinterpreted enharmonically *in a different key* (not in enharmonic keys, like G♭ and F♯), and the listener can hear this reinterpretation when these chords resolve.

One such sonority is the major-minor seventh, which can serve either as a V^7 or as a Ger^{+6} (Ex. 25-5a). Another is the diminished seventh chord, where any tone can serve as the leading tone (Ex. 25-5b). The other two possibilities are the augmented triad and the Fr^{+6} chord, although these chords are rarely reinterpreted enharmonically. Parallel major or minor keys could be substituted for the keys shown in Example 25-5 and in similar examples throughout this chapter.

EXAMPLE 25-5

a

Db: V^7 c: Ger^{+6}

b

a: vii$^{\circ 7}$ f#:   vii$^{\circ \frac{6}{5}}$ eb: vii$^{\circ \frac{4}{3}}$ c: vii$^{\circ \frac{4}{2}}$

The implications of all this are that when the listener hears a major-minor seventh or diminished seventh sonority, certain expectations will probably arise (such as, "This chord will resolve as a V^7 in Db"), only to be pleasantly thwarted on occasion by an equally logical enharmonic reinterpretation (such as, in this case, a Ger^{+6} in C). This process, which is often reserved for especially dramatic spots in a composition, is known as *enharmonic modulation.*

Checkpoint

1. Contrast enharmonic spelling for convenience and enharmonic modulation.
2. Make up a key scheme starting with Bb that might result in enharmonic spelling for the convenience of the performer.
3. What four sonorities can be reinterpreted enharmonically so that they occur in different keys?
4. Which two of these four sonorities are commonly used enharmonically in tonal music?

ENHARMONIC MODULATIONS USING THE MAJOR-MINOR SEVENTH SONORITY

The term *enharmonic modulation* is used to refer to a modulation in which the common chord is reinterpreted enharmonically to fit into the second key. The actual spelling of the chord is not important—it might be spelled as it would appear in the first key, or in the second key, or even in both if it occurs more than once. What is important is that the common chord can be *heard* as a sensible chord in both keys.

The person listening to Example 25-6 probably expects the fourth chord to resolve as a V^7/IV in G, as it does in the top staff. However, the possibility exists that it may be enharmonically reinterpreted as a Ger^{+6} in B, as seen on the bottom staff. This reinterpretation results in an enharmonic modulation from G to B. Play Example 25-6 several times, comparing the effect of the two resolutions of the major-minor seventh sonority.

EXAMPLE 25-6

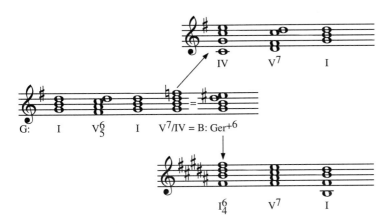

Now compare Example 25-6 with Example 25-7. The last chord in m. 41 of Example 25-7 sounds like a G^7 chord. Because the tonality at this point is G, the listener probably expects the next measure to begin with a C chord (IV in G). Instead, the G^7 is treated and spelled as a Ger^{+6} in B major.

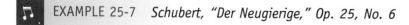

EXAMPLE 25-7   *Schubert, "Der Neugierige," Op. 25, No. 6*

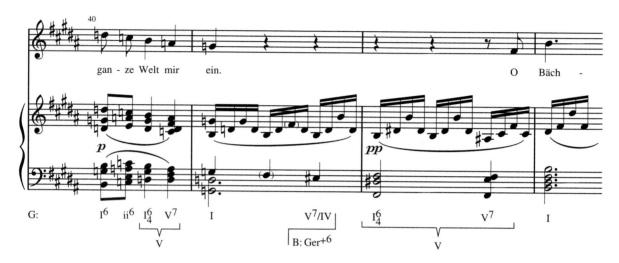

Any V^7 chord or secondary V^7 in the first key can be reinterpreted as a Ger^{+6} chord in the new key. The reverse is also possible—a Ger^{+6} in the first key can become a V^7 or secondary V^7 in the second key. However, in the majority of cases the common chord is a Ger^{+6} in the second key, presumably because of its more dramatic effect. Also, the major-minor seventh chord in the first key seems most often to be a V^7/IV. This common relationship, V^7/IV becoming Ger^{+6}, was illustrated in Examples 25-6 and 25-7. It would also be possible to use an It^{+6} as the enharmonic equivalent of an incomplete V^7, but this is not often encountered because of doubling problems.

ENHARMONIC MODULATIONS USING THE DIMINISHED SEVENTH CHORD

Surprisingly, the diminished seventh chord is not used as frequently as the major-minor seventh chord in enharmonic modulations, even though any diminished seventh chord can lead in four directions, compared to the two possible with the major-minor seventh (see Ex. 25-5). The top staff of Example 25-8 shows four resolutions of the same diminished seventh sonority. The bottom staff is similar, except that the diminished seventh chord in each case is followed by a V^7 before the resolution to tonic. Both methods—$vii°^7$–I and $vii°^7$–V^7–I—are used in enharmonic modulations. You should play through Example 25-8 to familiarize yourself with the sound of these resolutions.

EXAMPLE 25-8

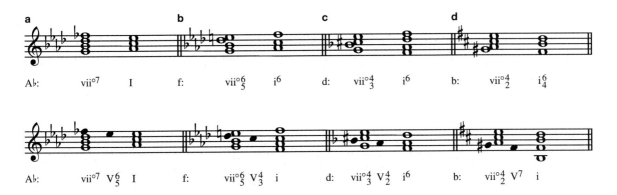

Example 25-9 is from the end of the first part of a movement by Haydn. The movement begins in f minor and modulates to A♭, the relative major. Because the composer is going to repeat the entire first section, he must modulate back to f minor before the repeat. Haydn prepares for the modulation in mm. 46 to 47 by using a g°⁷ chord (vii°⁷ in A♭), just as in the top staff of Example 25-8a. In the first ending, however, he uses the same sonority, respelled as vii°⁶₅ in f, and resolves it as in the bottom staff of Example 25-8b, bringing us back to f minor for the repeat.

EXAMPLE 25-9   *Haydn, Quartet Op. 20, No. 5, I*

Example 25-10 begins and ends in A major. A c♯°⁷ chord appears in m. 140, but the listener probably hears it as an a♯°⁷, which is a vii°$^6_5$/ii in A major (vii°⁷/IV would be another possibility). However, Beethoven treats this chord as a vii°$^4_2$ in F, the c♯ in the bass really acting like a d♭. This is similar to the bottom staff of Example 25-8d. When this same chord recurs in m. 145, it *sounds* like a vii°⁷/vi in F because it follows V and seems to imply a V–vii°⁷/vi–vi deceptive progression. Instead, it is treated (and notated) as an a♯°⁷, a vii°⁷/ii in A major.

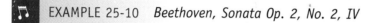

EXAMPLE 25-10   *Beethoven, Sonata Op. 2, No. 2, IV*

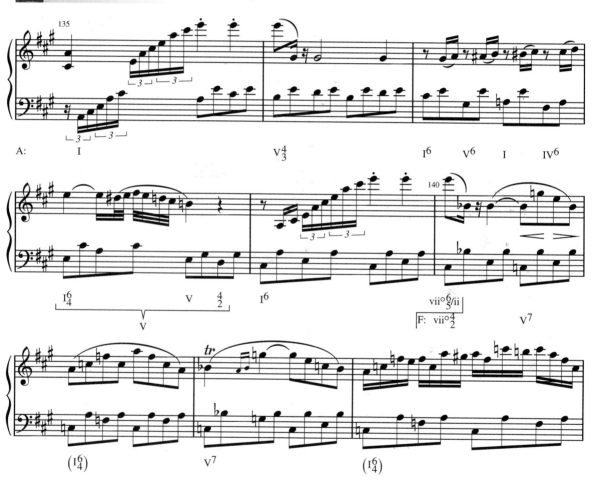

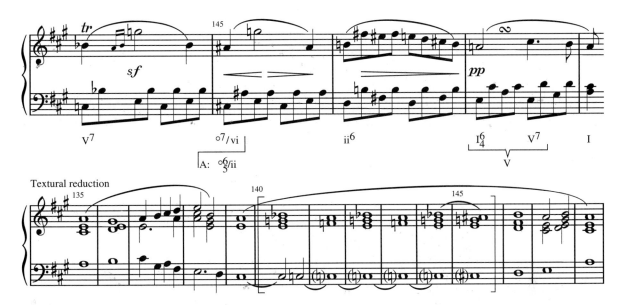

The textural reduction that appears below Example 25-10 is worth studying. Play it and listen to it, paying special attention to the bass line. You will find that mm. 140 to 145 constitute a harmonic digression, keeping the C♯ in m. 139 from reaching its goal, D, until m. 146. The entire example is a parallel period. The first phrase is four measures long, ending with a half cadence in m. 138. The second phrase begins like the first (thus the parallel structure), but it is expanded from four to ten measures by the tonicization of ♭VI in mm. 140 to 145. This expansion is indicated by the brackets in the reduction.

OTHER EXAMPLES OF ENHARMONICISM

Major-minor seventh chords and diminished seventh chords are sometimes used enharmonically at a more local level. In Example 25-11 there is a brief tonicization of a♭ (the minor Neapolitan!) in mm. 160 to 161, but it is much too brief to be a modulation. Measure 162 sounds like the same chord that was used in m. 160—a V7 of a♭—but here it functions as a Ger^{+6} in G. The extremely unusual minor Neapolitan comes about through a harmonic sequence: G7–c–E♭7–a♭.*

The original version of this impromptu is in G♭ instead of G, which means that it tonicizes a♭♭! Schubert was considerate, however, and wrote the key of a♭♭ enharmonically as g.

♫ EXAMPLE 25-11   *Schubert, Impromptu, Op. 90, No. 3*

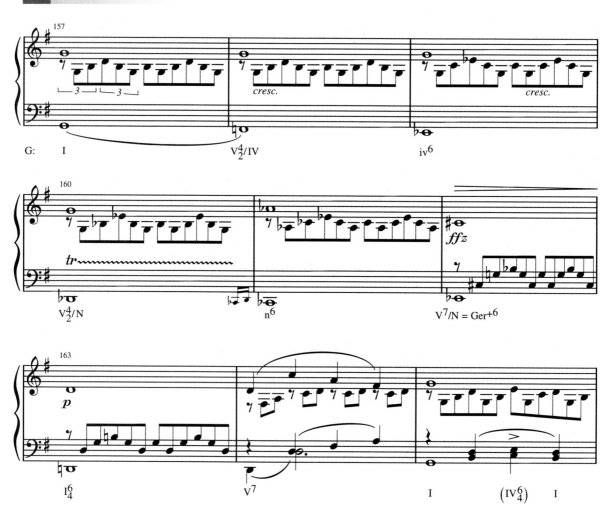

Summary

Enharmonic spellings are sometimes used when a composer wants to make the direction of a line more apparent to the performer—as in D–D♯–E as opposed to D–E♭–E—or when a composer simply wants to make something easier to read—by notating a passage in E instead of F♭, for example. These sorts of enharmonic spellings come about for the performer's convenience, but they are inaudible to the listener. *Enharmonic reinterpretations,* on the other hand, are audible because they reinterpret a chord in a new key as part of a modulation. Enharmonic modulations almost always use either a major-minor seventh chord or a diminished seventh chord as the common chord. The major-minor seventh chord will be heard as a German augmented sixth chord in one key and a V^7 (or secondary V^7) in the other. The diminished seventh chord used as a common chord will be a vii°^{7} (or secondary vii°^{7}) in both keys, but different pitch classes will serve as roots in the two keys.

Self-Test 25-1
(Answers begin on page 654.)

A.   Analyze the given chord. Then show any possible enharmonic reinterpretation(s) of that chord, keeping the same key signature. Each enharmonic reinterpretation should involve a new key, not just an enharmonically equivalent key (such as g♯ and a♭). Number 1 is given as an example.

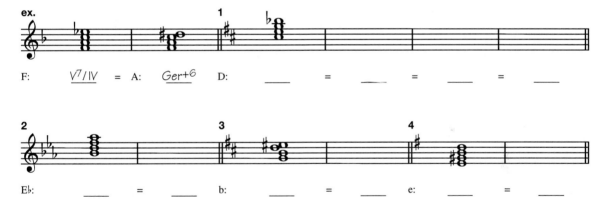

B.   Each of the following short examples contains an enharmonic modulation. Analyze each example *after* playing it slowly at the piano and listening for the point of modulation. Do not try to analyze these examples without hearing them.

C.   Analysis. Be sure to play as much of each excerpt at the piano as you can, simplifying the texture as necessary.

     1.   This excerpt begins in G♭ and ends in b♭ minor, although B♭ major is the eventual goal. Label all the chords. Can you relate the F–G♭–F figure in the last measure to anything that has happened earlier? That is, does it remind you of any other figure heard in this excerpt?

Beethoven, "Adelaide," Op. 46

2. Look back at the Schubert excerpt in Self-Test 19-1, part A2 (pp. 330–331). Is this an enharmonic modulation? Explain your answer.

3. This excerpt begins in B♭ and modulates to f♯. Before you try to analyze the modulation, play the excerpt slowly as block chords, listening carefully as you play.

Schubert, Piano Sonata, D. 960, I

4. This excerpt begins and ends in c minor. Label all the chords. This passage really represents an extended V–i cadence in c minor. An important role in extending the passage is played by the pitch class F♯/G♭. Make a list of all the chords containing F♯/G♭ and their locations.

Beethoven, Sonata Op. 10, No. 1, III

5. This passage begins in C and ends in E, although the eventual goal is the key of A. Label all chords in this excerpt. Is there an important pitch class in this excerpt similar to the F♯/G♭ in the previous passage? If so, which one do you think it is and why?

Schubert, Quartet Op. 125, No. 2, II

Exercise 25-1 See Workbook.

26

Further Elements of the Harmonic Vocabulary

INTRODUCTION

Tonal harmony, on the surface a simple and natural musical phenomenon, is really a very complex and variable set of relationships. Many people have devoted years to the study of tonal harmony and to the almost limitless number of musical structures for which it has provided the foundation. It surely represents one of the highest achievements of Western art and intellect.

Because the subject is so complex, we have been concerned throughout this text with those harmonic events in tonal music that could be thought of as the basic vocabulary of the system—those events that occur with a relatively high degree of frequency. This chapter deals with a few details that are perhaps less fundamental but that, nevertheless, deserve attention. However, of course, even with this chapter we will not completely exhaust the harmonic vocabulary. The variations in detail and exceptions to the norms found in tonal music are too numerous to codify; in fact, it is doubtful that they ever will be codified. This complexity is one of the really fascinating aspects of tonal music, an aspect you can look forward to exploring in your further study of the literature.

THE DOMINANT WITH A SUBSTITUTED 6TH

You may be familiar with the concept of added-note chords, such as the triad with an added 6th. Such chords were not really a standard part of the vocabulary of Western music before impressionism, but they were recognized as a possibility long before that time. For example, Jean Philippe Rameau (1683–1764), an influential French theorist and composer, considered the first chord in Example 26-1 to be a IV chord with an added 6th. Although you might prefer to label it as a ii$^6_5$, that approach does not explain the unresolved 7th (Bb3). Whichever analysis you choose, the cadence is plagal (review pp. 160–161).

EXAMPLE 26-1

Bb: IV^{add6} I
      (ii$^6_5$)

Although triads with added 6ths are not characteristic of most tonal music, the dominant chord with a *substituted 6th* is not uncommon, especially in the nineteenth century. In this case, the 6th above the root is substituted for the 5th, which does not appear. If you play the three cadences in Example 26-2, you will find that they have a similar effect. The first one, of course, is a familiar form of the perfect authentic cadence. Example 26-2b incorporates an escape tone that embellishes the 5th of the V chord. In Example 26-2c the A4 appears in place of the 5th—it is a substituted 6th (V$^{subs}_{6th}$). You might have noticed that the V$^{subs}_{6th}$ contains the same scale degrees as those found in a iii^6 chord, but the function is clearly dominant. To analyze the cadence in Example 26-2c as iii^6–I would certainly be an error.

EXAMPLE 26-2

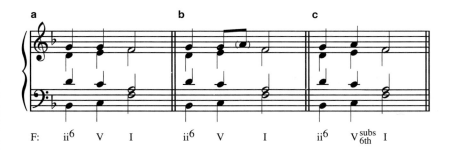

F: ii^6 V   I   ii^6 V   I   ii^6 V$^{subs}_{6th}$ I

Example 26-3 contains an illustration of the V$^{subs}_{6th}$. Notice that the E5, the pitch that would have been the 5th of the V chord, appears immediately before the F♯5. The V$^{subs}_{6th}$ is usually prepared in this manner, which leads some theorists to analyze the V$^{subs}_{6th}$ as a V chord with a metrical escape tone. Either approach is acceptable.

♫ EXAMPLE 26-3   *Haydn, Symphony No. 101, IV*

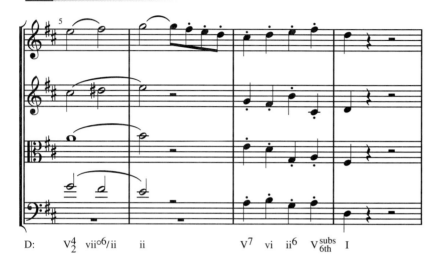

D: V$^4_2$ vii°^{6}/ii   ii   V^7 vi   ii^6 V$^{subs}_{6th}$ I

Example 26-4 is strikingly similar to the previous example, but it is in the minor mode. Notice again the preparation of the 6th.

♫ EXAMPLE 26-4   *Schumann, "Folk Song," Op. 68, No. 9*

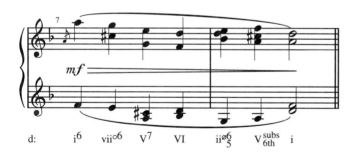

d: i^6 vii°^{6} V^7 VI   ii$^{ø6}_5$ V$^{subs}_{6th}$ i

The substituted 6th may appear in connection with the dominant triad, as in the examples above, or with the V^7, as in Example 26-5.

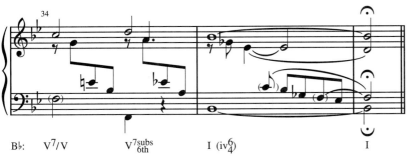

EXAMPLE 26-5 *Schumann,* Humoresque, *Op. 20*

The V_{6th}^{subs} and V_{6th}^{7subs} are usually found in root position with the substituted 6th in the top voice, and the 6th is always voiced higher than the 7th in the V_{6th}^{7subs}. The 6th resolves by leaping down to the tonic pitch.

THE DOMINANT WITH A RAISED 5TH

When the 5th of a V or V^7 is chromatically raised, the sonority that results is either an augmented triad (V^+) or an augmented minor-seventh chord (V^{+7}). This alteration is useful in that the raised 5th creates a leading tone to the 3rd of the tonic triad. The leading-tone effect would not be present if the tonic triad were minor, and for this reason the augmented dominant is not found resolving to a minor triad. These concepts are illustrated in Example 26-6.

EXAMPLE 26-6

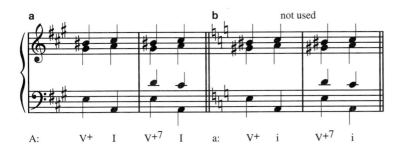

Notice that the V^{+7} may contain the interval of an $^+6$, depending on the voicing (between the soprano and tenor in Ex. 26-6a). Try not to confuse this altered dominant, whether in root position or inversion, with more conventional $^+6$ chords.

Most instances of V^+ and V^{+7} find the augmented dominant preceded by its diatonic form, which means that the $\sharp\hat{2}$ could also be analyzed as a chromatic passing tone. The C$\sharp$5 in Example 26-7 is a chromatic passing tone, but at the same time it creates a V^{+7} for a duration of four eighth notes.

EXAMPLE 26-7   Beethoven, Symphony No. 9, Op. 125, III (strings)

The V^+ and V^{+7} in the major mode are enharmonic with the V^{subs}_{6th} and V^{7subs}_{6th} in the minor mode, as Example 26-8 illustrates. The resolutions are quite different, however: the raised 5th of the V^+ moves up by half step to $\hat{3}$ (Ex. 26-8a), whereas the substituted 6th of the V^{subs}_{6th} leaps down to $\hat{1}$ (Ex. 26-8b).

EXAMPLE 26-8

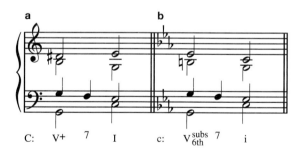

Example 26-9 begins with a V chord in the key of C♯, and the chord eventually resolves to a I, enharmonically spelled as D♭. In the second measure of the example, the E4 would appear to create a V^{7subs}_{6th}, but if you play the example, you will hear that the E4 is really a D×4, and the chord is a G♯$^{+7}$ (compare Ex. 26-8a). Chopin used this enharmonic spelling for the convenience of the performer, who would rather read G♯–E–F in the soprano than G♯–D×–F.

EXAMPLE 26-9 *Chopin, Nocturne Op. 48, No. 2*

C#/Db: V   V+7   I   V⁴₃

Secondary dominants may also appear in augmented form. Most common are the V⁺/IV and the V⁺⁷/IV, as in Example 26-10.

EXAMPLE 26-10 *Haydn, Quartet Op. 9, No. 2, I*

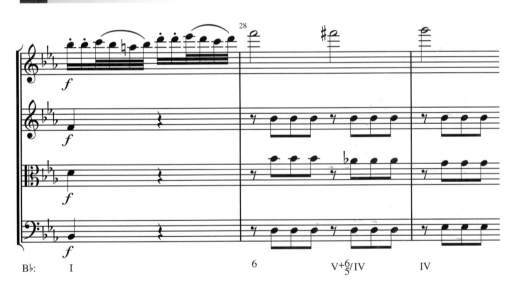

Bb: I   6   V+⁶₅/IV   IV

When a dominant seventh with a raised 5th appears in third inversion, it appears to be some kind of augmented sixth chord. In Example 26-11 the V⁺⁴₂/IV has an +6 between the outer parts (G♮–D♯), so in a sense it *is* a kind of augmented sixth chord, but the better analysis is the one shown.

EXAMPLE 26-11 *Schubert, Quartet Op. 29, IV*

A: V$^6_5$ V$^4_2$/IV IV^6 IV   V$^6_5$/IV   IV V+$^4_2$/IV IV^6

NINTH, ELEVENTH, AND THIRTEENTH CHORDS

Just as superimposed 3rds produce triads and seventh chords, continuation of that process yields ninth, eleventh, and thirteenth chords (which is not to say that this is the manner in which these sonorities evolved historically). These chords are shown in Example 26-12.

EXAMPLE 26-12

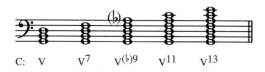

C: V   V^7 V$^{(\flat)9}$ V^{11} V^{13}

Interesting as these chords may be, the triad and the seventh chord were really the standard fare of music in the eighteenth and nineteenth centuries. True elevenths and thirteenths are rare before impressionism. Ninths occur throughout the tonal era, but the 9th of the chord often can be analyzed as an NCT and usually disappears before the chord resolves. The most common way to resolve the 9th is to slip down a step to double the root of the V^7. This is what happens in Example 26-13, where the minor-mode 9th, F$\flat$5, moves down by step to E$\flat$5, the root of the V^7.

EXAMPLE 26-13 *Beethoven, Sonata Op. 2, No. 1, I*

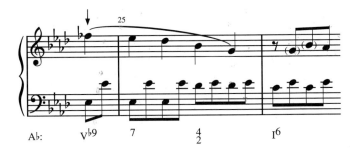

Another possibility, illustrated in Example 26-14, is to arpeggiate from the 9th of the chord down to the 7th.

EXAMPLE 26-14 *Beethoven, Quartet Op. 59, No. 2, III (piano reduction)*

Certainly, examples may be found of ninth chords that maintain the quality of a ninth chord right up to the resolution, at which point the 9th resolves down by step. This is illustrated in Example 26-15, where the 9th, F, resolves to E in the next chord.

EXAMPLE 26-15 *Schumann, "Leides Ahnung," Op. 124, No. 2*

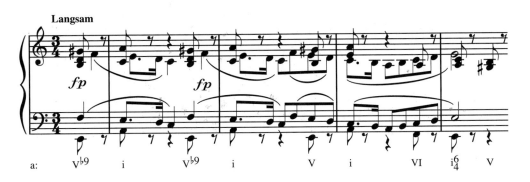

All the examples of ninth chords cited so far have been dominant ninths. Although dominant ninths are the most commonly encountered, other ninth chords do occur. Example 26-16 contains a clear instance of a iv^9.

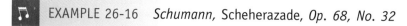

EXAMPLE 26-16   *Schumann, Scheherazade, Op. 68, No. 32*

The symbols used in the analysis of ninth chords are not standardized. The easiest approach is to let the roman numeral reflect the triad type, with the *9* simply appended to it. Inversions of ninth chords are not as common as inversions of triads and seventh chords. Moreover, the figured bass symbols for inversions of ninth chords are too cumbersome to be practicable. A useful, if unscientific, solution is to give in parentheses the figures used for inversions of seventh chords: $V^9(^6_5)$ and so on. This will not work in the case of a ninth chord in fourth inversion, but the fourth inversion is very uncommon.

THE COMMON-TONE DIMINISHED SEVENTH CHORD

Most diminished seventh chords function as leading-tone sevenths of tonic or of some other chord within the tonality. Although the enharmonic potential of the diminished seventh chord is occasionally exploited in enharmonic modulation, the resolution of the chord generally clarifies its function.

However, there is a diminished seventh chord usage that does not conform to the usual pattern. In this case, the diminished seventh chord progresses to a triad or dominant seventh chord, the *root* of which is the *same* as one of the notes of the $°7$ chord. In Example 26-17, G5, the 7th of the $a\sharp^{°7}$, is retained to become the root of the next chord. It is obvious that the $a\sharp^{°7}$ is not a leading-tone 7th of the G^6 or the G^6_5. We refer to a diminished seventh chord used in this way as a *common-tone diminished seventh* ($ct°7$). Remember that the tone in common is the root of the major triad or dominant seventh chord.

EXAMPLE 26-17

a♯°7   G⁶   a♯°7   G⁶₅

The function of a ct°⁷ is simply one of embellishment, and we put its analytical symbol in parentheses to indicate its weak harmonic function. A ct°⁷ can be used to embellish any triad or dominant seventh chord, but it is most often found progressing to I in major or V⁽⁷⁾ in major or minor. Most often the ct°⁷ has a distinctly nonessential flavor, acting as a neighbor chord (Exx. 26-18a and b) or as a passing chord (Ex. 26-18c). Notice the smooth voice leading in all the parts. Because the ct°⁷ has no theoretical root, no inversions should be indicated when labeling ct°⁷ chords.

EXAMPLE 26-18

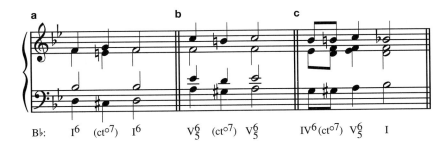

B♭:   I⁶   (ct°⁷)   I⁶   V⁶₅   (ct°⁷)   V⁶₅   IV⁶ (ct°⁷)   V⁶₅   I

Example 26-19 illustrates the ct°⁷–I progression interpolated between a pedal IV⁶₄ and its resolution back to I. The textural reduction of the accompaniment shows that the only significant harmonic event here is the presentation of the tonic triad. The V⁴₃ consists only of neighbor tones on a weak beat, whereas the IV⁶₄ and ct°⁷ in combination form a double neighbor group figure in the inner voices.

EXAMPLE 26-19   *Mozart, Sonata K. 545, II*

Textural reduction

Whereas ct°⁷ chords are usually complete, incomplete versions are sometimes encountered, as in Example 26-20, where the ct°⁷ chord is missing an A.

EXAMPLE 26-20   *Clara Wieck Schumann, Concert Variations, Op. 8, Var. 2*

V^9/ii ii $ii°^6$ I_4^6

The ct°7 chords in Example 26-21 embellish a dominant chord. Although ct°7 chords are clearly ornamental, their flavor is crucial to this passage and to the waltz that follows.

EXAMPLE 26-21   *Tchaikovsky,* Nutcracker Suite, *"Waltz of the Flowers"*
                                   (piano arrangement)

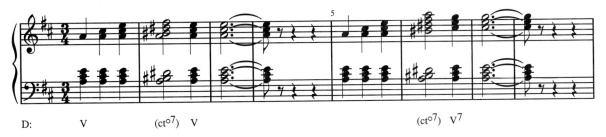

D: V   (ct°7)   V   (ct°7) V^7

Another prominent ct°7 embellishing V is seen in Example 26-22. The eight-measure introduction to this famous Sousa march is essentially a long dominant harmony.

EXAMPLE 26-22   *Sousa,* Semper Fidelis

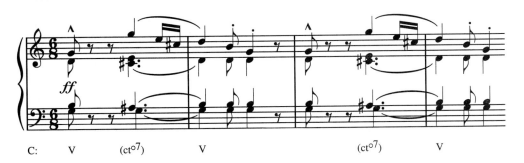

C: V   (ct°7)   V   (ct°7)   V

The ct°⁷ that embellishes I is usually spelled as a ♯ii°⁷ and that which embellishes V as a ♯vi°⁷, as in Example 26-18. However, enharmonic spellings are frequently found. In Example 26-23 Brahms spells the ct°⁷ embellishing I as a ♯iv°⁷ to clarify the F–A♭–F arpeggiation in the melody (instead of F–G♯–F).

One feature of the theme that begins in Example 26-23 is extensive use of mode mixture, and the A♭ introduces this technique more clearly than G♯ would have. This marvelous theme should be studied in its entirety (mm. 1–15), using a recording and a full score. You will discover not only mode mixture but also additional ct°⁷ chords, other altered chords, and polymeter (the aural effect of two or more different meters occurring at the same time). Motivic relationships are also of interest. For example, compare the melody in mm. 1 to 3 with the bass in mm. 3 to 5. Incidentally, the inner voices of this example have been included only to clarify the harmonies—they do not indicate Brahms' actual voice leading, which is too complicated for a piano reduction.

♫   **EXAMPLE 26-23**   *Brahms, Symphony No. 3, Op. 90, I (simplified texture)*

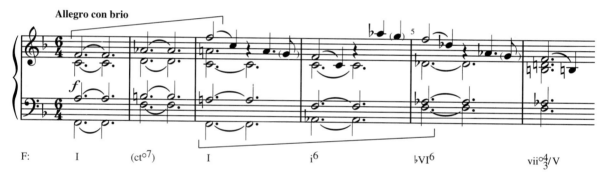

Lead sheet symbols will also occasionally imply an enharmonically spelled ct°⁷. The g♯°⁷ in Example 26-24 is spelled as a ♯i°⁷, but it is a ct°⁷ of V and would usually be spelled as an e♯°⁷.

♫   **EXAMPLE 26-24**   *Kern, "The Last Time I Saw Paris"*

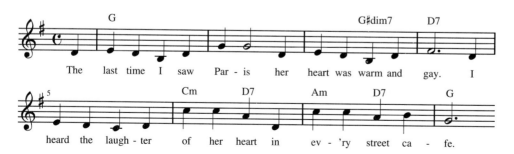

Words by Oscar Hammerstein II, music by Jerome Kern. International Copyright Secured, Copyright Renewed. Used by permission of Hal Leonard Corporation.

It is easy to confuse the vii°⁷/V with the ct°⁷ that embellishes the tonic because they are enharmonically equivalent and both are sometimes spelled enharmonically (review Chapter 25, p. 413). This is especially clear in Example 26-23, where the ct°⁷ is spelled as a vii°⁷/V (b°⁷). You should have no trouble if you will keep the following in mind:

Chord following the °7 chord:	Should be analyzed as:
I or I⁶	ct°⁷
V or I⁶₄	vii°⁷/V

In Example 26-25 Schumann spells the chord on the second beat of m. 15 as a d♯°⁷, a ct°⁷ of I, but its resolution to I⁶₄–V⁹ requires an analysis as a vii°⁷/V. The texture of this example is quite complex and features imitation between the soprano and alto parts.

♫ EXAMPLE 26-25   Schumann, "Lento espressivo," Op. 68, No. 21

Common-tone diminished seventh chords are sometimes used to embellish secondary dominants as well as the usual I and V chords. The climactic point in the passage in Example 26-26 is the a°⁷ chord in mm. 65 to 66, which is a ct°⁷ of the very short I⁶ chord in m. 67 or of the V⁷/ii that is the main harmony in the measure or both.

♫ EXAMPLE 26-26   Joplin, "Fig Leaf Rag"

$\text{(ct}^{\circ 7})$ V^4_3/ii 7 $\text{vii}^{\varnothing 6}_5/\text{V}$ V^7 I

                                        $(\text{I}^6?)$

In Example 26-27 a ct$^{\circ 7}$ chord is used enharmonically as part of a tonicization of the Neapolitan. When we first hear the diminished seventh chord in m. 12, we probably hear it as vii$^{\circ 7}$/vi and expect a vi to follow as a deceptive resolution of the preceding V^7. Instead, it functions as a ct$^{\circ 7}$ of the V^7/N that follows it. Notice also the unusual Ger^{+6} chord in m. 15.

♫ EXAMPLE 26-27 *Fanny Mendelssohn Hensel, "Beharre"*

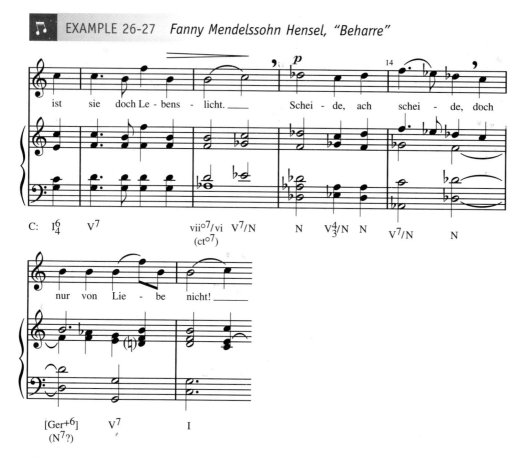

C: I^6_4 V^7 $\text{vii}^{\circ 7}/\text{vi}$ V^7/N N V^4_3/N N V^7/N N

                            $(\text{ct}^{\circ 7})$

[Ger^{+6}] V^7 I

    $(\text{N}^7?)$

Checkpoint

1. Is the V^{subs}_{6th} the same as a triad with an added sixth?
2. In the resolution of a V^{subs}_{6th}, how does the 6th resolve?
3. In a V^{7subs}_{6th}, is the 7th put above the 6th, or is it the reverse?
4. How does the raised 5th of a V^+ or a V^{+7} resolve?
5. In the progression $V^{9\flat}$–i, how does the 9th resolve?
6. What two chords are most likely to be embellished by a ct°⁷ chord?
7. What member of those chords (root, third, and so on) will be shared with the ct°⁷?
8. The ct°⁷ that embellishes _____ is usually spelled as a ♯ii°⁷, whereas the one that embellishes _____ is usually spelled as a ♯vi°⁷.

SIMULTANEITIES

We know that some chords in a passage have more of an embellishing function than other chords do. This was discussed in the preceding section and also in relationship to passing six-four chords, parallel sixth chords, and others. Sometimes the traditional label for an embellishing chord (that is, V, ii, and so on) seems particularly meaningless, and we might use the term *simultaneity* for such a sonority to distinguish it from a traditional *chord*. A frequently encountered example is the diminished seventh sonority fulfilling a passing function.

Consider Example 26-28. It employs a tonic pedal throughout. The chord roots and sonority types are these:

Roots:	D♭	G	/	A	D	/	E	E♭	/	A♭	/	D♭
Types:	M	°7	/	°7	°7	/	°7	ø7	/	Dom7	/	M

However, the real "chords" in this progression are

D: I   ii^{ø7}   V⁷   I

The diminished seventh chords are better understood as *simultaneities*—traditional sonorities used in nontraditional ways. Here the chromatically descending sonorities serve not as vii°⁷ or ct°⁷ chords but as passing chords connecting the I to the ii^{ø7}. Although these diminished seventh chords could be analyzed as a circle-of-fifths sequence (review p. 284), it is unlikely that we would hear them that way, so we do not use roman numerals in their analysis.

EXAMPLE 26-28   *Chopin, Nocturne Op. 27, No. 2*

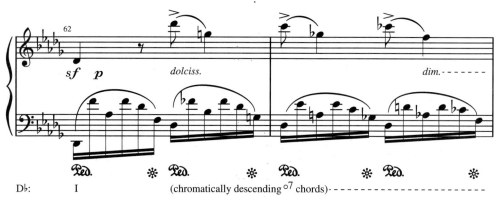

D♭:   I   (chromatically descending °7 chords)- -

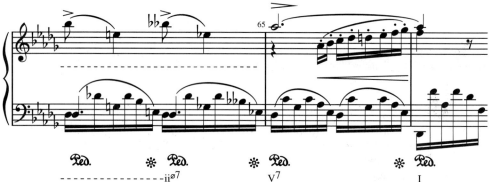

- - - - - - - - - - - - - - -ii∅7   V7   I

Example 26-29 is more complicated, and you should play through it several times before reading further. The phrase is in g minor, and it consists entirely of traditional sonorities. The NCTs, if there are any, are difficult to identify. The roots of the sonorities are labeled, with alternative analyses shown in two cases.

EXAMPLE 26-29   *Schumann, "Das verlassne Mägdelein," Op. 64, No. 2*

Two of the sonorities in this example are meaningless in the g minor context in which they occur: the B♭m in m. 2 and the It^{+6} over the C♭4 in m. 4. If we assume that these are simultaneities fulfilling a passing function, the phrase begins to make more sense. The analysis would be as follows:

| i | ii°$^6_4$ | | vii°$^4_2$ | i$^6_4$ | | IV^7 | ii°^{6} | | vii°$^4_3$ | i^6 |
| or VI | | | | | | | or iv | | | |

Now we can hear the phrase in two segments, each ending with a vii°^{7}–i progression, the first one being a weaker progression because the i chord is in six-four position. The only oddity in the phrase is the IV^7, which usually comes about through ascending melodic minor. Here it is caused by descending chromaticism in the alto line. An interesting detail of the passage is the imitation of the alto and bass in mm. 1 to 2 by the soprano and alto in mm. 3 to 4.

COLORISTIC CHORD SUCCESSIONS

Another way that a fundamental chord progression may be embellished is through the use of unexpected root movements to chords foreign to the key. Example 26-30 consists of an enormous I–V^7–I final cadence in C major, with the approach to the V^7 dramatized by a colorful series of unexpected chords. They do not seem to imply any tonicization or to function in a traditional sense in any key. In the analysis we simply indicate the root and sonority type of each chord.

EXAMPLE 26-30   *Liszt,* Orpheus *(reduction)*

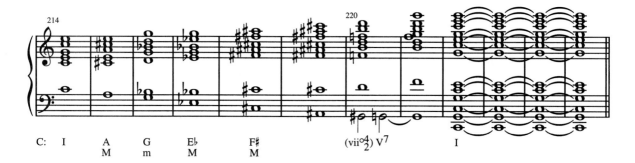

Coloristic successions often involve *chromatic mediant* relationships. Two triads are said to exhibit a chromatic mediant relationship if they are both major or both minor and their roots are a 3rd apart. In Example 26-30 the C to A and E♭ to F♯ relationships are both chromatic mediants. Even more distant is the *doubly chromatic mediant* relationship. In this case, the chords are of *opposite* mode (major/minor), have roots a 3rd apart, and share *no* common tones. Examples would be C to a♭ and C to e♭.

The A♭ major and e minor triads in Example 26-31 are in a doubly chromatic mediant relationship because A♭ and E are enharmonically a M3 apart and the two triads share no pitch classes. The listener would not be likely to guess that these chords will lead to an authentic cadence in f♯ minor.

EXAMPLE 26-31   *Puccini,* Tosca, *Act II*

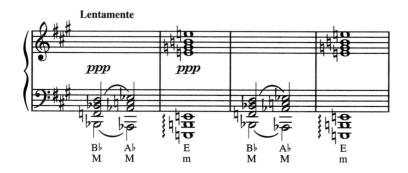

Summary

The *dominant with a substituted sixth* is a V or V^7 chord in which the 6th above the root ($\hat{3}$) is used *instead* of the 5th of the chord ($\hat{2}$). The 6th is usually approached by ascending step and left by descending leap: $\hat{2}$–$\hat{3}$–$\hat{1}$.

Augmented dominants (V^+ and V^{+7}) are not uncommon in the major mode. The raised 5th ($\#\hat{2}$) leads to the 3rd of the I chord. Secondary dominants may also be augmented.

Although *ninth, eleventh, and thirteenth chords* are theoretically possible, only the ninth chord appears with any frequency before the twentieth century. Most often the 9th of the chord disappears before the chord resolves. Otherwise, the 9th resolves down by step.

The *common-tone diminished seventh chord* has a tone in common with the root of the chord it embellishes, but be careful not to analyze the vii^{o7}/V as a ct^{o7} of a cadential I_4^6. The common-tone diminished seventh chord typically embellishes either a I chord (in which case it will usually be spelled as $\#ii^{o7}$) or a V chord (usually spelled as a $\#vi^{o7}$). Enharmonic spellings do occur.

Simultaneities is a term sometimes applied to traditional sonorities handled in a nontraditional fashion. Roman numerals are inappropriate for simultaneities.

A *coloristic chord succession* makes use of chords foreign to the key in unexpected and nontraditional ways. We do not include here, of course, an unexpected secondary dominant or a Neapolitan, for example; we refer to less traditional chords and progressions.

Self-Test 26-1
(Answers begin on page 656.)

A. In each exercise below, analyze the given chord. Then notate the specified chord in such a way that it leads smoothly into the given chord with acceptable voice leading. Some of the problems use a five-part texture for simpler voice leading.

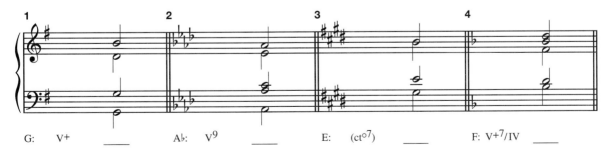

1
G: V^+ _____

2
A♭: V^9 _____

3
E: (ct^{o7})   _____

4
F: V^{+7}/IV _____

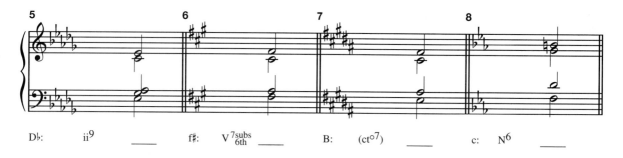

D♭:   ii⁹ _____   f♯:   V⁷subs ⁶th _____   B: (ct°⁷) _____   c: N⁶ _____

B.   Analysis. Throughout this section, highlight (using arrows and so on) any occurrences of the chords discussed in this chapter.

   1.   Label the chords in this excerpt. Pedal points occur in mm. 2 and 10.

   Schumann, "Das Schifflein," Op. 146, No. 5

   2.   This excerpt is in E throughout. What bass notes are implied in the second half of m. 90 and m. 94? The chord in mm. 96 to 97 appears to be unrelated to the chord in m. 98. Can you think of a better explanation? Label all chords.

Schumann, "Aus alten Märchen," Op. 48, No. 15

3. Label the chords in this excerpt, which modulates from E to A. The clarinets are in A and the horns are in E, but the harmonic analysis can be carried out by studying only the nontransposing instruments.

Beethoven, Symphony No. 7, Op. 92, II

4. This example is one of the thirteen short pieces that comprise Schumann's
Kinderszenen (*Scenes of Childhood*). Although it could be analyzed entirely in
F, your analysis should somehow reflect the strong tonicizations of C, g, and d.
How can the reharmonization heard in the last three measures be related to the
rest of the piece? Label chords and NCTs throughout, except for measures that
are exactly the same as earlier measures. What is the best name for the form of
this piece?

Schumann, "Träumerei," Op. 15, No. 7

5. This famous song has been the subject of several contradictory analyses. Phrase 1 (mm. 1–4) offers no problems; label the chords with roman numerals. The second chord in m. 4 is a simultaneity, as are most of the chords in phrase 2 (mm. 5–12). Label the roots of any simultaneities in mm. 5 to 8. Most of the seventh chords are passing simultaneities rather than true chords. How can you tell? What interval used in parallel motion forms the basis for mm. 5 to 8? Label the chords in mm. 9 to 12.

Schumann, "Ich grolle nicht," Op. 48, No. 7

Exercise 26-1 See Workbook.

PART VI

Late Romanticism and the Twentieth Century

Chapter 27

Tonal Harmony in the Late Nineteenth Century

INTRODUCTION

The forces that ultimately were to lead to the breakdown of the tonal system, or at least the end of its dominance of Western music traditions, may be viewed as the logical extension of the direction in which music had been developing since the beginning of the nineteenth century. Reference was made in Chapter 26 to certain harmonic practices that began to be found with increasing frequency as the end of the century drew near. These include the dominant with a substituted 6th, the prevalent use of chromatic mediant relationships, functional ninth chords, and coloristic chord successions. In attempting to identify characteristics that, as they evolved, eventually opened the door onto the new horizons of the twentieth century, we would certainly note the increasing preference for contrapuntal writing, the systematic blurring of essential harmonies by means of longer, stronger nonharmonic tones, the more rapid rate of change from one transient tonality to another, the tendency to avoid dominant-to-tonic cadences for longer periods of time, and frequently the total avoidance of any clear definition of a principal key center until well into the work. We might also note that melody was gradually released from its traditional harmonic associations, with the result that melodic and harmonic successions began to exist in their own coloristic right.

The period in which such practices became most pervasive lies roughly within the last two decades of the nineteenth century and the first two of the twentieth. Often referred to as the *post-Romantic era,* it is an elusive and intriguing epoch in many ways. Surely the trends that it spawned tended to develop in distinctly different directions as the twentieth century unfolded.

Of course, not all practices of the post-Romantic era were revolutionary. We have already encountered passages in the music of Mozart and Beethoven, even Bach, that defy tonal analysis, either written or aural. By the close of the nineteenth century, however, we find that this description applies to the greater part of the literature, as opposed to representing an occasional anachronistic curiosity.

Other developments that should be mentioned in passing include the expansion and modification of many of the accepted large forms, as seen in the symphonies of Bruckner and Mahler, the monumental music dramas of Wagner, and the tone poems of composers such as Liszt and Sibelius. When we are dealing with the concept of standard form, to be sure, we must note that the life cycle of any new musical venture is typically characterized by its introduction, gradual acceptance, standardization, and—shortly thereafter—rapid fall into disfavor through excessive use. Nowhere in Western musical history, however, can this process be observed more clearly than in the brief but turbulent span that preceded the dawn of the twentieth century.

Very much in evidence is an increasing emphasis on the dramatic and programmatic aspects of concert music. This trend may have inspired a spirit of nationalism on the part of numerous composers. Most notable among them are the so-called Russian Five: Cui, Balakirev, Borodin, Moussorgsky, and Rimsky-Korsakov. Much of their music is rich in historical allusions as well as in references to Russian folk legends. These five were by no means an isolated geographic phenomenon; other composers who drew on the heritage of their native lands include Edward MacDowell (United States), Sir Edward Elgar (England), Jean Sibelius (Finland), Edvard Grieg (Norway), and Antonin Dvořák (Bohemia), to name but a few. This reawakening of national awareness proved to be profoundly significant in its influence on the ensuing diversity of musical style. Although it is not within the scope of this brief chapter for us to deal with the aspects of structural evolution and nationalism cited above, it is nonetheless useful to recall that they were taking place more or less simultaneously with the technical details we will discuss here.

COUNTERPOINT

Although we will treat various elements of the post-Romantic style separately, you will notice that they are in a sense inseparable. Excessive melodic chromaticism will unavoidably affect harmonic movement; irregular resolutions must inevitably influence linear movement. Perhaps the dominant characteristic of this music is the prevalence of contrapuntal manipulation, particularly of supporting voices. Because these voices tend to be chromatically inflected and to move independently of the principal voice (if there is a principal voice), the individual harmonies and, hence, any clear sense of harmonic progression are blurred.

Richard Wagner, a prolific author as well as composer, is generally considered to have been the most influential single figure in the Late Romantic era, particularly in the sense that his compositional procedures seem to provide an obvious link between the mid-nineteenth century and the subsequent emergence of the twelve-tone system, to be discussed in Chapter 28.

The Prelude to *Tristan und Isolde,* shown in Example 27-1, illustrates how moving lines may serve to obscure, or even misrepresent, vertical harmonies.

♫ EXAMPLE 27-1   *Wagner,* Tristan und Isolde, *Prelude (piano reduction)*

The sonority found on the first beat of m. 2 suggests an $F^{\varnothing 7}$ chord (enharmonically spelled). Yet before this chord is allowed to function in any way, the G♯ resolves to A, creating a Fr^{+6} chord that seems to suggest the key of A. The ultimate conclusion of the phrase in m. 3 confirms the tonal center of A by means of its dominant. Although we anticipate a resolution to tonic, we are uncertain whether to expect a major or a minor chord. The voice leading in this example is worthy of mention. Notice the following points:

1. The bass line of mm. 2 to 3 echoes the alto of m. 1.

2. The soprano line beginning at m. 2 represents an *exact mirror* of the alto in mm. 1 to 3.

3. The tenor line mirrors, in reverse, the first and last pitches of the soprano line.

The Prelude then continues as follows (Ex. 27-2).

EXAMPLE 27-2 *Wagner,* Tristan und Isolde, *Prelude (piano reduction)*

Although the opening leap of B to G♯ appears to confirm A as tonal center, it serves instead as the link to a sequential passage that leads first to a half cadence in the key of C and finally to a reiterated half cadence in E. Of future significance here is the fact that we find these keys in mediant relationship (A, C, and E) subsequently serving as important tonal regions throughout the prelude. It should also be noted that the exceedingly slow tempo at which this piece is to be performed tends to further obscure the sense of harmonic direction.

The preceding examples exhibit an economy of motivic material. The prelude also, as we have noted, sets up certain tonal expectations that are unfulfilled. Contrapuntal activity can serve to weaken the original tonal center as well as obscuring the sense of motion toward a new one.

Example 27-3, also taken from *Tristan und Isolde,* illustrates a somewhat denser and more complex texture in which we hear several implied modulations, none of which reaches a conclusive cadence within the space of this passage. It may be seen as an example of Wagner's often stated goal of "endless melody," which characterizes many of his monumental music dramas. The excerpt begins in the key of G♭ major, a key that has been clearly established in the eight measures that precede the example. In mm. 726 and 727, we become aware that the G♭ tonality seems to be giving way to F. This shift occurs when the $F^{\varnothing 7}$, representing $vii^{\varnothing 7}$, is chromatically inflected to become a $B^{\varnothing 7}$, suggesting $vii^{\varnothing 7}/V$ in the new key. Note the tritone root relationship that exists between these two chords; note, too, the smoothness of the contrapuntal motion. Once again the linear distraction provided by the moving inner parts, with their pervasive non-chord tones, continues to propel the harmonic motion forward, though at the same time defying the listener's prediction of the eventual tonal outcome.

EXAMPLE 27-3   *Wagner,* Tristan und Isolde, *Act II, Scene 2 (piano-vocal score)*

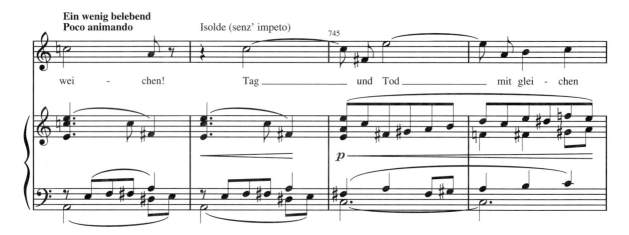

In m. 729, we see the tonality begin to shift once more as the C7 (which seemed to be leading us toward a cadence in F) resolves to F7 rather than a consonant triad. Over this implied dominant is heard the descending motive from the opening of the excerpt, supported with multiple chromatic lines, leading to m. 732 (Isolde's vocal entrance). In m. 733, the chromatic descending bass line leads to a G$^{\varnothing7}$ (suggesting vii$^{\varnothing7}$ in A♭, then (as in m. 727) chromatically inflected to become a C♯$^{\varnothing7}$, leading to a D7. As the D7 resolves to G7 (m. 736), we see the beginning of a rising chromatic line in the bass, which ultimately brings us to a temporary and somewhat unconvincing point of repose in A minor (m. 742). We should perhaps mention here that the *Liebesruhe* motif, which is played by the orchestra in the opening measure of the excerpt (m. 722), reappears frequently throughout this passage (with modifications) and is typical of the restless, somewhat angular style found in much of Wagner's vocal and instrumental writing.

The systematic blurring of tonality through contrapuntal activity might also involve nontraditional chord structures that, in some cases, might occur as linear accidents. Alexander Scriabin was fascinated with the juxtaposition of pitches that retained the implication of the traditional tonal suggestion but defied any attempt to relate them to traditional triadic chord structures. Listen to Example 27-4, by Scriabin.

EXAMPLE 27-4   *Scriabin, Fantastic Poem [C major], Op. 45, No. 2*

The opening five measures of Fantastic Poem provide an interesting example of this contrapuntal procedure. The excerpt is in C major, and the strategic placement of pitches (C, G, and B) would appear to support this tonality. However, the noncongruence of the melody, as well as the numerous accidentals, create a sense of hovering and a lack of harmonic motion. As you play this example, you are aware of pitches in whole-tone relationship. If, for example, you were to assemble the pitches found on beats 2 and 3 of the first complete measure, using D♯ as the lowest note, you would find that they form a scalar pattern built on whole steps.

Because a series of whole tones divides the octave into equal segments and allows neither for a perfect 5th nor for the half step needed to create a leading-tone relationship, any sense of clear, traditional tonality is impossible. Furthermore, because three consecutive whole steps will create a tritone as the framing interval, a certain restlessness is inevitable.

Note, too, the pitch collection that occurs on beat 3 of m. 4 of the excerpt. This sonority is sometimes referred to as the Mystic Chord and is particularly favored by Scriabin. When distributed in 4ths, as shown below, it creates the unstable, hovering sound that characterizes the example. The scale itself may be loosely related to the overtone series, beginning with the 8th partial (and omitting the 12th). Again, if we collapse the chord into a scalar configuration, we see that once again the whole tone is a very prominent interval. The whole-tone scale and its use in twentieth-century composition will be discussed further in Chapter 28.

TREATMENT OF DOMINANT HARMONY

The preceding examples, which deal primarily with contrapuntal manipulation, illustrate instances in which the *spirit* of dominant harmonic function is maintained, although in some cases its vertical structure is modified and often obscured.

In the Wagner excerpt (Ex. 27-3), for example, we see the use of a dominant pedal serving to support multiple chromatic lines. The vertical sonorities created strongly defy any attempt at functional analysis but serve to effect truly startling harmonic shifts.

Let us return now to the traditional major-minor seventh chord, which played such an important role in the establishment of the tonal system with which this book is primarily concerned.

Certainly the single structural bulwark on which the traditional tonal system rests is most aptly represented by the inviolability of the V–I progression. Rudolph Reti summed up this concept rather succinctly when he observed, in *Tonality in Modern Music:**

> *In fact the scheme I–x–V–I symbolizes, though naturally in a very summarizing way, the harmonic course of any composition from the Classical period. This x, usually appearing as a progression of chords, as a whole series, constitutes, as it were, the actual "music" within the scheme, which through the annexed formula V–I, is made into a unit, a group, or even a whole piece.*

Inevitably, then, when this traditional relationship is tampered with, the ensuing musical result, despite surface consonance, represents a significant historical digression.

The fourth movement of Brahms's Symphony No. 4, Op. 98, uses the process of continuous variation to define its structure. The theme that forms the basis for this truly monumental set of variations is as follows:

Its initial presentation is harmonized as shown below:

What is remarkable is the manner in which Brahms deftly avoids any clear use of dominant harmony throughout (note the "deceptive" resolution of V7/V to i6) until the penultimate chord, a French augmented sixth sonority resolving to a major tonic (which in turn serves as V/iv, thereby setting up the second statement of the theme).

---

*Rudolph Reti, *Tonality in Modern Music* (New York: Collier Books, 1962), p. 28. (Originally published as Tonality-Atonality-Pantonality.) Used by permission of Hutchinson Publishing Group Limited, London, England.

In Example 27-5 (Variation 10), we see a chain of major-minor seventh chords, each suggesting a dominant function but forced to resolve deceptively. Brahms has heightened the ambiguity of this brief passage still further by means of registral displacement and by alternating strings and winds from measure to measure. The effect thereby created is strikingly parallel and almost nontonal.

EXAMPLE 27-5 *Brahms, Symphony No. 4, Op. 98, IV (piano reduction)*

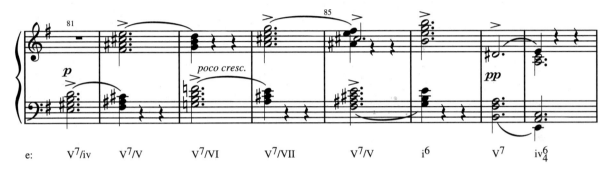

e: V^7/iv V^7/V V^7/VI V^7/VII V^7/V i^6 V^7 iv^6_4

In the following passage by Fauré, who is frequently mentioned as the most obvious predecessor of Debussy, we note V^7 sonorities, moving coloristically in parallel motion with no pretense of harmonic function, arriving finally at a brief but satisfying tonicization of E♭ (Ex. 27-6).

EXAMPLE 27-6 *Fauré, "L'hiver a cessé," Op. 61, No. 9*

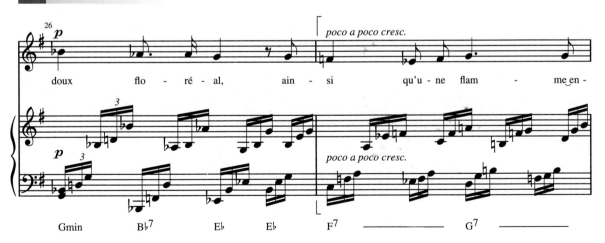

Gmin   B♭^{7} E♭   E♭   F^7 —————   G^7 —————

This interest in parallel motion of dominant 7th chords was eventually greatly expanded and further exploited by Claude Debussy, whose music will be discussed in Chapter 28.

Example 27-7, a Tchaikovsky excerpt, is essentially in B♭ major. There is no real harmonic motion involved but rather the harmonization of an ascending chromatic scale to enliven the progression from V to I. Although the succession of chord roots, as shown, is strictly parallel, the series of deceptive resolutions of major-minor seventh chords creates a pattern of intense harmonic activity.

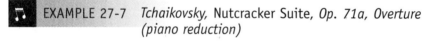

EXAMPLE 27-7   *Tchaikovsky,* Nutcracker Suite, *Op. 71a, Overture (piano reduction)*

SEQUENCE

The technique of sequence, illustrated in several of the preceding examples, played an important part in the music of many post-Romantic composers, especially in the process of modulation. The following example by Rimsky-Korsakov, whose influence was enormous not only on later Russian composers but also on the craft of orchestration, reveals procedures in which sequential activity serves to "legitimize" nontraditional relationships.

EXAMPLE 27-8   *Rimsky-Korsakov,* Scheherazade *(piano reduction)*

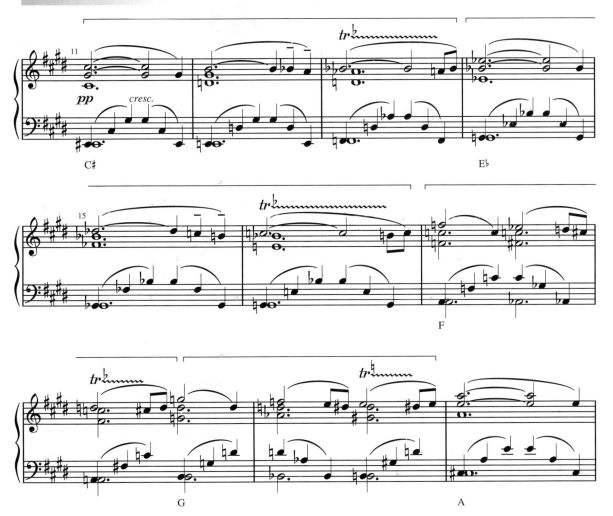

This passage, found near the beginning of the work, establishes the key of E major. The excerpt quoted here opens with C♯ major harmony, suggesting V/ii. The sequence that begins in the third measure of the excerpt moves through a series of tonicizations a whole step apart, from C♯ to A, and ultimately leads to a half cadence on B. Of interest is the second chord of the sequence, which vaguely suggests an ⁺6. This sonority, which embellishes the third chord of the pattern (V⁷ of the following tonal area), also shares a common tritone with it. The smoothness of the sequential movement renders convincingly the somewhat tenuous relationship between the series of chords thus tonicized (C♯–E♭–F–G–A) and the overall tonality of E major.

The earlier example by Tchaikovsky (Ex. 27-7) featured a series of dominant seventh sonorities resolving deceptively that are used to harmonize an ascending chromatic scale. The *omnibus,* a coloristic sequential succession of chords traditionally used to harmonize a *nonfunctional* chromatic bass line, is also a chromatically saturated chord succession. It is illustrated in Example 27-9.

EXAMPLE 27-9   *Omnibus*

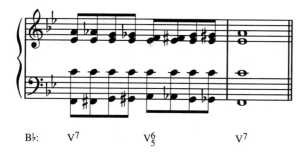

B♭:   V⁷   V⁶₅   V⁷

Although it would perhaps be possible to analyze the chords interpolated between root position V⁷ and V⁶₅ as tending to tonicize c minor (Ger⁺⁶–ii⁶₄–Ger⁺⁶), the bravura tempo at which such passages are normally performed will more likely suggest extended V⁷ harmony with chromatic passing tones in bass and soprano. The omnibus may also serve to harmonize a descending bass line as shown in Example 27-10.

EXAMPLE 27-10

You will notice that only one voice at a time is moving in contrary motion to the bass and that this function is passed back and forth between soprano, alto, and tenor. Notice, too, that the minor triads found as every third chord bear a mediant relationship to one another. When incorporated into a modulation, this sequential scheme facilitates quick motion between disjunct keys, with the smoothest possible voice leading.

An example of this device is found in the Sonata in A minor by Schubert, where it occurs as part of the transition leading to the second theme in C major (Ex. 27-11).

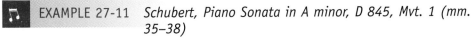

EXAMPLE 27-11 *Schubert, Piano Sonata in A minor, D 845, Mvt. 1 (mm. 35–38)*

Yet another example in which the omnibus is used to bring about a chromatic mediant modulation from G major to D♭ major is found in Example 27-12. The excerpt begins in E♭ major and opens with a root-position tonic chord. The addition of a C♯ creates a German sixth sonority, which leads to G major (I$_4^6$) in m. 12. In the following measure, we find B in the bass (I^6) and D in the soprano. As these two voices expand outward, the omnibus pattern leads us to a D♭ sonority in m. 16, clearly suggesting D♭ as the new tonic.

EXAMPLE 27-12   *R. Strauss, "Allerseelen," Op. 10, No. 8*

bei,   und laß uns wie-der von der Lie - be re - den, wie

einst   im   Mai.

EXPANDED TONALITY

The process of avoiding confirmation of tonic may sometimes be carried so far that the listener is never entirely sure of the primary tonal center of the piece. A surprisingly early
example of expanded tonality may be found in the Chopin Prelude in A minor (Op. 28,
No. 2). This intriguing miniature, shown in Example 27-13, has long provided a challenge
for theorists and historians alike.

EXAMPLE 27-13   *Chopin*, Prelude in A Minor, *Op. 28, No. 2*

Although the two introductory measures seem to suggest e minor, the cadence that occurs in m. 6 suggests V–I in G major (although the pervasive chromatic neighbor figure heard from the beginning alternates "teasingly" between E♮ and E♭). In m. 8, we are unexpectedly confronted with a b minor sonority and a compressed version of the tune heard in mm. 3 to 6. Unlike the earlier version, however, our expectation of a similar cadence in the mediant key of D is dashed by an enigmatic d♯^{ø7} (still accompanied by the chromatic neighbor figure), which slides down to an equally enigmatic d♯°7 (mm. 12–13). In m. 15, the bass line, which has been steadily descending since m. 8, finally arrives at E. Above it is heard what might be interpreted as an a minor $^6_4$, although with a nonconforming F♮ in the melody. The melodic gesture in mm. 17 to 18 concludes on D while beneath, we might almost hear the a minor $^6_4$ alternating with a b° triad (ii° in a minor perhaps?). Measures 21 to 22 bring the first decisive and "uncluttered" triads of the entire piece: E major to B major, then back to E major. Just as we hesitantly decide to accept E as tonic, however, Chopin once again dashes our expectations by adding a seventh to the chord (D♮), finally establishing a minor as the "official" key of the piece. With its pervasive chromaticism, slow tempo, and gradual downward shifting of multiple chromatic lines, the piece is reminiscent of the better-known Prelude No. 4 in e minor. Both of these works provide examples of relatively simple harmonic motion embellished by nonfunctional passing chords or simultaneities (discussed in Chapter 26), although the work discussed above clearly disguises, and draws the listener much farther from, the "home" key than does the e minor prelude.

    Now examine Example 27-14.

EXAMPLE 27-14   *Wolf, "Herr, was trägt der Boden"*

Actually, the opening measures might lead us to expect eventual resolution to b minor as tonic, although the key signature contradicts this. However, m. 2 negates the leading tone of A♯, and m. 3 with its g minor sonority all but destroys any previous expectations. In m. 4 (minor v?), m. 5 (iv⁶), and m. 6 (V⁷), we are brought seemingly back to b minor, only to be abruptly jarred by the d minor interruption of m. 7. It is not until the final measures of the piece (Ex. 27-15) that E (albeit E major) is at last allowed to serve as tonal center of gravity.

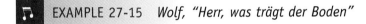

EXAMPLE 27-15   *Wolf, "Herr, was trägt der Boden"*

Even here we note a certain ambiguity suggested by the tonicization of the Neapolitan (m. 25), the harmonic enigma of the A♯/B♭, and the final attempt to hold back tonic by means of a deceptive cadence in m. 26. Still, the very functional root movement leading to the end (C♯–F♯–B–E) seems to compensate for the unexpectedness of this tonal goal.

The startling juxtaposition of F♯7 and d minor between mm. 6 and 7 (Example 27-14) is worthy of further comment. Here we have two sonorities whose roots are a third apart (mediant relationship) and are contrasting in quality (major vs. minor). We have often encountered the *diatonic* mediant relationship, which occurs naturally in major and minor keys (I–vi–IV–ii), in which the quality of chord naturally alternates between major and minor. In Chapter 19 we first encountered the *chromatic* mediant relationship involving two chords of like quality (major to major, minor to minor) whose roots were a third apart. This type of root movement will always involve one common tone, one chromatically inflected tone, and one new tone. The relationship of F♯ major to D minor, however, involves two chromatically altered tones and is usually referred to as a *double chromatic mediant*. The possibilities for double chromatic mediant relationship to F♯ major or f♯ minor are as follows:

F♯ major to d minor or a minor
f♯ minor to A♯ (B♭) major or D♯ (E♭) major

The main significance of the chord movement in Example 27-16 lies in the incompatibility of the two sonorities in terms of a single diatonic key and thus in the assurance of a startling tonal shift.

EXAMPLE 27-16   *Double chromatic mediant relationship*

Our final nineteenth-century example, by Mahler, also serves to illustrate the principle of what has aptly been described as *nonconcentric tonality,* that is, a change of tonal center between the opening and closing of a work or movement. The terms *concentric* or *centric* are sometimes used to designate the common tonal practice in which opening and closing keys are in agreement, providing a tonal framework for the composition. Example 27-17 illustrates a striking departure from that tradition.

EXAMPLE 27-17 *Mahler,* Kindertotenlieder, *No. 2*

The opening measures suggest g minor despite the key signature, which more logically would point to c minor. It is worthy of mention, in light of our preceding comments regarding the traditional inviolability of the dominant, that in both this example and the preceding ones by Wolf, the "wrong key" heard at the outset is, in fact, serving as a *minor* dominant for what ultimately proves to be the intended tonic. Let us note, too, that the tonicizing process for g minor takes place by means of Neapolitan and $^+6$ sonorities, which are much prized in post-Romantic music because they provide linear support with a minimum of functional root movement. Interestingly, at the point at which the music seems to move away from tonic toward the expected dominant, the tonality appears to be shifting toward E♭ (mm. 10–12).

Mahler's systematic manipulation of tendency tones within the established key is especially crafty. As you play through the example, note the G♮ in m. 13 (which our ear perceives as $\hat{3}$ in E♭, moving on to A♭, its expected destination). In the meantime, however, the bass E♭, which our ear has interpreted as a tonic passing tone headed for the leading tone of D♮, moves instead to D♭, and suddenly we find ourselves expecting a resolution to G♭ major, the soprano G♮ having been transformed into a leading tone to the supertonic. Yet before this is allowed to happen, our expectations are once again thwarted as the D♭^{7} in m. 14 is treated unexpectedly as an $^+6$ chord and drops to C major while the passing tone A♮, seeming to drive upward, resigns itself to function as a suspended submediant in C.

Example 27-18 represents the final twenty measures of the piece. We see mm. 54 to 57 continuing the pattern of restless, roving tonality that has characterized the work throughout by means of a series of deceptively resolving dominant seventh chords. Between mm. 57 and 58, however, the C♭ is enharmonically respelled to become the fifth of an e minor chord (iii$_4^6$ in C perhaps?), leading to vi7 (m. 59), to ii$^{\o}$ (m. 60), and to V9 in C major (m. 61), which in m. 62 seems to "resolve" to an augmented tonic chord. Notice the ongoing dissonance created by an inevitable "wrong note" in the sonorities that follow, until m. 66, where a consonant C major triad is at last realized. The measures that follow seem to tonicize C major in a relatively traditional fashion, until the penultimate sonority, a German sixth (m. 70) concludes the song on a doleful c minor chord.

♫ **EXAMPLE 27-18** *Mahler,* Kindertotenlieder, *No. 2 (mm. 54–74)*

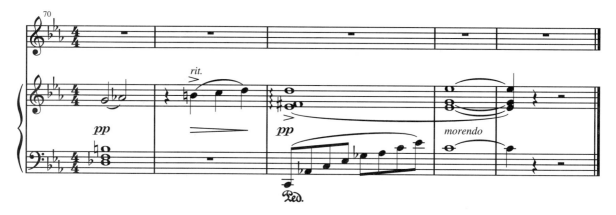

Elements of this music that contribute to its restless quality include the frequent use of augmented triads (although they may be the result of non-chord-tone activity), as in mm. 54, 56, and 62, and the prevalence of strongly accented non-chord tones. As was true in the examples by Wagner, the harmonies used by Mahler are often startling and tend to obscure the sense of tonality. What differs about the vocal lines, however, is their relative simplicity and the extent to which they seem almost to defy their rich chromatic environment. You might want to play mm. 54 to 57 and 60 to 67 of the vocal line without its accompaniment, noticing how straightforward they seem when compared with the more disjunct vocal melodies found in the earlier Wagner excerpts.

The techniques that have been discussed in this chapter represent those typical of the most prominent figures of the post-Romantic era. These are composers whose work is considered to represent the most striking and ultimately influential departures from established traditions. Although it is not within the scope of this chapter to address the influence of folk music on the further development of music in the twentieth century, it should be noted that its impact was profound. The work of Bartók clearly springs from his native roots, as does much of the music of Vaughan Williams. Traces of Spanish influence can be heard in many works of Debussy and Ravel, whereas elements of jazz have been incorporated into the music of composers such as Gershwin, Milhaud, and Stravinsky. Many historians, in fact, consider the interest in ethnic or folk music a significant cause for the extraordinary diversity that, as you are about to see, characterizes the twentieth century.

Summary

It is possible to identify a number of trends during the approximately forty-year period comprising the post-Romantic age. For one, we note a resurgence of interest in contrapuntal manipulation, particularly as a means of obscuring harmonic rhythm and tonality. The technique of sequence was increasingly used as a means of creating relationships between seemingly disparate musical elements, embellishing otherwise conventional relationships, or, in some cases, as a means of prolonging a single tonality. Composers began to lead toward less traditional key associations, particularly those that confound conventional analysis. The means for establishing a key became largely coloristic rather than functional. Irregular treatment of dominant harmony and a lessening of control by any single key as an organizing factor also represent a significant departure from the practices associated with earlier tonal music.

As we have noted, neither an investigation of larger formal practices nor an examination of ethnic music (including that of the United States) can be accommodated within the scope of this brief chapter. If you want to gain a more accurate understanding of this transitional period, you will need to study large musical structures. You will also need to gain some familiarity with the striking political, sociological, and philosophical movements that characterized the era.

Self-Test 27-1
(Answers begin on page 660.)

A. Harmonic and melodic procedures. The Prelude by Scriabin, though brief, illustrates some interesting departures from tradition. Play through the piece and answer the following questions:

1. What is the overall key of the piece? _____

2. In what way does the opening melody obscure this key? _____

_____

_____

3. Show roman numeral analysis for mm. 4 to 6.

_____   _____ / _____   _____

4. Mm. 7 to 8 contain two somewhat deceptive progressions. Where do these occur?

_____ and _____

5. Locate an augmented sixth chord in the composition. _____

6. What is unusual about the end of the piece? _____

_____

_____

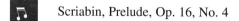 Scriabin, Prelude, Op. 16, No. 4

B. Mediant relationship of triads. You are given a triad built on F. Show all triads, above and below, that illustrate:

   1. Chromatic mediant relationship (one common tone with one chromatic alteration)

F

2. Double chromatic relationship (no common tones, two chromatic alterations)

F

C. In the excerpt below:

1. Show roman numeral analysis in mm. 1 to 16. Do all work on the music. Note the absence of a clear dominant-tonic cadence anywhere in the excerpt. Locate illustrations of avoided tonic cadence and describe the manner in which this is accomplished.

_____

_____

2. What other procedures mark this as a late Romantic work? _____

_____

_____

_____

Brahms, Symphony No. 1, Op. 68, II (piano reduction)

D. Chromatic sequence. Analyze the following chromatic sequences, then continue each as indicated.

E. Nontraditional harmonic movement. Although the Arietta by Grieg clearly begins and ends in E♭, the harmonic activity within the key is far from conventional. Answer the following questions about this short composition:

   1. How would you analyze the prevailing harmony in mm. 2 to 3? _____

    _____

   2. The chord succession in mm. 5 to 6 (repeated in mm. 7–8) suggests tonicization of the closely related key of _____ and may be analyzed with roman numerals as follows:

    / _____ _____ / _____ _____ /

3. What is unusual about the cadence that occurs in mm. 11 to 12? _____

_____

Where is this pattern found later in the piece? _____

4. Locate a deceptive cadence. _____

5. How would you describe the form of this piece? _____

Grieg, Arietta, Op. 12, No. 1

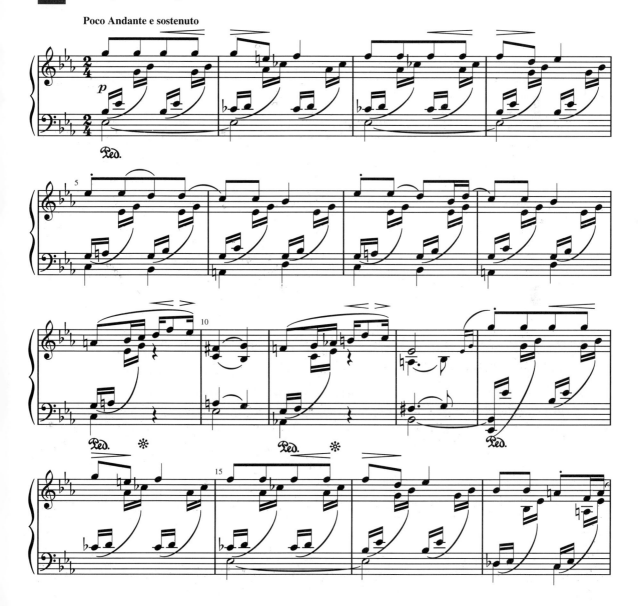

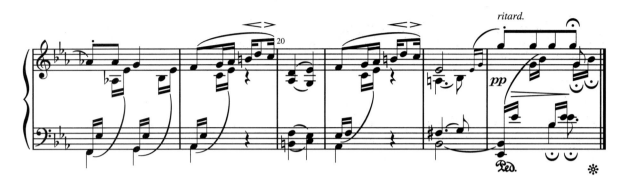

F. Nontraditional treatment of tonality. *Das Verlassene Mägdlein* by Hugo Wolf provides an interesting mixture of traditional and nontraditional procedures. Play through the piece (most of the essential harmonic notes are contained in the piano part) and answer the following questions:

1. What is the key of the piece? _____ By what means do the opening twelve measures establish that key? Can you assign roman numerals to this passage? In what way are the chord voicings nontraditional? _____

    _____

    _____

    _____

    _____

2. Measures 13 to 14 illustrate what type of relationship? _____

3. Measures 19 to 22 do not clearly define a tonality. Why not? _____

    _____

4. What tonal center is suggested in m. 27? _____

    How is it established? _____

5. Measure 38 returns to the opening material. In what way has this return been prepared in the preceding four measures? _____

    _____

    _____

6. How would you describe the overall form of the piece? _____

    _____

Wolf, Das verlassene Mägdlein

Trä - ne dann stür - zet her - nie - der; so kommt der Tag her-an

o ging'-er wie-der!

Exercise 27-1 See Workbook.

Chapter 28

An Introduction to Twentieth-Century Practices

INTRODUCTION

As the traditional tonal system was being stretched to its limits, composers became increasingly aware of the growing need for alternative means of musical organization and for a vocabulary that would adequately deal with new methods and concepts. Basic elements that seemed to lend themselves to significant modification included scale, chord structure, harmonic succession, rhythm and meter, and overall musical texture. The early experiments that took place seemed to lead along two somewhat different paths: one, an extension of the principles of ultrachromaticism; the other, a reaction against chromatic excess. The former path may be seen to have culminated in the development of the twelve-tone system, whereas the latter caused many composers to investigate the pre-tonal era, along with folk music, as a source of materials. Increasingly, many of today's musicians are turning to non-Western cultures as a source of fresh musical ideas.

Throughout the unfolding of the twentieth century, we have found each of these paths themselves branching off in various directions, creating a vast array of musical styles, philosophies, and practices. In some instances, one may observe the inexorable overlapping of seemingly disparate patterns of musical thought. In others, particularly the realm of film and commercial music, we note a continued reliance on principles of tonality. Worthy of note is the relative speed with which this expansion has taken place, especially in comparison with the time span from c. 1650 to 1900, sometimes referred to as the Common Practice period, during which Western music composition was based on the principles of tonal harmony.

The richness and diversity of today's musical experience present problems for any musician attempting to synthesize, codify, or define the prevailing trends in twentieth-century music, even as that very century draws to a close. This chapter will serve primarily as an overview of certain historically significant events that ultimately resulted in the definition of today's cultural environment. It may also provide a springboard for continued study and analysis.

IMPRESSIONISM

The term *impressionism* was first applied to a style of painting that sprang up in France and is most often associated with the work of Claude Monet (1840–1926) and his contemporaries. The primary aim of the artist was that of evoking a certain mood or atmosphere, using light and color in nontraditional ways. This concept was reflected in music by a turning away from more orderly formal procedures of the late eighteenth and early nineteenth centuries and a fascination with *color,* as expressed through harmony, instrumentation, and the use of rhythm.

Claude Debussy (1862–1918) is considered by many to have made some of the most significant contributions to the evolution of early twentieth-century musical thinking. His compositional style reveals departures from previous practices that, though easily accessible to the tonally oriented ear, clearly defy traditional tonal expectations.

You will notice the clear suggestion of G♭ major in Example 28-2.

♫ EXAMPLE 28-1 *Debussy, "La Fille aux cheveux de lin," from* Preludes, *Book I*

But notice, too, the nontraditional procedures he employs.

1. The opening measures outline an e♭⁷ chord, whose function is far from obvious.

2. The first cadence leading to tonic is plagal and thus avoids functional use of the leading tone.

3. The progression beginning in m. 5, with its predominance of mediant relationships, serves to render the G♭ tonic still more elusive.

In general, the most revealing aspects of early twentieth-century music may be discovered through an examination of the treatment of tonality. The analyst should ask the following questions: Does the piece seem to have a tonal center or centers? If so, how is tonality accomplished? If not, how is it avoided? The answers to these questions will do a great deal to shed light on a composer's style and musical inclinations.

SCALES

One reaction to the chromatic saturation of the late nineteenth century was a renewed interest in the church modes, shown in Example 28-2. The simplest way to represent each of the modes is by using the pitches of the C major scale, but with a pitch other than C serving as tonic, or *final,* for each mode.

EXAMPLE 28-2

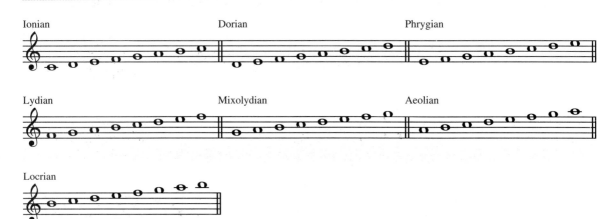

If we compare the modes directly to major and minor scales (Ex. 28-3), we find that the Ionian and Aeolian modes are identical to the major and natural minor scales, respectively, and that the remaining modes (except Locrian) may be likened either to a major scale or to a natural minor scale with one alteration. This method of identification has the advantage of providing an aural description, clearly related to familiar scales, of each modal pattern.

EXAMPLE 28-3

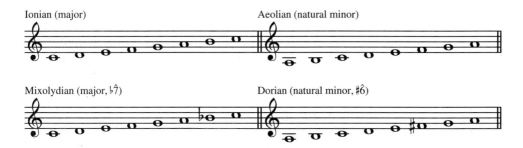

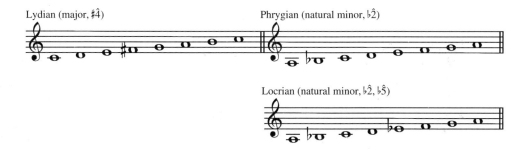

The Locrian mode, which requires two accidentals compared to natural minor and lacks a true dominant, is found far less often in musical composition, although it is commonly employed by jazz performers as a pattern for improvisation.

The modes may also be arranged as shown below, in decreasing relative order of "brightness," that is, according to the number of major or augmented intervals above the final. For comparison each mode in Example 28-4 is built on C.

EXAMPLE 28-4

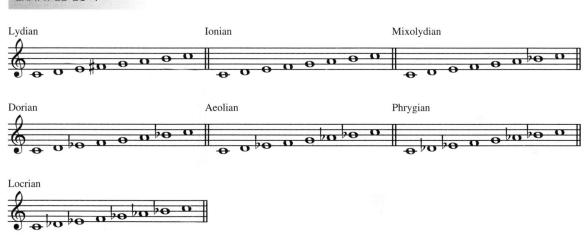

A scale that Debussy particularly favored is the Lydian-Mixolydian, or $\sharp\hat{4}$, $\flat\hat{7}$ scale. This hybrid collection of pitches may well have resulted from the juxtaposition of two major-minor seventh chords with roots a whole step apart, as indicated by the brackets in Example 28-5.

EXAMPLE 28-5

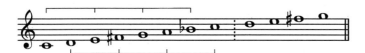

You will notice, given the presence of both B♭ and F♯, that it would be impossible to realize this scalar pattern using only the white keys of the piano. Just as each of the diatonic modes possesses unique color characteristics, the scale discussed above may be made to sound quite different with different pitches serving as "tonic." For example, beginning on D will result in a major scale with a ♭6̂ and ♭7̂. Likewise, beginning on A will yield a Phrygian/Dorian pattern (a minor with ♭2̂ and ♯6̂). When G is used, an ascending melodic minor scale is created.

When we start this scale on the note B♭, the resulting pattern begins with five pitches in whole-tone relationship to one another. For this reason, you may occasionally see the designation *4 + 1,* indicating that this type of scale may be arranged so as to consist of four whole steps, separated by a half step from the one remaining whole step, as follows:

$$B♭ - C - D - E - F♯ - G - A - B♭$$

Accordingly, the white key scale could be designated *3 + 2* when arranged as follows:

$$F - G - A - B - C - D - E - F$$

Obviously the nonspecific nature of these labels would be useful only to distinguish between the two scalar patterns used, say, in a passage that contains no clear tonal center.

Example 28-6 shows this scale resulting from the canonic mirroring of two voices. You will notice that while the pitches of the example represent those of an ascending melodic minor scale on C, the emphasis on D and A in the top voice tends to negate any clear sense of C as tonic.

EXAMPLE 28-6   *Bartók, "Subject and Reflection,"* Mikrokosmos *No. 141*

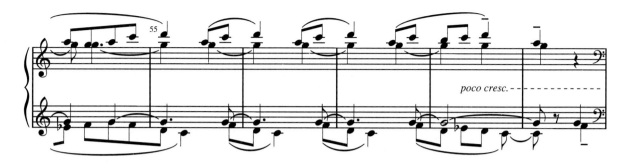

The *pentatonic,* or five-note, scale has played a significant role in music, particularly non-Western music, for centuries. Although the term *pentatonic* literally denotes any collection of five pitches, the two forms of the scale shown in Example 28-7 tend to be encountered the most frequently in the literature.

EXAMPLE 28-7

Both of these pitch sets can obviously occur within a diatonic series. You will notice, however, that there are no half steps or tritones in the anhemitonic scale, which may be likened to the pattern of the black keys on the piano. Any one of its five pitches may be made to serve as tonic by means of reiteration and metric accent. The effect of the scale is likely to be harmonically static, however, particularly if its use is prolonged. For this reason, a composer will seldom use the pentatonic scale as the basis for a composition of any length.

If you refer back to Example 28-1, you will notice that with the exception of the passing F in m. 3, the melody of the first six measures is based entirely on the "black-key" pentatonic scale. A somewhat more sophisticated use may be observed in Example 28-8.

EXAMPLE 28-8   *Debussy, "Nuages," from* Nocturnes *(piano reduction)*

Used by permission of Edward B. Marks Music Company.

The pentatonic tune, appearing in octaves, centers around F♯ and is harmonized by d♯ minor and G♯ major sonorities. To the traditional ear, this might possibly suggest ii–V in C♯ major or perhaps a D♯ Dorian key center. At no point in the piece, however, is either C♯ or D♯ permitted to function decisively as tonic. Notice, too, the closing two measures of the excerpt in which two quasi-pentatonic melodic fragments are harmonized (respectively) by G♯ 6 7th (m. 71) and G♯ Mm 7th (m. 72). The relationship of these two sonorities is an interesting one, in that each mirrors the other in terms of its construction. Debussy is particularly fond of the sense of "harmonic hovering" created by their juxtaposition, and he employs it frequently.

The pitch collections we have discussed so far bear a clear resemblance to scales or fragments of scales associated with the diatonic system. Composers have also, however, made extensive use of *artificial,* or *synthetic, scales.* One of the most prominent of these, the *whole-tone scale,* composed entirely of major 2nds, was also a favorite of Debussy's. This scale is used in Example 28-9. It is of interest to note that "Voiles," the closing section of which appears below, is composed in ABA structure, the B section being based exclusively on the pentatonic scale.

EXAMPLE 28-9 *Debussy, "Voiles," from* Preludes, *Book I*

Like the pentatonic scale, the whole-tone scale possesses several structural limitations because it contains basically only three intervals: the major 2nd, the major 3rd, and the tritone (along with their inversions). Its symmetry and its total lack of perfect intervals (and hence of major and minor triads) bestows on it an elusive, tonally ambiguous quality that has proved attractive to many composers. The augmented triad is, in fact, the only tertian triad possible within this pitch collection.

The vertical sonorities that may result from whole-tone simultaneities are often referred to as *whole-tone chords*. (The Fr^{+6} chord, though used in tonal contexts, may be structurally derived from the whole-tone scale.)

The available variety of synthetic scales is, obviously, limited only by the composer's imagination. We will mention here only two additional ones (Ex. 28-10) that are interesting because of their symmetrical structure: the *octatonic*, or *diminished, scale*, derived from the superimposition of two diminished seventh chords at the interval of a half or whole step, and the *half-step minor 3rd scale*, derived from the juxtaposition of two augmented triads at the interval of the half step.

EXAMPLE 28-10

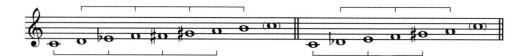

Example 28-11 shows the interesting possibilities for chord structures derived from the octatonic scale. Note the alternation of major triads in second inversion with minor first-inversion triads in the first part of the example. Note, too, the exotic result when a seventh above the bass is added to each of the sonorities. This scale, frequently employed by composers from the Russian Five (mentioned in Chapter 27), also intrigued Olivier Messiaen (1908–1992), who applied symmetrical procedures to rhythm as well as to pitch.

EXAMPLE 28-11

Four-note chords in the octatonic scale

Triads in the octatonic scale

D   f   B   d   A♭   b   F   g♯

The term *dodecaphonic* refers to music based on a twelve-note scale. Although seemingly synonymous with the more traditional term *chromatic,* its use tends to avoid any implication of "functional" tendency tones (the significance of ♯6 vs. ♭7 and so on) in nontonal music.

The opening four measures of Example 28-12 make use of all twelve pitch classes. Although the note F is heard throughout and obviously represents an important reference point, the simultaneities formed by the moving chromatic lines do not suggest functional harmony and fail to confirm F as a strong tonal center.

EXAMPLE 28-12   *Kennan, Prelude No. 1*

Self-Test 28-1
(Answers begin on page 663.)

A.   Scale characteristics.

1.   Which three of the diatonic modes are essentially major in quality?

     _____ , _____ , and _____

2.   Which *two* of the seven diatonic modes begin with a minor second?

     _____ and _____

3.   Name two six-note symmetrical scales and the derivation of each.

     _____ and _____

     Derivation: _____

4.   What scale is created by the juxtaposition of two major-minor seventh chords whose roots are one whole step apart?

     _____

5.   What traditional seventh chord type forms the basis for derivation of the octatonic scale? _____

6.   Three of the four traditional triad types may be derived from the octatonic scale. They are _____ , _____ , and _____

7.   What two intervals are missing from the anhemitonic (diatonic) pentatonic scale?

     _____ and _____

B. Add the appropriate accidentals to create the type of scale asked for:

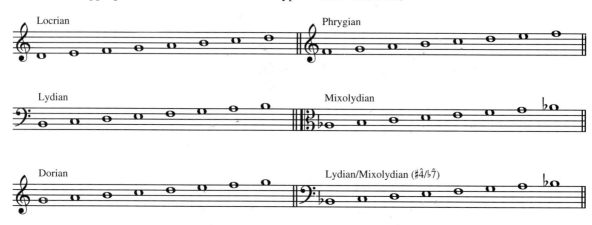

C. Scale transposition.

1. Taking the pentatonic pattern C–D–E–G–A as a model, transpose the set so that the set will begin, respectively, on each of the pitches indicated:

2. Notate whole-tone scales starting on each of the following pitches (remembering that it is permissible, in a six-note scale, to mix sharps and flats):

3. Notate the following modal scales in the clef indicated:

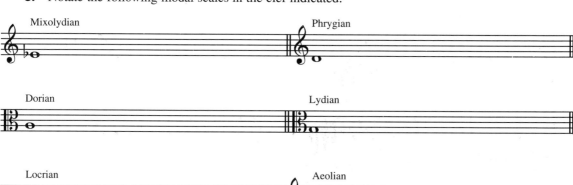

D. Identify the scale that forms the basis of each of the following melodies:

Exercise 28-1 (A–G) See Workbook.

CHORD STRUCTURE

You will recall a brief discussion in Chapter 26 regarding the occasional use of ninth chords in tonal music. In most cases, these sonorities represent dominant function, with the ninth often treated as a non-chord tone and resolving down by step. Functional dominant ninth chords, although far less common than dominant seventh chords, may be found in the music of such composers as Schumann, Chopin, and Beethoven. Eleventh and thirteenth chords, on the other hand, were rarely encountered prior to the twentieth century. For that reason, the increased use of ninth, eleventh, and thirteenth chords on the part of some twentieth-century composers represents an obvious extension of the post-Romantic tradition of tertian harmony. These chords may occur in both functional and nonfunctional settings.

Example 28-13, by Ravel, illustrates a coloristic use of tall chords in the sense that traditional rules of resolution fail to apply. Notice the clear sense of root movement in mm. 1 to 3, as indicated in the analysis. The texture of succeeding measures continues to employ tall chords, created through the scalewise motion of the bass line. The effect of this passage is to prolong the sense of C as tonal center until the music slips unobtrusively into G in m. 7 of the excerpt, again employing a functional bass line.

EXAMPLE 28-13 *Ravel, "Rigaudon," from* Le Tombeau de Couperin

As has been noted in Chapter 26, tall chords are created through the stacking of major and minor 3rds. Frequently, in the interests of lightening up the texture and achieving greater flexibility, a composer may omit some components of a tall chord, such as the 5th or the 11th. Depending on the context, this omission may tend to alter the listener's perception of the basic chord structure. Play the three chords of Example 28-14.

EXAMPLE 28-14

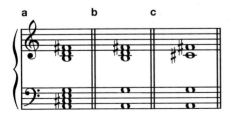

Example 28-14a is clearly a thirteenth chord. If we interpret the root A as being a dominant, we can see that all pitches of the D major scale are being sounded. This adds a certain

heaviness to the sonority, which a composer might prefer to avoid. The omission of the 3rd and 5th of the chord, as shown in Example 28-14b, does little to alter our perception of the sonority. In Example 28-14c, however, when we systematically omit the 5th, 9th, and 11th, we might interpret the sonority as a V^{7subs}_{6th}, or we might even hear the F♯ as a nonharmonic tone. The "correct" interpretation is obviously dependent not only on the previous musical experience that the listener brings to it but also on the context in which the chord occurs. For example, a popular song arrangement that features almost exclusively tall tertian sonorities will logically suggest analyzing such a chord as a thirteenth chord.

Yet another extended tertian harmony is the *polychord*—superimposed triads—several versions of which are shown in Example 28-15.

EXAMPLE 28-15

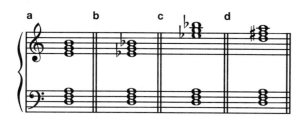

In Example 28-15a the diatonic relationship of the pitches might well suggest a chord of the thirteenth. Example 28-15b might still be perceived as a d minor ninth chord with upper extensions, but the chromatic inflection of the upper triad is far more likely to suggest two independent triads with their roots a m9 apart. This effect is greatly enhanced by the separation occurring in Example 28-15c between the two sets of pitches. The sonority occurring in Example 28-15d is often referred to as a *split-third chord,* as it represents both major and minor quality built on the same root.

Now play Example 28-16 which is polychordal.

EXAMPLE 28-16

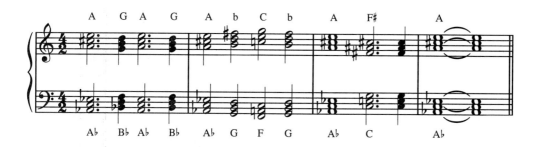

Notice the sharp dissonance created by (1) chords whose roots are a half step or tritone apart and (2) chords containing even a single contrasting chromatic inflection, such as G/B♭, as opposed to pairs of chords that may be found in the same key signature, such as F/C or G/b minor.

Example 28-17 is taken from "Eglogue" from *Four Sketches for Piano*, by Darius Milhaud, a prominent member of a group of French composers known as Les Six, whose members included, among others, Francis Poulenc and Arthur Honegger. The excerpt begins at m. 43 with a somewhat angular melody doubled in widely spaced minor thirds. The following two measures make use of a split third chord (f minor against A♮ in the left hand) in a passage that remains tonally ambiguous. Although G major appears to be the tonal center of the following three measures, the shifting accidentals in the right hand strongly suggest B major (m. 46) followed by D major (m. 47), creating fleeting moments of dissonance that are typical of Milhaud's writing.

EXAMPLE 28-17   *Darius Milhaud, "Eglogue," Four Sketches No. 1, mm. 43–48*

When two or more key centers are heard at the same time—which occurs considerably less frequently than polychordality—we refer to *bitonality* or *polytonality*. In order for the listener to perceive duality of key, it is necessary for the harmonic motion of each key to be relatively uncomplicated and very diatonic. Bitonality is illustrated in Example 28-18.

EXAMPLE 28-18   *Bartók, "Playsong," Mikrokosmos No. 105*

Although we may theorize about the possibility of three or more independent and simultaneous tonal centers, as suggested by the term *polytonality,* we would nonetheless be hard pressed to locate examples of literature in which this tonal multiplicity is obvious to the listener.

This observation suggests an interesting aspect of sonorities found in twentieth-century composition. Whereas in the tonal system the pitches of a tertian triad or seventh chord may be perceived as a discrete and identifiable unit, despite doubling, inversion, and even the presence of non-chord tones, the aural effect of sonorities in a less traditional setting is far more dependent on doubling, spacing, and arrangement in general.

Example 28-19 shows five possible arrangements of the pitches of a pentatonic scale. As you play each of the five, you will probably hear in turn:

1. a major triad with added 6th and 2nd

2. a stack of perfect 5ths

3. a 4th-rich sonority

4. an implied V^9 with suspension

5. a tone cluster (chord built from 2nds)

EXAMPLE 28-19

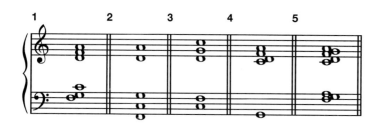

It may well have been the intervallic "accidents" occurring as the result of tall stacks of 3rds that suggested to composers the possibility of experimenting with other intervals for constructing chords. The P5 and its inversion, the P4, seem particularly well suited to avoiding any commitment to traditional major or minor implications. Example 28-20 illustrates the use of chords built in 5ths and 4ths.

EXAMPLE 28-20 *Debussy, "La Cathédrale engloutie," from* Preludes, *Book I*

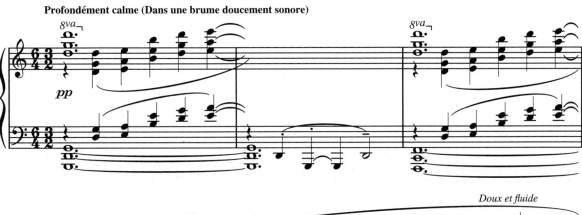

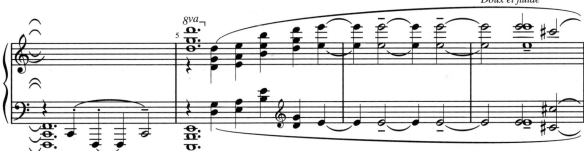

Except for the moving bass line, the pitches used adhere strictly to the diatonic pentatonic scale (G–A–B–D–E). If we view the pentatonic scale in terms of its derivation from stacked 5ths (G–D–A–E–B), this interdependence of scale and chords seems almost inevitable.

A predominantly *quartal* harmony (based primarily on 4ths) may be observed in Example 28-21.

EXAMPLE 28-21 *Hindemith, Flute Sonata, II*

Notice how the sense of B as tonal center is maintained by the bass line, which consists of a descending Dorian scale based on B, as well as frequent reference to F♯ by the solo flute and in the right hand of the accompaniment.

The use of 2nds as a method of chord construction also proved attractive to many composers. Example 28-22 illustrates the use of secundal harmony by Ross Lee Finney.

EXAMPLE 28-22 *Finney, "Playing Tag"*

Notice how, in addition to the accentuation and forward motion provided by the secundal chords, the fragmentary melody is based primarily on 2nds as well.

Any collection of three or more pitches in secundal relationship may correctly be referred to as a *tone cluster*. The term was coined by the American composer Henry Cowell, whose early experiments called for pianists to play certain passages with fists, palms, and, frequently, the entire forearm. Example 28-23, an excerpt from *The Tides of Manaunaun,* illustrates this technique. The sonorities thus created are powerful and richly programmatic.

EXAMPLE 28-23   *Cowell,* The Tides of Manaunaun

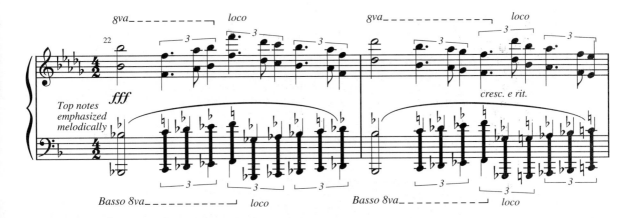

The concept of cluster chords, especially when used in conjunction with the rich timbral palette of an orchestra or chamber group, has continued to prove extremely useful for composers in the latter half of the twentieth century and will be further explored in this chapter.

PARALLELISM   *planing*

You may have noticed by now that the treatment of texture plays a significant role in our perception of twentieth-century music. The instrumental timbre, the structure of the chords, the doublings, the vertical spacing, the melodic construction, and the method of movement from one musical event to another—all these aspects contribute significantly to our impression of the piece as having a tonal center or not.

One of the earliest indications of a break with traditional procedures of harmonic progression was the use of parallelism. In some forms, of course, parallelism has been known before the twentieth century; you have already been exposed to parallel sixth chords in a tonal context, as illustrated in Example 28-24.

EXAMPLE 28-24

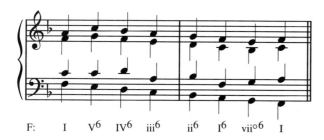

Even in this diatonic, triadic progression, the ear experiences at least a brief confusion in the space between the beginning and the ending tonic chords because of the sliding effect produced by parallel movement between the outer voices.

Even more challenging to the ear is Debussy's use of parallel movement of inverted dominant seventh chords, contrasted in the intervening measure with parallel movement of augmented triads (Ex. 28-25). The term *planing*, essentially synonymous with *parallelism*, is frequently used to describe this device when it occurs in twentieth-century music—perhaps to avoid the pejorative connotations of the formerly used term.

EXAMPLE 28-25 *Debussy, "Nuages," from* Nocturnes *(piano reduction)*

Used by permission of Edward B. Marks Music Company.

Following the first beat of mm. 61 and 63 the melody outlines the pitches of a dominant ninth chord on A♭, enharmonically respelled for convenience. The planing observed in this example is referred to as strict because the vertical intervals remain unchanged. This type of parallel motion will inevitably require a substantial number of accidentals because such consistent chord quality does not normally occur within a diatonic key; as a result, the feeling of tonal center will be unclear. In contrast, diatonic planing involves parallel movement of vertical sonorities whose quality is determined by the prevailing diatonic scale. Example 28-26 shows parallel triads used to harmonize a chantlike melody in C.

EXAMPLE 28-26 *Debussy, "La Cathédrale engloutie," from* Preludes, *Book I*

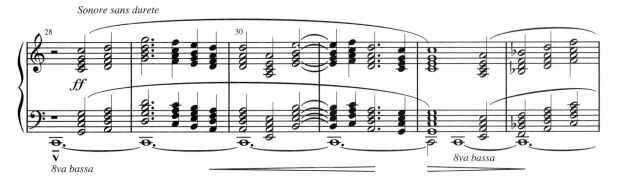

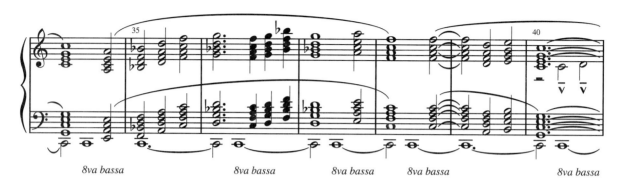

The pedal on C and the rhythmic emphasis on C, E, and G all serve to maintain a strong sense of C as tonal center of gravity. Notice, however, that B♭ is substituted for B♮ in the melodic line to maintain the consonant quality of major and minor triads. Although the B♭ could suggest a Mixolydian scale on C, the previous establishment of C major causes us instead to hear merely a brief tonicization of the subdominant, with C functioning temporarily as $\hat{5}$.

We occasionally encounter parallel chord movement that can be explained neither by consistency of chord type nor by the limitations of a single scale. Such a passage is shown in Example 28-27.

EXAMPLE 28-27   *Debussy, "Fêtes," from* Nocturnes *(piano reduction)*

Used by permission of Edward B. Marks Music Company.

In this case, the composer's aim is harmonization of the upper fourth of the chromatic scale below A (A–G♯–G–F♯–F–E). This descending line is further enhanced by the secondary line (C♯–B–B♭–A–A♭), which doubles it in 3rds. The concluding A♭ might be considered a misspelled leading tone in A. This seems especially plausible when we encounter a recurrence of this material in the closing section of the work (Ex. 28-28), harmonized to sound almost functional in the key of A. Here the juxtaposition of A♭ against B♭ clearly suggests an ⁺6, serving as a means of tonicization.

EXAMPLE 28-28 *Debussy, "Fêtes," from* Nocturnes *(piano reduction)*

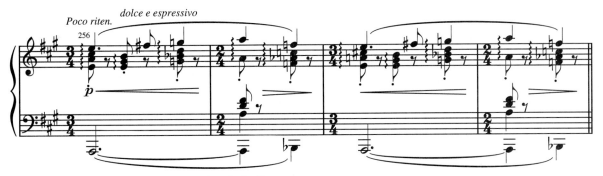

Obviously, the principle of parallelism may be applied to other structures, such as quintal and quartal chords, as well as to simple melodic doubling at intervals other than the traditional octave.

The second movement of Bartók's *Concerto for Orchestra* provides us with a virtual catalogue of doublings. The movement opens with a duet for bassoons doubled at the 6th, as illustrated in Example 28-29.

EXAMPLE 28-29 *Bartók,* Concerto for Orchestra, *II (reduction)*

This is followed by a passage featuring new material for oboes (Ex. 28-30), doubled at the m3 with an occasional M3.

EXAMPLE 28-30 *Bartók,* Concerto for Orchestra, *II (reduction)*

Following a brief transition by the strings, the work continues with other pairs of instruments: clarinets doubled at the m7, flutes doubled at the P5, and trumpets playing parallel major 2nds.

PANDIATONICISM

The technique of *pandiatonicism* represents an attempt to equalize the seven pitches of the diatonic scale so that no single pitch is heard as tonic. In Example 28-6 we observed that although C was a consistent point of reference, and the pitches used were those of a c minor scale, there was no clear sense of C as a tonal center, thereby suggesting the technique of pandiatonicism. In looking back at Example 28-13, we might also consider mm. 3 to 5 as a brief pandiatonic passage.

Example 28-31, by Samuel Barber, uses a key signature of G♭ major and features some recurrence of G♭ (tonic) and considerable recurrence of D♭ (dominant). Nonetheless (although we are aware of the music being centered in the scale of G♭), we get no sense of functional harmonic movement as we play or listen to this passage. The bass alternation of D♭ and E♭ the irregular division of the meter, and the structural inconsistency of the chords all contribute to the seeming absence of tonal direction.

EXAMPLE 28-31   *Barber, Excursions, III, mm. 49–55*

Frequently we will find that pandiatonic passages tend to be somewhat contrapuntal, employing multiple lines of music that more or less "saturate" the texture with the entire scalar pitch collection. Example 28-32 provides an example of a pandiatonic passage, taken from Stravinsky's ballet *Petrouchka*. Although the piano reduction used here does not permit us to view individual lines, it demonstrates the density of the music.

EXAMPLE 28-32 *Stravinsky, "Danse russe," from* Petrouchka *(piano reduction)*

Used by permission of Edward B. Marks Music Company.

Using C, the lowest pitch, as a reference point, we discover the excerpt to be based on a $\sharp\hat{4}, \flat\hat{7}$ scale; yet at no point is the ear permitted to accept C as tonic. In this instance the designation *4 + 1* scale might prove useful.

In another example from the same ballet (Ex. 28-33), E♭ seems to serve as a kind of tonal center. The reduction provided here gives some idea of the variety of melodic material played by the various instruments. You may also notice the relationship of the meter signature to the subdivisions within the measures. The combining of multiple rhythmic streams in this manner will be discussed in the following section, which deals with rhythm and meter.

EXAMPLE 28-33   *Stravinsky, "The Masqueraders," from* Petrouchka *(piano reduction)*

© Copyright 1912 by Hawkes & Son (London) Ltd. Copyright Renewed. Revised edition © Copyright 1947 by Hawkes & Son (London) Ltd. Copyright Renewed. Reprinted by permission of Boosey & Hawkes, Inc.

Self-Test 28-2
(Answers begin on page 665.)

A. Vertical sonorities

Review the nontraditional chord structures described in Chapter 28. Then describe
the structure of the chords shown below.

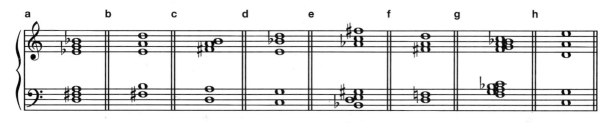

a   b   c   d   e   f   g   h

_____   _____   _____   _____   _____   _____   _____   _____

B. Analysis

1. Identify the scale on which the following composition is based.

_____

2. What is the tonal center at the opening of the piece? _____

In what measure does it change? _____ To what? _____

3. What technique is used for most of the accompaniment? _____

4. What is the most prominent melodic interval in this composition? _____

5. Where do you notice *hemiola* occurring? _____

Payne, *Skipping*

C. Sequence construction

   1. Harmonize the following phrase by continuing the parallel motion of dominant
         ninth chords in the spacing indicated.

   2. Now provide a quartal harmonization, again continuing to use the chord struc-
         ture provided for the first chord.

D. Composition (piano)

Using the following ostinato pattern for the left-hand part in each case, compose one or two brief phrases of music that demonstrate the following techniques:

Example #1: pandiatonicism

Example #2: secundal harmony/tone clusters

Example #3: bitonality

3

Exercise 28-1 (H–N) See Workbook.

RHYTHM AND METER

Because the study of pitch associations constitutes the primary bulwark of the traditional tonal system, it would seem reasonable that most attempts to establish alternative systems of organization would tend to concentrate on that area. Nonetheless, the mainstream of early twentieth-century composition saw significant innovations in the areas of rhythm and meter, procedures that impart a distinctive twentieth-century flavor to the music involved.

In the previous section dealing with pandiatonicism, we saw examples of irregular rhythmic organization. The first occurred in Example 28-31 by Barber in which, despite a meter signature of ¢ (cut time), each measure was clearly subdivided into seven quarter-note beats. Example 28-33 by Stravinsky featured multiple instrumental lines, each operating with a slightly different temporal organization despite the meter signature of $\frac{5}{8}$. In this particular example, we hear no clear reference beat but rather a shimmering palette of sound.

Composers seemed primarily interested in escaping the established norm of regular recurring pulses subdivided into groups of two or three. Various procedures have been employed in an effort to achieve this end, and the results are fascinating. Perhaps the most common of these is that of asymmetric meter, such as $\frac{5}{4}$ or $\frac{7}{8}$, or a composite meter, such as $\frac{3+3+2}{8}$, which we encounter frequently in the music of Bartók. These are used to provide what we might describe as a "regular irregularity" in that the groupings in a $\frac{5}{4}$ piece are likely to occur consistently as either 2+3 or 3+2. When these two groupings alternate, however, the effect becomes one of considerably more unpredictability.

A composer may achieve this desired irregularity either by cross accentuation, or by rapidly changing meter signatures—a process referred to as *mixed meter.* This latter technique is illustrated in Example 28-34, where we also observe irregular subdivision of the $\frac{5}{8}$ measures.

EXAMPLE 28-34   *Adler, "Capriccio"*

Both these procedures provide the listener with a sense of intense rhythmic activity coupled with constantly shifting metric accentuation. Because the effect on the listener is one of unequal groupings of subdivisions being added together, the process may be referred to as *additive* rhythm.

The term *polyrhythm* has been coined to denote a musical texture in which the listener is made aware of more than one musical stream or layer, each responding to an independently recurring metric downbeat. In some instances the listener may be unaware of the presence of any downbeats in the texture. (This phenomenon occurs in the example by Messiaen, Ex. 28-57.) In the following example by Copland, we observe a chorale-like passage being played by the strings. Irregular note values and ties across the bar line make it difficult to ascertain a downbeat. The flute part, however, maintains a militantly duple obbligato line that appears to exist in a separate rhythmic stream. Notice the beginning of a polytonal section (F and A) in the last two measures of the excerpt.

EXAMPLE 28-35   *Copland,* Appalachian Spring, *mm. 86–98*

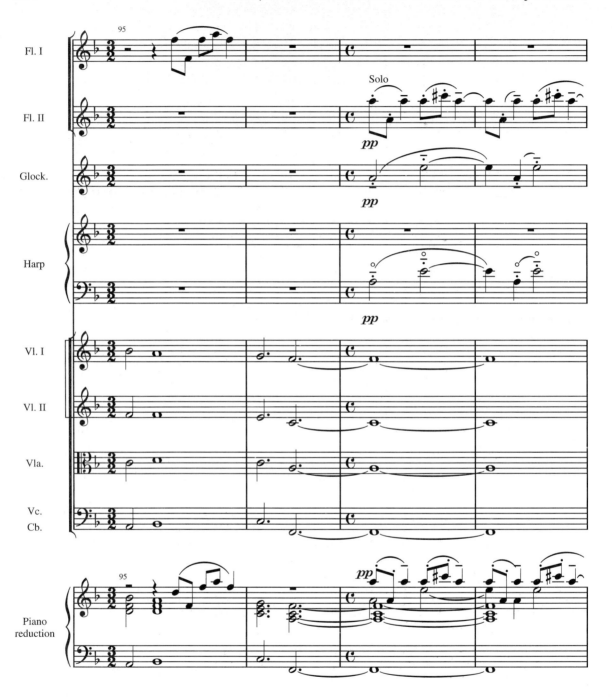

The term *polyrhythm* is sometimes confused with another term in common usage, *polymeter.* We use the former to denote the aural phenomenon of simultaneous rhythmic streams and the latter to refer to the notation of two or more meters at once. It is possible for a passage to be polyrhythmic and polymetric at the same time, as shown in Example 28-36.

EXAMPLE 28-36 *Stravinsky, "Danse de la foire," from* Petrouchka *(piano reduction)*

Used by permission of Edward B. Marks Music Company.

The effect of this passage on the listener may imply a total lack of bar lines. Instead, one is aware of a constant triplet background against which seemingly spontaneous bursts of rhythmic activity occur. You should keep in mind that *Petrouchka,* which we most often hear performed in the concert hall, was first composed as a ballet score. In this particular scene, the conflicting musical events represent specific actions taking place on the stage.

The term *metric modulation* was used by Elliott Carter to describe a method of changing tempo by equating a particular note value to a proportional value of that, or another, note value.

A simple example of this procedure might be as follows:

A somewhat more complex illustration of this concept may be found in the second movement of Carter's 2nd String Quartet, shown in Example 28-37.

EXAMPLE 28-37   *Carter, Second String Quartet, Mvt. 2, mm. 181–186*

The final rhythmic concept we will present is that of *added value,* which is not to be confused with *additive rhythm,* mentioned earlier. Like metric modulation, this process—developed largely by Olivier Messiaen and described at length in his book *The Technique of My Musical Language*—creates rhythmic irregularity through the addition of a note, a dot, a tie, or a rest to what otherwise appears to be a perfectly regular rhythmic pattern. For example, consider the following grouping:

This figure might be transformed in any of the following ways, to mention but a few of what are almost limitless possibilities:

Messiaen himself admitted to a fondness for the subtleties of Indian rhythms, and we see abundant evidence of this in much of his music. Example 28-38 shows the principles of added value in operation.

EXAMPLE 28-38   *Messiaen, "Dance of Fury for Seven Trumpets," from* Quartet for the End of Time

The opening two measures, except for one sixteenth beat, would fit a $\frac{4}{4}$ framework. The third measure contains one eighth-note value too many, whereas the fourth measure has been lengthened by three sixteenths. As the movement proceeds, any comparison with a time signature becomes pointless; in fact, the listener would have difficulty perceiving an implied regular meter even at the beginning.

At the beginning of this chapter, we observed that at least two major and divergent compositional paths emerged from the post-Romantic era. One of these was based on the expansion and further development of certain elements of tonality, including scales, chords, principles of harmonic progression, texture, and use of folk music. Our emphasis thus far has been centered on those procedures that reflect the goals of composers in the more traditional stream.

The second path was a somewhat more revolutionary one that embraced and expanded the principle of chromatic saturation found in the music of composers such as Wagner, Mahler, Richard Strauss, and others, as a means of emancipating music from principles of tonality. In the following pages, we will further explore these developments that brought about profound changes in attitudes and approaches to the craft of music composition.

Self-Test 28-3
(Answers begin on page 667.)

Which of the rhythmic procedures mentioned in Chapter 28 are illustrated by the following examples?

SET THEORY

Much music of the post-Romantic period remained sufficiently tonal to yield, albeit imperfectly, to traditional methods of analysis. However, even as early as the first decade of the twentieth century, some composers were creating music that resists any application of traditional harmonic theory.

Listen to or play Example 28-39, the opening measures of a piece that was composed in 1909. Most analysts consider this to be one of Schoenberg's *atonal* works, meaning a musical composition without a tonal center or centers. (Schoenberg, incidentally, despised the term and preferred *pantonal* instead.) It is possible to find tonal structures in this excerpt that are also found in tonal music, such as the D7 chord outlined in m. 8, but they lose their identities when placed in this atonal setting.

EXAMPLE 28-39   *Schoenberg, Three Piano Pieces, Op. 11, No. 1*

Used by permission of Belmont Music Publishers, Pacific Palisades, CA 90272.

Theorists and composers who are faced with the task of analyzing music such as this found, of course, that many of their traditional tools were of little use. A new vocabulary was especially critical if they were going to be able to describe in a systematic way the new pitch structures that composers were using. While notable attempts were made in this regard by Paul Hindemith and Howard Hanson, the method that is in wide use today was first codified and refined by Allen Forte in *The Structure of Atonal Music.** This method is based upon a theory called *pitch class set theory* or simply *set theory*.

*Allen Forte, The Structure of Atonal Music (New Haven, Conn.: Yale University Press, 1973).

The first step in analyzing a piece using set theory is to *segment* the piece into groups of notes called *sets* or *cells.* The segmenting takes into account various musical considerations (phrasing, register, rhythm, and so on) as well as what has been learned from analyzing earlier sets. In Example 28-39, for example, one might segment the opening five-note melody as a single five-note set, or one might take just the first three notes as a set because of the longer duration of the third note.

Analysis of the sets is usually carried out at the same time as the segmentation, and here we encounter the main topic of this section. In common-practice music we could easily identify the triads and seventh chords by name because they were so few in number, but in music that departs radically from that system any combination of pitches is possible. Set theory offers us a consistent method of naming any possible combination of pitches. We will go through the process step by step.

Step 1. Put the set in normal order. What this means is to arrange the pitch classes so that they cover the smallest range possible, similar to what we do when we put a triad in root position. You can often figure out the normal order just by looking at the set. For example, the normal order (or NO) of the first three notes of the melody in Example 28-39 would be G–G♯–B, and the NO of the first five notes would be F–G–G♯–A–B. The NOs of the first two three-note chords (or trichords) are a little harder to visualize because of the spacing, but they would be F–G♭–B and A–B♭–D♭. The normal orders of all four sets are shown in Example 28-40.

EXAMPLE 28-40

Notice that in Example 28-40 we notated the sets as ascending scales rather than as chords to make them easier to read; this is the conventional way of notating a NO. Notice also that we spelled one note in the third set enharmonically (F♯ instead of G♭); because we are dealing with pitch classes, you can use any enharmonic spellings that you want.

You will find that some sets cannot be put into NO as easily as those in Example 28-40. For example, consider the five-note set (or pentachord) that occurs three times in the tenor voice: D–F♯–A–A♯–B. It is difficult to decide what arrangement of the set would cover the smallest range possible. In cases such as this, you will need to follow the following step.

Step 1a. Notate the set as a scale, going up to the octave, and find the largest interval. The top *note of the largest interval will be the* bottom *note of the normal order.* We have notated the pentachord as an ascending scale in Example 28-41a. Notice that we went up to the octave, an easy step to forget. The largest interval (be careful with enharmonic spellings here) is the major third, D–F♯, so the NO begins on F♯, the *top* note of that interval, as in Example 28-41b.

EXAMPLE 28-41

Occasionally you will encounter a set where there is more than one occurrence of the largest interval. This doesn't happen often, but it happens frequently enough to be a nuisance. You can see that the set in Example 28-42a (not from the Schoenberg excerpt) contains two occurrences of a M3, which is the largest interval. To break the tie, we have to consider the two candidates for the NO, one beginning on G (Ex. 28-42b) and one beginning on C (Ex. 28-42c). We break the tie by comparing the *lowest* intervals of the two candidates, selecting the one with the smaller interval as the NO. In this case, Example 28-42b begins with a smaller interval (a m2) than does Example 28-42c (a M2), so Example 28-42b is the NO.

EXAMPLE 28-42

That's all there is to know about finding the normal order, but we have a couple of steps still to go. Pitch class set theory invokes the theory of *inversional equivalence,* which sounds more intimidating than it is. You are already familiar with equivalence in music. *Octave equivalence* allows you to say that there are only 12 pitch classes on the keyboard instead of 88 or that a C major triad is a C major triad no matter what register it is in or how it is voiced. *Transpositional equivalence* allows you to say that "Happy Birthday" is the same song no matter what key you sing it in. Both of those are theories, although they do have an acoustical foundation. Inversional equivalence is the third step, and its premise is that a set and its mirror inversion are two representations of the same thing. For example, the NO of the first three notes of the Schoenberg excerpt is G–G♯–B (Ex. 28-43a), whereas the NO of the notes in the right hand in m. 3 is C♯–E–F (Ex. 28-43b). Although these sets are not transpositionally equivalent, they are inversionally equivalent: Example 28-43a consists of a m3 on top of a m2, whereas Example 28-43b consists of a m2 on top of a m3.

EXAMPLE 28-43

Because inversionally related sets are considered in set theory to be equivalent, we will need to compare our original NO with the NO of its inversion to find the *best normal order* (BNO).

Step 2. Invert the normal order of the set and put the inversion into normal order. There are various ways to invert a set in normal order, but the easiest is to keep the lowest and highest notes the same while reversing the order of the intervals between them. Example 28-44 shows the NO of the pentachord in Example 28-42 and its inversion. Notice how the order of the intervals has been reversed.

EXAMPLE 28-44

In the majority of cases, if you invert the NO of a set, you will get the NO of the inversion of the set. However, if there was more than one occurrence of the largest interval when you were figuring out the NO of the set, then you have to consider all the possible candidates for the NO of the inversion as well. The set in Example 28-44 comes from Example 28-42, where we found two occurrences of a M3. Therefore, we have to consider two candidates for the NO of the inversion and break the tie the same way as we did before.

EXAMPLE 28-45

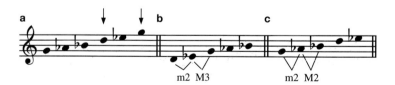

This time, however, we find that the two candidates for NO (Examples 28-45b and c) begin with the same interval—a m2. When this happens, we have to continue to the next interval, which breaks the tie in favor of Example 28-45c because its M2 is smaller than the M3 in Example 28-45b. This gives us the NO of the inversion. (However, let us reiterate that, in most cases, if you invert the NO of a set, you will get the NO of the inversion without having to do anything further.)

Step 3. Compare the two normal orders to find the best normal order. This part is easy. You simply compare the NO of the original set with the NO of the inversion to find the best normal order (BNO). Because they will always span the same interval, you break the tie the same way you did before—by comparing the bottom interval, then the next, and so on, until one NO has a smaller interval than the other. That NO then becomes the BNO.†
In Example 28-46 we have the two normal orders side by side, and you can see that Example 28-46b is the BNO because its M2 is smaller than the M3 in Example 28-46a. If all the intervals are identical, then you have discovered an *inversionally symmetrical* set. This is not an uncommon occurrence. Examples of inversionally symmetrical sets include the augmented triad and the octatonic scale.

EXAMPLE 28-46

It is time now to provide a name for our pitch-class set, a unique name that will stand for our original set and its inversion and all their transpositions. That name is called the *prime form* of a set.

Step 4. Use the best normal order to construct the prime form. To construct the prime form (sometimes called the *set type* or *set class*), calculate the number of half steps each member of the BNO is above its lowest note:

Note	Half Steps Above G
E♭	8
D	7
B♭	3
A♭	1
G	0

Then put the numbers in order in this form:

[0,1,3,7,8]

†*If you are thinking that "best normal order" should really be "better normal order," you are absolutely correct. However, this grammatical anomaly seems to be with us to stay.*

Although there is much more to pitch-class set theory, you now have the vocabulary to do some basic analysis. Do not expect to find that entire pieces are composed by means of one or two prime forms because such pieces are quite rare. You may find, however, that a few set types account for many or most of the notes in a given passage or that they are subsets or supersets of other segmentations. In any case, set theory offers another way of listening to some kinds of music, a method of listening for intervallic relationships in music in which traditional harmonic relationships are nonexistent.

Self-Test 28-4
(Answers begin on page 667.)

A. The opening trichord

   1. We saw in Example 28-43 that the notes in the right hand in m. 3 are an inversion of the first three notes. This means they are members of the same set class. What is its prime form?

   2. List some other occurrences of this set type in the excerpt. Try to make your segmentations musically defensible. You may omit obvious repetitions.

   3. Which of those occurrences uses the same pitch classes as the opening three notes?

B. Other segmentations

   1. There are four half-note trichords. Label them a through d and provide the prime form of each.

   2. Each of those trichords is of a different set type, but each one can be related to each of the others in one way or another. Try to do this (Be creative!).

   3. What is the prime form of the opening two measures of the melody? Of the opening three measures? Which of these is inversionally symmetrical? How can you tell?

   4. An expansion of the opening two measures appears in mm. 9 to 10. What is the prime form of this set? How does it compare to the original? Is it inversionally symmetrical?

   5. What is the prime form of the recurring five-note figure in the tenor in mm. 4 to 8? Is it inversionally symmetrical?

   6. Bonus question: The opening three measures of the melody can be partitioned into four trichords that are the same set classes as those used for the half-note chords. This can be done in such a way that each trichord is used only once and every note of the melody is used at least once. Try it. (This may not be of consequence analytically, but it's good practice and kind of fun.)

Exercise 28-1 (O–P) See Workbook.

THE TWELVE-TONE TECHNIQUE

The procedure for composing with twelve tones is perhaps the most methodically revolutionary technique of the twentieth century. The Viennese-born composer, Arnold Schoenberg is generally credited with developing and codifying this system that he believed would negate a sense of tonal center. Having been profoundly influenced by the music of Wagner, Mahler, and Brahms, his earlier works embody many elements of the post-Romantic style. Ultimately he found this style to be unsatisfactory and consciously sought to create a new harmonic language through the use of angular melodies, sudden and extreme contrasts of dynamics and texture, and use of instruments and the voice in non-traditional ways. You have already encountered an early work of Schoenberg, the style of which provides a sharp departure from the compositional styles that we have studied thus far.

Even before Schoenberg had organized his ideas into an actual method of composition, certain procedures were operational in his music, such as the following:

1. Avoidance of the 8ve, either as melodic component or harmonic interval.

2. Avoidance of traditional pitch collections, that is, any that might suggest major or minor triads and hence a tonic.

3. Avoidance of more than three successive pitches that might be identified with the same diatonic scale.

4. Use of wide-ranging and extremely disjunct melodies.

The principles mentioned above continued to hold true in much of Schoenberg's twelve-tone music as well as in that of his early followers, especially Webern and Berg. His system was designed to methodically equalize all pitches of the dodecaphonic scale by the following means:

1. A twelve-tone composition is to be based on an arrangement or series of the twelve pitches that is determined by the composer. This arrangement is the *tone row* or *set*.

2. No pitch may be used again until all other pitches have been sounded. There is one exception to this restriction: a pitch may be repeated immediately after it is heard. Repetition may also occur within the context of a trill or tremolo figure.

3. The tone row may, within the confines of the system, legitimately be used in retrograde (reversed order), inversion (mirroring of each interval), or retrograde inversion (reverse order of the mirrored form).

It is important to remember that the row is not necessarily intended to represent a "theme" or "melody" but is more of a tool used by the composer to arrive at new musical gestures or vertical structures that he or she might not consciously have thought of. Before discussing more complex illustrations of this technique, let us examine a simple composition composed using the twelve-tone method. The piece, entitled "All Alone," is taken from a set of *24 Piano Inventions* composed by Ross Lee Finney, all of which are based on the use of a twelve-tone row. The row and its retrograde are shown in Example 28-47.

EXAMPLE 28-47   *Tone Row from 24 Piano Inventions*

The twelve notes of the scale are in the following order in the first four bars,

But in the next four measures their sequence is turned backwards:

and at the very end they are used as chords:

Example 28-48 shows "All Alone" in its entirety. You will notice that the D at the end of the fourth measure has two identities: one as the 12th note of the prime form of the row and one as the starting pitch of the retrograde form, which begins in bar 5. Notice too that the A in m. 8 is allowed to remain as the bass note throughout the remainder of the piece. Although this example illustrates the most basic use of this technique, we can see the possibilities for creating a very expressive melody and for variety in texture.

EXAMPLE 28-48   *Finney, "All Alone," No. 14, 24 Piano Inventions*

Now let us examine another row that forms the basis for the Symphony Op. 21 by Anton Webern, one of Schoenberg's most devoted followers (Ex. 28-49).

EXAMPLE 28-49   *Webern, Row forms of Symphony Op. 21*

Prime zero (P^0)

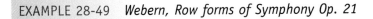

[0,   1,   3]   [0,   1,   4]   [0,   1,   4]   [0,   1,   3]

Retrograde zero (R^0)

Inversion zero (I^0)

Retrograde inversion zero (RI^0)

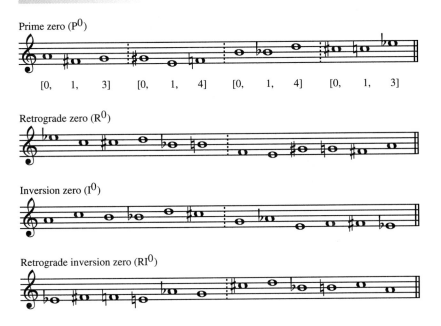

Note the consistency and symmetry of arrangement in the trichords that comprise the row. [0,1,3] begins and ends the set, whereas two versions of [0,1,4] appear in the middle.

Any one of these forms may be transposed to begin at any pitch level; thus the process may yield up to forty-eight versions of the row (in most instances). It is important to remember that the original series of pitches is in no way comparable to the theme of a theme and variations. Although the intervallic arrangement of the row may tend to bring about the recurrence of melodic and harmonic cells, tremendous variety results from the rhythmic manipulation and octave displacement typically found in early twelve-tone works.

When you examine a twelve-tone composition, it is helpful to have immediate access to the forty-eight possible forms of the series. This is most conveniently obtained by use of a *matrix,* illustrated in Example 28-50 with the original or prime form of the series of Example 28-49 shown as its top row of pitches. The inversion zero form is laid out in the first vertical column, from top to bottom. This is accomplished by inverting or mirroring the intervals in P^0, that is, A–F♯ (M6 up) inverts to A–C (M6 down). F♯–G (m2) equates with C–B. The symmetry of this operation may be viewed in the following diagram, in which the note A serves as the axis of involution.

EXAMPLE 28-50

Twelve-tone matrix.

	I												
	0	9	10	11	7	8	2	1	5	4	3	6	
0	A	F#	G	Ab	E	F	B	Bb	D	C#	C	Eb	0
3	C												3
2	B												2
1	Bb												1
5	D												5
4	C#												4
10	G												10
11	Ab												11
7	E												7
8	F												8
9	F#												0
6	Eb												6
	0	9	10	11	7	8	2	1	5	4	3	6	

P → (left)　　R ← (right)　　RI (bottom)

Using this method, we find that the interval that begins each prime row form will be a M6. Thus A–F# will be followed by C–A, then B–G# (Ab), and so on.

Index numbers on each side of the matrix designate levels of transposition, arranged in ascending chromatic order from zero. The P^0 set, for example, transposed up a M3 to begin on C#, would be designated as P^4. You will note that the index number reflects, in each case, the number of half steps contained within the interval of transposition. The retrograde P^4 would be labeled as R^4 and would begin on G. When correctly done, the sum of the index numbers for a prime form and its inversion should equal 12—that is, P,3+I,9; P,2+I,10, and so on. Likewise, RI,3 will correspond with R,9, and so on.

We should mention here that the actual procedure for labeling set forms tends to vary somewhat, depending on the theorist cited. In the writings of earlier twelve-tone composers, we find the term *original* used in place of *prime*. The inevitable confusion arising between the letter "o" (original) and the numeral "0" (zero) may have prompted the change in terminology. Precise intervallic spellings are unnecessary; for example, the half-step transposition of D–F may be represented by E♭–F♯ because the music under discussion is not governed by traditional rules of consonance and dissonance. It is advisable, however, to strive for consistency: always choose F♯ rather than G♭, for example, or vice versa. Example 28-51 illustrates the completed matrix.

EXAMPLE 28-51

	0	9	10	11	7	8	2 (I)	1	5	4	3	6	
0	A	F♯	G	A♭	E	F	B	B♭	D	C♯	C	E♭	0
3	C	A	B♭	B	G	A♭	D	C♯	F	E	E♭	F♯	3
2	B	A♭	A	B♭	F♯	G	C♯	C	E	E♭	D	F	2
1	B♭	G	A♭	A	F	F♯	C	B	E♭	D	C♯	E	1
5	D	B	C	C♯	A	B♭	E	E♭	G	F♯	F	A♭	5
4 (P)	C♯	B♭	B	C	A♭	A	E♭	D	F♯	F	E	G	4 (R)
10	G	E	F	F♯	D	E♭	A	A♭	C	B	B♭	C♯	10
11	A♭	F	F♯	G	E♭	E	B♭	A	C♯	C	B	D	11
7	E	C♯	D	E♭	B	C	F♯	F	A	A♭	G	B♭	7
8	F	D	E♭	E	C	C♯	G	F♯	B♭	A	A♭	B	8
9	F♯	E♭	E	F	C♯	D	A♭	G	B	B♭	A	c	9
6	E♭	C	C♭	D	B♭	B	F	E	A♭	G	F♯	A	6
	0	9	10	11	7	8	2 (RI)	1	5	4	3	6	

The construction of the Op. 21 pitch set is an interesting one from many standpoints. Each half of the row is made up of adjacent pitches of the chromatic scale. In addition the second *hexachord* (set of six pitches) represents the retrograde of the first. On comparing R^6 (the retrograde of the row, transposed up a °5), we discover that it is identical with P^0. We may then assume that for each transposition of the prime set, there is a matching retrograde pattern; likewise, for each inversion, there will be a matching retrograde inversion form.

This built-in correlation between set forms will, of necessity, reduce the available pitch series to twenty-four possibilities rather than the usual forty-eight. The term *combinatoriality* is often used to describe this feature. The distinguishing property of a combinatorial set is its capability of generating a number of hexachords that are mutually exclusive, that is, in which no pitches are duplicated.

Example 28-52 shows the opening of the Theme of the *Variationen* (Movement II) from the Symphony Op. 21. As you examine this excerpt with the matrix, you will see that the clarinet states the I-8 form of the set, whereas the horns and harp together outline the pitches of I-2, its matching retrograde form. Note, too, the consistent tritone relationship between the starting pitches of these related sets, which are exploited throughout the movement. The texture of this brief excerpt is sparse, as is the case with much of Webern's work.

EXAMPLE 28-52   *Webern,* Variationen, Symphony *Op. 21, mm. 1–11*

The availability of complementary hexachords will often play an important role in a composer's choice of particular set forms and will tend to bring about maximum structural cohesion in a work. To be sure, not all combinatorial rows exhibit the intricate symmetrical relationships found in Webern's. An exhaustive discussion of combinatoriality is better suited to advanced study in serial techniques than to this introductory chapter. If you would like to pursue these topics further, you should look into the writings of George Perle or Milton Babbitt.

Certain rows, such as those of Example 28-53, have achieved a certain reknown by virtue of their having formed the basis for well-known serial compositions.

EXAMPLE 28-53

Berg, Tone row for Violin Concerto

Dallapiccola, Tone row for *Quaderno musicale di Annalibera*

These rows illustrate the care composers lavished on the melodic and harmonic possibilities of the original set. The predominance of the 3rd in the Berg row, for example, plays an important role in bringing about an almost triadic texture within the body of the work. Also in the Berg row, pitches 1, 3, 5, and 7 of the series (bracketed) represent the open strings of the violin, whereas the last four pitches, which comprise a segment of a whole-tone scale, represent the opening notes of "Es ist genug," the Bach chorale prominently featured in the last movement. The second example, from Dallapiccola's *Quaderno musicale di Annalibera,* illustrates an all-interval set, in which eleven different intervals make up the series.

Example 28-54 illustrates two processes, both of which occur with some frequency in atonal music. The first is the atomization of the melodic line, a process known as *pointillism.* The second is the deliberate juxtaposition of minute melodic fragments of contrasting timbre and register; this compositional device, in which melody is in a sense created by the rapid shifting of tone colors, is referred to as *Klangfarbenmelodie,* or, literally, "sound color melody," and it is a concept that continues to fascinate many composers in the second half of the twentieth century. As you listen to a recording of this work, it may be helpful to try to suspend previously studied tonal listening habits.

EXAMPLE 28-54   *Webern, Concerto Op. 24*

This composition, like most compositions by Webern, lends itself to analysis of set types. Notice the consistency of use of [0,1,2] and [0,1,4] trichords, several of which are labeled.

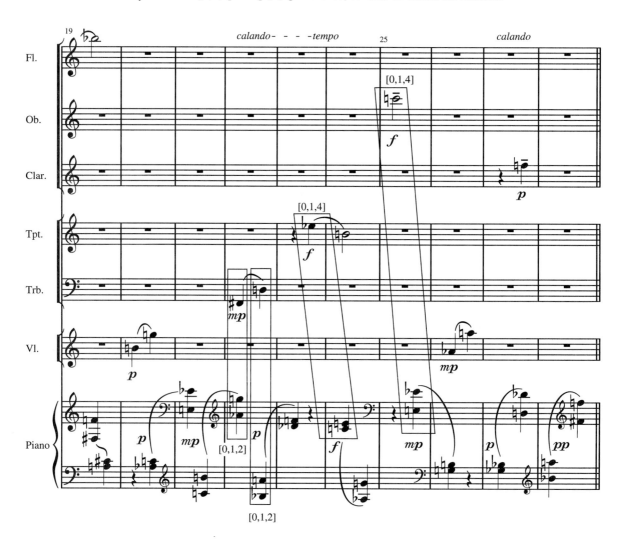

We should also mention here that the twelve-tone procedure, although conceived specifically as a systematic means for avoiding (or rather for providing alternatives to) tonality, has been adapted by later composers as an effective means for organizing more tonally oriented music. The row may even be employed as a quasi-pandiatonic procedure. Stravinsky, for example, makes use of a twenty-eight-note series for the variations found in the second movement of his Sonata for Two Pianos and a five-note set for *In Memoriam Dylan Thomas,* consisting of the pitch series E–E♭–C–C♯–D.

Self-Test 28-5
(Answers begin on page 668.)

A. Twelve-tone exercise. The row given below forms the basis for Schoenberg's String Quartet, No. 4, Op. 37. Notate the inversion of the row on the blank staff, then fill in the matrix using the guidelines found on page 538.

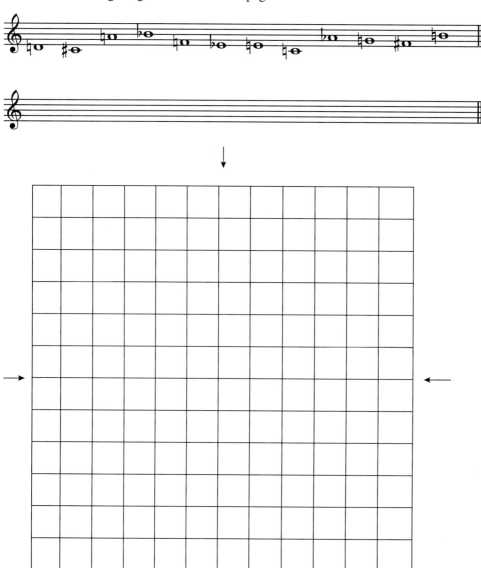

B. Using the Schoenberg row for which you have just constructed a matrix, compose a twelve-tone piece using the structural design of "All Alone" by Ross Lee Finney (Ex. 28-48). Your piece need not be slow and sad, but it should be constructed using (1) the prime form of the row, (2) the retrograde or perhaps another set form taken from your matrix, and (3) chords based on the prime form. Keep in mind that the use of one or more rhythmic motives is helpful in establishing the mood of a piece.

Exercise 28-1 (Q–V) See Workbook.

TOTAL SERIALIZATION

Inevitably, as composers became fascinated with the concept of ordering pitches, there evolved a keen interest in ordering other parameters of a piece, such as rhythm, dynamics, and articulation. The term *serialization,* which earlier in the twentieth century has been considered by some to be synonymous with *twelve-tone method,* came to denote the process whereby such aspects of music as the subdivisions of the beat, dynamic level of individual pitches, and, in the case of instrumental music, choice of timbre were decided on by means of a predetermined rhythmic, dynamic, and/or timbral series. It is sometimes referred to as *integral serialism.* Two composers associated with the origins of this practice are Anton Webern, whose fascination with the problem of ordering we have already observed, and Olivier Messiaen, whose 1949 piano etude *Mode de valeurs et d'intensités* exerted a profound influence on his pupil, Pierre Boulez. Example 28-55 shows the Messiaen pitch set, along with its rhythmic, dynamic, registral, and attack characteristics, whereas Example 28-56 illustrates the set used by Boulez in *Structures.* We perceive Boulez's debt to his teacher in the fact that the pitch set used is identical to Series I of the Messiaen piece.

EXAMPLE 28-55   *Messiaen, Set forms for* Mode de valeurs et d'intensités

EXAMPLE 28-56 *Boulez, Set forms for* Structures, *Ia*

	1	2	3	4	5	6	7	8	9	10	11	12
Notes (P0)	E♭	D	A	A♭	G	F♯	E	C♯	C	B♭	F	B
Durations	♪	♪	♪.	♪	♪♪	♪.	♪..	♩	♩♪	♩♪	♩♪.	♩
Dynamics	*pppp*	*ppp*	*pp*	*p*	*quasi p*	*mp*	*mf*	*quasi f*	*f*	*ff*	*fff*	*ffff*
Mode of Attack	>	>̣	.		normal	⌢	′	*sfz* ∧	>̣		̇	⌢

On the introductory page of *Mode de valeurs,* Messiaen explains that he has employed a thirty-six pitch series (that is, three separate pitch sets, each of which is assigned to a specific register of the piano) and twelve methods of attack as follows:

>	′	.	–	⌢	>̣	>̣	≥	⌢.	*sf* >	*sf* >̣	"normal", no sign
1	2	3	4	5	6	7	8	9	10	11	12

He notes that there are seven dynamic levels ranging from *ppp* to *fff* while the register is to a certain extent controlled by the pitch series being used. Thus no two appearances of the same pitch class will be identical.

Example 28-57 shows the beginning of the Messiaen work. Clearly the range of dynamic shading called for presents a singular challenge in pianistic control and a still more formidable challenge to even the most sophisticated listener.

EXAMPLE 28-57   *Messiaen,* Mode de valeurs et d'intensités

As you might imagine, the mathematical possibilities for systematic ordering or reordering of sets are virtually limitless, and they continue to present a fascinating avenue of exploration for many composers as well as a challenge for speculative theorists. The term *stochastic music* refers to music composed through computer-generated choices based on the laws of probability. This procedure, which has been used by Lejaren Hiller and Iannis Xenakis, may be viewed as the ultimate extension of total serialization.

There can be a striking similarity between two seemingly contradictory compositional processes—namely, the effort to achieve total control and the effort to abdicate control entirely through chance or aleatory procedures. Both of these processes reflect a composer's desire to break free from conscious aural choices, thereby discovering sounds or effects that might not otherwise occur to him or her. In the following pages of this chapter, we will briefly explore a few early examples of aleatory music, along with some subsequent compositional directions that it may have spawned.

ALEATORY OR CHANCE MUSIC

Aleatory refers to music in which various elements of a composition are, in varying degrees, determined by chance. Although the term is essentially a twentieth-century addition to the vocabulary of music, the idea of chance is by no means new to the realities of musical performance. Composers have long been at the mercy of poor performers, inadequate instruments, cough-racked audiences, and imprecise musical notation.

To a certain extent, the time-honored practice of improvisation, especially as it pertains to the spontaneous music-making of a group of jazz performers, may be considered to involve the element of chance, although obviously to a more predictable degree than the events mentioned above.

The application of *chance* to music composition may manifest itself in one of two ways: the overall plan of the piece may be precisely notated, with specific details left either to the performer or to chance, or the compositional process itself may be indeterminate. The best-known, and perhaps the earliest, advocate of indeterminacy as a valid approach to music performance and composition was the American John Cage.

The piece with which Cage was most widely identified may well be the one usually referred to as 4′33″. The first performance (from which the title derives) took place at Woodstock, New York, on August 29, 1952, and featured David Tudor, a pianist and long-time professional associate of Cage. The piece consisted at that time of three movements, the beginnings of which were indicated by the closing of the keyboard lid; the opening of the keyboard lid signaled the end of each movement. For the duration of each movement (33″, 2′40″, and 1′20″, respectively), the pianist remained motionless on stage. The published score of the piece consists of a single page and gives the playing instructions "Tacet" for each movement. It further specifies that the work is "playable" by any instrument or instrumental ensemble and that it may last any length of time. The chief importance of this seemingly tongue-in-cheek work, whose aural effect relies entirely on miscellaneous noises occurring in the concert hall, lies in the obligation it places on the listener to incorporate what would normally be disturbing noises (a cough, the hiss of a radiator, the rustling of a program, a plane passing overhead) into the framework of a musical experience.

His *Imaginary Landscape for 12 Radios* is a model of precise notation. Each pair of twenty-four performers is furnished with a radio and an individual part, on which is indicated tuning, volume, and tone control. There is, in addition, a conductor equipped with a stopwatch. Obviously, despite the precision of performance instructions, every performance will differ greatly from every other one, depending on geographic location and time of day. A performance in New York City, for example, will always be a totally different experience than one in Omaha, Nebraska (where the premiere performance took place in 1951).

Cage's pioneer efforts inspired a host of followers, and the result was an incredible diversity of experimentation. The length to which Cage's disciples carried his original ideas may be seen in a group of pieces by Max Neuhaus, composed between 1966 and 1968. The set comprises six sound-oriented compositions, specifically designed for a situation other than that of the concert hall. The first of these, "Listen," specifies that the audience, who arrive expecting a concert or lecture, are to be put on a bus, have their hands stamped with the word "Listen," and then driven through an existing sound environment. One such "performance," for example, took place in the Consolidated Edison Power Station at Fourteenth Street and Avenue D in New York City. "Drive-In Music," the fifth piece in the group, is designed for people in automobiles. The original score consists of a street map of a small area in Buffalo, New York, designating the streets along which the listener is to drive. At various locations along the route, radio transmitters, which may be heard only through an AM radio, are mounted on telephone poles or trees. Their broadcast areas are designed to overlap, so that at any given time the listener is hearing a combination of signals. Because the actual "music" heard by the concertgoer is subject to such a multitude of fluctuations, brought about not only by the choice of sounds (which might range anywhere from noise to snippets of classical repertoire) but also by the weather, speed of travel, engine noise, and so on, we simply cannot conceptualize or describe the resulting musical effect without having experienced it.

Compositions such as those just described tend, of necessity, to be notated either by means of specific verbal instructions or in a graphic manner. The earliest use of graphic notation was often viewed as a means of saving the composer tedious hours of copying while providing a more dramatic and descriptive representation of his or her musical intent to the performer. However, the unique notational requirements of some types of aleatoric music spawned an interest in the artistic layout of the score itself, even in the case of music intended for performance by traditional instruments.

One such example, scored for solo piano and showing a great deal of pitch and rhythm detail, is illustrated in Example 28-58, by George Crumb.

EXAMPLE 28-58 *Crumb, "The Magic Circle of Infinity," from* Makrokosmos I

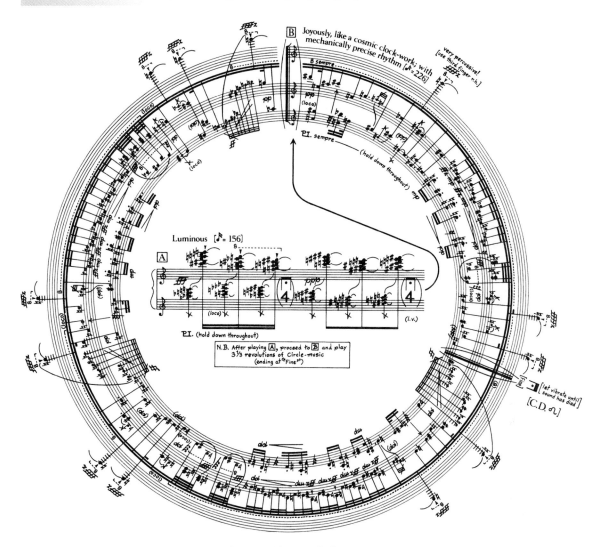

This work, which received its premiere performance in 1973, was intended by the composer to pay homage to two composers whom he greatly admired: Bartók and Debussy. There are twelve pieces in the set, each associated with a sign of the zodiac. The score calls for amplified piano and carries very specific directions for pizzicato plucking of strings inside the piano and for accurate marking of the strings with bits of tape to ensure precise harmonics.

It should be noted here that Crumb's interest in exploring all available timbral possibilities (creating in many cases extraordinary challenges for the performer!) has been widely recognized and acclaimed.

The concept of *phase* or *process* music may be seen as a logical extension of the aleatoric procedure. Use of this terminology is generally credited to Steve Reich, who introduced the technique in a 1965 tape piece, *It's Gonna Rain,* and later applied it to an instrumental work, *Piano Phase* (1967). Phase music consists of the constant repetition, over an extended period of time, of a given number of musical elements by an ensemble that may or may not be precisely specified. The musical segments are most often performed in a predetermined order; the unique property of this music results from the indeterminacy of the time lapse between each event, thus causing the instruments to move in and out of "phase" with each other as the music progresses. *Piano Phase* consists of thirty-two musical fragments, to be played either by two pianos or two marimbas.

The instructions and first page of the score of *Piano Phase* are given in Example 28-59.

In "Music as a Gradual process," taken from his book of essays, *Writings about Music,* Reich articulates the type of thinking that led to this procedure:[‡]

> *I do not mean the process of composition, but rather pieces of music that are, literally, processes. The distinctive thing about musical processes is that they determine all the note-to-note (sound-to-sound) details and the over all form simultaneously. (Think of a round or infinite canon.) I am interested in perceptible processes. I want to be able to hear the process happening throughout the sounding music. To facilitate closely detailed listening a musical process should happen extremely gradually.*
>
> *Performing and listening to a gradual musical process resembles: pulling back a swing, releasing it, and observing it gradually come to rest; turning over an hour glass and watching the sand slowly run through to the bottom; placing your feet in the sand by the ocean's edge and watching, feeling, and listening to the waves gradually bury them.*

EXAMPLE 28-59   *Reich, Piano Phase*

Directions for Performance

Repeats

The number of repeats of each bar is not fixed but may vary more or less within the limits appearing at each bar. Generally speaking a number of repeats more than the minimum and less than the maximum should be aimed for. The point throughout, however, is not to count repeats, but to listen to the two voice relationship and as you hear it clearly and have absorbed it, move on to the next bar.

Duration

Although duration may obviously vary, experience has shown that it should be about 20 minutes.

Performance

The first performer starts at bar 1 and, after about 4 to 8 repeats, the second gradually fades in, in unison, at bar 2. After about 12 to 18 repeats getting into a comfortable and stable unison, the second performer gradually increases his or her tempo very slightly and begins to move very slowly ahead of the first until, after about 4 to 16 repeats, he or she is one sixteenth note ahead, as shown at bar 3. This relationship is then held steadily for about 16 to 24 repeats as outlined above. The dotted lines indicate this gradual movement of the second performer and the consequent shift of phase relation between both performers. This process of gradual phase shifting and then holding the new stable relationship is continued with the second pianist becoming an eighth (bar 4), a dotted eighth (bar 5), a quarter note (bar 6), etc. ahead of the first performer until he or she passes through all twelve

‡*Steve Reich,* Writings about Music *(Halifax: The Press of the Nova Scotia College of Art and Design, 1974), p. 9.*

relationships and returns to unison at bar 14. The second performer then gradually fades out and the first continues alone at bar 15. The first performer changes the basic pattern at bar 16 and the second performer gradually fades in with still another pattern at bar 17. The second performer again very slowly increases his or her tempo and slowly moves ahead and out of phase until he or she arrives one sixteenth note ahead as shown at bar 18. This relationship is then held steadily as before. After moving through all eight relationships in this way the second performer returns to his or her starting point at bar 25. The first performer then gradually fades out and the second performer continues alone at bar 26. The second performer changes the basic pattern at bar 27 and the first fades in, in unison, at bar 28. The second performer again slowly increases his or her tempo and moves ahead and out of phase as before until he or she returns to unison at bar 32. After several repeats in unison one performer nods his or her head on the downbeat and, after 4 repeats, both performers end together.

Rehearsal

When first rehearsing the piece it may be useful for the first performer to play bar 1 and keep on repeating it while the second performer tries to enter directly at bar 3 exactly one sixteenth note ahead *without trying to phase there*. After listening to this two voice relationship for a while the second performer should stop, join the first performer in unison and only then try to increase very slightly his or her tempo so that he or she gradually moves one sixteenth note ahead into bar 3. This approach of first jumping in directly to bar 3, 4, 5, etc., listening to it and only then trying to phase into it is based on the principle that *hearing* what it sounds like to be 1, 2 or more sixteenth notes ahead will then enable the performer to phase there without increasing tempo too much and passing into a further bar, or phasing ahead a bit and then sliding back to where one started. Several rehearsals spread over several weeks before performance will help produce smooth phase movements and the tendency to phase too quickly from one bar to the next will be overcome allowing performers to spend due time—the slower the better—in the gradual shifts of phase between bars.

Instruments

When two pianos are used they should be as identical as possible. The lids should both be open or removed. The pianos should be arranged as follows:

AUDIENCE

When two marimbas are used they should be as identical as possible. Soft rubber mallets are suggested. *The piece may be played an octave lower than written, when played on marimbas.* The marimbas may be moderately amplified by conventional microphones if the hall holds more than 200 people. The marimbas should be arranged as follows:

AUDIENCE

piano phase

for two pianos
or two marimbas*

steve reich

hold tempo 1 / Tempo 1 fortsetzen / tenir le tempo 1.

* *The piece may be played an octave lower than written, when played on marimbas. / Wenn Marimbas verwendet werden, kann das Stück eine Oktave tiefer als notiert gespielt werden. / La pièce pourra etre jouée à l'octave inférieure quand elle est executée par des marimbas.*

a.v.s. *= accelerando very slightly. / sehr gerinfügiges accelerando. / très légèrement accelerando.*

In addition to Reich, both Philip Glass and Terry Riley have used this approach, which is sometimes referred to as *minimalism* because of the extreme economy of means that it represents.

Terry Riley's *In C* (1964) is composed of fifty-three melodic fragments, to be played in order and in tempo by an ensemble. The group may consist of any number of players and may comprise any instrumental combination. Each player decides for himself or herself (1) when to enter and (2) whether, and how often, to repeat each fragment. Pulse is maintained by a pianist playing steady eighth notes on the top two C's of a grand piano. The aesthetic effect of a performance, which in some cases may extend beyond an hour, depends in large part on the attitude and expectation brought to it by the listener. The subtle counterpoint and shifting pitches and colors can be compelling despite the lack of a sense of forward motion.

More recently, John Adams has introduced more traditional rhythmic procedures into his use of the minimalist technique. One of his more recent works, *Short Ride in a Fast Machine,* was commissioned for the opening concert of the Great Woods Festival in Mansfield, Massachusetts, in 1986. It is a joyfully exuberant piece with a pervasive and infectious motor rhythm. Scored for full orchestra with the persistent presence of wood block, the work is occasionally suggestive of the earlier orchestral scores of Stravinsky. At the same time, the listener is aware of a new and contemporary language, one indigenous to the present day.

TEXTURE AND EXPANDED INSTRUMENTAL RESOURCES

We have seen the increasingly important role played by texture in the evolution of twentieth-century musical thought. One reason for this lies in its capability to provide a convincing means of musical organization free from the traditional conventions of key and chord. Even in the relatively conservative textural style of Debussy we find an unusual preponderance of unaccompanied, angular melodies; figuration independent of functional considerations; and vertical sonorities used solely for the sake of color.

As composers turned their attention to further explorations of texture, changes occurred not only in the performance demands placed on players of traditional instruments but also in the structure and size of ensembles. The massive orchestral forces favored by Berlioz and Mahler gave way to a renewed interest in chamber groups. Stravinsky's interest in nontraditional groupings of instruments did a great deal to legitimize the concept of a smaller, more heterogeneous instrumental body. His *L'Histoire du soldat* (1918), scored for clarinet, bassoon, horn, trombone, percussion, violin, and bass, became a model of innovative procedure that many composers chose to follow. Featured along with the varied instrumental forces found in this work was the aspect of theater music; it includes a part for narrator as well as speaking roles for one or more characters and specific directions for stage movement and dance (possibly indicative of Stravinsky's intense and continuing interest in music for the ballet.)

Other methods of exploiting the coloristic properties of traditional instruments proved attractive to later composers. We have already noted Henry Cowell's experimentation with tone clusters on the piano in the 1920s. Another early work by Cowell, entitled *The*

Banshee, calls for the performer to play inside the instrument. Effects created by plucking the strings or drawing the finger or fingernail across the length of the string are eerie and reminiscent of the legendary figure of Irish folklore for which the piece is named.

John Cage, known for his pioneering efforts in the area of aleatory music, is also known for his use of "prepared piano," involving the placement of various objects and/or materials (such as screws, bolts made of metal or rubber, plastic, felt, and coins) on the strings at a precisely specified location. His Concerto for Piano (Prepared) and Chamber Orchestra (1960) calls not only for extensive adjustments of the piano strings but also for a large battery of percussion.

The role of percussion has been greatly expanded in the twentieth century. One of the earliest landmarks in this field is Edgar Varèse's *Ionisation,* composed in 1931. This work calls for thirteen musicians to play a total of thirty-seven percussion instruments, including, in addition to the standard battery, two sirens, bongos, guiros, slapsticks, Chinese blocks in three registers, maracas, and a number of less usual instruments. Despite the presence of chimes, celesta, and piano (all of which are saved exclusively for the Finale), the piece is essentially a study in nonpitched sonorities; its novelty has perhaps never been surpassed.

American composers, including John Cage and Lou Harrison, have experimented extensively with new percussive effects and music for percussion ensembles. Nontraditional instruments and techniques include brake drums and bowing of mallet instruments. In many cases, these composers have modeled their works on Eastern traditions, such as the gamelan. Also interested in oriental music and philosophy is American Harry Partch, known primarily as the inventor of new percussion instruments.

An important work, composed in 1960, *Threnody for the Victims of Hiroshima* by Krzysztof Penderecki, represents a striking departure from the conventional use of string sonorities. Although other composers had experimented with this medium, *Threnody* is generally considered a landmark work in the literature. Examine Example 28-60, a page from the score of this work.

EXAMPLE 28-60 *Penderecki,* Threnody for the Victims of Hiroshima

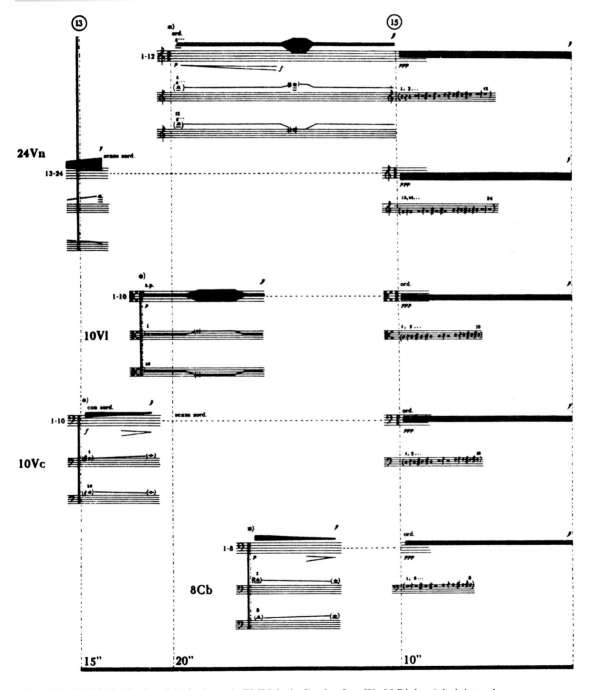

The cluster effect, shown graphically in the score, involves very specific pitch indications on each player's individual part. For rhythmic direction, the performers must obviously rely heavily on cues from the conductor. This example shows the traditional concept of "chord" or vertical "event" being replaced by a shifting, iridescent fabric of sound.

In addition to the sustained cluster effects, one finds the composer employing nontraditional instrumental techniques. At various times the players are asked, for example, to raise or lower the pitch by a 1/4 or 3/4 tone, to play between the bridge and tailpiece, to play an arpeggio on the four strings behind the bridge, to play on the tailpiece or on the bridge, or to create a percussive effect by striking the upper sounding board of the violin with the nut or the fingertips. It is, in fact, the subtle alternation of tone clusters and percussive effects that ultimately creates the formal structure of the piece.

The composer Georgy Lygeti is also widely recognized for compositions which feature sustained chromatic clusters. His *Atmospheres* for orchestra (1961) and *Volumnia* for organ (1961–62) both served as models for subsequent composers.

In terms of vocal effects, the technique of *sprechstimme,* a cross between singing and dramatic declamation, was used by Schoenberg in *Pierrot Lunaire* (1912), a work that calls for reciter accompanied by an ensemble consisting of five instrumentalists. The effect has been widely used since then, as have techniques of whistling, whispering, clucking, cooing, and laughing. Composers such as Penderecki, Stockhausen, and Oliveros have employed these sounds on a wide scale.

Further exploration of coloristic possibilities has resulted from the gradual incorporation of jazz techniques into concert literature. Besides its unique harmonic language, jazz represents a characteristic and readily identifiable approach to instrumentation. This frequently involves electric guitar, electric bass, keyboard synthesizers (to be discussed later), and extensive use of contact microphones.

Finally, one may find crystal wine glasses pressed into musical service by composers such as Crumb, Schwantner, Mayuzumi, Kagel, and Haubenstock-Ramati. The goblets, usually of varying sizes, produce beautifully pure pitches when stroked around the rim with wet fingers.

ELECTRONIC MUSIC

Inevitably, with the mounting interest in coloristic effects, the possibilities for electronic sound generation began to be investigated more closely. The earliest instruments to have practical applications were developed in the 1920s and included the theremin, the trautonium, and the ondes martenot. All three instruments made use of electronic oscillators as tone generators; they differed only in the manner by which the performer played the instrument. The theremin enjoyed a period of renewed interest in 1945 when employed by Miklos Rozsa in the films *Spellbound* and *Lost Weekend.*

Toward the midpoint of the twentieth century, technical developments in the tape recorder resulted in the growing popularity of *musique concrète,* in which natural sounds—such as a voice, an instrument, or the ticking of a clock—were first recorded, then subjected to modification by means of altered playback speed, reversed tape direction, fragmentation and splicing of the tape, creation of a tape loop, echo effect, and other timbral manipulations. In 1948 Pierre Schaeffer, who is generally credited with introducing the above term, presented a concert featuring *musique concrète* exclusively over French radio.

Although the distinction would almost certainly not be audible to the listener, the term electronic music, strictly speaking, was initially reserved for music that was generated synthetically by means of an oscillator. The tones thus produced may be precisely controlled in terms of frequency, amplitude, and waveform. Discrete types of sound waves produced by these generators include the "sine" wave (a sound without overtones, suggestive of an open flute), the "sawtooth" wave (a jagged, nasal tone that contains all overtones), and the "rectangular" or "square" wave (a pitch containing only odd-numbered harmonics). The "white noise" generator produces a "hissing" sound, composed of all the audible frequencies at random amplitudes. These basic sounds were then manipulated by means of amplifiers, filters, modulators, equalizers, sequencers, and reverberation units.

Toward the middle of the twentieth century, many of the most important developments in electronic music composition took place at the Studio for Electronic Music of the West German Radio in Cologne. Herbert Eimert and Karlheinz Stockhausen, who were involved in the founding and subsequent work that was carried on in Germany, were also intrigued by the possibilities of total serialization as well as its applications to electronic composition.

The first published score of a composition based entirely on sine-wave tones was Stockhausen's *Elektronische Studie II* (1954). Its composition was based on a number of electronically generated tone mixtures for which specific frequencies were determined mathematically. In the preface to the score, the composer indicates that volumes levels in decibels (shown at the bottom of the score) correspond with frequency/timbre indications at the top. The duration of the individual "sound mixture" is indicated as a tape length (in centimeters) that corresponds to the graphic indicators for pitch and volume. Despite the precisely controlled structure of all parameters of the music, variations caused by "noise" of conflicting overtones and the effect of reverberation are inevitable. The opening of the score, shown in Example 28-61, is included here primarily as an item of historical interest. Following the publication of this early work, Stockhausen has continued to make important contributions to the literature as well as to the continued evolution of musical thought.

EXAMPLE 28-61   *Stockhausen,* Studie II, *graphic score notation (opening)*

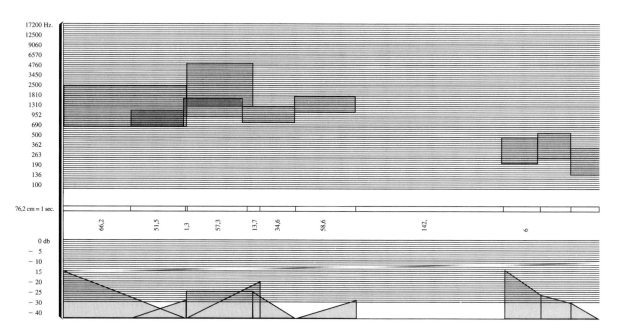

It was the development of synthesizers around the midpoint of the twentieth century that allowed the composer freedom to generate and combine sounds without the former need for laborious splicing and mixing of tape. Edgar Varèse's *Poème Electronique,* performed at the Brussels World's Fair in 1958, was created directly on magnetic tape. It took place in a pavilion designed by Le Corbusier and specified the installation of four hundred loudspeakers that filled the curved space of the pavilion with continuous waves of sound. The *Poème* was accompanied by a series of film projections which interacted randomly with the music. The visual and sonic synthesis of this extraordinary work evoked reactions ranging from wild enthusiasm to stark terror among its audience.

The inevitable loss of drama in performances of purely electronic music was found by many composers to be an unacceptable trade-off. This spawned efforts to combine live performers and taped sound. Composers who experimented with this form of collaboration included Bruno Maderna, Vladimir Ussachevsky, Otto Luening, and Milton Babbitt. Champions of indeterminacy, such as John Cage, found that the theatrical possibilities of this combination were well suited to their musical philosophies. More recent composers especially well known for their work in this medium include Mario Davidovsky and Jacob Druckman. Davidovsky's eight *Synchronisms* for various solo instruments and tape, along with Druckman's series of compositions entitled *Animus* for tape and trombone, voice/ percussion, and clarinet, respectively, have become part of the standard contemporary recital literature for these instruments. In some instances, the collaboration calls for the performer to play into a tape recorder. The sounds thus generated are electronically modified and played back, providing an improvisatory partnership. In other cases, pre-recorded music by the solo instrument is combined on tape with electronic or *concrète* sounds. The final product may be the result either of strict control on the part of the composer or may represent processes of indeterminacy.

The first two pages of Davidovsky's *Synchronisms No. 6* for Piano and Electric Sounds is shown in Example 28-62. The work was premiered in 1970 and requires a tape playback unit of high professional quality. In his introduction to the work, Davidovsky states, "In the particular piece, the electronic sounds in many instances modulate the acoustical characteristics of the piano by affecting its decay and attack characteristics. The electronic segment should perhaps not be viewed as an independent polyphonic line, but rather as if it were inlaid into the piano part."

EXAMPLE 28-62   *Davidovsky, Synchronisms No. 6, first two pages*

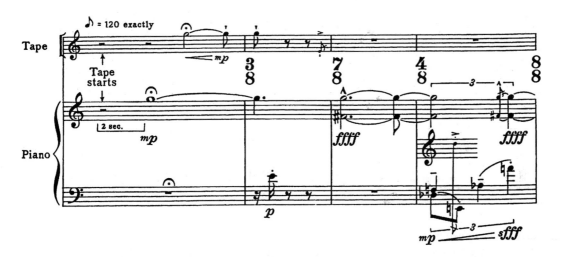

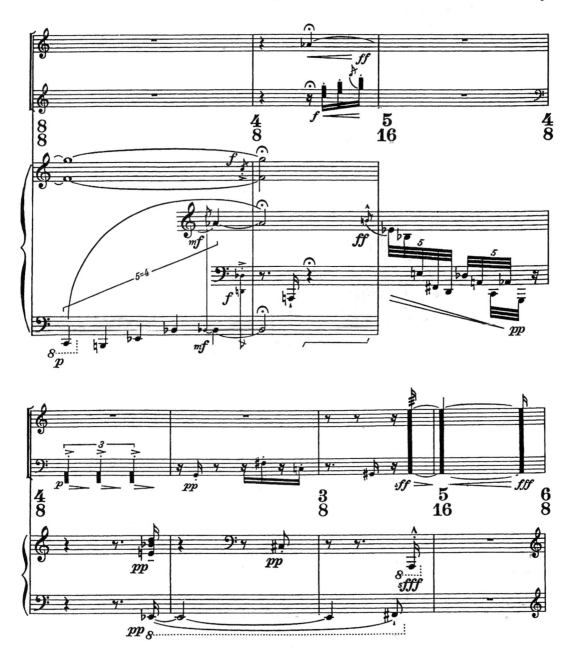

You will note the composer's tempo marking ($\flat$ = 120 exactly), indicating the obvious need for precise coordination with the tape. The metric challenges of this "collaboration" may remind you of those found in Messiaen's *Mode de Valeurs* (Ex. 28-57), a work based on the principle of total serialization. In this example, however, the taped "cues" provide a sense of partnership, making for an exciting and musically rewarding result.

The subsequent introduction of modular synthesizers, marketed under trade names of Moog, Buchla, and ARP, offered a wide palette of new sounds. An interesting offshoot of this development may be found in the "Switched-On-Bach" series: a realization of the Bach Brandenburg Concerti and various orchestral works. The album was recorded entirely with a modular analog synthesizer. Some contend that the 1968 release of this album by Wendy Carlos, using the then exotic sounds of a modular Moog, in a sense may have launched the synthesizer era. Other synthesized adaptations of standard repertoire followed in rapid succession and achieved widespread (if, in some cases, brief) popularity.

Digital synthesizers, such as the Yamaha DX series and various sound-sampling devices, such as the Ensoniq Mirage, the Emulator II, and the Kurzweil, represented an important development in the evolution of electronic music. The Yamaha has become the mainstay of many popular music groups not only because of its variety of timbres but also because of its relative portability. Its essential unit is a digital oscillator, which enables the composer to control the various parameters of a musical sound, creating new colors as well as accurately simulating those of many acoustic instruments. The sampling devices, on the other hand, have the capability of recording and storing precise information concerning a given sound. The actual sampling involves the encoding of an analog signal by reading its level at precisely spaced intervals of time. The sound thus encoded may then be reproduced either singly or in combination with other material.

It was the introduction of MIDI (Musical Instrument Digital Interface) that virtually revolutionized the field of electronic music. MIDI originally allowed the keyboard of one synthesizer to drive the sound generators of another, making possible the use of audio processors, drum machines, and even the control of multiple computers by a single performer. It could expedite changes in key velocity, pitch bend, and modulation; units are now available that notate a piece of music as it is being played or composed. Through the use of a *sequencer,* a digital recorder that stores "sequences" of musical information rather than actual sounds, a composer may significantly modify the timbre, tempo, or texture of a previously encoded piece.

The implications of these technological developments for performing musicians, and indeed for the future of the music profession as a whole, are incalculable, especially in the field of popular and commercial music. Whereas the production of a new recording at one time involved the services of a composer, studio musicians, a copyist, a recording engineer, and an editor (to name but a few), many of today's audio production studios make it possible for the composer working alone to accomplish all the above functions in a fraction of the time formerly required and often with a resulting product of high quality.

Although it is impossible within the scope of this brief overview to fully cover the myriad developments now taking place in the field of music technology, the foregoing information may serve as a springboard for future exploration of the extraordinary expansion of this field and its implications for the future of music composition and performance.

Summary and Forward Look

We have observed that the early twentieth century was characterized by a curious dichotomy: on the one hand, an extension of post-Romantic tendencies, and, on the other, a conscious (at times almost militant) attempt to establish a totally new musical language. Composers in both camps succeeded in developing distinctly new methods of expression that were clearly indigenous to their age. This early ambivalence has continued to manifest itself in the continuing diversity of musical language.

No one at present can know just how future historians will regard our era and evaluate the primary direction of our musical culture. Surely no component of musical style—pitch, harmony, rhythm, texture, form—has remained untouched by the stylistic explosion that marked the turn of the century. Yet as the century draws to a close, there seems to be an attempt by many to draw from earlier developments rather than to strike out on totally individual and innovative paths. We can see, in some cases, a fusion of trends that at one time seemed headed in opposite directions.

The idea of serialism, for example, which was conceived as a systematic means of escape from the deeply entrenched conventions of tonality, has indeed been pressed into the service of what we hear as very tonal music. Recent efforts in electronic music frequently reflect a consolidation of ideas of color and movement from very early in the century. Some compositions borrow heavily from the jazz idiom while many contemporary jazz groups perform works that are scarcely distinguishable from today's "serious" concert music. The pace of technological development has wrought profound changes on the music profession itself. However, whatever the direction we seem to be taking, it is indeed a challenging and exciting time in which to be a musician.

Self-Test 28-6
(Answers begin on page 670.)

A.

1. How does the process of total serialization differ from the original twelve-tone method?

_____

_____

2. Name two composers who experimented with this technique.

_____ and _____

B.

1. Define the term *aleatory* as it is applied to music.

_____

_____

2. What is the significance of the composition entitled *4'33"* by John Cage?

_____

_____

3. What contemporary compositional technique is derived from aleatory proce-

dures? _____ Name at least three composers who

are known for their compositions featuring this process:_____ ,

_____ , and _____ .

Chapter 28   *An Introduction to Twentieth-Century Practices*

C. Name at least three composers who have made use of expanded instrumental resources through nontraditional use of instruments or voice and briefly describe the techniques they used.

_____

_____

_____

_____

_____

_____

D. Briefly define the following terms associated with electronic music:

1. sine wave _____

2. white noise _____

3. oscillator _____

4. *musique concrète* _____

5. MIDI _____

Exercise 28-1 (W) See Workbook.

Appendix A

Instrumental Ranges and Transpositions

In this appendix we suggest some practical ranges to assist you in composing exercises to be performed in class. These are not extreme ranges, by any means, but the extreme highs and lows of even these ranges should be used cautiously, especially the brasses.

Instrument	*Abbreviation*	*Sounding range*	*Written range*
Flute	Fl.		Same
Oboe	Ob.		Same
B♭ Clarinet	Clar. in B♭		Treble clef, M2 higher
Bassoon	Bsn.		Same
E♭ Alto Sax	A. Sax in E♭		Treble clef, M6 higher
B♭ Tenor Sax	T. Sax in B♭		Treble clef, M9 higher

Instrument	Abbreviation	Sounding range	Written range
French horn	Hn. in F		P5 higher
B♭ Trumpet	Tpt. in B♭		Treble clef, M2 higher
Trombone	Trb.		Same
Tuba	Tuba		Same
Violin	Vl.		Same
Viola	Vla.		Same
Cello	Vc.		Same; tenor clef also used when convenient
Bass	D.B.		P8 higher

Appendix B

Answers to Self-Tests

The answers given in certain kinds of Self-Test problems must be considered to be suggested solutions because more than one correct answer might be possible. When you have questions, consult your teacher.

CHAPTER 1

Self-Test 1-1
Part A, p. 5.

1. C1   **2.** E2   **3.** F3   **4.** B4   **5.** A5   **6.** G6   **7.** D7

Part B, p. 5.

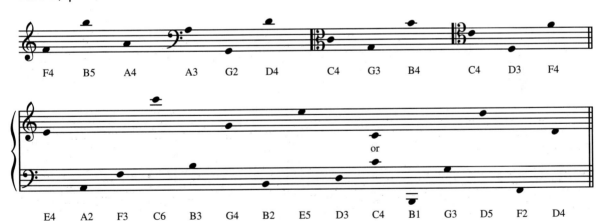

Self-Test 1-2

Part A, p. 12.

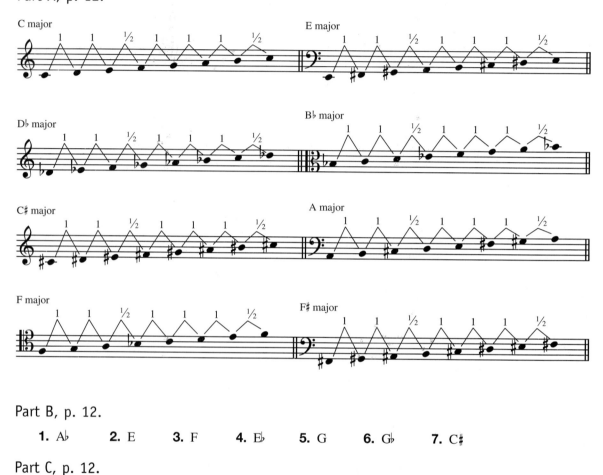

Part B, p. 12.

1. A♭   **2.** E   **3.** F   **4.** E♭   **5.** G   **6.** G♭   **7.** C♯

Part C, p. 12.

Part D, p. 13.

1. E♭	**2.** C♯	**3.** two sharps	**4.** F	**5.** four flats
6. five sharps	**7.** G♭	**8.** two flats	**9.** G	**10.** D♭
11. six sharps	**12.** seven flats	**13.** E	**14.** three sharps	

Self-Test 1-3
Part A, p. 16.

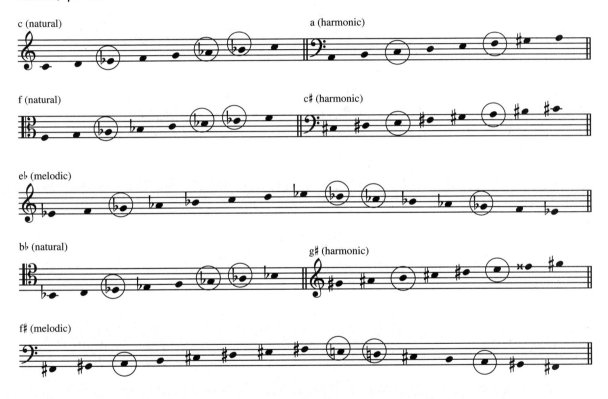

Part B, p. 17.

1. g **2.** e **3.** c♯ **4.** f **5.** a♭ **6.** d♯ **7.** e♭

Part C, p. 17.

Part D, p. 17.

1. one flat   **2.** e♭   **3.** c♯   **4.** three sharps   **5.** d♯

6. five flats   **7.** seven sharps   **8.** g   **9.** four flats   **10.** two sharps

11. c   **12.** seven flats   **13.** e   **14.** g♯

Self-Test 1-4
p. 20.

1. 2   **2.** 5   **3.** 7   **4.** 1   **5.** 3

6. 4   **7.** 8   **8.** 6   **9.** 4   **10.** 2

11. 6   **12.** 7   **13.** 8   **14.** 3   **15.** 5

Self-Test 1-5

Part A, p. 22.

All are "P" except nos. 4 and 7.

Part B, p. 22.

1. M   **2.** m   **3.** m   **4.** M   **5.** m

6. m   **7.** m   **8.** M   **9.** M   **10.** m

Part C, p. 22.

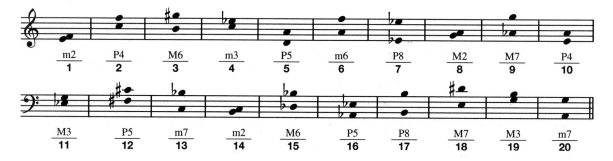

Self-Test 1-6
Part A, p. 26.

1. +5   **2.** °7   **3.** M3   **4.** °4   **5.** +2

6. m7   **7.** °5   **8.** °3   **9.** +6   **10.** +4

Part B, p. 26.

1. P5   **2.** m2   **3.** °7   **4.** m6   **5.** +4

6. M7   **7.** M3   **8.** °3

Part C, p. 26.

P5	m7	m3	M6	+4	M7	+5	m6	M2	°7
1	**2**	**3**	**4**	**5**	**6**	**7**	**8**	**9**	**10**

Part D, p. 27.

1. m3   **2.** P1   **3.** m6   **4.** P8   **5.** M3

6. P4   **7.** m3   **8.** °5   **9.** m2   **10.** +1

11. m2   **12.** M7

CHAPTER 2

Self-Test 2-1
Part A, p. 30.

1. 2   **2.** 4   **3.** 3   **4.** 8   **5.** 4   **6.** 3

7. 4   **8.** 7   **9.** 5   **10.** 6   **11.** 2   **12.** 4

13. 8   **14.** 4   **15.** 2   **16.** 12

Part B, p. 31.

1. triple   **2.** duple (or quadruple)   **3.** quadruple (or duple)

4. duple (or quadruple)   **5.** triple

Part C, p. 31.

1. B♭	**2.** A♭	**3.** E	**4.** D♯	**5.** E
6. B	**7.** B♭	**8.** E♭	**9.** A♭	**10.** A
11. G	**12.** G♯	**13.** F	**14.** C♯	**15.** C♯

Self-Test 2-2
p. 32.

1. simple quadruple (or simple duple)

2. compound duple (or compound quadruple)

3. simple triple

4. simple duple (or simple quadruple)

5. compound duple (or compound quadruple)

Self-Test 2-3
Part A, p. 34.

1. ♩♩ ; 2/4

2. simple triple; ♪ ; ♫

3. simple duple; ♩ ; 2/2

4. ♪ ; 3/8

5. ♫ ; 3/16

Part B, p. 34.

Self-Test 2-4
Part A, pp. 36–37.

1. ♪♪♩; ⁶⁄₈   **2.** compound triple; ♩.; ♩ ♩ ♩

3. compound duple; ♩ ♩ ♩; ⁶⁄₄   **4.** ♪.; ¹²⁄₁₆   **5.** compound triple; ♩.; ⁹⁄₈

Part B, p. 37.

1.

2.

3.

Self-Test 2-5
Part A, pp. 40–41.

1. simple quadruple; ♩; ♫   **2.** ♪♪♩; ⁶⁄₈   **3.** simple duple; ♪; ♫

4. ♩.; ⁶⁄₄   **5.** simple triple; ♩; ³⁄₂   **6.** compound quadruple; ♪.; ¹²⁄₁₆

Part B, p. 41.

1. 𝄾   **2.** 𝄾. (or 𝄾𝄾)   **3.** 𝄾𝄾 (or 𝄾𝄾𝄾)   **4.** 𝄾   **5.** 𝄾   **6.** 𝄿𝄿 (or −)

Notice that ▬ would not be a good answer for no. 3 because this rest would obscure the beats in the measure (see p. 38).

Part C, p. 41.

1. ⁹₄   2. ⁴₄ or ²₂ or 𝄴 or 𝄵   3. ³₈   4. ⁶₁₆   5. ¹²₈   **6.** same as no. 2

Part D, p. 42.

Part E, p. 42.

1.

2.

Part F, p. 42.

1. simple duple (or quadruple); 2 (or 4) over some note value (1, 2, 4, 8, and so
   on)

2. compound quadruple (or duple); 12 (or 6) over some note value

3. sounds like compound duple or compound single, but notated as simple triple
   (see p. 36); 3 over some note value

4. simple quadruple (or duple); 4 (or 2) over some note value

5. compound duple (or quadruple); 6 (or 12) over some note value

Part G, pp. 42–43.

    1. f   **2.** G   **3.** c♯   **4.** A   **5.** B♭

    6. c   **7.** D   **8.** E♭   **9.** b   **10.** F

    11. g   **12.** f♯   **13.** E   **14.** A♭

Part H, p. 43.

Part I, p. 43.

CHAPTER 3

Self-Test 3-1

Part A, p. 45.

    1. b♭: B♭ D♭ F   **2.** E: E G♯ B   **3.** g°: G B♭ D♭   **4.** f°: F A♭ C♭

    5. c: C E♭ G   **6.** D⁺: D F♯ A♯   **7.** A: A C♯ E   **8.** d: D F A

    9. G♭: G♭ B♭ D♭   **10.** B: B D♯ F♯   **11.** a♭: A♭ C♭ E♭   **12.** c♯: C♯ E G♯

Part B, p. 46.

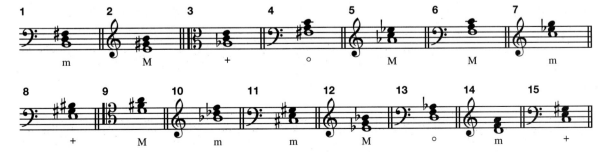

Part C, p. 46.

	1.	2.	3.	4.	5.	6.	7.	8.	9.	10.
Fifth	C♯	B♭	F♯	D♯	G♭	A	E	C♭	G♯	B
Third	A	G♭	D	B	E♭	F♯	C♯	A♭	E	G♯
Root	F	E♭	B	G	C♭	D♯	A	F	C♯	E
Type	+	m	m	+	M	°	M	°	m	M

Part D, p. 46.

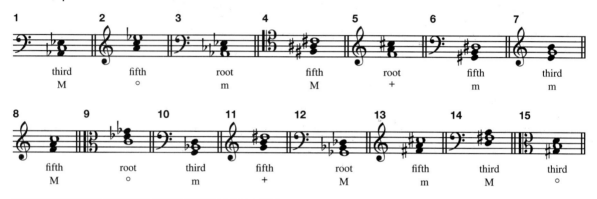

Self-Test 3-2

Part A, p. 48.

1. m7	2. M7	3. ᴓ7	4. ᴓ7	5. M7
6. ᴓ7	7. m7	8. Mm7	9. M7	10. Mm7
11. °7	12. °7	13. Mm7	14. °7	15. m7

Part B, p. 48.

Part C, p. 48.

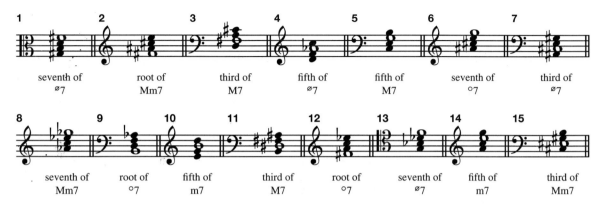

1	2	3	4	5	6	7	
seventh of	root of	third of	fifth of	fifth of	seventh of	third of
ø7	Mm7	M7	ø7	M7	°7	ø7

8	9	10	11	12	13	14	15
seventh of	root of	fifth of	third of	root of	seventh of	fifth of	third of
Mm7	°7	m7	M7	°7	ø7	m7	Mm7

Self-Test 3-3
Part A, pp. 53-54.

	1	2	3	4	5	6	7	8	9	10	11	12	13	14
Root	E	A	G♯	E	C♯	D	E	G	B	E♭	F♯	G	E	D
Type	m7	M	°7	Mm7	m	ø7	M7	m	ø7	M	°7	m7	°	Mm7
Inversion symbol	$\frac{6}{5}$	6	$\frac{4}{3}$	$\frac{4}{3}$	$\frac{6}{4}$	$\frac{4}{2}$	7	6	$\frac{4}{3}$	$\frac{6}{4}$	$\frac{6}{5}$	7	6	$\frac{4}{2}$

Part B, p. 54.

1. GM **2.** C♯° **3.** DM **4.** D♯°

5. D♯°7 **6.** BMm7 **7.** Em **8.** F♯Mm7 **9.** Bm

10. EM **11.** AM **12.** EM **13.** AM

Part C, p. 55.

Self-Test 3-4
Part A, p. 58.

	1	2	3	4	5	6	7	8	9	10	11
Root	F	A♯	E	F	B	G	C	F♯	D♭	C	F♯
Type	m7	°7	M	m	Mm7	ø7	M	M	Mm7	°7	M7
Inversion symbol	7	$\frac{6}{5}$		$\frac{6}{4}$	$\frac{4}{2}$	$\frac{6}{5}$	6	$\frac{6}{4}$	7	$\frac{4}{2}$	7

Part B, pp. 59–60.

1. Schubert.

	1	2	3	4	5	6	7	8	9	10	11	12
Root	D♭	G♭	E♭	A♭	D♭	G♭	D♭	D♭	A♭	B♭	A♭	D♭
Type	M	M	Mm7	M	M	M	M	M	M	m	Mm7	M
Inversion symbol	6		$\frac{6}{5}$		6		6		6		7	

2. Byrd.

	1	2	3	4	5	6	7
Root	F	C	F	E♭	A	B♭	F
Type	m	M	M	M	°	M	M
Inversion symbol					6		

3. Fischer.

	1	2	3	4	5	6	7	8	9	10	11	12	13
Root	E	G♯	A	F	B	F	G	C	D	B	D	G	C
Type	M	°7	m	M7	ø7	M	Mm7	M	m7	°	m	Mm7	M
Inversion symbol		$\frac{4}{3}$	6	7	$\frac{4}{3}$		$\frac{4}{2}$	6	7	6		7	$\frac{6}{4}$

CHAPTER 4

Self-Test 4-1

Part A, pp. 65–66.

1. V **2.** iv⁶ **3.** ii **4.** III⁶ **5.** ii

6. vii° **7.** I **8.** ii° **9.** iii **10.** vii°

11. V$_4^6$ **12.** IV **13.** i **14.** vi **15.** III$_4^6$

Part B, p. 66.

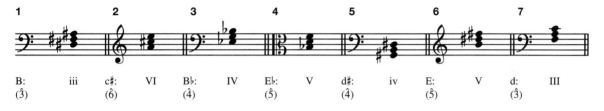

B: iii   c#: VI   Bb: IV   Eb: V   d#: iv   E: V   d: III
($\hat{3}$)   ($\hat{6}$)   ($\hat{4}$)   ($\hat{5}$)   ($\hat{4}$)   ($\hat{5}$)   ($\hat{3}$)

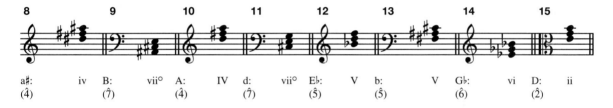

a#: iv   B: vii°   A: IV   d: vii°   Eb: V   b: V   Gb: vi   D: ii
($\hat{4}$)   ($\hat{7}$)   ($\hat{4}$)   ($\hat{7}$)   ($\hat{5}$)   ($\hat{5}$)   ($\hat{6}$)   ($\hat{2}$)

Part C, pp. 66–68.

1. IV **2.** V **3.** IV⁶ **4.** V **5.** I⁶

6. IV **7.** V **8.** V **9.** I **10.** iii

11. IV **12.** iii⁶ **13.** iii **14.** IV **15.** I

16. I **17.** V **18.** I **19.** IV **20.** IV⁶

21. I **22.** ii **23.** vi **24.** vi **25.** V

26. V **27.** IV **28.** vii°⁶ **29.** I **30.** V⁶

31. I **32.** I **33.** V **34.** IV **35.** iii⁶

36. vi **37.** iii⁶ **38.** IV **39.** I **40.** I

41. V **42.** ii **43.** iii **44.** vi **45.** iii⁶

46. IV **47.** I **48.** I

Self-Test 4-2

Part A, p. 71.

1. iv^7 **2.** I^{M6}_5 **3.** iii^7 **4.** $ii^{\varnothing4}_3$ **5.** VI^{M7}

6. IV^{M7} **7.** $vii^{\varnothing7}$ **8.** i^7 **9.** vii^{o7} **10.** vi^6_5

11. V^4_2 **12.** V^7 **13.** $ii^{\varnothing7}$ **14.** iii^4_3 **15.** I^{M7}

Part B, p. 71.

b: i^7 Eb: V^7 f#: iv^7 A: V^7 f: vii^{o7} D: I^{M7} G: $vii^{\varnothing7}$
($\hat1$)   ($\hat5$)   ($\hat4$)   ($\hat5$)   ($\hat7$)   ($\hat1$)   ($\hat7$)

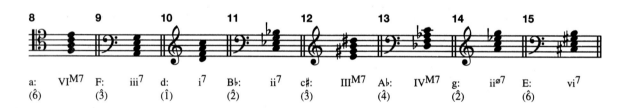

a: VI^{M7} F: iii^7 d: i^7 Bb: ii^7 c#: III^{M7} Ab: IV^{M7} g: $ii^{\varnothing7}$ E: vi^7
($\hat6$)   ($\hat3$)   ($\hat1$)   ($\hat2$)   ($\hat3$)   ($\hat4$)   ($\hat2$)   ($\hat6$)

Part C, p. 72.

1. Bach.

1. I **2.** vi **3.** iii **4.** IV **5.** IV^{M7}

6. V^4_2 **7.** I^6 **8.** ii^6_5 **9.** V **10.** I

2. Schumann.

1. I **2.** vii^{o6} **3.** I^6 **4.** vii^{o6} **5.** I

6. ii^6_5 **7.** V **8.** I **9.** I **10.** I^6

11. IV **12.** I^6 **13.** V^4_3 **14.** I **15.** V

CHAPTER 5

Self-Test 5-1
Part A, p. 77.

1.

G: I V I IV V I IV V I

a. Resolve $\hat{7}$ to $\hat{1}$.

b. Not in a IV chord.

c. Two leaps should outline a triad.

d. Two focal points.

2.

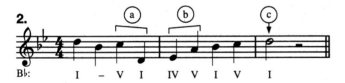

B♭: I – V I IV V I V I

a. Leap of a 7th.

b. Leap of an $^{+}4$.

c. Two focal points.

3.

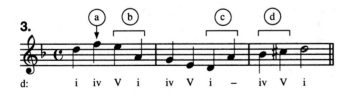

d: i iv V i iv V i – iv V i

a. Not in a iv chord.

b. Large leap should be preceded and followed by ascending motion.

c. Follow leap with descending motion.

d. Interval of $^{+}2$.

Part B, p. 77 (sample solutions).

1.

I   V   I   IV   I   –   vi   ii   V   I

2.

i   iv   i   –   V   –   i   iv   V   i

3.

I   V   vi   IV   I   IV   ii   V   I

Self-Test 5-2
Part A, p. 81.

$$\frac{i}{C} \Big/ \frac{i}{C} \quad \frac{V^6}{O} \quad \frac{i}{O} \quad \frac{iv^6}{C} \Big/ \frac{V}{O} \quad \frac{V^4_2}{O} \Big/ \frac{i^6}{O} \quad \frac{vii^{o6}}{O} \quad \frac{i}{C} \quad \frac{ii^{o6}}{C} \Big/ \frac{V}{C}$$

Part B, p. 81.

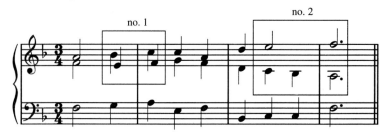

Part C, p. 82 (alternative solutions in parentheses).

G: I   f: V   Bb: IV   f#:   III

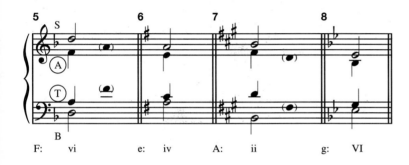

F: vi   e: iv   A: ii   g: VI

Self-Test 5-3
Part A, p. 88.

The progression is G: I / IV I / V / vi V / I /

Parallel 6ths: S/A, m. 1; S/T, mm. 3–4

Parallel 3rds: S/T, mm. 1–3; S/B, m. 3

Part B, p. 88.

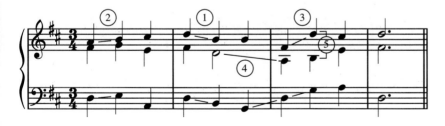

Part C, p. 89.

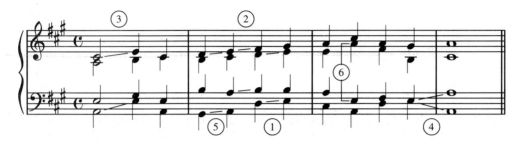

CHAPTER 6

Self-Test 6-1
p. 92 (sample solutions).*

Solutions to this and similar exercises throughout the book are sample solutions only. Many other correct solutions are possible.

Self-Test 6-2
Part A, p. 94.

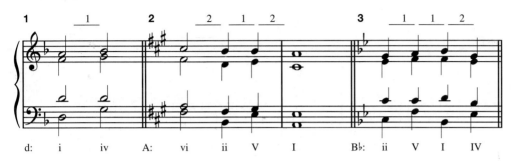

d: i   iv   A: vi   ii   V   I   Bb: ii   V   I   IV

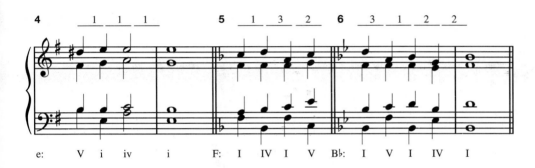

e: V   i   iv   i   F: I   IV   I   V   Bb: I   V   I   IV   I

Part B, p. 95.

G: I   V   I   IV   I   Eb: vi   ii   V   I   d: i   iv   i

Self-Test 6-3
Part A, p. 96.

B♭: vi IV ii V   f♯: i VI iv i   G: I iii vi ii V – I

Part B, pp. 96–97.

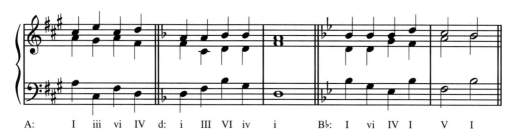

A: I iii vi IV   d: i III VI iv i   B♭: I vi IV I V I

Self-Test 6-4
Part A, p. 99.

Part B, p. 100.

1.

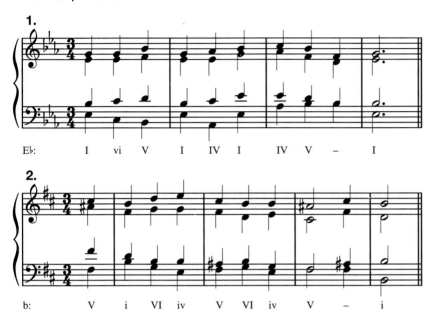

Eb: I   vi   V   I   IV I   IV   V   –   I

2.

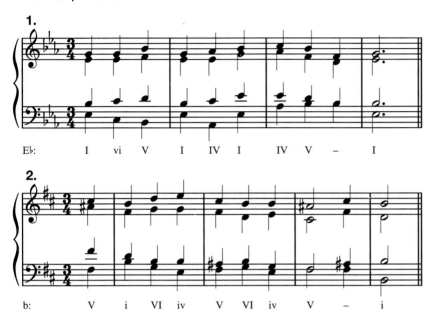

b: V   i   VI iv   V   VI iv   V   –   i

Part C, p. 100.

1.

a: i   V   i   VI   iv   V   i

2.

D: I   iii vi IV   V   vi   IV ii   V   I

Self-Test 6-5
Part A, p. 103.

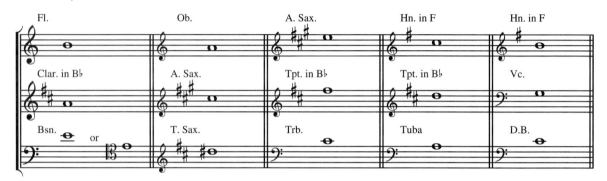

Part B, p. 103.

1.

F: I   vi   ii   V   I

2.

Part C, p. 104.
"Aura Lee"

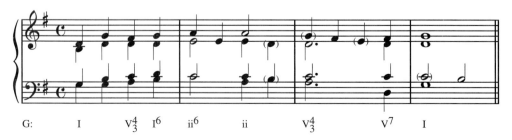

G: I V_3^4 I^6 ii^6 ii V_3^4 V^7 I

CHAPTER 7

Self-Test 7-1
Part A, p. 119.

1. iii or V   **2.** I or ii   **3.** I or vi

4. iii or vi   **5.** ii or IV   **6.** I

Part B, p. 119.

1. $\overline{\text{V} \quad \text{ii}}$ **2.** $\overline{\text{VII} \quad \text{I}}$ **3.** $\overline{\text{IV} \quad \text{iii}}$ **4.** none

Part C, pp. 119–121.

1. Bach.   I / $\overline{\text{vi} \quad \text{iii}}$ IV V^7 / vi   V   I /

2. Vivaldi.

Part D, p. 121.

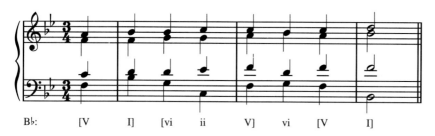

B♭:   [V   I]   [vi   ii   V]   vi   [V   I]

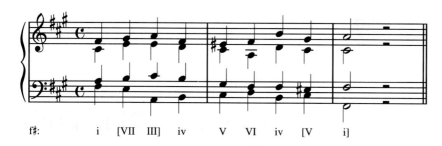

f♯:   i   [VII III]   iv   V   VI   iv   [V   i]

Part E, p. 121.

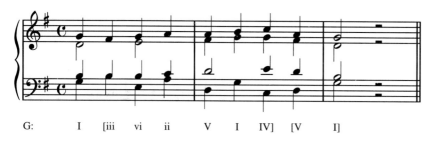

G: I   [iii   vi   ii   V   I   IV]   [V   I]

Part F, p. 122.

1. Three-part chorus (SAB)

F: I   V   vi   V   –   I   IV   I   –   ii   V   I

2. Four-part chorus (SATB)

e: i   iv   i   V   VI   iv   V   i

3. Four-part chorus (SATB)

E♭:   I   ii   V   I   V   I   vi   IV   V   I

4. Four-part chorus (SATB)

d: i   V   i   iv   V   VI   V   —   i

5. Three-part chorus (SAB)

A: I   IV   V   I   V   vi   ii   V   I

Part G, p. 123.

Part H, p. 123.

1. V^6_5	**2.** IV^6	**3.** iv^7	**4.** I^{M7}	**5.** $ii^{ø6}_5$
6. vi^7	**7.** V^4_2	**8.** vii^{o6}_5	**9.** ii^6	**10.** V^4_3
11. iv^4_2	**12.** I^6_4	**13.** VI	**14.** I^{M4}_3	**15.** V^6

CHAPTER 8

Self-Test 8-1
Part A, pp. 138–140.

1. The voice-leading features parallel 4ths (arpeggiated in the right hand), as in Example 8-9.

2. i / iv^7 iv^6 V V$^4_2$ / i^6 vii^{o6} i   i / vii^{o7} i V

The i^6 and iv^6 use the doubling in Example 8-10a; the vii^{o6} uses Example 8-10c.

Notice that Bach uses parallel motion only once in the outer-voice counterpoint: beats 2 to 3 of m. 1.

3. / i / / V$_5^6$ / / i / vii°^{6} or V$_3^4$ / i^6 ii°^{6} / V

With a little imagination, we can find most of the bass line, both forward and backward, in the melody

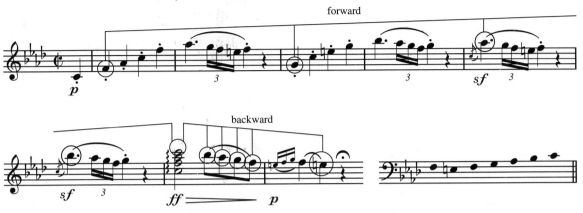

Part B, p. 141.

Mozart, *Eine kleine Nachtmusik,* K. 525, I

The simplification of the outer-voice counterpoint shown below the example makes it easier to see the imitation in the first three measures.

Part C, pp. 141–142.

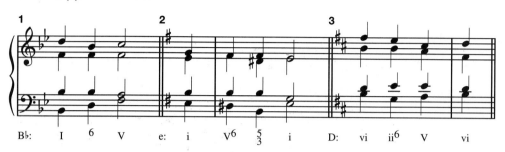

Bb: I   6   V   e: i   V6   5/3   i   D: vi   ii6   V   vi

Eb: IV   V   I6   IV6   f#:   i   V6   i   iv   d: i6   iv6   V   i

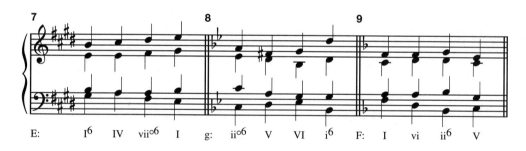

E: I6   IV   vii°6   I   g: ii°6   V   VI   i6   F: I   vi   ii6   V

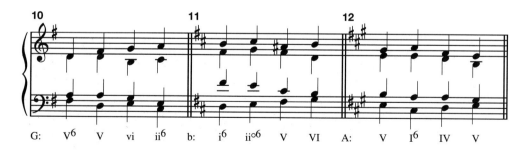

G: V6   V   vi   ii6   b: i6   ii°6   V   VI   A: V   I6   IV   V

Part D, p. 142.

Bb: I   6   V   e: i   V6   5/3   i   D: vi   ii6   V   vi

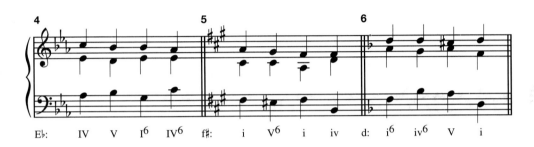

Eb: IV   V   I6   IV6   f#: i   V6   i   iv   d: i6   iv6   V   i

Part E, p. 142.

A: I   V6   I   ii6   V   vi   ii6   vii°6   I

g: i   V6   i   iv6   ii°6   V   i6   vii°6   i   V

Part F, p. 142.

Bach, French Suite No. 5

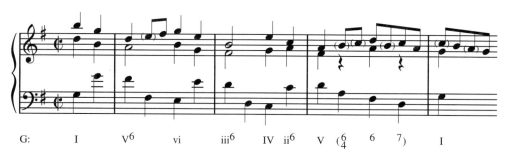

G: I   V⁶   vi   iii⁶   IV   ii⁶   V   (⁶₄   6   7)   I

Part G, p. 143.

F: I   V⁶   I   ii⁶   V   I   ⁶   V   —   I

b: i   vii°⁶ i⁶   ii°⁶   V   i⁶   i   V⁶   i   iv⁶   V   i

Part H and I, p. 143. (Compare to Ex. 7-4 and Ex. 8-7b.)

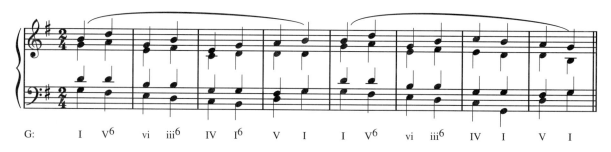

G: I   V⁶   vi   iii⁶   IV   I⁶   V   I   I   V⁶   vi   iii⁶   IV   I   V   I

CHAPTER 9

Self-Test 9-1
Part A, pp. 154–155.

1. g: i / (iv$_4^6$) / − / i / vii°$_5^6$ i^6 / vii°$_5^6$ i^6 /

The iv$_4^6$ is a pedal six-four chord.

2. I V^6 / − IV^6 I$_4^6$ V^7 / I IV I /

The I$_4^6$ is a cadential six-four.

3. I IV^6 (I$_4^6$) V$_2^4$ I^6 I I^6 IV

The I$_4^6$ is a passing six-four.

Part B, p. 155.

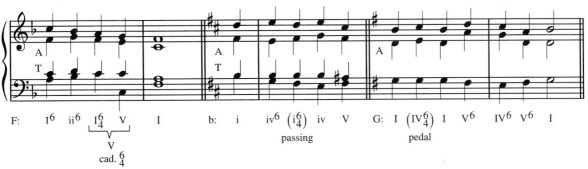

Part C, p. 155.

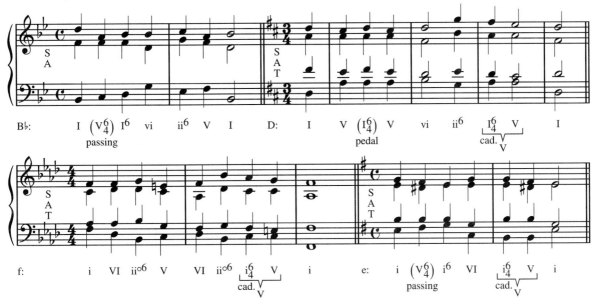

CHAPTER 10

Self-Test 10-1
Part A, pp. 172–175.

1. This excerpt is a repeated parallel period.

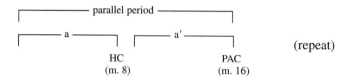

    1. I   **2.** V_3^4 **3.** I^6 **4.** I   **5.** V^6 **6.** V   **7.** I

2. There are modified sequences in the melody in mm. 1 to 4, 5 to 6, 9 to 12, and 13 to 14.

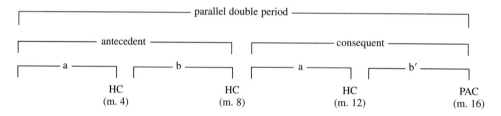

3. Because mm. 1 to 8 constitute a contrasting period, the whole theme can be heard as a contrasting period with a repeated and extended consequent phrase.

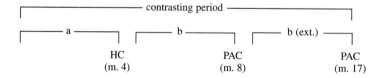

4. This excerpt is a repeated parallel period (not a double period). Octaves by contrary motion occur between melody and bass in mm. 7 to 8 and mm. 15 to 16.

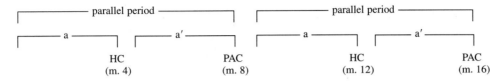

Part B, p. 176.

1.

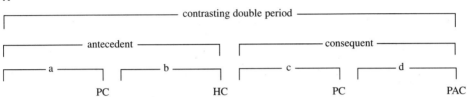

2.

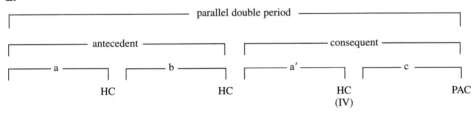

Part C, p. 176.

CHAPTER 11

Self-Test 11-1
Part A, p. 190.

1.

Measure	Treble	Bass
1	p	
2	n	p
3	7-6	
5	p	
6	p	p
7	4-3	

2. soprano: p; alto: p, p; tenor: 7-6, p, p

3. The only voice-leading problem seen in the reduction is found in m. 4, where direct 5ths (review pp. 85–86) occur between the I and IV chords. Bach disguised these through the use of passing tones. The parallel 5ths in m. 2 are not objectionable because the second 5th is a °5 and because the bass is not involved in the 5ths (review p. 85). Slightly unusual is the proportion of chords with a doubled 3rd: four out of sixteen.

Eb: I   V $^{(7)}$ vi V^6 I   6   V^7 I   V^6 I   IV^6 I   IV   I^6 V^7 I

Textural reduction

Part B, p. 191.

Part C, p. 192.

Bach, "Herr Christ, der ein'ge Gott's-Sohn"

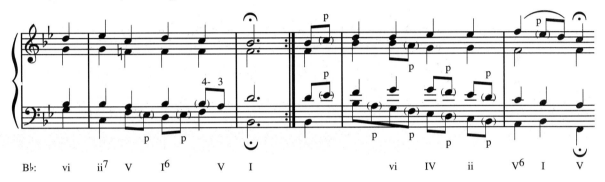

CHAPTER 12

Self-Test 12-1
Part A, p. 202.

1. m. 1: p; m. 3: p, p, app; m. 4: app, p

2. m. 24: app, app; m. 25: app, app; m. 26: app, p, p

3. m. 72: n, n; m. 74: 7-6; m. 75: 7-6, app, p; m. 76: p, p; m. 77: (melody) ant, (alto) ant

4. Notice (1) the scalar motion in all voices, inspired, of course, by the melody; (2) the incomplete IV, which contributes to the scalar motion; (3) the root position vii°, appearing here in one of its few typical usages; (4) the $\hat{7}$-$\hat{3}$ movement at the cadence—not unusual for Bach in an inner voice; and (5) the avoidance of parallel motion in the outer-voice counterpoint.

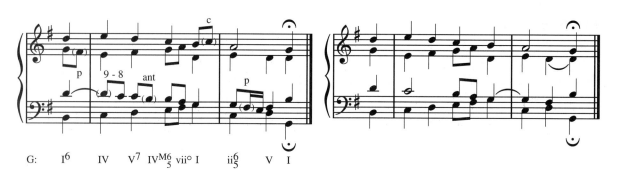

G: I^6 IV V^7 $\text{IV}^{\text{M}6}_5$ vii° I ii^6_5 V I

5.

D: (V)   I   vi ii^6 V^7 I ii^6 I^6_4 V   I
                                                                                        V

(V)   I   vi ii^6 V^7

I ii^6 I^6_4 V^7 I
                        V

*We label this as an appoggiatura rather than as a passing tone because of the effect of the $^+2$.

Part B, p. 204.

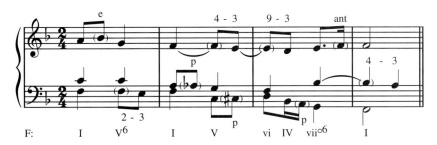

Part C, p. 204.

Mozart, Sonata K. 330, III

CHAPTER 13

Self-Test 13-1
Part A, p. 215.

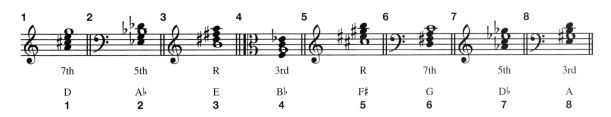

Part B, p. 215.

m. 1 V^7–vi deceptive progression. With $\hat{7}$ in an inner voice and in the major mode, it may move down to $\hat{6}$ instead of up to $\hat{1}$. The 7th resolves normally. All voices move by step.

m. 2 V^7 ornamented by a neighbor and a 4-3 suspension. The V^7 is complete, but the I is incomplete because of the resolution of the leading tone in the alto. The 7th resolves down by step.

m. 5 Another ornamented V^7, but in this case the leading tone is frustrated, leading to a complete I chord. The 7th resolves down by step.

Part C, pp. 215–216.

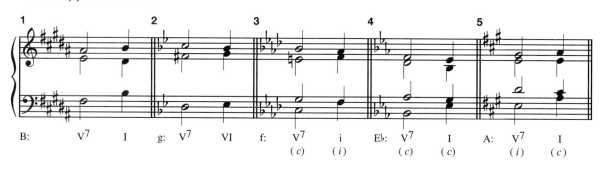

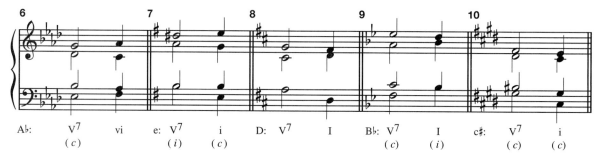

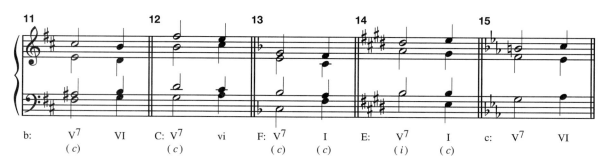

Part D, p. 216.

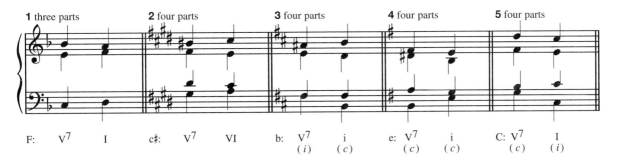

F: V⁷   I   c♯: V⁷   VI   b: V⁷   i   e: V⁷   i   C: V⁷   I

Part E, pp. 216–217.

1. Bach, "Kommt her zu mir, spricht Gottes Sohn"

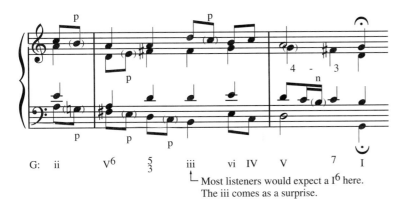

G: ii   V⁶   ⁵₃   iii   vi IV   V   ⁷   I

                  ⌐ Most listeners would expect a I⁶ here.
                    The iii comes as a surprise.

2. Bach, "Jesu, der du meine Seele"

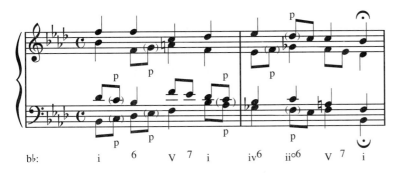

b♭:   i   6   V ⁷ i   iv⁶ ii°⁶ V ⁷ i

Part F, p. 217.

Ab: I   V⁷   vi   V⁶   V   I   ii⁶   I⁶₄   V⁷   I

Self-Test 13-2
Part A, p. 223.

C: V⁶₅   e: V⁴₃   Bb: V⁴₂   G: V⁴₃   A: V⁴₂   g: V⁶₅   f♯:   V⁴₂   Ab: V⁶₅

Part B, p. 223.

1. The leading tone (G♯3) resolves up to tonic. The 7th (D3) is approached by a suspension figure and resolves down by step to 3̂.

2. The leading tone (F♯4) resolves up to 1̂. The 7th (C5) is approached by a passing tone figure and resolves down by step to 3̂.

3. There is no leading tone in this chord. The 7th (F4) is approached by an appoggiatura figure and resolves down by step to 3̂.

Part C, p. 224.

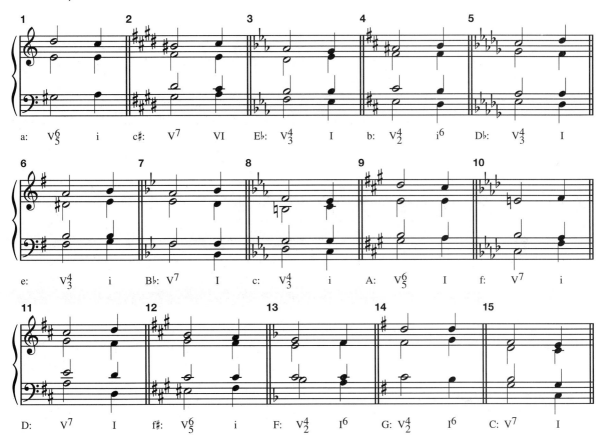

Part D, p. 224.

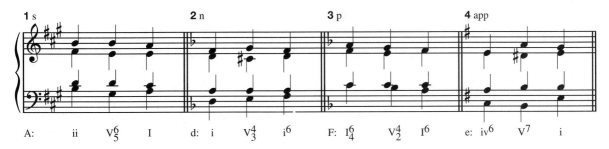

Part E, p. 225.

1. F	**2.** A	**3.** E♭	**4.** G, g	**5.** E
6. d	**7.** B♭	**8.** D	**9.** E, e	**10.** A♭
11. D	**12.** c♯	**13.** B♭	**14.** g	**15.** b

CHAPTER 14

Self-Test 14-1
Part A, p. 235.

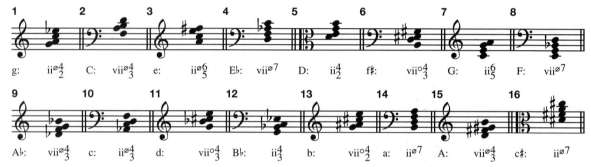

Part B, p. 236.

1. ii$^6_5$	**2.** ii$^4_2$	**3.** vii^{ø7}	**4.** ii$^{ø6}_5$	**5.** vii$^{°7}$
6. vii$^{ø4}_3$	**7.** ii^{ø7}	**8.** vii$^{°4}_3$		

Part C, pp. 236–237.

1. The ii$^{ø4}_2$ has its 7th approached as a suspension (from the previous chord tone). The large leap in the tenor (C4–F♯3) is necessary because of the motion in the upper voices. The 7th of the vii$^{°7}$ is approached as an appoggiatura. The resolution of both tritones leads to a tonic triad with doubled 3rd. In the last complete measure notice the 5-4 suspension, which "works" because of the dissonance with the G4, and the tonic pedal under the final i–iv^7–vii°–i progression.

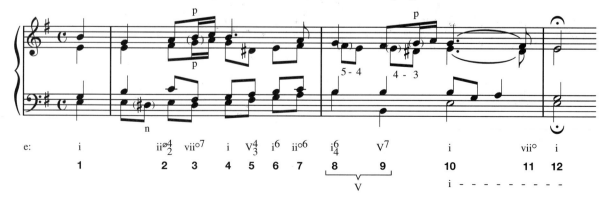

2. The 7th of the vii°⁷ is approached as an appoggiatura. It is left by arpeggiation, although one could hear it as leading to the B5–A5 in the next measure.

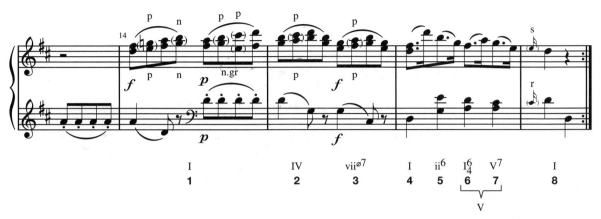

I	IV	vii°⁷	I	ii⁶	I⁶₄	V⁷	I
1	**2**	**3**	**4**	**5**	**6**	**7**	**8**

3. The 7th of the ii°⁶₅ is approached as a suspension. Resolution from the ii°⁴₃ is normal, the 7th becoming part of a 4-3 suspension. The main rhythmic motive (♩ ♪. ♪ | ♩) appears three times in the vocal part and three times in the accompaniment, alternating between the two.

4. The 7th of the ii^7 is prepared as a suspension in another voice (the bass in the previous measure). The texture thickens to five parts before the ii^7 resolves normally to the V^7. The asterisks indicate when the damper pedal is to be released. The reduction helps us to appreciate Chopin's imaginative elaboration of a simple progression. Notice that the C5 in m. 15 is analyzed as a passing tone that connects B4 to D5.

Part D, pp. 238–239.

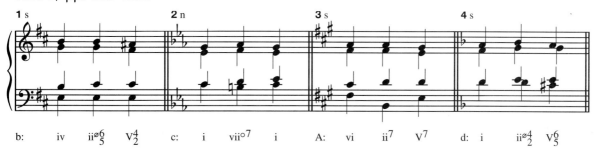

b: iv   ii$^{\varnothing 6}_{5}$ V$^{4}_{2}$ c: i   vii$^{\circ 7}$ i   A: vi   ii^{7} V^{7} d: i   ii$^{\varnothing 4}_{2}$ V$^{6}_{5}$

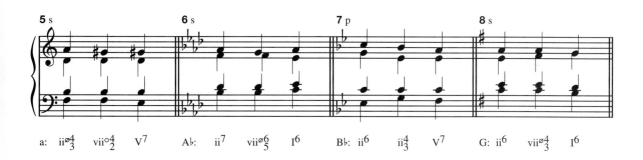

a: ii$^{\varnothing 4}_{3}$ vii$^{\circ 4}_{2}$ V^{7} A♭:   ii^{7} vii$^{\varnothing 6}_{5}$ I^{6} B♭:   ii^{6} ii$^{4}_{3}$ V^{7} G: ii^{6} vii$^{\varnothing 4}_{3}$ I^{6}

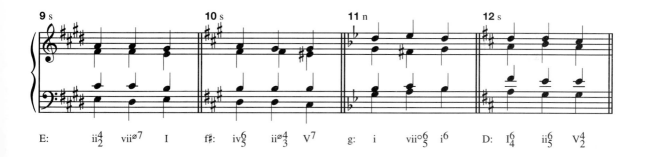

E: ii$^{4}_{2}$ vii$^{\varnothing 7}$ I   f♯:   iv$^{6}_{5}$ ii$^{\varnothing 4}_{3}$ V^{7} g: i   vii$^{\circ 6}_{5}$ i^{6} D: I$^{6}_{4}$ ii$^{6}_{5}$ V$^{4}_{2}$

Part E, p. 239.

Corelli, Trio Sonata Op. 3, No. 2, II

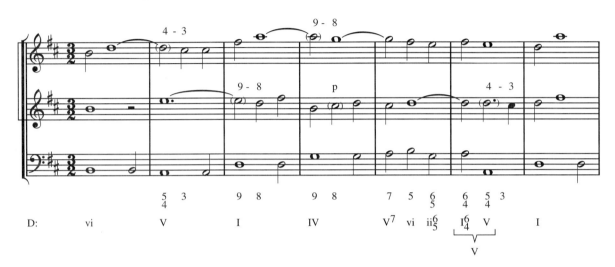

Part F, p. 240.

1. Bach, "Jesu, der du meine Seele"

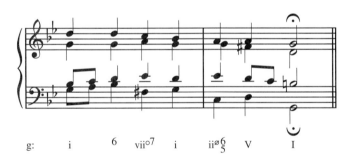

2. Bach, "Wie schön leuchtet der Morgenstern"

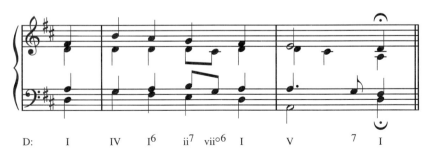

CHAPTER 15

Self-Test 15-1
Part A, p. 251.

C: vi$^4_3$ f: IV$^6_5$ B♭: IV$^{M6}_5$ e: i^7 c: VI^{M7} F: iii^7 f♯: iv$^4_2$ D: I$^{M4}_3$

G: IV^{M7} b: III$^{M4}_2$ a: ♯vi$^{ø6}_5$ E♭: I$^{M6}_5$ c♯: iv$^4_3$ E: vi$^4_2$ d: i$^4_3$ g: VI$^{M6}_5$

Part B, p. 251.

1. III$^{M6}_5$ **2.** vi$^4_3$ **3.** iv^7 **4.** ♯vi$^{ø4}_2$ **5.** I$^{M4}_2$

6. VI$^{M4}_3$ **7.** IV$^{M6}_5$ **8.** i$^4_2$

Part C, pp. 251–252.

1. The alto and tenor parts cross, and the soprano is more than an octave from its nearest neighbor (all of this in the second half of the first measure). This certainly could have been avoided (you might try it yourself) but at the expense of the sweeping lines in the inner voices. The 7th of the IV$^{M6}_5$ is approached as a suspension.

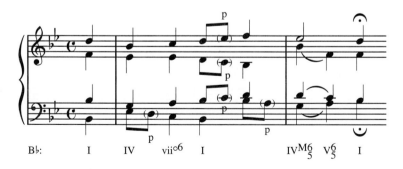

B♭:   I   IV   vii^{o6} I   IV$^{M6}_5$ V$^6_5$ I

2. The 7th of the vi⁷ is approached as a suspension. The resolution is slightly
unusual in that the ii has a doubled 3rd. However, if the tenor had gone to A3,
the line would not have been as satisfactory, and parallel 5ths would have been
formed with the alto.

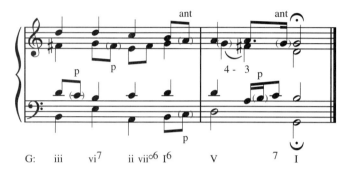

G: iii   vi⁷   ii vii°⁶ I⁶   V   7   I

3. Circle of fifths; 5th; it would proceed downward by step, one note per measure:
F4–E♭4–D♭4–C4.

i   iv⁷   /   VII⁷   III^M7   /   VI^M7   ii^ø7   /   V⁷   i

Part D, pp. 252–253.

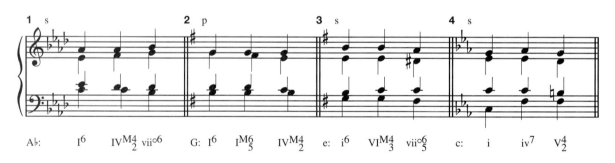

A♭:   I⁶   IV^M4/2 vii°⁶   G: I⁶   I^M6/5   IV^M4/2   e: i⁶   VI^M4/3 vii°6/5   c: i   iv⁷   V4/2

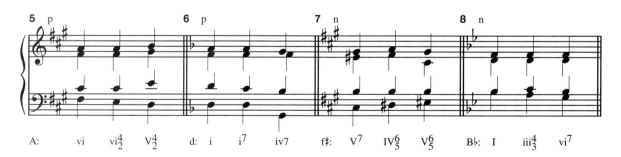

A: vi   vi4/2   V4/2   d: i   i⁷   iv7   f♯:   V⁷   IV6/5   V6/5   B♭: I   iii4/3   vi⁷

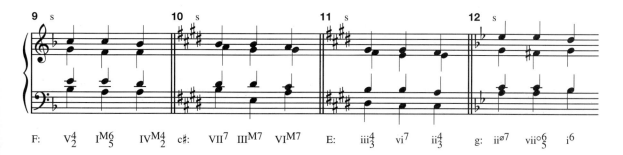

F: V$^4_2$ I$^{M6}_5$ IV$^{M4}_2$ c#:   VII^7 III^{M7} VI^{M7} E: iii$^4_3$ vi^7 ii$^4_3$ g: ii^{ø7} vii$^{o6}_5$ i^6

Part E, p. 253.

Notice the similarities between this excerpt and the one in Part C, no. 3.

Bach, French Suite No. 1, Minuet

Part F, p. 254.

1.

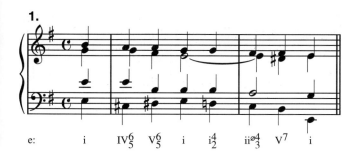

e: i   IV$^6_5$ V$^6_5$ i   i$^4_2$ ii$^{ø4}_3$ V^7 i

2.

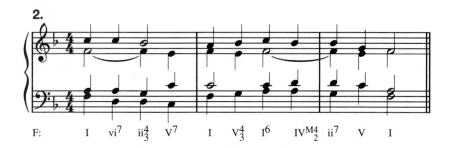

F: I   vi⁷   ii⁴₃   V⁷   I   V⁴₃   I⁶   IVᴹ⁴₂   ii⁷   V   I

CHAPTER 16

Self-Test 16-1
Part A, p. 261.

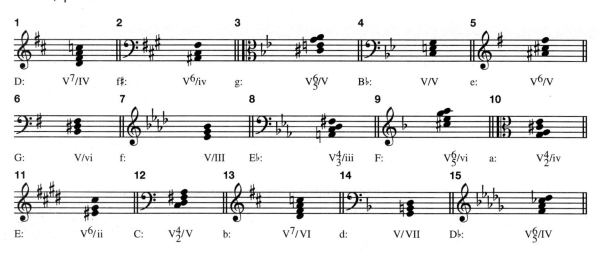

D: V⁷/IV   f#:   V⁶/iv   g: V⁶₅/V   B♭:   V/V   e: V⁶/V

G: V/vi   f: V/III   E♭:   V⁴₃/iii   F: V⁶₅/vi   a: V⁴₂/iv

E: V⁶/ii   C: V⁴₂/V   b: V⁷/VI   d: V/VII   D♭:   V⁶₅/IV

Part B, p. 261.

1. V⁶/ii	**2.** X	**3.** V⁴₂/V	**4.** X	**5.** V⁴₃/iv
6. V⁶₅/vi	**7.** V⁷/III	**8.** V/V	**9.** X	**10.** V⁴₂/IV
11. X	**12.** V⁴₃/VI	**13.** V⁶/iii	**14.** V⁷/iv	**15.** V⁴₃/V

Self-Test 16-2

Part A, pp. 267–271.

1.

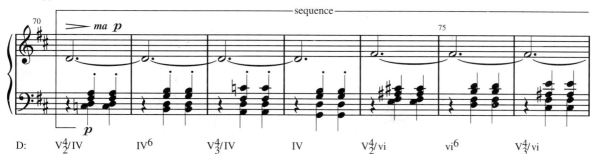

D: V_2^4/IV   IV^6 V_3^4/IV   IV V_2^4/vi   vi^6 V_3^4/vi

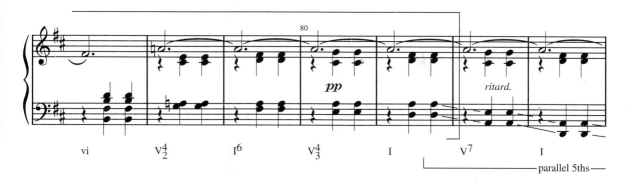

vi V_2^4 I^6 V_3^4 I   V^7 I

parallel 5ths

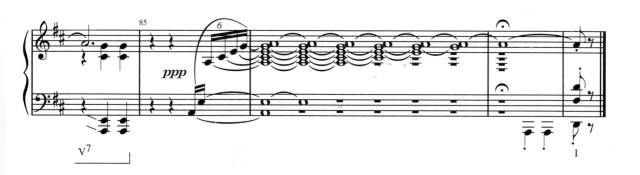

V^7 I

2.

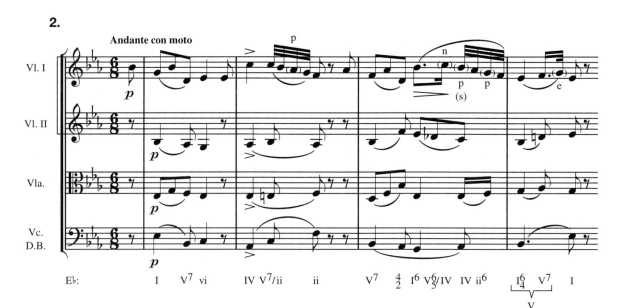

3. Measures 1 to 2 return at a different pitch level in mm. 5 to 6. This is not really
a sequence because mm. 3 to 4 intervene. Counting from the bottom, parts 1
and 2 double at the octave. Part 4 doubles 7 (the melody) until the second half
of m. 7. Other parallel octaves occur occasionally, as between parts 3 and 6
over the bar line from m. 2 to m. 3.

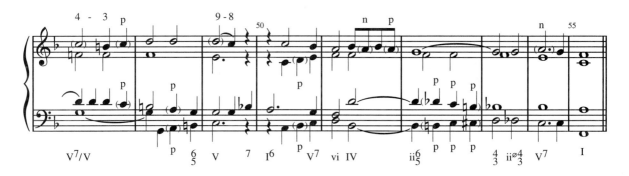

6.

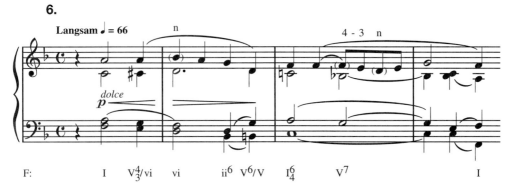

7. Yes, the four accompanying parts follow conventional voice-leading principles.
The melody is an independent line for the most part, but it doubles an inner
voice in mm. 2 to 3.

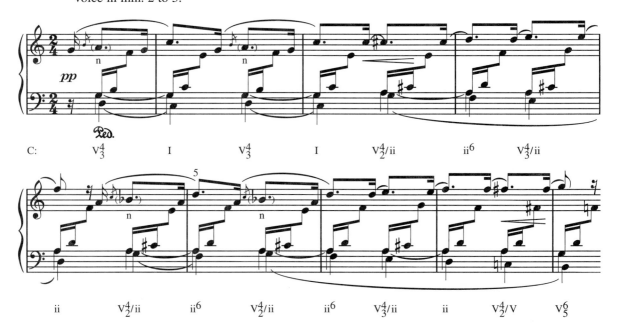

Part B, p. 271.

Ab: V⁷ V⁷/IV   IV   f#: ii°⁶ V⁶/V   V   e: ii°⁶ V⁴₃/iv   iv   D: V V⁶/vi vi   E: ii V⁷/ii V⁷/V

Eb: vi⁷ V⁷/V   V⁷   b: iv V⁷/III III^M7   Bb: V⁶₅ V⁴₃/vi   vi   d: i V⁴₂/V V⁶   Ab: I V⁶₅/ii   ii⁴₂

Part C, p. 272.

1. V⁽⁷⁾/V, V⁽⁷⁾/VII   **2.** V⁽⁷⁾/ii, V⁽⁷⁾/V, V⁷/iii

3. V⁽⁷⁾/V, V⁷/vi   **4.** V⁷/ii, V⁷/IV

5. V⁽⁷⁾/ii, V⁽⁷⁾/vi, V⁷/IV   **6.** V⁽⁷⁾/iii, V⁽⁷⁾/vi

7. V⁷/IV, V⁷/V   **8.** V⁽⁷⁾/III, V⁽⁷⁾/V

9. V⁽⁷⁾/III, V⁽⁷⁾/VII   **10.** V⁽⁷⁾/iv, v⁽⁷⁾/VII, V⁷/V

Part D, p. 272.

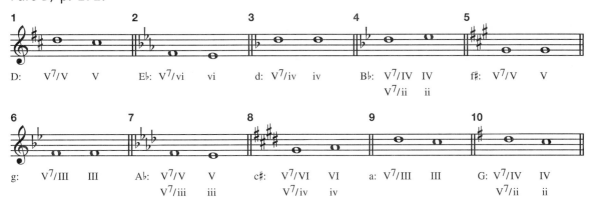

D: V⁷/V   V   Eb: V⁷/vi vi   d: V⁷/iv iv   Bb: V⁷/IV IV   f#: V⁷/V   V
                                                      V⁷/ii ii

g: V⁷/III III   Ab: V⁷/V   V   c#: V⁷/VI VI   a: V⁷/III III   G: V⁷/IV IV
                        V⁷/iii iii   V⁷/iv iv   V⁷/ii ii

Part E, pp. 272–273.

1. Bach, "Herzlich thut mich verlangen"

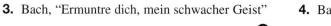

A: V$_5^6$ I   V^6 IV^6 (I$_4^6$)   V$_5^6$/V V   I

2. Bach, "Christus, der ist mein Leben"

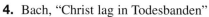

F: I   –   V^6 V$_2^4$/IV IV^6 V   I

3. Bach, "Ermuntre dich, mein schwacher Geist"

e: i V$_3^4$ i^6 V$_{(5)}^6$/iv iv V$_5^6$ V   7 i

4. Bach, "Christ lag in Todesbanden"

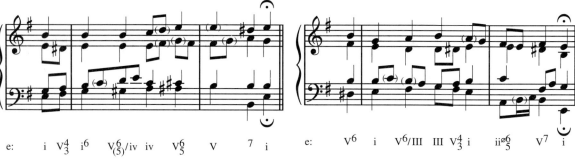

e: V^6 i V^6/III III V$_3^4$ i   ii$^{ø6}_5$ V^7 i

Part F, p. 274.

1.

D: I V$_5^6$/vi vi V$_2^4$/V   V^6 V$_2^4$/IV IV^6 V^7 I

2.

g: i V/III III V$_5^6$/iv iv V$_5^6$/V V   VI   ii$^{ø6}_5$ V   i

CHAPTER 17

Self-Test 17-1
Part A, p. 277.

Part B, p. 278.

1. vii°7/vi   **2.** X   **3.** vii°6/VI   **4.** vii°6/5/IV   **5.** vii°7/VII

6. X   **7.** vii°7/III   **8.** X   **9.** vii°7/ii   **10.** vii°6/5/V

11. vii°94/3/V   **12.** X   **13.** vii°6/iv   **14.** vii°6/V   **15.** X

Self-Test 17-2
Part A, pp. 293–298.

1.

a: i   6   5/3   V   vii°7/iv   iv   vii°7/V   V

2.

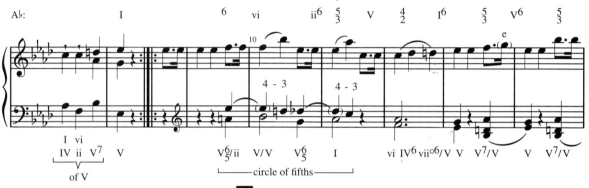

3. The G4 might be heard as part of an incomplete passing tone figure
(A–G–F♯–E, with the F♯ omitted) or as an escape tone from the F♯4 that
occurred a beat earlier (as F♯–G–E).

5. The excerpt is not a period because the second cadence is not more conclusive than the first. The first cadence (m. 4) is a PAC, whereas the second (m. 8) is a HC.

The 5-4 suspension is marked with an exclamation point because it involves a note that is consonant with the bass resolving to one that is dissonant with the bass, exactly the reverse of the commonly accepted definition of a suspension.

Part B, p. 298.

B♭: vi vii°⁶/V V   E♭: I⁶ vii°⁶/ii ii⁶   A♭: V⁷ vii°⁷/vi vi   A: vi⁶ vii°⁶/vi vi   C: vi vii∅⁴₃/V V⁶

f♯: iv⁶ vii°⁷/VI VI   C: vi vii°⁴₃/ii ii⁶   E: I⁶ vii°⁷/iii iii   G: ii⁴₂ vii°⁴₃/V V⁶   c♯: VI vii°⁶₅/iv iv⁶

Part C, p. 299.

1. Bach, "Du grosser Schmerzensmann"

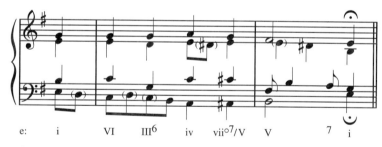

e: i   VI   III⁶   iv   vii°⁷/V   V   7   i

2. Bach, "Ach, Gott, wie manches Herzeleid"

A: V   I   V⁶/vi   vi   vii°⁶/ii   ii   I⁶   V

3. Bach, "Ein' feste Burg ist unser Gott"

e: i   III   V/III   V$^6_5$ i   V

                       (7)

                  V   V$^6_5$/vi   vi

                       of III

Part D, p. 299.

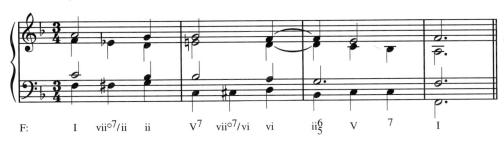

F: I   vii°^{7}/ii   ii   V^7 vii°^{7}/vi   vi   ii$^6_5$ V ^{7} I

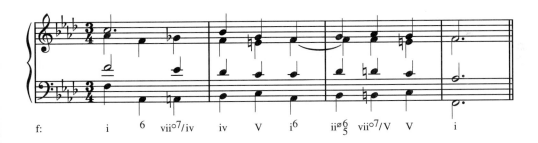

f: i ^{6} vii°^{7}/iv   iv   V   i^6 ii$^{ø6}_5$ vii°^{7}/V   V   i

CHAPTER 18

Self-Test 18-1
Part A, p. 304.

1. b	**2.** D♭	**3.** A	**4.** a♭	**5.** d
6. F♯	**7.** c♯	**8.** A♭	**9.** c	**10.** B

Part B, p. 304.

1. c, d, E♭, F, g

2. e♭, f, G♭, A♭, b♭

3. E♭, f, g, A♭, B♭

4. C♯, d♯, e♯, F♯, G♯

5. E, f♯, g♯, A, B

6. b, c♯, D, E, f♯

Part C, p. 304.

1. foreign

2. closely related

3. enharmonic

4. closely related

5. relative and closely related

6. closely related

7. parallel

8. foreign

9. relative and closely related

10. foreign

Self-Test 18-2
Part A, pp. 304–314.

1.

2. If the last chord in m. 7 were a ii$_5^6$, the 7th (E5) would resolve by step.

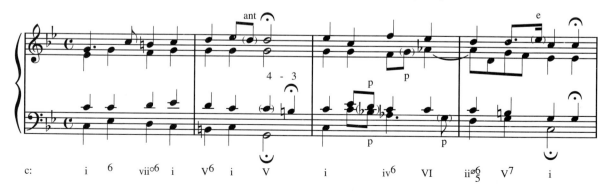

3.

4.

5. The outer voices in the sequence in mm. 9 to 11 could be heard as an elaboration of this pattern.

Part B, p. 314.

1. F   **2.** A   **3.** a   **4.** f♯   **5.** A♭

Part C, p. 315.

1. First key, A♭:   I   ii   IV   vi

      Triads: A♭   b♭   D♭   f

      Second key, D♭:   V   vi   I   iii

2. First key, c: iv   VI

      Triads: f   A♭

      Second key, f: i   III

3. First key, a: i   III   iv   VI

      Triads: a   C   d   F

      Second key, F: iii   V   vi   I

4. First key, G: I   iii   V   vi

      Triads: G   b   D   e

      Second key, D: IV   vi   I   ii

5. First key, c♯:   i   ii°   III   iv   VI

      Triads: c♯   d♯°   E   f♯   A

      Second key, E: vi   vii°   I   ii   IV

6. First key, D: I   iii   V   vi

      Triads: D   f♯   A   b

      Second key, f♯:   VI   i   III   iv

Part D, p. 315.

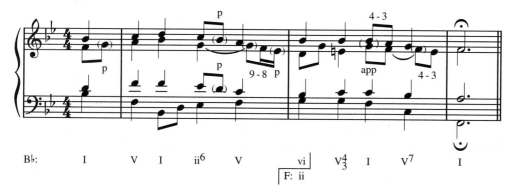

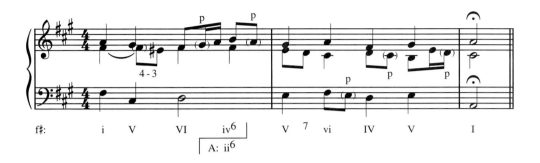

Part E, p. 316.

Bach, "Freu' dich sehr, o meine Seele"

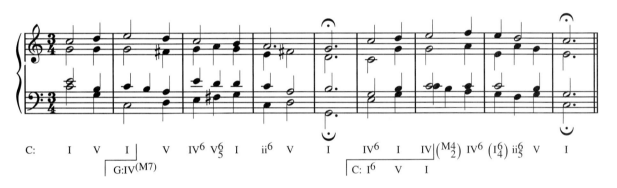

Part F, p. 316.

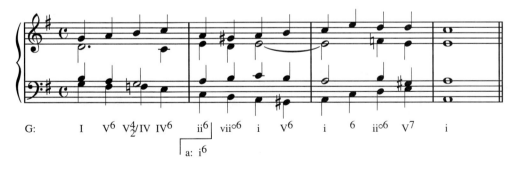

CHAPTER 19

Self-Test 19-1
Part A, pp. 329–333.

1. This modulation might also be analyzed as a phrase modulation.

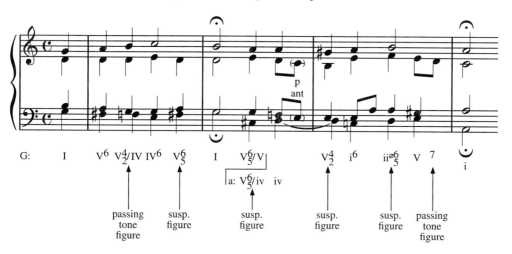

2. Yes, D♭ major and A major are in a chromatic mediant relationship, but it is enharmonically spelled (compare C♯–A). The modulation is effected through a common tone, also enharmonically spelled.

3. The modulation from g minor to f minor is sequential. The modulation back to
g minor is a direct modulation.

g: i / iv⁶ / V⁷ / f: iv⁶ / V⁷ / i ⁶ V / i V g: iv / i⁶₄ V / i⁶₄ V / i

4. The two keys are G major and E♭ major. A monophonic modulation is accomplished in mm. 121 to 123. The relationship between G and E♭ could be described in at least two ways. For one, there is a chromatic mediant relationship between the two keys. Also, E♭ is VI in g minor, the parallel minor of G major.

Part B, p. 333.

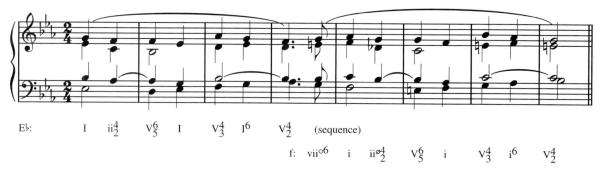

Part C, p. 334.

Bach, "Hilf, Herr Jesu, lass gelingen"

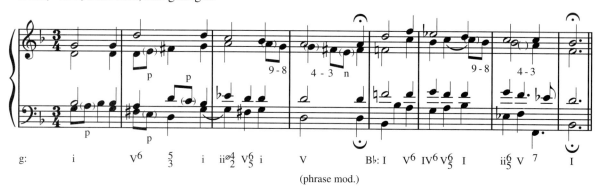

CHAPTER 20

Self-Test 20-1
Part A, p. 347.

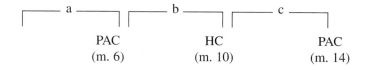

Or b and c could be considered one phrase. Either way, the form is sectional binary, unless you want to use the term *phrase group* (review p. 171).

Part B, pp. 347–349.
Two-reprise continuous rounded binary.

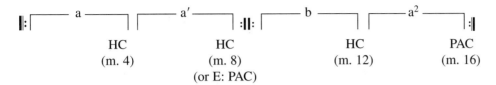

	a	a′	b	a²
	HC	HC	HC	PAC
	(m. 4)	(m. 8)	(m. 12)	(m. 16)
		(or E: PAC)		

1. The first G4 is the 7th of a V^7/IV. The other is part of a 4-3 suspension.

2. End of m. 6: A: I = E: IV

3. The melodic figures resemble the opening motive (leap up, stepwise down), whereas the bass line is related to the first two bass notes.

4. m. 7, beat 3.

5. m. 7, beat 4 to m. 8, soprano and bass.

Part C, pp. 349–350.
Two-reprise sectional binary.

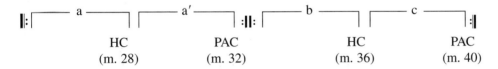

	a	a′	b	c
	HC	PAC	HC	PAC
	(m. 28)	(m. 32)	(m. 36)	(m. 40)

1. The first violins (or the melody) at the octave.

2. Part of a vii°⁶/V.

3. In mm. 4 to 5, perhaps explainable as occurring between phrases.

Part D, pp. 350–351.
Continuous ternary.

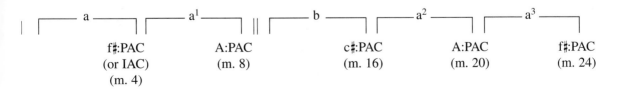

	a	a¹	b	a²	a³
	f♯:PAC	A:PAC	c♯:PAC	A:PAC	f♯:PAC
	(or IAC)	(m. 8)	(m. 16)	(m. 20)	(m. 24)
	(m. 4)				

1. Schumann moves from i to the relative major (III) to the minor dominant (v) and then back the same way (III, then i). The tonicized pitch classes arpeggiate the tonic triad: F♯–A–C♯–A–F♯

2. A: vii°⁷/ii / ii / V⁴₃/V V⁷ / I / f♯: i V / VI^M7 iv⁷ / $\underbrace{i^6_4\ V^7}_{V}$ / i / /

3. In mm. 21 to 22, V–VI^M7, there are parallel 5ths between the bass and tenor. They are hidden by the anticipation (A3) in the tenor.

4. The double bar after m. 8.

CHAPTER 21

Self-Test 21-1
Part A, p. 364.

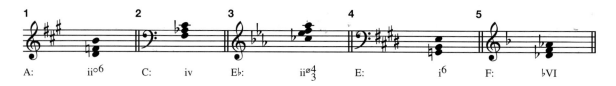

A: ii°⁶   C: iv   E♭:   ii⌀⁴₃   E: i⁶   F: ♭VI

g: I   B♭:   vii°⁶₅   A♭:   iv⁶   G: ♭III   D: ii⌀⁶₅

Part B, p. 364.

1. ii°⁶ **2.** iv⁶ **3.** vii°⁴₃ **4.** i **5.** ♭VI

6. I **7.** vii°⁶₅ **8.** ♭III **9.** ii⌀⁴₂ **10.** iv

Part C, p. 364–369.

1.

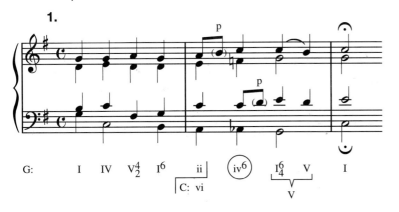

2.

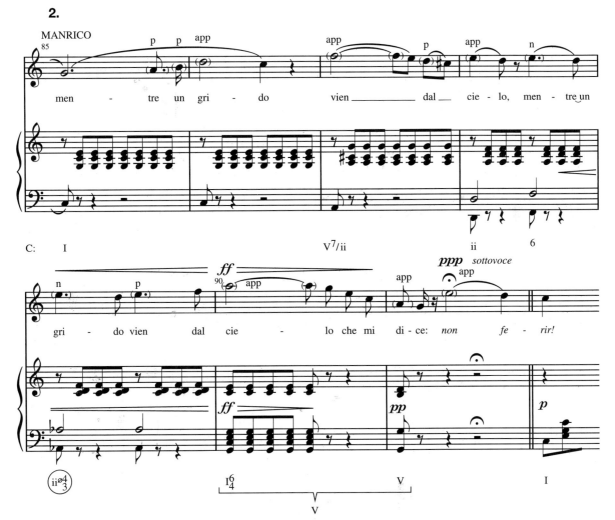

3. The flutes double the violas in mm. 47 to 51.

A: V V$_2^4$/ii / ii^6 / V$_2^4$ I^6 / IV$^{M4}_2$ ii ⟨♭VI^6⟩ / V$_5^6$ I ii^6 V^7 / vi V$_5^6$/V / V^7 / I /

or

vii^{o6}

4. Measures 5 and 6 contain diminished seventh chords. Both contain a °5 and a $^+$4, and in both cases the tendency of the °5 to resolve inward and of the $^+$4 to resolve outward is followed. The chords of resolution then have doubled 3rds.

B♭: I^6 / V$_2^4$ / I^6 V / I / vii^{o7}/ii ii / ⟨vii^{o7}⟩ I / IV V^6/V / V

5. The first modulation is from a♭ minor to its relative major, C♭, by means of the common chord in m. 5 (a♭: i = C♭: vi). A change of mode to c♭ minor follows in m. 9, notated as b minor. This change of mode simplifies the second modulation, from c♭/b to its relative major, E♭♭/D, through the common chord in m. 14 (b: iv = D: ii).

Part D, p. 369.

1.

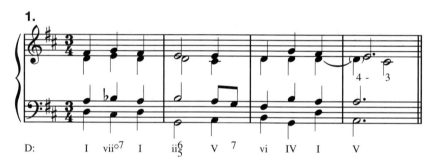

D: I   vii^{o7} I   ii$_5^6$ V   7   vi   IV   I   V

2.

F: I   vii^{o7}/ii   ii   vii^{o7} I   ii$^{ø6}_5$ V   I

Part E, p. 370.

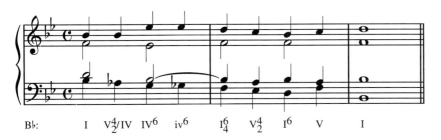

Bb: I   V$^4_2$/IV   IV^6 iv^6 I$^6_4$ V$^4_2$ I^6 V   I

CHAPTER 22

Self-Test 22-1

Part A, p. 380.

1. ii$^{\circ 6}$ **2.** vii$^{\varnothing 7}$/IV   **3.** vii$^{\circ 7}$/ii   **4.** N^6 **5.** N^6

6. N^6 **7.** N   **8.** iv^6 **9.** V$^6_5$/V   **10.** N

Part B, p. 380.

c: vii$^{\circ 4}_3$/iv   f#:   N^6 Ab: bVI   e: N^6 d: N

F: vii$^{\circ 6}$/ii   Eb: N^6 D: V$^4_2$/V   E: ii$^{\varnothing 4}_3$ bb: N^6

Part C, pp. 380–383.

1. d: vii$^{\circ 6}_5$ / i^6 V$^6_5$/iv / N^6 vii$^{\circ 7}$/V / i$^6_4$ V i$^6_4$ V^7 i$^6_4$ / V / /

or
VI^6/iv

with the bracket under "i$^6_4$ V i$^6_4$ V^7 i$^6_4$ / V" labeled V

2. a. c#: / i iv$_4^6$ / i / V^7 i$_4^6$ /

V^7 i$_4^6$ V$_2^4$ / i^6 / N^6 / i$_4^6$ V^7 / i /

b. The first three $_4^6$ chords are pedal $_4^6$ chords.

The fourth one is a cadential $_4^6$.

c. The form is a period. Most listeners would probably call it a parallel period, even though only the first four notes of the two phrases are similar.

3.

b: i   V^7/N   N

                        vii°^{7} V^7 i   ii^{ø7} vii°^{7} VI   V   7

4. Notice that the excerpt begins with a long circle-of-fifths sequence.

a: i^6 iv / VII^6 III / VI^6 ii° / V^6 i / N^6 |

F: IV^6 V^7 / I / V$_3^4$ I / IV$_4^6$ I / V$_5^6$ I /

Part D, p. 383.

Part E, p. 383.

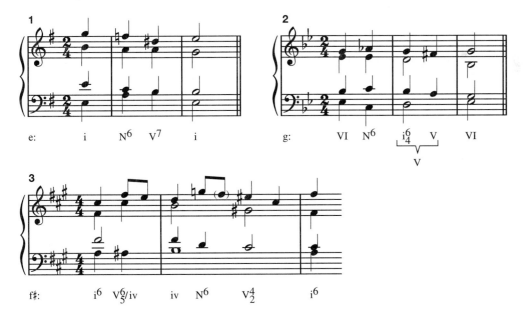

Part F, p. 384.

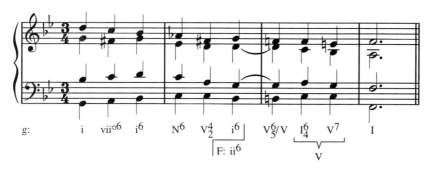

g: i   vii°⁶ i⁶   N⁶ V⁴₂ i⁶   V⁶₅/V i⁶₄ V⁷   I
                                  └─F: ii⁶─┘   └──V──┘

Part G, p. 384.

CHAPTER 23

Self-Test 23-1
Part A, pp. 394–395.

1. Ger⁺⁶   **2.** Fr⁺⁶   **3.** vii°⁶/V   **4.** Ger⁺⁶   **5.** vii°⁴₂

6. It⁺⁶   **7.** Fr⁺⁶   **8.** ii°⁴₃   **9.** iv⁶₅   **10.** It⁺⁶

Part B, p. 395.

f: Ger⁺⁶   E: Fr⁺⁶   c♯:   N⁶   D♭:   Ger⁺⁶   F: It⁺⁶

a: Fr⁺⁶   E♭:   V⁶₅/ii   g: Ger⁺⁶   D: iv⁶   b: It⁺⁶

Part C, pp. 396–399.

1. The ♯$\hat{4}$ and ♭$\hat{6}$ expand to an octave on $\hat{5}$, as expected. Parallel 5ths are avoided by resolving to a i⁶₄ chord. Notice the unusual unprepared escape tone in m. 4, creating a sharp dissonance with the V chord beneath it.

a: vii°⁶₅/V / Ger⁺⁶ / i⁶₄ VI i⁶₄ vii°⁷/V / i⁶₄ VI ii⌀⁶₅ V / i

2. The resolution of the Fr⁺⁶ is ornamented with a 4-3 suspension in the second violin. The ♭$\hat{6}$ and ♯$\hat{4}$ expand to an 8ve on $\hat{5}$.

B: I / ii⁶ / V ⁷ / I / V⁶ |
                        | F♯: I⁶ V⁶₅ / I IV⁶ Fr⁺⁶ / V / I /

3. The ♭$\hat{6}$ and ♯$\hat{4}$ expand to an 8ve on $\hat{5}$. Parallel 5ths are avoided by resolving to a i⁶₄ chord.

b: i / i⁴₂ / Ger⁺⁶ i⁶₄ / V⁴₂/N N⁶ /
    V⁴₂ i⁶ / ii⌀⁷ V⁷ / i

4. The chromatic passing tone occurs at the beginning of m. 6 in the first violin. In both Ger⁺⁶ chords the viola has the 5th above the bass. The parallels are avoided in the first instance by leaping up to $\hat{5}$. In the second Ger⁺⁶ the parallels are disguised by means of a 6-5 suspension. In the first Ger⁺⁶ the resolution of ♯$\hat{4}$ in the second violin is taken by the viola, allowing the violin to leap up to $\hat{2}$ (the 5th of the V chord).

f: i / vii°⁷ V⁶₅ / i / iv⁶ / Ger⁺⁶ / V vii°⁷/V / V Ger⁺⁶ / V / /

5. In m. 9, $\sharp\hat{4}$ moves down by half step to provide the 7th of the V^7 chord. In m. 26, $\flat\hat{6}$ and $\sharp\hat{4}$ move to an 8ve on $\hat{5}$.

$$C: \ I \ / \ / \ / \ / \ / \ I \ V^6_5 \ I \ / \ \underset{V}{\underbrace{I^6_4 \ V}} \ / \ / \ / \ It^{+6} \ V^7 \ / \ I$$

$$V^4_3 \ / \ i \ / \ It^{+6} \ / \ V \ / \ ^7$$

Part D, p. 400.

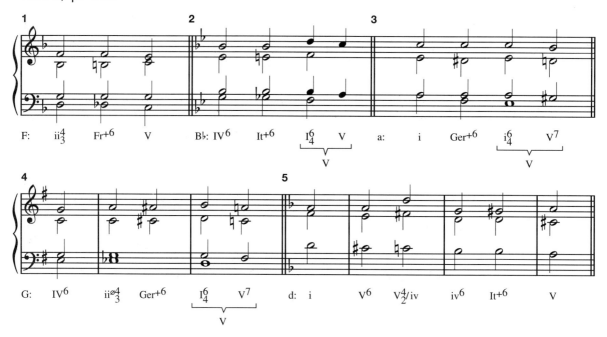

Part E, p. 400.

Part F, p. 401.

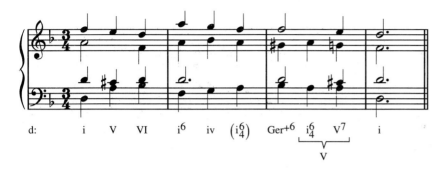

d: i   V   VI   i^6 iv   (i$^6_4$)   Ger^{+6} i$^6_4$ V^7 i

                                                        V

CHAPTER 24

Self-Test 24-1
Part A, p. 410.

   1. Ger^{+6} V   **2.** It^{+6}/iv iv   **3.** V$^6_5$/iv iv   **4.** Ger^{+6} I$^6_4$ V$^4_2$ **5.** Ger^{+6} I

                                                                     V

   6. [Ger^{+6}] i   **7.** $^{+6}$ V   **8.** It^{+6} V^6 **9.** Fr^{+6}/I I   **10.** N^6 vii$^{\circ 7}$/V V

Part B, pp. 410–412.

   1. e: N^6 Ger^{+6} / i$^6_4$ V^7 / I   **2.** e: / [Ger^{+6}] / i^6 / [Ger^{+6}] / i^6

                                 V

   3.

Schwer-ter __ klir - ren und bli - tzen;   dann   steig' ich ge-waff - net her - vor aus dem Grab, den

G: I   V$^4_3$ I   V   I   6

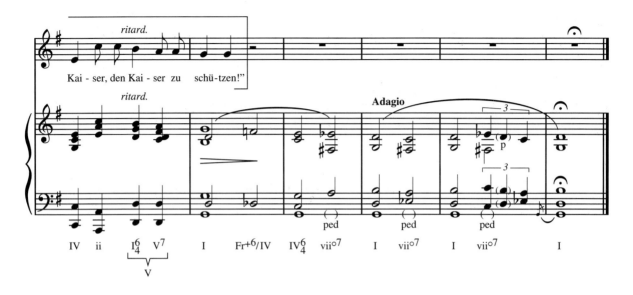

4. a: / i / V⁷ / i / [Ger⁺⁶] / i / / V⁷ / i /

CHAPTER 25

Self-Test 25-1
Part A, p. 423.

Other correct answers in addition to those given above are possible. For example, the third chord in no. 1 could have been spelled and analyzed as a vii°⁴₃ in g♯ (or G♯), or as a vii°⁴₃/V in c♯, and so on.

Part B, p. 424.

1. E: I / vii°⁷ / I / V$^4_3$ / I⁶ $^5_3$ / vii°⁷ |

| G: vii°$^4_2$ / V⁷ / I / V⁷ / I /

2. c: i V$^4_2$ / i⁶ ii$^{ø6}_5$ / vii°⁷/V |

| e: vii°$^6_5$ V$^4_3$ / i⁶ / ii$^{ø6}_5$ V⁷ / i /

3. D: I iii IV / I⁶ V$^4_3$ I V⁷/IV |

| f♯: Ger⁺⁶ / i$^6_4$ V ⁷ / i /

Part C, pp. 424–429.

1. The F–G♭–F figure in m. 65 may be related to the voice line in mm. 58 to 62 (B♭–C♭–B♭) and to the bass in mm. 59 to 63 (F–G♭–F).

G♭: I / V$^6_5$ / I / V$^6_5$ / I V⁷/IV |

| b♭: Ger⁺⁶ / V ⁶ i ⁶ / V $^6_5$ i ⁶ / V

2. No, this is not an enharmonic modulation. The real key relationships here are D♭ (I) to B♭♭ (♭VI). Anyone would rather read music written in A instead of B♭♭, so the flats are written enharmonically as sharps beginning in m. 39. But the listener is completely unaware of the enharmonicism—the true test of an enharmonic modulation.

3. Notice that a single °7 chord is heard in mm. 45 to 46, and, although the listener is unaware of the shift to sharps at the end of m. 46, the unexpected resolution to a C♯°⁷ is clearly audible. We have analyzed the °7 chord in B♭ as a vii°$^4_3$/ii because Schubert spelled it that way. However, it has other enharmonic possibilities in B♭—vii°$^6_5$/IV, for example—and these are equally valid analyses.

B♭: V⁷ (I$^6_4$) V / (I$^6_4$) V (I$^6_4$) V⁷ / / vii°$^4_3$/ii | /

| f♯: vii°⁷ / / V⁷ / i /

4. c: V⁷ Ger⁺⁶ / V$^6_5$/V i$^6_4$ V⁷ / i / / Ger⁺⁶ |
                                V | D♭: V⁷ / / / / / / I V$^4_2$ I⁶ /

V⁷ / I ii⁶ V$^6_5$/V / V / I V$^4_2$ I⁶ / V⁷ / vii°⁷/vi |

| c:vii°$^6_5$/V / i$^6_4$ V / i
                                          V

m. 98	c: Ger^{+6}	m. 99	c: V$^6_5$/V
mm. 102–106	c: Ger^{+6} = D♭: V^7	m. 107	D♭: V$^4_2$
m. 108	D♭: V^7	m. 109	D♭: ii^6
m. 111	D♭: V$^4_2$	m. 112	D♭: V^7
m. 113	D♭: vii$^{\circ 7}$/vi = c: vii$^{\circ 6}_5$/V		

Also note the importance of F♯/G♭ as a melodic pitch in this passage.

5. B♭/A♯ is an important pitch class in this passage. It appears melodically as the 7th of the vii$^{\circ 7}$/ii four times in mm. 34 to 41 (the first time accented), and it is used as the enharmonic hinge between the keys of C and E in m. 43.

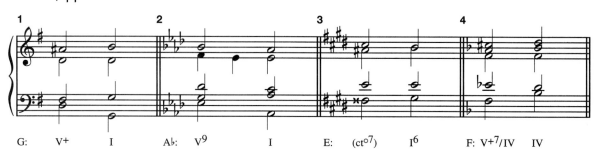

C: I vii$^{\circ 6}_5$/ii / ii^6 / / V$^6_5$ / I vii$^{\circ 7}$/ii ii vii$^{\varnothing 6}_5$ / I^6 vii$^{\circ 6}_5$/ii ii^6 / ii$^{\varnothing 6}_5$ V$^4_2$ /

I^6 i^6 (V$^6_4$) vii$^{\circ 7}$/ii / ii V$^6_5$ / I V$^4_2$/IV

E: Ger^{+6} i$^6_4$ V^7 / I V$^6_5$ I / V $^4_2$ I^6 V$^6_5$ / I

V

CHAPTER 26

Self-Test 26-1
Part A, pp. 449–450.

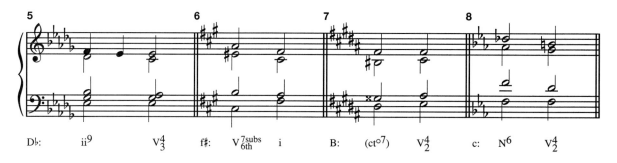

G: V+   I   A♭:   V^9 I   E: (ct$^{\circ 7}$)   I^6 F: V^{+7}/IV   IV

D♭:   ii^9 V$^4_3$ f♯:   V$^{7\text{subs}}_{6\text{th}}$ i   B: (ct$^{\circ 7}$)   V$^4_2$ c: N^6 V$^4_2$

Part B, pp. 450–456.

1.

E: I / V / V$_2^4$/IV / IV^6 / (I$_4^6$) / vii$^{\circ 7}$/V /

V$_2^4$ / I^6 V^{+6}/IV / IV / vii$^{\circ 7}$/ii ii^6 / V^7 / vi / ii / V^7 / I /

2.

3. E: I / V^7 / I / ⟨ct$^{\circ 7}$⟩ / V$_2^4$/IV / ⟨ct$^{\circ 7}$⟩ / V$_2^4$/IV / ⟨ct$^{\circ 7}$⟩ ⌐ A: vii$^{\circ 6}_5$/ii / ii^6 / I$_4^6$ V^7 / I

4.   The form of this piece is continuous ternary.

5. I / IV⁶ $\frac{5}{3}$ / ii°⁷ V⁷ / I C / vi C / F A / D F / B ii⁴₃ / V⁷ V⁷/V /

V IV⁶ / (ct°⁷) V⁶₅ / I

The chords in mm. 5 to 8 appear to be simultaneities because they do not create
a logical progression and because the chord 7ths do not resolve. Parallel 10ths
above the bass can be traced throughout these measures.

CHAPTER 27

Self-Test 27-1
Part A, pp. 481–482.

1. e♭ minor

2. The melody is very angular and contains no leading tone. It does not clearly imply a harmonic background. The phrase concludes on scale degree $\hat{3}$ rather than tonic.

3. VII⁷ III⁷ / VI⁷ II⁹⁷ / V (very traditional!)

3. VII^7 III^7 / VI^7 II^{97} / V (very traditional!)

4. Measure 8, beat 1: we are led to expect G♭ major because of emphasis on the D♭ dominant seventh chord. Measure 8, end of beat 3: we have been set up for a♭ minor here, especially with G♮ suggesting a leading tone.

5. Measure 9, last two beats feature a Ger^{+6} in E♭.

6. There is no melodic "closure"; that is, the closing phrase is identical to the antecedent phrase that opened the composition. Also, the cadential harmonic motion consists of I$^6_4$ moving directly to I in root position.

Part B, pp. 482–483.

Note: enharmonic spelling is acceptable.

Part C, pp. 483–484.

1. Measure 6 introduces a $^6_4$ chord, which might suggest a shift to B as tonic. However it "resolves" deceptively to the borrowed subtonic as shown. After lingering on dominant harmony in mm. 9 to 10, the resolution to V of IV rather than a tonic triad is unexpected. In m. 15, the brief movement to vii/V with *tonic as bass* is used to prepare a half cadence in E.

2. Extended use of non-chord tones is prevalent, as in m. 5. In mm. 8 to 12, we find a succession of strong non-chord tones in the melody. Note too the persistent use of a minor tonic $^6_4$. Rapid harmonic rhythm (mm. 1–2, 12–13) is interspersed with much slower harmonic motion.

Brahms, Symphony No. 1, Op. 68, II (piano reduction)

Part D, p. 484.

1.

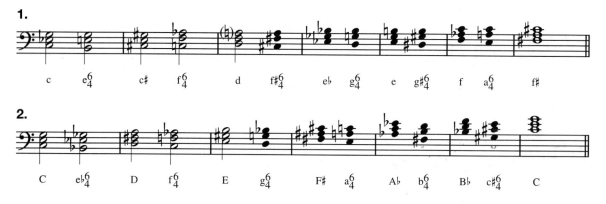

2.

Part E, pp. 484–486.

1. Leading tone seventh in E♭ (vii°⁷) over tonic pedal.

2. g minor; ii$^6_5$–VI$^4_3$–ii⁷–VI$^4_2$ (It might also be possible to consider the persistent E♭ as an inner pedal and analyze: ii$^6_5$–i⁶–ii⁷–i$^6_4$)

3. ii$^6_5$ moves to I$^6_4$, which ends the phrase. This pattern is repeated in mm. 21 to 22, although here the $^6_4$ moves directly to root position I, which in turn closes the piece.

4. Measure 20.

5. Binary or two-part.

Part F, pp. 486–489.

1. a minor. The opening measure may be heard as VI (retrospectively) or as part of an implied supertonic extending throughout the first three measures and leading to V. Because of the dominant preparation, m. 5 will be heard as tonic (a minor), followed by VI–ii°–vii°⁷ (V). Measure 9 will be heard as tonic with added 6th, proceeding to iv⁷ (m. 10), Fr⁺⁶ (m. 11, including "A" from the vocal part), and V (m. 12). The voicing is extremely angular, perhaps intending to picture the distraught state of mind of a young woman who has been betrayed by her lover.

2. Chromatic mediant (A major/C♯ dominant seventh)

3. Both triads are augmented, although their roots (A♭/E♭) are 5th-related.

4. B♭ major. Note use of an augmented V chord in m. 28.

5. Measures 34 to 37 systematically prepare a minor through introduction of the leading tone of V (D♯ in m. 34), minor dominant (m. 35), major dominant (m. 36), and addition of seventh to dominant harmony (m. 37).

6. Ternary. Mm. 1 to 12 = A; mm. 13 to 37 = B, which is essentially divided into two sections and might be heard as almost developmental in nature; mm. 37 to 52 = A and Codetta.

CHAPTER 28

Self-Test 28-1
Part A, p. 499.

1. Ionian, Lydian, Mixolydian.

2. Phrygian, Locrian.

3. Whole-Tone and Half-Step/Minor Third. Both are derived from the augmented triad, in one case superimposed at the interval of a whole step, and in the other, a half step.

4. Lydian-Mixolydian (♯4/♭7).

5. Fully diminished seventh chord, juxtaposed at the interval of a half step or whole step.

6. Diminished, major, minor

7. Minor, 2nd and tritone.

Part B, p. 500.

Part C, p. 500.

1.

2.

3.

Part D, pp. 501–502.

1. Dorian   **2.** Octatonic

3. Dorian   **4.** Phrygian

5. Lydian-Mixolydian   **6.** Aeolian

7. Mixolydian   **8.** Locrian

Self-Test 28-2
Part A, p. 517.

a. polychord

b. quartal chord

c. added 6th chord

d. dominant 9th

e. whole-tone chord

f. split-third chord

g. secundal chord (cluster)

h. quintal chord

Part B, pp. 517–518.

1. Anhemitonic pentatonic.

2. B♭. In m. 6 it changes briefly to D because of the altered bass pattern.

3. Ostinato.

4. Perfect 4th (prominent in the melody and accompaniment as well).

5. Measures 12 to 13, within the $\frac{6}{8}$ meter. Measures 8 to 9, although notated in $\frac{3}{4}$, will also suggest hemiola to the listener because of the suggested articulation.

Part C, p. 518.

1.

2.

Part D, pp. 519–520.

Obviously the sample solution for each of these exercises represents only one of numerous other possibilities. You will observe the following features:

1. Notice how the right-hand melody is designed so as not to reinforce the G major and F major chords that constitute the ostinato pattern. Although the last measure of the phrase may suggest V7 in the key of C, there has been no suggestion of C as tonal center earlier in the piece, leaving us still unaware of any clear tonal center.

2. In addition to featuring secundal harmony, this phrase also seems to wander tonally. The sustained clusters that conclude the phrase do nothing to establish or clarify any sense of key.

3. The right hand clearly emphasizes tonic and dominant in the key of F♯, thereby setting up a sense of bitonality in relation to the "white-key" ostinato found in the left hand.

Self-Test 28-3
p. 528.
The procedures illustrated are:

   a.   asymmetric meter

   b.   mixed meter

   c.   added value

   d.   metric modulation

Self-Test 28-4
Part A, p. 534.

   1.   [0,1,4]

   2.   Measure 3, the half-note chord

   Measure 4, G–B♭–B♮ (right hand)

   Measures 4 to 5, G–G♯–B (chord)

   Measures 4 to 5, F♯–A–A♯ (tenor)

   Measure 10, right hand

   3.   The chord in mm. 4 to 5

Part B, p. 534.

   1.   **a.**   [0,1,6]

   b.   [0,1,4]

   c.   [0,2,4]

   d.   [0,2,6]

   2.   a and b   The M7 on the bottom of a moves up a M3 to become the bottom of b.

   a and c   Both have G♭2 as their bass notes.

   a and d   Both contain a B/F tritone.

   b and c   The top two notes of b appear a P4 lower as the top 2 notes of c.

   b and d   Both contain a M3.

   c and d   The m7 on the bottom of c moves up a m2 to become the outer notes of d.

3. Measures 1 to 2:   [0,2,3,4,6]

Measures 1 to 3:   [0,1,3,4,5,7]

The [0,2,3,4,6] is inversionally symmetrical. When you invert it, you get the same intervals in the same order as in the original.

4. [0,2,3,6,8] They might be compared in at least two ways. First, the [4,6] of the first set has been transposed up a M2 to become [6,8] in the second set. Second, the [4] in the first set has been replaced with [8] in the second set. [0,2,3,6,8] is not inversionally symmetrical.

5. [0,3,4,5,8] No.

6.

	B	G♯	G	A	F	E
[0,1,6]	x				x	x
[0,1,4]	x	x	x			
[0,2,4]			x	x	x	
[0,2,6]	x			x	x	

Self-Test 28-5
Part A, p. 546.

P  R

I  RI

I

	0	11	7	8	3	1	2	10	6	5	4	9	
0	D	C♯	A	B♭	F	E♭	E	C	A♭	G	F♯	B	0
1	E♭	D	B♭	B	F♯	E	F	C♯	A	A♭	G	C	1
5	G	F♯	D	E♭	B♭	A♭	A	F	D♭	C	B	E	5
4	F♯	F	C♯	D	A	G	G♯	E	C	B	B♭	E♭	4
9	B	A♯	F♯	G	D	C	C♯	A	F	E	E♭	A♭	9
11	C♯	C	G♯	A	E	D	D♯	B	G	G♭	F	B♭	11
10	C	B♭	G	A♭	E♭	D♭	D	B♭	G♭	F	E	A	10
2	E	D♯	B	C	G	F	F♯	D	B♭	A	A♭	D♭	2
6	G♯	G	E♭	E	B	A	A♯	F♯	D	D♭	C	F	6
7	A	A♭	E	F	C	B♭	B	G	E♭	D	D♭	G♭	7
8	B♭	A	F	F♯	C♯	B	C	G♯	E	E♭	D	G	8
3	F	E	C	C♯	G♯	F♯	G	E♭	B	B♭	A	D	3
	0	11	7	8	3	1	2	10	6	5	4	9	

P →   ← R

RI

Part B, p. 547.

This sample solution might be titled "Seconds and Sevenths." Notice how prominently these dissonant intervals are featured until the third section of the piece, after which we find more consonant sonorities leading to a calmer and more peaceful conclusion.

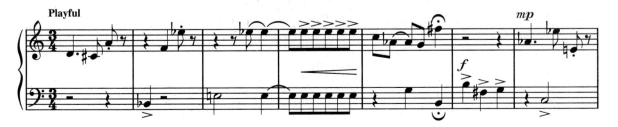

Self-Test 28-6
Part A, p. 567.

1. Total serialization is the process whereby nonpitch aspects of a piece are subjected to a predetermined order.

2. Composers such as Boulez and his teacher, Messiaen, were influential in the development of this compositional technique.

Part B, p. 567.

1. The term *aleatory* is used to describe music in which various elements of a composition are, in varying degrees, determined by chance.

2. Because of the way it "frames" or "organizes" silence, *4'33"* heightens the listener's awareness of surrounding sounds or noises, causing what might ordinarily be heard as distractions to become a part of the aesthetic of the listening experience.

3. Minimalism. Steve Reich, Terry Riley, Philip Glass, John Adams.

Part C, p. 568.

George Crumb. Amplified piano, pizzicato plucking of strings inside the piano

John Cage. Prepared piano

Henry Cowell. Playing on strings inside the piano

Edgar Varese. Use of sirens as part of percussion ensemble

Lou Harrison. Bowing of mallet instruments; use of brake drums

Penderecki. Use of sustained, microtonal clusters; striking various areas of the violin (and other stringed instruments) to create a percussive effect

Schoenberg. Use of *sprechstimme*

Part D, p. 568.

1. sine wave: a sound without overtones.

2. white noise: nonpitched hissing sound consisting of all audible frequencies at random amplitudes.

3. oscillator: tone generator.

4. *musique concrète:* natural sounds that have been recorded on tape and then subjected to modification by means of altered playback speed, reversal of tape direction, fragmentation, tape loop, and other technical manipulations.

5. MIDI: Musical Instrument Digital Interface, a process whereby the keyboard of one synthesizer can be made to drive the sound generators of another, thereby greatly enhancing the capabilities of a single performer.

Index of Musical Examples

Subject Index